PUBLIC ART AND ARCHITECTURE IN NEW MEXICO 1933–1943

A GUIDE TO THE NEW DEAL LEGACY

Public Art and Architecture in New Mexico 1933–1943

A Guide to the New Deal Legacy

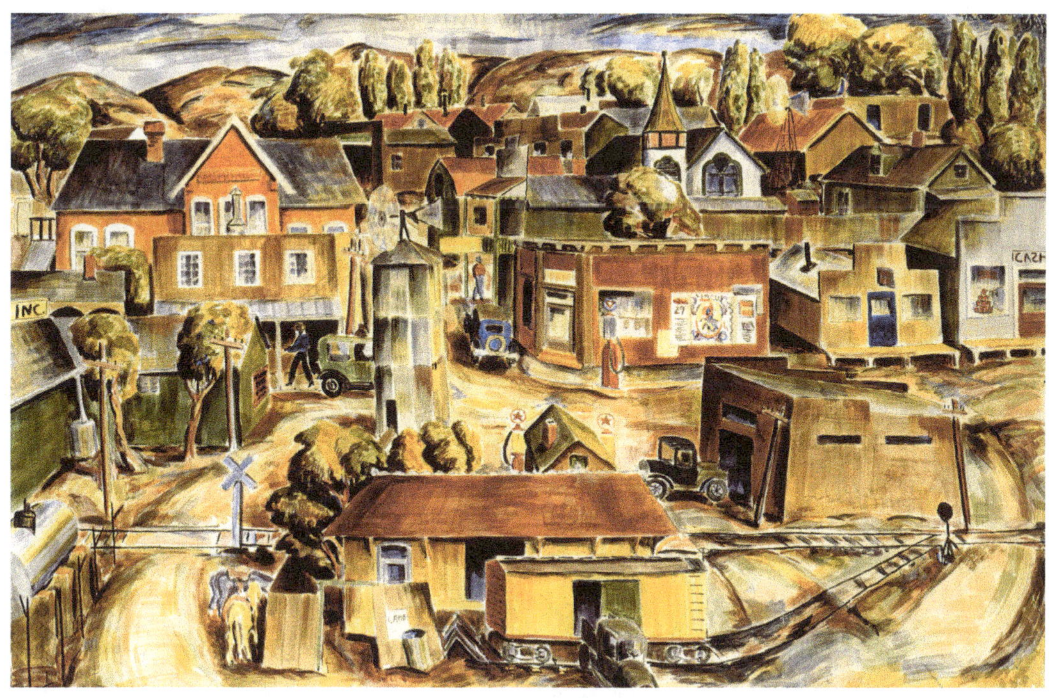

Compiled
by
Kathryn A. Flynn

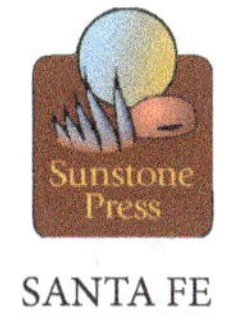

SANTA FE

Sunstone books may be purchased for educational, business, or sales promotional use. For information please write: Special Markets Department, Sunstone Press, P.O. Box 2321, Santa Fe, New Mexico 87504-2321.

Book and Cover design › Vicki Ahl
Body typeface › Minion Pro
Printed on acid-free paper
♾

Library of Congress Cataloging-in-Publication Data

Library of Congress Cataloging-in-Publication Data

Public art and architecture in New Mexico 1933-1943 : a guide to the New Deal legacy / compiled by Kathryn A. Flynn.
pages cm
Includes bibliographical references and index.
ISBN 978-0-86534-881-3 (hardcover : alk. paper) -- ISBN 978-0-86534-882-0 (softcover : alk. paper)
1. Public art--New Mexico--History--20th century--Guidebooks. 2. New Deal art--New Mexico--Guidebooks. 3. Public architecture--New Mexico--History--20th century--Guidebooks. I. Flynn, Kathryn A., 1936-
N6530.N6P83 2012
709.789'09043--dc23

2012007834

WWW.SUNSTONEPRESS.COM
SUNSTONE PRESS / POST OFFICE BOX 2321 / SANTA FE, NM 87504-2321 /USA
(505) 988-4418 / ORDERS ONLY (800) 243-5644 / FAX (505) 988-1025

Dedicated to

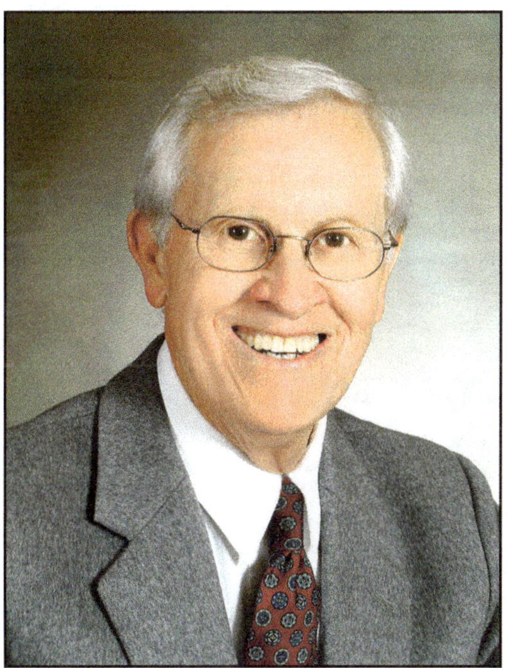

J. Paul Taylor from Mesilla loves New Mexico as did the fifteen generations before him in his family. As an educator and a state legislator he became an inportant figure working for outstanding education for the state's children and adults, for preserving the state's history and its treasures, and supporting those programs that are necessary to improve the daily lives of his fellow citizens. Also a lover of fine art, Taylor combined this love with his passion for New Mexico history and virtually became a major influence through his legislative activities, thereby making it possible to save the state's varied New Deal treasures and exposing these treasures to all.

CONTENTS

INTRODUCTION

This is a guide and reference book that will give readers information on New Mexico's New Deal Public Treasures, sharing what was created, who created them and where those treasures are today. My goals have been to:

Provide helpful information for any researcher/scholar about the New Deal's accomplishments in New Mexico;
Provide New Mexico citizens and tourists guidance on where to look for these treasures;
Assist communities all over the state to become aware of the treasures they have and preserve them and share them with the world;
Expose the younger generations to what their family elders provided for them today; and
Honor and thank all those who made and left these treasures for us to enjoy, appreciate and respect how they improved their their lives and ours.

My earlier book on this subject, *Treasures on New Mexico Trails*, was published by Sunstone Press in 1995, and I could not turn loose of a healthy addiction that focuses on finding the treasures: art and buildings, the artists, and their stories. Since then I have discovered much more through the sleuthing activities that came about as a result of this enjoyable "addiction or passion." Unfortunately, those artists and artisans have virtually all passed on, leaving behind their creations. In some cases, their talents and techniques have also been passed on to their children and grandchildren to carry on their legacy. For that, we are thankful.

In despite of my efforts, there are many people who have never noticed most of our New Deal public art treasures in New Deal public buildings as they regularly venture in and out of them on business. Actually, most of these structures and their public art and interior fixtures are generally taken for granted but still continue to serve their citizens, as they have for the past seventy-five or more years. Others would never think about going to a courthouse, other county and federal buildings, or even local libraries to look for art in addition to searching out art galleries. Or who ever thinks or wonders about how their water or sewer systems got there? Or who has ever noticed the WPA stamp on their city sidewalks, or how many have even noticed the rock walls around cemeteries or football fields? The public buildings created then were the first examples of America's own architectural style—leaving behind the massive European granite columns and other European features. All of these treasures were created by someone's grandfathers, uncles and aunts and neighbors sometime between 1933–1943. That period was such a difficult time in the nation's history, and yet beauty came out of it.

As a fifth grader growing up out here in the American Southwest, I remember the horrendous dust storms of that era in Portales that attacked our days and nights so severely. Some days it was even hard to see anything while I was sitting at my school desk next to an outside window. It was awful, but others, like those in northeastern New Mexico and the panhandle areas of Texas and Oklahoma, had even worse daily experiences because of that terrible drought and those ferocious dust storms that destroyed crops and livestock.

I hope that this guide to the New Deal Legacy will give the reader an insight into some of the ways we as Americans and New Mexicans dealt successfully with the economic problems that faced the country between 1929–1943. For many it can be a chance to refresh memories of that period when the federal government developed needed projects to employ its citizens who could use their skills and talents to support themselves and their families while maintaining their pride. For New Deal scholars, art historians and architecture students, this will serve as a guide to structures known and unknown. For younger folks, this book may provide a new view of a part of the state's history by revealing the visual records that remain. For all, it should open our eyes to the quality and quantity of the varied accomplishments of that Depression Era. We still use many of the public buildings (schools, post offices, courthouses, etc.) roads, rock walls, campgrounds, dams and furniture; and in many of these public places there is outstanding fine art.

Over the years, many have asked how and why this author got into this project. Here are some of the answers.

Finding and organizing this information grew out of my compiling the *New Mexico Blue Book*, which is published every two years by the New Mexico Office of the Secretary of State. New Deal information was featured in the 1991–92, 1993–94 and 1995–96 editions.

There was a enthusiastic response from readers. That response created the catalyst for developing and coordinating a series of local art exhibits around the state in May 1992 in conjunction with the National Historic Preservation Week and National Tourism Week. In order to utilize these designated weeks to showcase the state's New Deal treasures, we met with state and local representatives of both groups, and soon thirteen communities began developing ways to show off their New Deal treasures during these first two weeks of May. Those communities included Alamogordo, Albuquerque, Clayton, Clovis, Fort Sumner, Gallup, Las Cruces, Melrose, Raton, Santa Fe, Silver City, Taos and Truth or Consequences. An exhibit in the Governor's Gallery at the State Capitol kicked off the two week New Deal Treasure Hunt. Since then other traveling photo exhibits have continued to tour the state to reinforce the awareness of this little known gold mine.

Since then, various state and federal agencies have become involved in helping research the New Deal public art treasures for which they were responsible. However, this has not always been simple since there appeared to be no centralized official records of the accomplishments of that era. Therefore this New Deal detective was forced to go to Washington to research and unravel the stories relating to the public art and artists, some of whom were forgotten or unknown. At that time (1995) only 19 of the 165 artists identified were still alive and many of the records had big gaps since the federal government directed the states to destroy their copies of documents, believing that Washington had all the information. That turned out to be untrue, which frustrated this lead detective, but I would not and have not been deterred from my quest. Fortunately I was able to get each of their stories since today, they also are no longer with us. Those nineteen included Narcisco Abeyta, Harrison Begay, Pop Chalee, Ted Egri, Allan Houser, John Jellicoe, Nat Kaplan, Gene Kloss, Oliver LaGrone, Tom Lea, Abad Lucero, Bill Lumpkins, Ila McAfee, Eliseo Rodriguez, Jose Rey Toledo, Andrew Tsihnahjinnie, Pablita Velarde, Bill Warder, and James Ridgely Whiteman.

These New Mexico artists created public art treasures in the early years of 1930 based on employment in the various public art programs—the Public Works of Art Program (PWAP); the Treasury Section of Painting and Sculpture (The Section); the Treasury Relief Art Project (TRAP); and the Works Progress (and later Projects) Administration's Federal Art Project (WPA/FAP). The majority were in the first programs and later (1935) looked to the WPA/FAP for employment. This last program continued for a longer period of time, even after World War II began when it transferred its focus to designing graphics for selling war bonds and other related war graphics.

After I finished my first book, doctoral student, Tey Mariana Nunn, successfully sleuthed records everywhere to locate all the Hispanic artists who worked in these programs. It was a challenge since most were frequently identified as "assistants" with little information as to who they were. She found 108 artists not included in my earlier book and has compiled an outstanding publication, *Sin Nombre: Hispana and Hispano of the New Deal Era,* which is rich with information previously uncovered.

But despite my and others' efforts, there is still some public art missing. A chapter in the present book is included to share with you what paintings are still on what I call the Unsolved Mystery List. What happened to those paintings is unknown except for those that were burned in school fires or were painted over. Some may have "walked or been carried" into private homes and offices, but in those cases, they still remain public art owned by our citizens, paid for with public funds. I encourage the reader to help us solve the Unsolved Mysteries of New Mexico-New Deal public art identified in Chapter 4 and encourage any current "owner" to donate them back to public spaces. One unknown painting was found as recently as March 2011 up in the rafters of a public building in Gallup. Maybe there are others out in other hidden areas.

In addition to the programs focusing on public art, we found that there were many other programs with different focuses, all meant to provide work for our citizens and meet the enormous variety of public needs. There was a title and an acronym or name for every program (WPA, CCC, NYA, REA, TVA, PWA, CWA, FERA and FDIC to name a few) and all fell under the generic New Deal umbrella. Most of these programs were focused on building public facilities and/or caring for our land and other institutions.

In Chapter 1, each New Mexico town with known New Deal public art and buildings is identified, but there could be some we have missed. Within each town the information is organized so readers will be able to identify the New Deal buildings with New Deal art, other public buildings with New Deal art, and then the identification of other New Deal accomplishments. Some towns have a little or a lot of everything in every category while others are more limited.

The men and women in these other programs were hired primarily to do construction projects; those programs included the WPA program, the Civilian Conservation Corps (CCC) and National Youth Administration (NYA). The latter two programs were established to help find work and education for the state's youth. Some 56,000 young men enrolled in the New Mexico CCC program were between the ages of 18 to 23, but in reality a number of the enrollees were even younger since they misrepresented their ages to get into the programs to help themselves and their families. The NYA enrollees were usually 16 to 24 and worked in their schools where their actual ages were known. All the CCC and NYA alumni have been pleased to be interviewed and given the opportunity to share about a time in their lives that "made them the stronger person they were to become." Most felt it was the most important thing that happened in their lives. And the CCC participants have created an alumni association nationwide and the few remaining members continue to meet and share that memorable legacy. They also encourage others to join.

Others who were also unemployed and needing work were architects and engineers. Charles E. Peterson, a young architect with the National Park Service, drafted a proposal in 1933 to develop a national program called the Historic American Buildings Survey (HABS) that would provide employment for architects and students in the field by having them survey America's historical buildings and structures up to 1860 in a systematic and uniform manner. It was submitted, approved, funded and put in place within two months. Peterson became the director and the West got special attention since Peterson made sure that older structures like Native American pueblos were included despite the date cap. One might wonder if he was strongly influenced by one of his regional advisory board members, John Gaw Meem. Taos, Acoma and Chaco's Pueblo Bonito pueblos were among the earliest sites surveyed along with Zuni villages. The survey results from those sites are included in the 28,226 building surveys done between 1933 and up to 1993 and are filed in the Library of Congress. These documents are reportedly the most frequently reproduced collections in that institution.

Today the program continues and is administered by the National Park Service. Architects are still being sent out all over the country to survey selected structures for a variety of reasons. Early in 2000, HABS surveyors were in Mesilla, New Mexico surveying the historic home of J. Paul Taylor, to whom we have dedicated this book. Mr. Taylor and his family donated the family home and its contents to the New Mexico Museum system upon his death and the museum attempted to determine what is included in this gift. A humorous tidbit shared with former Representative Taylor was there was so much "in" the house that the surveyors were having difficulty getting the measurements of the structure. For example, they determined that there are currently eighty-seven chairs of varying sizes located throughout the house.

In 2001, the New Mexico Historic Preservation Division of the New Mexico Department of Cultural Affairs and the National Parks Service with financial help from many individuals and group sponsors published a book, *Recording a Vanishing Legacy:The Historic American Buildings Survey in New Mexico.* Today at least 100 detailed surveys of New Mexico buildings are referenced in this document. Also noted in this book are all the New Mexico repositories of the New Mexico HABS surveys. In Albuquerque they can be found at the University of New Mexico Fine Arts Library, University of New Mexico Center for Southwest Research/ John Gaw Meem Archive and in Santa Fe, the History Library at the Palace of the Governors, Southwest Room of the New Mexico State Library, Collections Department, the National Park Service's Intermountain Regional office and other Office of Cultural Affairs' Historic Preservation Division. In Las Cruces they can be found in the New Mexico State University Library's Special Collections Department.

This approach to problem solving is still a viable approach and/or alternative which needs to be seriously considered by our current administration. Learning from our past accomplishments and failures is always valid and as Roosevelt's good friend, Winston Churchill once said, "A nation that forgets its past has no future."

In my earlier book on the subject, we included forty-eight communities with New Deal Treasures that included 65 murals or large paintings, 657 easel paintings and other media offerings, 10 pieces of sculpture, 10 pieces of pottery, 43 wood carvings, numerous pieces of furniture and craft items and some buildings. In this edition you will find more artists and places and more information about some items that were in the original book. Now nearly ninety communities are included—almost no town has been left out. Based on my experience over the past seventeen years, I'm guessing that you will find even more as you begin your treasure hunt. You should also include a search in Washington, DC for New Mexico treasures, and even in other states. Some treasure hunters may select their home state, to pursue their New Deal Treasure Hunt. I can say with confidence that it will be equally challenging and rewarding. We recommend you keep the following goals in mind as you do your sleuthing:

- Locate and identify New Mexico's or other states' New Deal treasures;
- Celebrate the accomplishments of the New Deal projects in New Mexico and elsewhere;
- Give our citizens of today an appreciation of those accomplishments; and
- Instill that same sense of hope provided in that time of depression to be applied to our current times that are including some similar economic and social difficulties.

As noted earlier, this sleuthing caused this New Deal Detective to help form a national organization to feature, save, and protect these treasures nationwide. The National New Deal Preservation Association (NNDPA) was founded in Santa Fe, New Mexico in December 1998 by people from across the nation who were similarly addicted. The New Mexico Chapter of NNDPA has raised and spent over $500,000 as of 2011, conserving, preserving, and restoring New Deal public art. There is more to be done so you, the reader, are encouraged and welcome to join the non-profit organization and become a New Deal Detective. You can do so by contacting NNDPA at P. O. Box 602, Santa Fe, New Mexico 87504 or by visiting the group's website at www.newdeallegacy.org. You can also call (505) 473-3985 or (505) 690-5845.

Why was the New Deal a good deal? In summary, we conclude that in New Mexico:

It was social purpose in action;
It provided the chance for our people to survive and produce with pride;
It recorded and presented the essence of New Mexico—geographically, culturally, artistically, architecturally, agriculturally and even environmentally;
It was the beginning of highlighting the unique New Mexico style, in particular assisting Hispanic artists in marketing their unique goods for the first time;
and
It exposed our citizenry to actual fine art for the first time rather than just seeing it as reproductions in books and calendars.

Today, that New Deal is still sharing its legacy. When you look at its buildings and fine art, you will know that each is a good reason why it was a good deal—then and now. It is important that in our appreciation of these treasures, we make sure we preserve and protect them from those who may or may not be aware of their significance and value, and for those young people who may want to know more about the past someday.

So go exploring in this Land of Enchantment and beyond and Happy Sleuthing!

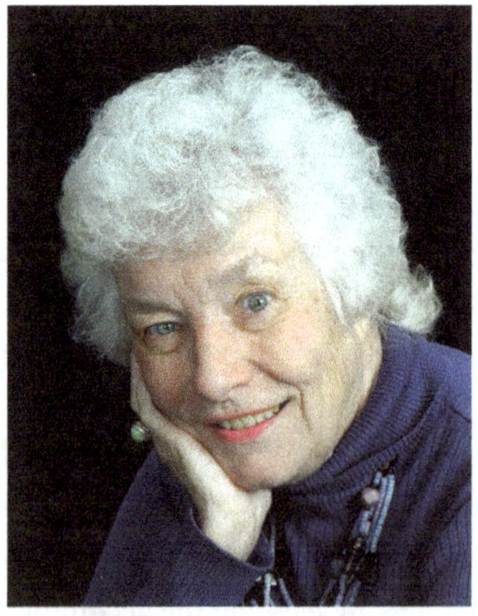

—Kathryn A. Flynn
National New Deal Preservation Association—NNDPA,
New Mexico's New Deal Executive Director

ABBREVIATIONS

AAA: Agricultural Adjustment Administration (1933)
CCC: Civilian Conservation Corps (1933)
CWA: Civil Works Administration (1933)
ERA: Emergency Relief Act (1935)
FCA: Farm Credit Administration (1933)
FCC: Federal Communication Commission (1934)
FSA: Farm Security Administration (1937)
FDIC: Federal Deposit Insurance Corporation (1933)
FERA: Federal Emergency Relief Act (1933)
FERA: Federal Emergency Relief Administration (1933)
HABS: Historical American Building Surveys (1933)
HRS: Historical Records Survey (1935)
NIRA: National Industrial Recovery Act (1933)
NLA: National Labor Board (1933)
NLRB: National Labor Relations Board (1934)
NPS: National Park Service (1916)
NRA: National Recovery Administration (1933)
NYA: National Youth Administration (1933)
PWA: Public Works Administration (1933)
PWAP: Public Works of Art Project (1933)
REA: Rural Electric Administration (1935)
RA: Resettlement Administration (1935)
SECTION: Treasury Section of the Painting and Sculpture (1934)
SEC: Securities and Exchange Commission (1934)
SSA: Social Security Administration (1935)
SCS: Soil Conservation Service (1935)
TRAP: Treasury Relief Art Project (1935)
TVA: Tennessee Valley Authority (1933)
U.S. Maritime Commission (1936)
WPA: Works Progress Administration (1935)*
- FAP: Federal Art Project (1935)
- FDP: Federal Dance Project (1935)
- FMP: Federal Music Project (1935)
- FTP: Federal Theater Project (1935)
- FWP: Federal Writers Project (1935)

*Changed to Works Projects Administration in 1939.

1

WHAT TOWNS HAVE NEW DEAL ART AND ARCHITECTURE?

In this chapter, New Deal accomplishments are identified in the following categories:

New Deal Public Buildings with New Deal Public Art
New Deal Public Art in Public Buildings
Other New Deal Buildings, Structures and Programs
Mystery Artwork (art still missing)

Some towns have items in all categories while others may be more limited in one or more categories. The categories in the towns where there was no activity are not listed.

In addition at the end of this chapter we have included information on over 400 rural schools that were built in rural New Mexico by the WPA that may be in addition to the towns mentioned earlier in this chapter. Some of those rural towns and their schools may no longer exist or have very little of the buildings still standing.

For an overview of New Deal artists and public art in New Mexico, see *A More Abundant Life, New Deal Artists and Public Art in New Mexico* by Jacqueline Hoefer, published by Sunstone Press.

ALAMOGORDO

"Painting a mural challenges a painter like composing a symphony does a composer. A landscape painting by comparison, would be like the composers tone poem."

—Peter Hurd, *The National Observer*, February 8, 1971

NEW DEAL PUBLIC ART IN NEW DEAL PUBLIC BUILDINGS

ALAMOGORDO WOMEN'S CLUB
12th and Indiana Boulevard
State Register of Cultural Properties SRCP 1831

This New Deal building was constructed in 1936 by the WPA program and is still being used by the Women's Club and other community organizations for public gatherings. It is an adobe structure and officially entered in the National Register of Historic Places on August 4, 2003.

Three J. R. Willis paintings funded by the WPA-Federal Art Project (FAP) in 1937 enhance the large room and are arranged around the fireplace. The smallest one hangs over the fireplace, "Pack Outfit, Hondo Canyon," and two larger works can be seen on each side of fireplace, "Landscape Mural-Native Americans on Horseback" and Landscape Mural-Village Scene."

Professional art conservation of these paintings was done in 2005 by Dale Kronkright and the funding was shared between the Women's Club and the New Mexico Chapter of the National New Deal Preservation Association (NNDPA).

OTERO COUNTY OFFICES
(Formerly U. S. FEDERAL BUILDING which housed the post office and later the Lincoln Forest Service.)
1101 New York Avenue
State Register of Cultural Properties SCRP 1793

This building, which was built in 1938 as a post office in the New Deal's Public Works Administration (PWA) project, is designed in the Southwest pueblo adobe style with corbels, vigas and a portal on the front exterior. On the wall of this exterior reside four Peter Hurd frescos painted in 1942. Framing the front door of the building are two of the frescos titled, "Sun and Rain," while the other two smaller pieces, "Sorghum" and "Yucca," are further from the center of the wall. Hurd reported in a letter to the federal funding source that he had been haunted by a desire to portray "a sort of hymn to the blessings of sun and rain in our arid land."

The *Alamogordo Daily News* wrote in 1941 about the central section of this art, "The scene on the left of the main entrance portrays the sunshine and the green things that it brings from the earth, a beautiful scene of trees and flowers with Peter Hurd's own home in nearby Picacho in the foreground, and the St. Andreas Mountains and White Sands in the background. The life-size woman in the picture is Miss Edna Imhoff, teacher in schools at Rebenton and the child picking flowers is Della Joiner, daughter of the postmaster in Hondo. At the right of the entrance is an old Mexican shepherd praying for rain. This shepherd is Dorothel Montoya, well-known to the big sheep outfits in the Hondo Valley, and back of him is the state flower with Sierra Blanca in the far background."

Below the shepherd with one hand raised to the sky in thanks of rain is inscribed, "Ven lluvia ven a acariciat la tierra serdiento" (Come blessed rain, come caress the thirsty land). Below Miss Imhoff, who has paused while hoeing in the garden to watch her daughter play, is inscribed, "Come sunlight after rain to bring green life out of the earth."[1]

Hurd chose to work in fresco due to the influence of the Mexican muralist, Diego Rivera, whom Hurd had previously met.[2] This is a style of painting in segments of wet plaster before it dries which captures the artwork as an integral part of the actual surface. All these murals were restored by Santa Fe art conservator, Steve Prins, in 1998.

1. "Peter Hurd Completes Beautiful Murals at Alamo Post Office," *Alamogordo Daily News,* Vol.45, No. 16, April 16, 1943.
2. Frank Paine, *New Mexico Magazine,* January, 1977.

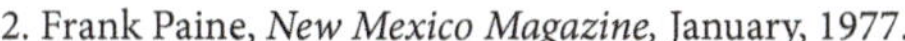

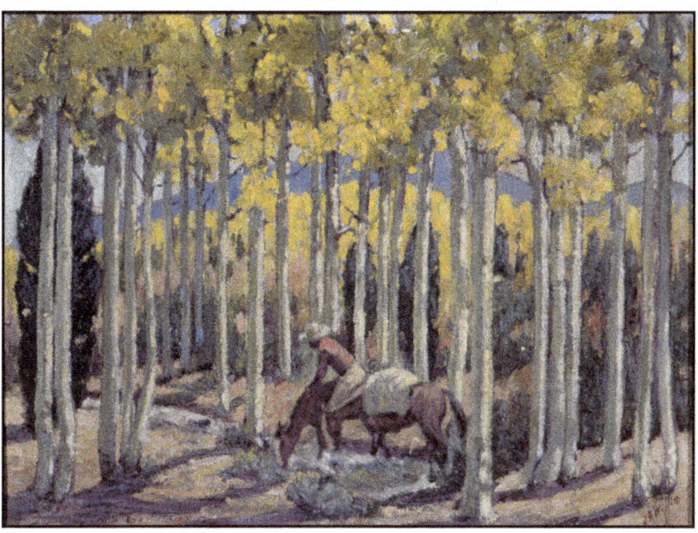

New Deal artist, J. R. Willis, painted three landscapes that have hung in the Alamogordo Women's Club since it was built by the WPA. They were conserved in 2005. Another group of three done by him can be found in the Gallup schools and portray major historical scenes in the state's history. Photograph by Pat Berrett from *A More Abundant Life, New Deal Artists and Public Art in New Mexico*, courtesy of Sunstone Press.

NEW DEAL PUBLIC ART IN OTHER BUILDINGS—Unknown

NEW DEAL BUILDINGS, STRUCTURES and PROGRAMS

NEW MEXICO SCHOOL FOR THE VISUALLY HANDICAPPED
100 North White Sands Boulevard
(575) 437-3505

Various improvements were made by the WPA on this campus including landscaping and maintenance structures. Both the Central Receiving Building and the Infirmary Building are New Deal structures and are on the State Register of Cultural Properties. SRCP 1475 and 1476.

RURAL ELECTRIC COOPERATIVE (REA), a New Deal program, provides electricity to the rural New Mexicans of this area of the state through the Otero County Electric program with main offices in Cloudcroft.

WHITE SANDS NATIONAL MONUMENT
White Sands National Monument Historic District (#1491)
New Mexico State Register 9-9-98, National Register 6-23-88

The Historic District at White Sands National Monument (WSNM) consists of eight Pueblo Revival buildings constructed in the late 1930s by Civil Works Administration workers as a Recreation Demonstration and Emergency Conservation Work project. It is understood to have been done at the cost of $31,000. This included the main Visitor Center including the museum and structures with similar architectural styles used for housing staff and maintenance activities.

The centerpiece of the district is the Monument Administration and Museum Building, constructed in 1936–37. This two-story building with patios and portals was beautifully finished inside with exposed viga and latilla ceilings, a corner fireplace, tin work fixtures which were made by the National Youth Administration (NYA) girls at Camp Capitan in Baca Canyon in nearby Capitan, New Mexico. The Colonial style furnishings were created by CCC workers.

Landscaping with native plants was done at the time of construction along with the trails and roads throughout the park. The CCC was also responsible for this. The White Sands New Mexico Historic District was found eligible to be included in the National Register for its architecture and its association with the history of the National Park Service (NPS), particularly the NPS emphasis on use of local materials and rustic styles in construction of park buildings.

OTHER BUILDINGS, INFRASTRUCTURE and PROGRAMS

According to the survey report done for the state's Historic Preservation Office by

David Kammer, PhD, with the research assistance of Jeff Rose, the following facilities, structures and infrastructures were accomplishments by the WPA workers:

Otero Courthouse improvements
School (North Elementary), gymnasium and school improvements
Relief and Security Authority Building
Town Office
Alameda Public Park improvements
Municipal golf course improvements
Rifle range improvements
Water System improvements
Road improvements, drains, walls, bridges, reservoirs
Athletic field improvements
Sewing Room Operation
Index and catalog court records
Public Works of the CCC in Lincoln National Forest—SHR#1491
Wofford Lookout Tower out of Cloudcroft is on SHR#1446.

MYSTERY ARTWORK **See Chapter 4 (Kloss and Nordfeldt)**

ALBUQUERQUE

"The Thirties was our golden age, the only humane era in our history, the one brief period when we permitted ourselves to be good."

—Edward Laning, WPA muralist

One of the best sources for the New Deal accomplishments in Albuquerque can be found in Charles Biebel's book, *Making the Most of It, Public Works in Albuquerque During the Great Depression 1929–1942.*

NEW DEAL PUBLIC ART IN NEW DEAL PUBLIC BUILDINGS

ALBUQUERQUE SPECIAL COLLECTIONS LIBRARY
423 Central NE

This building was built earlier than the New Deal era but an addition and some landscaping was done by the New Deal program. A Fremont Ellis painting entitled "Old House at Chimayo" (22"x 30") hangs in this library. There is also a portfolio of Indian rugs done by Ruth Connely. It is only one of two known portfolios done by this artist. The other is located at the Laboratory of Anthropology in Santa Fe on Museum Hill. This author would like to learn more about this artist since she has found very little about her.

NEW DEAL PUBLIC ART IN PUBLIC BUILDINGS

ALBUQUERQUE MUSEUM
2000 Mountain Road NE

This outstanding museum and gallery has become the repository for the WPA artwork that was originally placed in the U.S. Veterans Hospital and also the New Deal collection of Albuquerque High School:

Bisttram, Emil
"Juanita" oil 33" x 44"
"Old Hunter" oil 27" x 36"
Fleck, Joseph
"Don Quixote" oil 32" x 45"
Kloss, Gene
"Rain Priest" oil
McAfee, Ila
"Antelope" oil 36" x 41"

AMY BIEHL SCHOOL (formerly Albuquerque Post Office)
123 Fourth Street SW
(505) 299-9209

Two paintings were identified as being created for this original space but have never been located by the school, GSA or the USPS. They were: "At Arroyo Hondo" by E. Martin Hennings and "New Mexico Fall" by Carl Redin.

BERNALILLO CITY/COUNTY BUILDING
County Commissioners Chambers
One Civic Plaza

An oil painting titled "Bison" by Ila McAfee done through the WPA Federal Art Project (FAP) hangs in these chambers. It is owned by Carrie Tingley Hospital for Crippled Children but was placed on a long term loan to the City of Albuquerque following the restoration of this painting by art conservator, Suzanne Frend, of California in the middle of the 1990s. The restoration was paid for by the New Mexico Chapter of the NNDPA and the city's 1% for Public Art funds.

CARRIE TINGLEY HOSPITAL FOR CRIPPLED CHILDREN
1127 University NE
(505) 277-5200 or (800) 472-3235

This state funded hospital was originally located in Hot Springs, New Mexico, the town now known as Truth or Consequences, New Mexico. This New Deal facility was built in that community to take advantage of the available hot mineral springs which was an early treatment for polio. In 1981 the hospital program was transferred to Albuquerque in order to better serve medically the children with different and more complicated orthopedic conditions. The hospital structure in Truth or Consequences now houses a veterans' retirement facility.

A large collection of WPA artwork from the Truth or Consequences facility was also transferred at the time of the move to Albuquerque and placed throughout the new building to continue its purpose. The collection included fourteen oil paintings and a sculpture of a mother and child by New Deal artists. Most all of these paintings have had professional art conservation work on them as purchased by the Carrie Tingley Hospital Foundation. At the time of this writing (2009), the artwork can be found in the following locations.

"Mercy," the mother/child sculpture, was created by Oliver LaGrone and it now resides in the Bill and Barbara Richardson Wing of the Children's Hospital at University of New Mexico Hospital. Previously this life size plaster statue was routinely located in the clinic lobby of the clinic area in Truth or Consequences and later in the clinic at the Albuquerque program at 1127 University NE where the children liked to climb up and stand by it. The statue is the creation of the artist's memory of his mother nursing him through malaria as a young child in Albuquerque. The sculptor later became the first African-American to graduate from the University of New Mexico Art Department and went on to become a professor for many years in North Carolina prior to his death. The statue was not bronzed until 1993 when funds were obtained through the City's Art in Public Places funding. During that project a second casting of the piece was done and now stands in the Albuquerque Museum's Statue Garden in Old Town. Dr. LaGrone returned to his hometown for the unveiling of the "finally completed" bronzed sculptures and shared his memories of his life and his creating the piece sixty years earlier thanks to the New Deal funding.

Two large untitled paintings, by Gisella Loeffler, both 72" x 120", were painted on fiber board for the hospitalized children in Hot Springs. They reflect the artist's childhood in the Austro-Hungarian Empire with strong influences of the folk art found there. Both are painted in a highly colorful and decorative combination of oil and gold paints with one featuring Indian and Hispanic dances and customs including a nativity scene in the foreground and the other filled with children fairy tale characters as portrayed in Loeffler's own imaginative style. Her daughter, Undine, remembers watching her mother paint them in their living room in Taos as she was recuperating from a childhood disease. Both pieces were restored and conserved by Albuquerque art conservator, Luis Neri-Zagal, shortly after the move from Truth or Consequences and can be found in the hospital's outpatient cafeteria.

The remaining WPA/FAP easel oil paintings can be found throughout the hospital. They include:

Ellis, Fremont
"Winter Scene"
"April Landscape"
Hullenkremer, Odon
"Boy in Helmet"
"Kids on Teeter-Totter" oil (actually the sisters of the "Boy in Helmet" who were neighbors of the artist in Santa Fe)
"Convicts" oil (construction scene)
Jones, D. Paul
"Hernandez Church"
Parsons, Sheldon
"Autumn House with Gold Tree"
"Golden Trees with Flowers"
"Poppies"
"Purple and Gold Iris"
"Lavender Iris"
Trevors, Franz
"Autumn Fields"

Note: Another oil painting, "Bisons" by Ila McAfee, is on a long-term loan to Albuquerque and hangs in their City-County Chambers Auditorium in City Building at One Civic Plaza. Prior to being placed in this facility, the painting was in need of great repair due to the fact that someone had removed it from its frame and stretcher and folded it causing ripping of the canvas and painting. The New Mexico Chapter of the NNDPA paid to have Suzanne Frend, art conservator in California, totally restore it.

KIRTLAND AIR FORCE BASE

The Old Officer's Club on this base was originally the Sandia Girls School, a private school built by the Simms family. It had art and furniture created specifically for it but most has been lost. Six of the pieces created by Lloyd Moylan were conserved and still hang in the cocktail lounge of the East Officer's Club. They are a series of different Indian dances including Buffalo, Butterfly, Clown, Deer, Eagle and Matachinas. Originally there were at least seven paintings and maybe more, but the missing paintings may have disappeared during a fire. Other unusual craft items also missing are the pieces of furniture that were crafted for the space which included ranch style chairs with propellers carved into the arms of the chairs.

PLAZA DE SOL BUILDING—A city building.
600 Second Street

A large, cardboard, topographic state map can be found in the lobby of this building and was created during the New Deal. It was restored by Duane Chartier, art conservator, in the late 1990s. Nothing like it has been found anywhere else in New

Mexico but we are aware of a few others in other locations including one of the entire city of San Francisco as it existed at that time.

THE RAYMOND JONSON GALLERY
1017 Fine Arts Center/Popejoy Hall
(505) 277-8927

This collection is now part of the University of New Mexico Art Museum located in the Popejoy building primarily on the lower level. It was earlier housed in the former home of Raymond Jonson (1891–1982) and includes many of his works from the New Deal era. Jonson was one of the University of New Mexico professors and was known for making and selling paints to the other artists. The six abstract works (60" x 105") which he called "The Cycle of Science" were done to match the Willard Nash six panels that have been at this gallery. They include "Mathematics," "Biology," "Astronomy," "Engineering," "Physics," and "Chemistry." He also created another group called "The Study for Art."

Of the Science series, Jonson wrote in his *Technical Notes*, "These studies represent my concept of the spiritual side of modern youth, with the idea that contemporary knowledge offers an emotional and spiritual approach. When the panes are finished I hope to have created not only an ideal wall decoration but works possessing a spiritual quality. I think of them as symphonic compositions consistent with my medium and honest to the highest ideal I stand for."

Commenting on Nash's large paintings that were planned to match his Science Series, Jonson wrote in 1936 to Dr. J. F. Zimmerman, the president of University of New Mexico, "I want to say that I think Nash's panels worked out very well and it seems to me that they serve the function as intended by him. Many may not like them—that does not matter. I believe artists will like them, for they contain much in regard to plastic work, and contain, for him who can and will see, a considerable amount of interest."

UNIVERSITY OF NEW MEXICO ART MUSEUM
1017 Fine Arts Center/Popejoy Hall
(505) 277-7313

There is quite a large collection of New Deal public artwork in this museum. Within the collection are six oils by Willard Nash (1898–1943) done in 1934 which were originally hung for five years opposite six Raymond Jonson murals in Zimmerman Library. These two sets of large paintings were done to portray the physical and spiritual side of mankind. Nash's works depicted the physical side via various athletic activities and later ended up in Carlisle Gymnasium for a number of years. Nash, like Jonson, was a Modernist, but his experiments with human form were more moderate and possibly inspired by Cezanne and Picasso.

Most of these pieces had water damage to them so they were restored in 2007 by Albuquerque art conservator, Luis Neri Zagal. This was paid for by the New Mexico Chapter of NNDPA and University of New Mexico. Jonson's set of 1934 paintings was of his typical Transcedental style with vivid colors and abstract images and have been kept in the Jonson Gallery collection over the years. All twelve of the Jonson/Nash paintings were hung together once again in 2008 after 75 years for an exhibit to commemorate the 75th anniversary of the New Deal program's creation.

The other New Deal artworks in this museum's collection include:

Abelman, Ida*
"Janitor's Kids"
Abramoritz, Albert*
"Santa Monica"
Adams, Kenneth
"Church at San Antonio" oil 1934
Anderson, Carlos*
"Thirty Miles Upstate"
Arnold, A. Grant
"Serenity"
Barton, Harold
"Abstraction" oil 1939
"Dead Tree" oil 1939
"Dead Tree" oil 1938
"South Second" oil 1939
Breslow, Louis*
"Puppet Show in Park"
Borne, Mortimer*
"Manhattan from Brooklyn"
Botts, Hugh*
"Skyline"
Campbell, Blendon*
"New Hampshire Auction"
Chaney, Ruth
"Subway Excavation"
Chapman, Manville
"Mountain Village"
Davis, Hubert*
"Holiday"
Dorman, John
"House on Canyon Road"
Dwight, Mabel*
"Christmas in Paris"
Easton, Cora
"Hollyhocks and House" oil 1939
Eklred, Thomas*
"Keeler Lane"
Fruhauf, Aline*
"Hotel at South Jersey"
Good, Minetta*
"November"
Grossman, Elias*
"The Church on Henry Street"
Hicks, William*
"Farm Buildings, Long Island"
Higgins, Victor
"Ranchos Church" w/c 1934
Imhoff, Joseph
"The Storm" lithograph
Jonson, Raymond
"Variation on Rhythm-D"
"New Mexican Village"
"Ranchito New Mexico"
"Twilight Scene"
"Snow Scene"
Kloss, Gene
"Twilight Scene" oil 1934
"Remote Village"
"Sanctuary-Chimayo
"Winter Mass"
"Penitente, Good Friday"
"Acoma"
Koune, Saul*
"Wind"
Kruse, Alexander
"Jennie"

Limbach, Russell*
"Brown's Woods"
Lowell, Nat*
"Fulton Market"
Mongel, Max*
"Cargo Boat"
Morang, Dorothy
"Still Life Fruit on Green Bowl"
"Fiesta on Acequia Madre"
"Acrobat at Fiesta"
"Sunlit Walls"
"Landscape—Mountains from Tesuque"
"Sunset Glow"
"Aspen on the Sangre de Cristo"
"Two Wine Bottles"
Morris, James
"Breakfast Tray" oil 1939
"Mountain Village" oil 1939
"Spring Morning, Santa Fe"
Moylan, Lloyd
"Navajo Runners"
(There is a similar mural by Moylan in a Colorado Springs high school also titled "Navajo Runners.")
"Two Men" lithograph
"Acrobat"
Murphy, Minnie Lois
"Hurdy Gurdy"
Nash, Willard
"A Tree Study" oil
(The additional six paintings discussed earlier depict football-boxing, men's tennis and track, shotput, woman swimmer, women's tennis and basketball.)
Naumer, Helmuth
"Oak Tree in Winter" oil 1940
"Mexican Houses" oil 1940
"Two Pines"
Nooney, Ann*
"April"
Parish, Betty*
"Village"
Pillin, Polia
"Five Domestic Science panels"
Sanger, William*
"A Bit of Albany"
Skolfield, Raymond*
"Caravan Theater"
Steffen, Bernard*
"Mine Village"
Supfer, Blanche*
"Morning on the Plaza"
"Chichicastenango"
Ufer, Walter
"Blaze and Buckskin" oil 1934
Wahl, Theodore*
"Colorado Ranch"
Weissbuch, Oscar*
"Cape Cod Coast"

*These paintings were done by New Deal artists from other states and most likely were included in a traveling WPA/FAP traveling art exhibit and were at the University of New Mexico at the time the WPA program was closed around 1943. At that time, it was determined that all traveling exhibit items would remain at their current site. A study of these artists and their works elsewhere would be interesting since none were New Mexico artists.

UNIVERSITY OF NEW MEXICO PRESIDENT'S HOME

This fine home was built between 1927–1931 which was prior to the New Deal programs. It was designed by George Williamson and Miles Brittelle and constructed for approximately $21,750. It does include a tin chandelier in the Dining Room likely done by Eddie Delgado, a New Deal tinsmith from Santa Fe. Miscellaneous New Deal chairs are also to be found in the house. A great deal of the university's New Deal furniture created for various buildings was thrown out. Some was saved by staff for their homes and offices.

U. S. FEDERAL BUILDING/DISTRICT COURTHOUSE
421 Gold SW
(505) 766-8834 (Office of GSA Buildings Manager)
SR#700 State Register 10-20-78, National Register 11-22-80

Completed in 1930, this Federal Building is a striking combination of Mediterranean style and decorative Indian design motifs. The lower portion of the six-story building is pale matte-lazed terra cotta above a stone foundation; the upper stories are of glazed brick in varying shades of tan. The top story is set off by a row of white tile and arched windows. The red tile roof is hipped and flat-topped. The exterior embellishments include patterned tile courses with motifs from Indian decorative arts while the interior features strong Indian motifs.

The interior lobby highlights two murals. One, a 1936 WPA supported mural of the "Pueblo Rebellion of 1680" by Loren Mozley, was designed to fit above and around the elevators in the entry area on the first floor. This brightly colored mural is filled with highly stylized figures engaged in the dramatic revolt by the Pueblo Indians against the then Spanish rulers of New Mexico. The mural was conserved by Santa Fe art conservator, Steve Prins, in 1996.

The second mural was done by Emil Bisttram originally for the U.S. Post Office and Federal Courthouse in Roswell and was placed there in November 1937. That building was later demolished and unknown to most, prior to the demolition, the mural's three pieces were rolled up and taken to Albuquerque and placed in the basement of that Federal Courthouse. Later found and totally restored by U.S. General Services Administration, all three pieces now also hang in the lobby and are entitled "Justice Tempered with Mercy—Uphold the Right, Prevent the Wrong." Bisttram also created another mural which won a first prize and was placed in the U.S. Justice Department Building in Washington, DC and is entitled "Justice for Women and Children." In New Mexico, Bisttram served as a supervisor of the creation of murals by other artists around the state.

A painting done by W. Herbert Dunton, "Bull and Cow Elk" is displayed on the

6th floor in an office area. Dunton was known for his western scenes which frequently featured the wild animals he loved to hunt and paint. One painting he did of a large, black bear hung in President Roosevelt's office and now is in the Museum of American Art in Washington, DC.

VETERAN'S HOSPITAL

Building No.1 which currently houses the Psychology Department was one of the buildings constructed during the WPA activities and has unusually fine carved animal heads on the corbels which are at the ends of the ceiling vigas. The carver or carvers are unknown. WPA handmade furniture is located throughout the building.

NEW DEAL PUBLIC BUILDINGS, STRUCTURES and PROGRAMS

Some of the buildings at the University of New Mexico were designed by John Gaw Meem and were the landmarks for creating the Santa Fe style architecture for which he is famous.

ALBUQUERQUE LITTLE THEATER
224 San Pasqual Avenue SW
(505) 242-4750

This building designed by Meem was built over seven months by thirty-one workers for $28,000. It was furnished with furniture created by the National Youth Administration (NYA) along with colcha embroidered cushions pillows and stage curtains, tin work by Eddie Delgado and a fresco on the front exterior of the building by Dorothy Stewart in 1936. The fresco was later destroyed during a building expansion project. Another mural was also located in the ladies lounge and is also gone. Restoration of some of the tin work plus new pieces was done by Delgado's great-grandson, Jason Younis, in 2007.

At the dedication ceremony on Sept. 23, 1936 the keynote speaker was Harry Hopkins, the national director of the WPA.

The theater administration plans that the desired educational wing, also designed by Meem at the time of the construction of the theater, will be constructed if funds become available. At that time the early fresco will be re-created.

ALBUQUERQUE PUBLIC SCHOOLS BUILDINGS

A number of other buildings were constructed, remodeled or had additions built as the result of this source of funding. Adjacent school playgrounds, ball fields, etc. were also created. The schools include: Armijo, Bandelier, Coronado,* Duranes, Five Points School, Harwood High School, Jefferson Middle School, John Marshall, La Mesa, Lew Wallace, Lincoln, Los Candelarias, Pajarito, Roosevelt, San Jose,* Santa

Barbara, Stronghurst and Washington Junior High. For specific information on each of these, refer to the Albuquerque Museum Monograph by Charles Biebel which may be out of print.

*These schools are listed on the State Register #1644 and #1645.

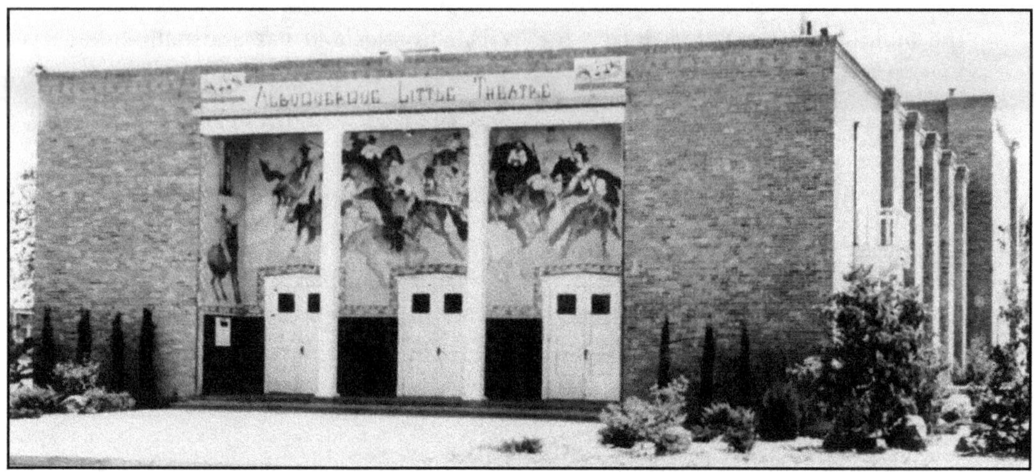

The Albuquerque Little Theater as it originally appeared with a mural/fresco called "Los Moros" by Dorothy Stewart. It was destroyed during a renovation some years ago. There are plans to reproduce it when funds are available. Photograph from *A More Abundant Life, New Deal Artists and Public Art in New Mexico*, courtesy of Sunstone Press.

ART WORK for the schools. According to Biebel, artists were hired to create 31 oil paintings and 21 watercolors to be placed in the schools. One wonders where they are now. The art collection at Albuquerque High School which was supposedly donated each year by the senior class for some years is now part of the collection at the Albuquerque Museum.

BARELAS COMMUNITY CENTER
801 Barelas Road SW

BASALT MASONRY WALL in Old Town Plaza, now demolished.

BUENA VISTA COMMUNITY PLAYGROUND
Location unknown but it was constructed by the youth in the National Youth Administration.

CITY HALL, POLICE AND JAIL ADDITION was completed with $116,000 of Public Works Administration (PWA).

CIVILIAN CONSERVATION CORPS CAMPGROUND
The Kiwanis Hut is a rock structure built by the CCC in the Sandia Mountains near

the camp area. Other CCC sites in the area are the Juan Tabo Recreation Area and La Cueva Campground. The young men from the camps near Albuquerque built picnic grounds at these sites and numerous ones in town. They built cabins, ski runs, tows, lodges, signs, and markers and strung telephone lines.

EL VADO DAM and RESERVOIR
Built to save flooding in the North Valley and downtown areas of Albuquerque.

HEIGHTS COMMUNITY CENTER
823 Buena Vista SE
(505) 848-1334

This New Deal project done by the NYA in 1938 is still serving its original purpose to provide the community with space for a variety of services and many happy hours of enjoyment. There have been expansions to the original building which is located near Albuquerque's Technical Vocational Institute now called Central New Mexico Community College.

LOS POBLANOS HISTORIC INN/FARM
Los Ranchos de Albuquerque

The original property was a WPA era stimulus project around an 800 acre working ranch and also the original site of Creamland Dairy.

MILNE STADIUM
1200 Hazeldine SE
(505) 880-3700
An Albuquerque public school facility.

MONTE VISTA FIRE STATION (currently a restaurant)
3201 Central Avenue NE
SR #849 State Register 12-18-81, National Register 3-19-87

The Monte Vista Fire Station, designed by City Architect, E. H. Blumenthal, was built with PWA funds and completed in 1936. As with all New Deal projects this hollow block and stucco building was constructed with local materials, using local labor. The exposed wooden lintels, projecting viga ends, ladders on the upper floors, and undulating parapets give the station its Pueblo Revival effect.

NEW MEXICO STATE FAIRGROUNDS BUILDINGS

Wilfred Stedman designed the grandstand, paddock, track and clubhouses as part of this WPA project. Other New Deal buildings at the fairgrounds include the Fine Arts Building and the Bolack Building (Agriculture) both done in 1942. This latter building is on the State Register of Cultural Properties SRCP #1492. When built between 1936–1938, most residents felt "it was too far out to attract exhibits and visitors—it was like an outpost in a desert and the now famous Central Avenue Gate Tower was a most useless structure," as noted in a State Fair document. Over 200 laborers laid a million or more adobes to construct the buildings including the grandstand, barns, administration building, exhibit buildings and jockey room and moved 170,000 cubic yards of dirt for the racetrack.

OLD ALBUQUERQUE HIGH SCHOOL
401 Central Avenue NE, Suite #102
(505) 764-3700
SR #464 State Register 6-20-77, National Register 11-17-78

Three of the Gothic Revival buildings in the Old Albuquerque High School complex were designed by Louis Hesselden and built by the PWA using labor supplied by the WPA. The buildings included the administration building, gymnasium and library. This whole complex has been restored and converted into business units and residential condominiums called The Lofts at Albuquerque High. The public art created for this building was transferred to the Albuquerque Museum collection when the building was released by the Albuquerque Public Schools.

OLD ALBUQUERQUE MUNICIPAL AIRPORT
2920 Yale Boulevard SE
SR #482 State Register 12-20-76, National Register 5-5-89

The 1939 municipal airport building is a flat-roofed, two story Pueblo Revival style structure that was designed by City Architect Ernest H. Blumenthal and built of adobe brick and other local materials by WPA workers. Adobe bricks were made on site and covered the reinforced concrete frame. Vigas and other wood elements were cut in the Jemez Mountains and milled or hand carved on site. The flagstones for the floors were cut and brought from the nearby Sandia Mountains. The interior is also Pueblo Revival with viga and herringbone-pattern latilla ceilings and walls of roughened stucco above tongue-and-groove wainscoting. The lobby was decorated with tinwork chandeliers, Indian rugs, hand-carved wooden screens and WPA created furniture. At some point, there were large paintings created by Pop Chalee which now hang in the current Albuquerque International Airport, but she reported she was commissioned to paint those by Howard Hughes, pilot and movie producer.

OLD CHAMBER OF COMMERCE BUILDING
Built in September, 1935 for $7,500 but demolished later.

REMODELING OF ARMORY
This building has been demolished.

RIO GRANDE ZOOLOGICAL PARK
903 Tenth Street SW
This city facility was enlarged with New Deal funds.

ROOSEVELT PARK
501 Sycamore Street SE
State Register # 1646

This large park was first called Terrace Park possibly because this flat terrain was changed with additional dirt filled hills and terraces. Two acres were made available to the City and the Albuquerque Public schools gave the City a long term lease on an additional eleven acres. Retaining walls and a water system were constructed and nearby streets were improved. Most of this work was paid for with Civil Works Administration (CWA) funds. Two hundred seventy-five workers planted trees, shrubs and totally changed the environment at a cost of $126,065. Tingley changed the name to Roosevelt Park on February 1934 as a tribute to President Roosevelt's great leadership. After its completion 800-1,000 school children being served by the WPA's Federal Music Project put on a Christmas program there.

TINGLEY BEACH
1800 Tingley Drive SW

An early swimming hole and city landmark first called the Conservancy Beach but later named after Clyde Tingley, Mayor and later Governor. The adjacent lake was drained and workers cleaned out the algae, moss and seaweed before refilling it.

TINGLEY FIELD STADIUM

This was a New Deal constructed baseball field where the Albuquerque Dukes played their first games. The buildings including 4,000 seat grandstand, concession stands, dug out, and wall were built for $41,000 by 90 workers. All these were later demolished and now the area is virtually all part of the park near the Rio Grande Zoological Garden on Tenth Street.

UNDERPASSES at CENTRAL AVENUE and TIJERAS AVENUE

UNIVERSITY OF NEW MEXICO ANTHROPOLOGY BUILDING (formerly the Old Student Union Building)

Meem designed this building that was completed in 1937. It includes 27,880 square feet and the construction costs were $127,553 according to Van Dorn Hooker's book, *Only in New Mexico*. WPA handcrafted furniture also adorned the interior.

UNIVERSITY OF NEW MEXICO SCHOLES HALL
SR #388 State Register 6-20-75, National Register 9-22-88

Built in 1936 as the Administration and Laboratory Building of the University of New Mexico, the building was designed by John Gaw Meem and funded by Public Works Administration (PWA) for $262,410. The H-shaped building with two story wings and a three story central section is Spanish-Pueblo Revival Style and features two towers designed to be reminiscent of those of the Mission of Acoma. The building including 49,210 square feet initially housed administration, anthropology, physics, psychology, and geology departments. WPA craftspersons built furniture that blended well with the type of architecture. Over the years there has been much interior remodeling but the exterior is still very much as it was when the New Deal funded construction was completed.

UNIVERSITY OF NEW MEXICO ZIMMERMAN LIBRARY

An example of John Gaw Meem's design of Santa Fe Style architecture came into being with federal funding ($341,424) as a (PWA) project in 1938. Furniture and tin work can be found throughout the building created by New Deal craft persons and as a result Meem once commented that this was probably the most expensive building created on campus when one includes the amount spent on all the fine handicrafts. The total estimated cost was actually $460,080 according to Van Dorn Hooker. Meem shared that this building which includes 61,578 square feet was probably his finest work. There have been additions to this building since. There are other outstanding murals in the building that are not New Deal creations, but were funded by the Carnegie and Ford foundations.

The Center for Southwest Research in this facility is a gold mine of New Mexico's New Deal information. A must if you are doing research on this subject. (505) 277-1389 is the phone number for a knowledgeable reference specialist. Collections of the papers of various key New Mexico New Dealers including John Gaw Meem and Helen Chandler Ryan, head of the New Mexico Federal Music Project, are located here. See Appendix for more reference information from this facility.

OTHER UNIVERSITY OF NEW MEXICO STRUCTURES

Dates, costs and square feet information from Van Dorn Hooker's book, *Only in New Mexico: An Architectural History of the University of New Mexico. The First Century, 1889–1989.*

Bandelier West, men's dorm, 1941 ($92,124 and 15,073 square feet). Meem designed.

Marron Hall East, women's dorm, 1940 ($91,427 and 19,982 square feet). Meem designed.

Mesa Vista #1, men's cooperative dorm, student infirmary, and Navy ROTC, 1941 ($66,142 estimated and 12,040 square feet). It is the only adobe building on campus. Meem designed and constructed by University of New Mexico staff directed by Earl Bowdich.

Heating Plant and Engineering Lab, 1936 ($158,413 and 17,324 square feet). Meem designed.

Football stadium, 1934 ($129,000 but later torn down to make way for Ortega Hall).

State Public Health Laboratory, 1941 ($51,627 and 9,823 square feet). Meem designed. Now Navy ROTC program.
Golf course
Swimming pool
Tennis courts, University Heights addition
Press building
Landscaping and sidewalks done by CCC

VETERANS COMMUNITY CENTER
East Tijeras and Broadway

Programs to serve the veterans were administered here as was the administration of the WPA program.

OTHER STRUCTURES AND IMPROVEMENTS including water works, waste disposal plant, roads, streets, gutters, miles of sidewalks.

PROGRAMS

Hot school lunches.
Mosquito eradication to reduce malaria.
Poison control for major grasshopper infestations in surrounding land to city.
Teachers provided for kindergarten programs.
Sewing classes with clothes and mattress covers made and distributed to destitute families.
Beef slaughtered and frozen to be distributed to destitute families.
Surveys for flood and erosion control.
Public health programs for mothers of newborns.
Redecoration of City Library and City Hall.

MYSTERY ARTWORK, see Chapter 4

AMISTAD

NEW DEAL PUBLIC BUILDINGS and STRUCTURES

SCHOOL
State Register #1622

In 1937 a small public school with a gymnasium was built to provide educational opportunities for the children of ranching families in this northeastern area of the state. The facility is now used as a community center and is in excellent shape possibly because the gym was built with adobe bricks reinforced with steel. In addition to many basketball games, there were stage shows, musical events and other kinds of programs.

The stage curtain was originally from the Forrest High School when it closed in 1957 as were also their basketball uniforms. The curtain is now hanging in the cafeteria. The people in that area of the state are very proud of this facility and are dedicated to keeping it in good condition. While in this little village, don't miss a small museum in a remaining house just across the street.

RURAL ELECTRIC ADMINISTRATION (REA)

Southwestern Electric Cooperative continues to serve this primarily rural area of the state making their daily living and work activities far more easy and comfortable. This is near the heart of the Dust Bowl area which prompted so much to be done for Americans and New Mexicans between 1933–1943.

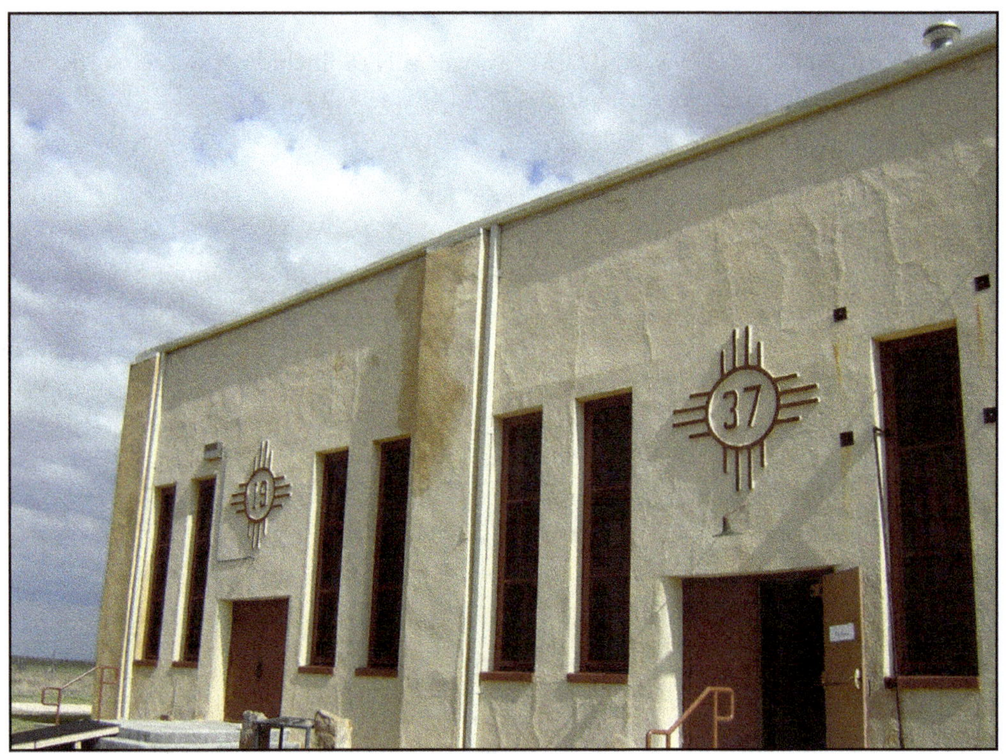

This WPA adobe gymnasium with its WPA 1937 boldly identified on the front of the building is still in use as part of the Amistad Community Center. Photograph by the author.

ARTESIA

Although there is no known New Deal public art in other buildings in this community, there are original field notes from the WPA-Writers Project created by Katherine Rosedale Caudle located in the town's History Museum and Art Center. This facility also is in possession of a WPA chair and table made in 1938.

NEW DEAL BUILDNGS AND STRUCTURES

ARTESIA MUNICIPAL HOSPITAL Originally called Artesia Memorial Hospital when built in 1939 by PWA funds and landscaping was also done. That building is currently closed for public use but may in the future become a nursing home facility.

OLD CITY HALL This structure was built in 1939 but is now being used as a real estate office and looks much as it did then.

OLD FIRE STATION This New Deal building was torn down and the lot is currently vacant but possible plans being considered involve a city office complex.

OLD SWIMMING POOL, ROCK BATHOUSE, GYMNASIUM

MORRIS ATHLETIC FIELD This is the high school football field built in 1939 and still in use. The rock wall enclosing it is particularly unique because of the various rock designs (flowers, hat, cross, etc.) built into the walls at various locations. Most people may not even notice them until they have been pointed out, and then they are quite visible to the viewer.

OLD CITY LIBRARY This was built with Public Works Administration (PWA) funds and currently serves as a city office building.

McMILLAN DAM

RURAL ELECTRIC COOPERATIVE
1505 North Thirteenth Street
(575) 746-3571

This is the office of Central Valley Electric Cooperative, a New Deal program that continues to serve Americans/New Mexicans today. This cooperative has approximately 12,134 consumers in its area of the state.

OTHER IMPROVEMENTS The WPA and CCC were also responsible for road construction, erosion control, telephone line construction, fencing and stock tank construction, sidewalks, curbs, gutters, cemetery road improvements, water and sewer system improvements, and personnel help at the library.

AZTEC

NEW DEAL ART IN NEW DEAL BUILDINGS

AZTEC RUINS NATIONAL MONUMENT

This historic site was created by early pueblo people (Chacoans and Mesa Verdeans) and became a national monument much later in 1923. The New Deal Public

Works Administration (PWA) and the Civil Works Administration (CWA) monies and programs provided the opportunity to do restoration work on the pueblo ruins, build park structures and cataloging of the undocumented assortment of accrued specimens which are still in use and available today. The New Deal 1934 restoration of the kiva is said to be the only reconstructed great kiva in the Southwest. Art work in the exhibit displays were done by a New Deal unknown artist, 'Bergen', who may have lived in California since the paintings originated in the Western Museum Laboratory in Berkeley. The titles of these watercolors include:

"Reconstruction of the Pueblo"
"Pueblo Weaver"
"Pueblo Hunters"
"Pueblo Women Grinding Corn"
"Pueblo Corn Field"
"Pueblo Potters"
"Pueblo Men Chipping Flint"
"Bread Making"

NEW DEAL BUILDINGS, STRUCTURES and PROGRAM

CITY HALL Built in 1936 and now houses the Aztec Museum downtown.

LIBRARY An adobe structure built in 1936 and on State Register of Cultural Properties SRCP 906.

OTHER STRUCTURES AND IMPROVEMENTS included schools, roads, Animas River bank repair, two bridges relocated, ditches, channel improvements, sewer construction, sidewalks, water system repairs and park improvements including pool, field and tennis courts.

PROGRAM Sewing rooms operations.

MYSTERY ARTWORK, see Chapter 4 (Kloss)

BANDELIER NATIONAL MONUMENT

15 Entrance Road
Los Alamos, New Mexico 87544
(505) 672-3861
State Register SRCP 56, 5-20-69, National Register 10-15-66

"In spite of Depression gloom, there was a new and positive sense of the artist's place in American society and a more confident attitude toward American art. I have never heard an artist who lived through those years complain about WPA art projects. It still remains for many a golden age."

—Milton W. Brown. "New Deal Art Projects–Boondoggle or Bargain?" *Art News*, April, 1982

NEW DEAL PUBLIC ART IN NEW DEAL BUILDING

Between 1936 and 1940 Bandelier National Monument participated as part of the WPA by employing a number of New Mexico artisans to create special artworks for their CCC built structures. These buildings are now on the State and National Registers of Historic Places.

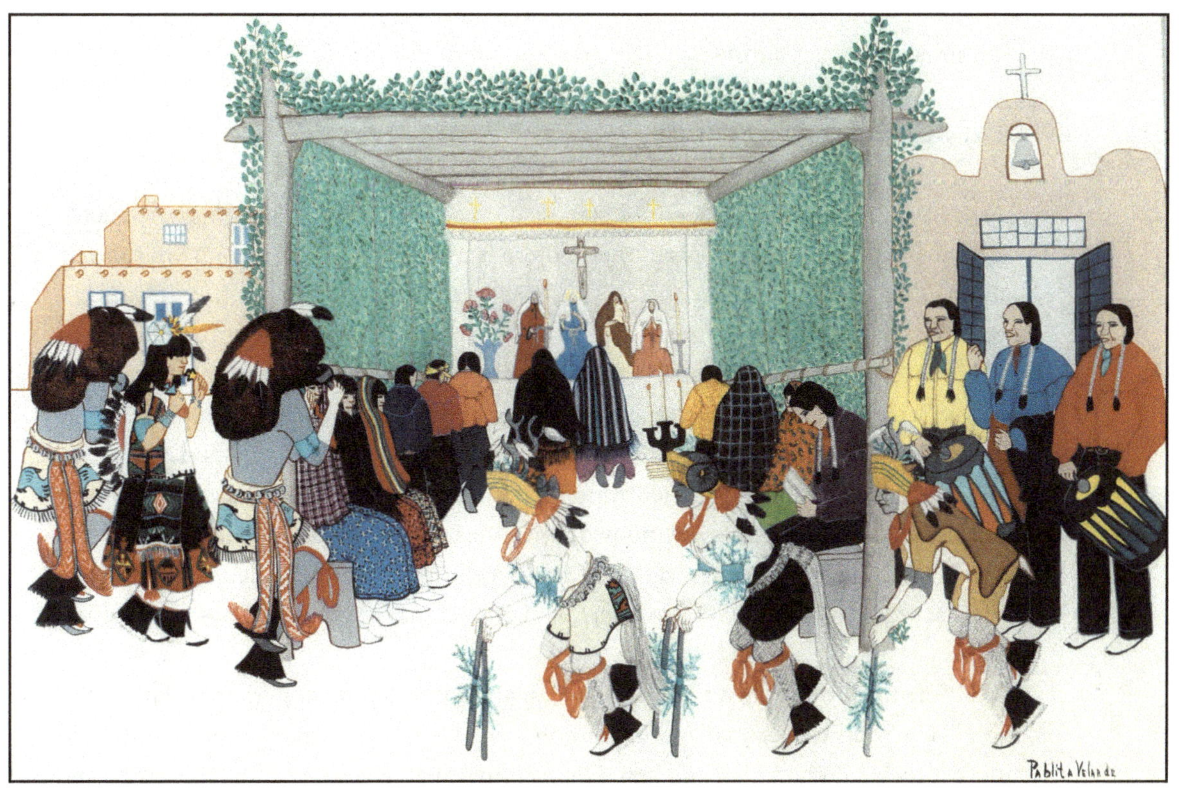

Pablita Velarde's 1939 casein "Ceremony" is part of a large collection (over 80) of casein watercolors in the Bandelier National Monument Archives. Photograph by Pat Berrett from *A More Abundant Life, New Deal Artists and Public Art in New Mexico*, courtesy of Sunstone Press.

Pablita Velarde from Santa Clara Pueblo was commissioned by the National Park Service (NPS) and paid by WPA to do large murals and easel paintings. They are primarily casein on masonite boards and on glass. In the past Velarde's art has been in storage but was shown in its entirety in 2008 at an exhibit at the Museum of Indian

Arts and Culture in Santa Fe. The remodeling of the Visitor Center was completed in the summer of 2010 and it is planned that the Velarde collection will be seen more frequently on site. These works express her basic integrity and faithful portrayal of her people and their Native American culture. The entire collection includes over eighty paintings and the elders of her pueblo were not happy with her for portraying everyday life in the pueblo. Defying "the system etc." was standard behavior for Pablita all her life and certainly even before the expansion of women's roles were accepted particularly in her Native culture.

Legoria Tafoya, one of Pablita's sisters, created both a Santa Clara pottery making series and black and white photographs of her pottery making techniques. Helmuth Naumer's fourteen pastels express the timeless Pueblo Indian landscape and Frijoles Canyon. E. J. Austin's works are primarily drawings and prehistoric site location maps and Indian facial sculptures.

NEW DEAL BUILDINGS and STRUCTURES

In addition to working on the stabilization of the remarkable prehistoric pueblo ruins at Bandelier National Monument, there is a historic district comprising thirty-one buildings constructed by the CCC as well as the road down into the site and the paths throughout the park area. Built in the Pueblo Revival style, the rock buildings formed a complete development for the National Monument—everything from a Visitor Center and offices for staff to lodging for guests and housing for employees. The guest lodging now houses more staff offices. The buildings were built of locally quarried stone and connected to each other by portals, stone walls, and flagstone walks. Exterior details include wooden doors, window frames, viga ends and post and decorated corbel portals. The interiors feature viga and latilla ceilings, corner fireplaces, bancos and hand carved wood. The CCC also built Spanish-Colonial style furnishings for the guest lodges.

The main office area also includes a snack bar and gift shop and was laid out to look like a Southwestern village surrounding three sides of a plaza where visitors can now eat their lunches, visit and rest. Detailed masonry drinking fountains, curbs and retaining walls give the entire complex a pleasing unity.

BELEN

NEW DEAL BUILDINGS, STRUCTURES and PROGRAMS

JUNIOR HIGH and other school improvements. Building no longer exists.

CITY HALL Became the Police Headquarters, but is now abandoned and in terrible shape.

COMMUNITY CENTER Became a public library and is now a florist shop.

POLICE DEPARTMENT Status unknown.

PUBLIC WELFARE BUILDING Destroyed to build new Welfare Office and MVD building.

SCHOOLS, GYMNASIUM, ATHLETIC FIELD. Status unknown.

RECREATIONAL BEACH The Boys Beach off the Rio Grande east of Belen was built prior to the New Deal but WPA may have been used to make improvements there.

RURAL ELECTRIC ADMINISTRATION (REA) Central New Mexico Cooperative- This New Deal program continues to serve the rural areas near this community.

OTHER STRUCTURES and PROGRAMS include tennis courts, sidewalks, curbs, gutters, sewer and water plant improvements, community garden project, canal constructing, canning center, and sewing project.

MYSTERY ARTWORK, see Chapter 4 (Kloss)

BERNALILLO

NEW DEAL ART IN NEW DEAL BUILDINGS

CORONADO STATE MONUMENT
State Register of Cultural Properties SRCP 1515

This is a New Deal structure on the site of the Kuaua, a thriving pueblo in the 1500s. The monument houses a collection in the early Pueblo kiva of Native American art. During the New Deal era, individuals were hired to do excavation of Kuaua Ruins and Native American artist, Velino Shije Herrera, was hired by the WPA-Federal Art Project, along with some others to restore the early artwork.

NEW DEAL BUILDINGS, STRUCTURES and PROGRAMS

ROOSEVELT ELEMENTARY SCHOOL Currently housing K-2 grade classrooms.
State Register of Cultural Properties SRCP 1619.

HIGH SCHOOL ADDITION

COUNTY HEALTH CENTER

PUBLIC WELFARE BUILDING

OTHER STRUCTURES and PROGRAMS include roads, schools, sewing room, canning and clothing projects, ditch drainage improvements and desert regional garden exhibit.

MYSTERY ARTWORK, see Chapter 4 (Kloss)

BLOOMFIELD

SALMON RUINS MUSEUM AND RESEARCH LIBRARY
P. O. Box 125
Bloomfield, New Mexico 87413
(505) 632-2013, (505) 632-8633 (Fax)
www.salmonruins.com

This facility has acquired the research work of Jim Snyder, their deceased librarian, which includes one hundred seventeen three inch binders of materials and maps about the CCC work in that area, as well as Chaco Canyon and Guernsey, Wyoming.

BOSQUE FARMS

NEW DEAL PUBLIC BUILDINGS and STRUCTURES

BOSQUE COOPERATIVE BUILDING State Historic Register #1632.

ELEMENTARY SCHOOL This is also a New Deal structure.

NEW DEAL RESETTLEMENT TOWN

This is the only Resettlement Town known in New Mexico. It is an area near Belen where farmers in the 1930–1940s were resettled with funding from one of the New Deal agricultural programs. The Joe Arvizu home and outbuildings have been well kept in their original form and have been awarded New Mexico Historic Sites status and plaque #1409. Other such resettlement farms in the area still exist but have made major changes to their structures. The Woodall House is also on the State Register #1789.

RURAL ELECTRIC ADMINSTRATION (REA) The Central New Mexico Electric Cooperative continues to provide electricity to the rural areas of this part of the state.

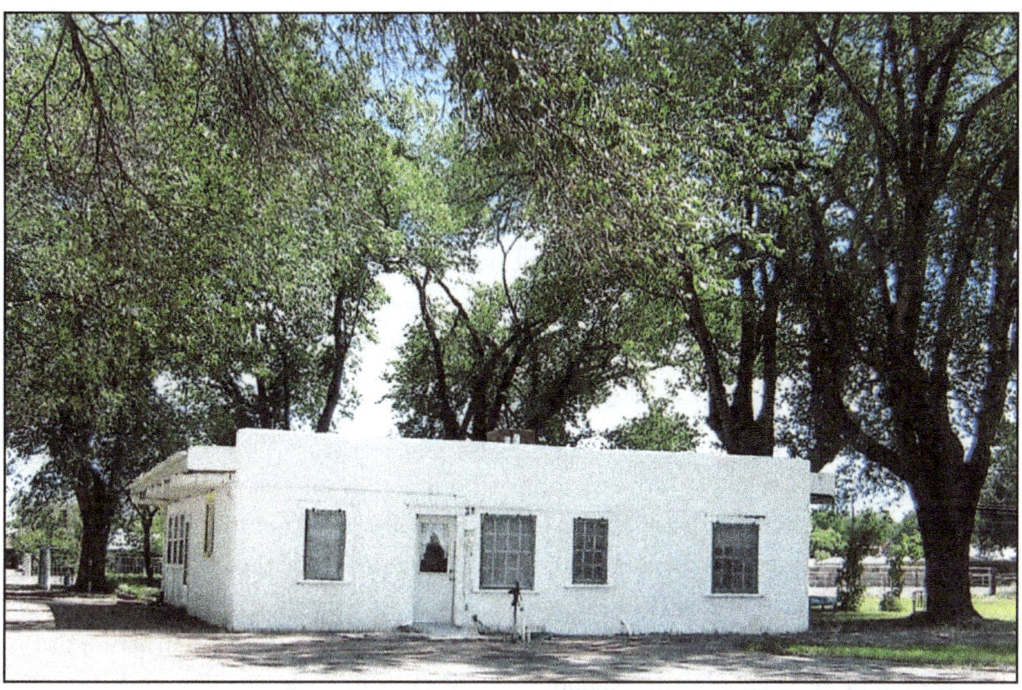

This Bosque Farms house and all its original farm outbuildings have been kept up in pristine condition with no changes over the years, therefore it is on the New Mexico State Historical Register. The New Deal resettlement program gave many families across the state and nation a chance to start over after their previous farm land had been badly eroded and was no longer useable to live on or raise agriculture products.

BUEYEROS

A two room school house was built in 1939 and continued as such until the early 1950s when small rural schools were consolidated into larger nearby towns. It is in need of restoration but sometimes used as a community center. It has been placed on the State Register for Cultural Properties #1621. Note: If you are in the area to see the school or otherwise, the Bueyeros Church has been restored and the church rectory is now a Bed and Breakfast—an upscale accommodation for that part of the country.

CAPITAN

NEW DEAL BUILDINGS, STRUCTURES and PROGRAMS

CAMP CAPITAN

This was a National Youth Administration (NYA) camp for unemployed girls and was located between Capitan and Lincoln in Baca Canyon. The site started out as a forestry department site, then CCC camp and finally a girl's camp. It was the first of its kind in the U.S., originating in 1935 under the administration of the Women's and Professional Project of the WPA then transferred to NYA. Like the CCC program, the girls received $5 per month plus $25 going to their families back home. They came from all over the state and were educated and also trained in various skills including household management, arts and crafts, sewing and reportedly there were murals covering the walls of the recreational building known as the Baca Canyon Opera House. This program lasted for three years at this site and during that time the girls sewed state flags, clothes for children at Carrie Tingley Hospital for Crippled Children and tin work light fixtures for White Sands National Monument among other things.

PUBLIC SCHOOL

The first schools were one room school houses on area ranches followed by a public school building paid for by a local citizen in 1900. After the area became a state in 1912, the legislature mandated high schools created throughout the state and a high school was completed in 1913 in Capitan. It was replaced by a WPA funded school in 1936. By 1945 a new high school was needed and built and the 1936 structure became the junior high school. Other school structures remain including a shop building, and landscaping.

RURAL ELECTRIC ADMINISTRATION (REA)

This rural area of the state is provided electricity thanks to the 1930s New Deal program by the Otero County Electric Cooperative. As of 2011, it had 13,480 consumers in Chaves, Lincoln, Otero and Socorro counties.

VILLAGE HALL/FIRE STATION

In 1941 a municipal building was constructed for $46,240 and continues to be used in this way. Earlier in 1935 a fire station was built but that building no longer exits.

OTHER STRUCTURES Water works construction, Ranger Station, and roads.

MYSTERY ARTWORK

None known but curiosity about where the murals are and the other arts and crafts (including furniture) that were done by the young ladies at Camp Capitan.

CAPULIN

The road leading up and around Capulin Volcano National Monument in Union County was constructed by the Civil Works Administration (CWA) by twenty-five local men between December 1933 and April 1934 thanks to the leadership of Homer Farr who was a local power figure and the first director of this site. They also created campgrounds. He communicated with the Roosevelt Administration tirelessly in order to provide employment for the local men and to get the road done. He was most likely responsible for also getting the Federal Emergency Relief Administration (FERA), another New Deal program, to do the retaining wall around the Visitor Center parking area. For more information, contact the Ranger at (575) 278-2201.

CARLSBAD

"...the federal art project might be termed the guardian of many artists and we believe it is bridging a span of time which might have been disastrous to art developments when discouragement occurred from lack of patronage."

—Russell Vernon Hunter, Federal Art Project Director. "WPA Project Bringing Art Education Appreciation," *The Santa Fe New Mexican*, February 22, 1926

NEW DEAL ART IN NEW DEAL BUILDINGS

CARLSBAD CAVERNS NATIONAL PARK
Carlsbad Caverns National Park Historic District
3225 National Park Highway
Carlsbad, New Mexico 88220
(575) 887-0275
State Register #269, 2-20-73, National Register 8-18-88

The Historic District at Carlsbad Caverns National Park comprises a number of Pueblo Revival buildings constructed by park personnel in the 1920s and 1930s and several stuccoed adobe buildings in the New Mexico Territorial Revival style by the CCC in the early 1940s. Some of the trails and landscaping were also done by the CCC, but most predate this program.

The District is eligible for the National Register both because of its architectural significance and landscaped setting and because of its association with the CCC and WPA. Furniture and tin work were also created for these structures and still they are in use today.

Will Shuster, Santa Fe artist, created five paintings of the caverns in 1934 and 1939 during his New Deal painting days. Most of these works are now in the Western Archaeological Conference Center and storage area in Tucson, which is part of the National Park Service, but some are back at the Cavern's Visitor Center.

Early New Deal posters included a selected piece possibly from Shuster's earlier set of art created during a trip with Walter Mruk in 1926, works that "were objective in form and highlighted in white, grays, and blues. The later paintings were done under electric lighting and were warmer and utilize more color than the earlier canvasses," wrote Joseph Dispenza and Louise Turner in *Will Shuster, A Santa Fe Legend.* A newer book by Lois Manno is called *Visions Underground: Carlsbad Caverns through the Artist's Eye*. It discusses Shuster's work and more about the history of the park.

NEW DEAL ART IN PUBLIC BUILDINGS

CARLSBAD MUSEUM AND ART CENTER
318 W. Fox Street
(575) 387-0276

"The Jicarilla Apache Trading Post", 42" x 50," was painted by La Verne Nelson Black as part of the New Deal Treasury Relief Art Project (TRAP). This program paid for artwork to be placed in newly constructed New Deal buildings so it would be interesting to determine what the original site for this painting was since this museum is not a New Deal structure. The painting is a dramatic work of Jicarilla Apache Indians at the trading post some of whom are on horseback.

A Juan Sanchez santo done as part of his New Deal work is also in the collection on loan from the Museum of Fine Art in Santa Fe. Other retablos from the same source may also still be on loan there.

NEW DEAL BUILDINGS, STRUCTURES and PROGRAMS

ALTERNATIVE HIGH SCHOOL—Possibly Edison/Phoenix Project

BEACH, RIVERWALK, PARK AND BATHHOUSE

These buildings were created along the Pecos River. It was originally known as the Carlsbad Metropolitan Park. All these facilities are still a popular attraction in the community today particularly in the summer and even with a special event around Christmas featuring local boats lit up with Christmas decorations and parades down the river during that holiday period.

EDDY COUNTY COURTHOUSE

The courthouse was begun in 1801 with additions in 1914 and 1939. The 1939 addition was done by WPA for $185,000.

P. R. LEYBA SCHOOL Built 1940 and still in use.

RATTLESNAKE SPRINGS HISTORIC DISTRICT A New Deal CCC project that is on the State Register # 1496.

RURAL ELECTRIC ADMINISTRATION (REA) The rural areas surrounding Carlsbad are provided electricity by the Central Valley Electric cooperative based in Artesia.

SITTING BULL FALLS FACILITIES. On State Register #1740. Most of the work done by the CCC.

OTHER STRUCTURES AND PROGRAMS include National Guard armory and stables, Unemployment Office, bridge, roads, sidewalks, water system improvements, cemetery improvements, clothing project, city census, airport and construction.

MYSTERY ARTWORK, see Chapter 4

CARRIZOZO

NEW DEAL BUILDINGS, STRUCTURES and PROGRAM

COMMUNITY CENTER. The original building may have been built in 1927 with a gymnasium and stage added to it by the WPA. It is now a market.

COUNTRY CLUB

HIGH SCHOOL. The original building (1940) has been renovated.

LINCOLN COUNTY COURTHOUSE

The first courthouse was built in 1913 when the county seat was moved in 1909 from Lincoln to Carrizozo. Later a newer facility was created in 1940 with New Deal funds and included a jail. In 1964 another new courthouse was created and the 1940 portion is now the annex to the newer structure.

RURAL ELECTRIC COOPERATIVE (REA), a New Deal Project, continues to serve this rural area of the state via the Otero County Electric Cooperative with the office in Cloudcroft.

SCHOOL BOOK DEPOSITORY

This New Deal structure was built in 1937 and was the site where school teachers got their school books. It was similar to a library and book repairs and cataloging were carried out by WPA workers. Later it served as a law office, an abstract and insurance office and is now a private home.

WOMEN'S CLUB. On State Register for Cultural Properties SRCP 1833. In 2011 the building is still in use celebrating its 90th anniversary.

OTHER STRUCTURES AND IMPROVEMENTS included roads, waterworks, ditches, bridges, parks, septic tank construction, curbs and gutters, and demolition of the railroad roundhouse.

CEDARVALE

NEW DEAL BUILDINGS and STRUCTURES

The WPA added a gymnasium to the school house in 1936. Both are still standing but are in poor condition. The owner of the property would like to restore them. Similar poor conditions for buildings can be seen in the New Deal WPA school buildings in Monticello and Claunch.

CHACO CANYON

It must have been a challenge for young CCC boys to work stabilizing the rock structures at this site. The museum was built by the WPA in 1935 for $4,550 and excavation and repair of ruins was done at that same time. The CCC was also active in this project. No known New Deal art has been identified at this monument.

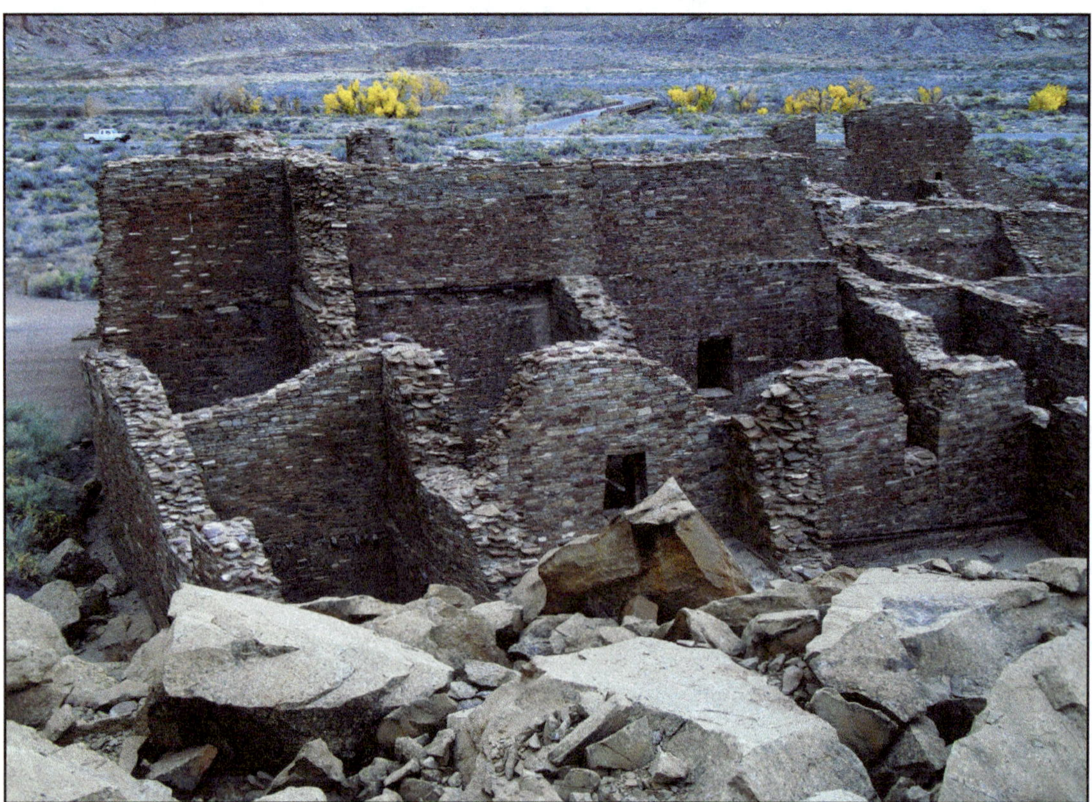

The Civilian Conservation Corps (CCC) young men worked hard in this area stabilizing the ruins and the WPA built the structure in 1935 housing the museum. All are still available for tourists and campers to continue to experience today.

CHAMA

NEW DEAL BUILDINGS AND STRUCTURES

RURAL ELECTRIC COOPERATIVE (REA)
1135 Camino Escondido
Chama, New Mexico 87520
(575) 756-2181

This portion of New Mexico is still being served today by the New Deal and making 2,880 consumers' daily lives easier and more productive every day.

SCHOOL, GYMNASIUM and some additions and ROADS

CIMARRON

NEW DEAL ART IN PUBLIC BUILDINGS

Furniture in the City Hall was created by local citizens in either the WPA-Federal Art Project or the Vocational Programs in the schools. These funds were frequently shared in order to get the jobs done that included teaching woodworking skills, employing those in need of work and furnishing public buildings.

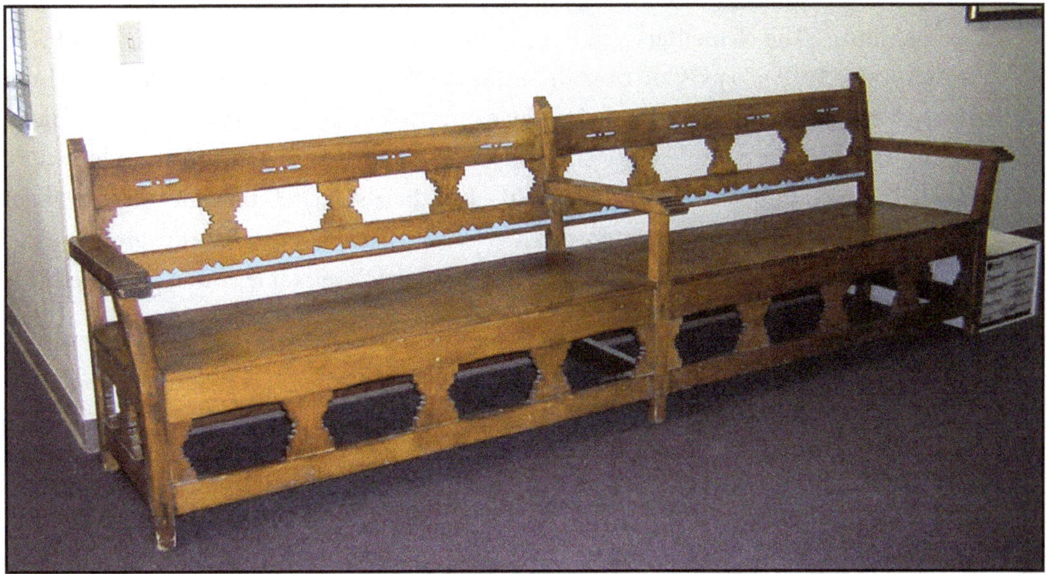

This small village's City Hall still enjoys and appreciates the early southwestern style furniture created for their community building. Similar furniture can be found in public buildings all over the state. Some of it has, however, migrated into private homes.

NEW DEAL BUILDINGS, STRUCTURES and PROGRAM

The RURAL ELECTRIC ADMINISTRATION (REA)'s Kit Carson Electric Cooperative out of Taos continues to serve 22,363 consumers in the rural areas of this county and Rio Arriba and Taos counties.

SCHOOL GYMNASIUM and improvements and roads.

CLAUNCH

(40 miles south of Mountainair on State Road 14)

"The PWA brought new facilities, a high standard of construction, and safety to school buildings across the U. S. By 1936, over 7% of all school construction came through the PWA."
—Faulkner Hamlin Talbot, *Architecture and Government*, Pencil Points, May 19, 1938.

NEW DEAL BUILDINGS and PROGRAMS

The RURAL ELECTRIC ADMINISTRATION (REA) Socorro Electric Cooperative is still serving this rural area of the state as it began doing early in the 1940s.

SCHOOL

Still standing (without a roof) is a rock structure which was once the community school house. The elementary section was built in 1936, the high school in 1939. The inscription, "WPA," is visible over the front doors of both buildings. These buildings using New Deal funds were created by the hand work of the CCC and NYA work forces. Many of them were designed by Wilfred Stedman of the Krueger and Clark architectural firm. They are in bad condition as of 2011 but their signs tell the story. Many of our elder New Mexicans, including former Governor Bruce King, were educated in these structures all over the state. His home WPA school was in Stanley but it is now gone.

CLAYTON

"Even the bootleggers did their bit, in absentia. From all over the northern section of the county, students and ranchmen brought in whiskey stills to the Clayton schools—scores of them abandoned years before when their operators took hasty retreat. The fine copper they contained took form as massive wastebaskets for the schools."
—Elvon L. Howe, "The Man Who Saved Union County,"
Rocky Mountain Empire Magazine, May 16, 1948

NEW DEAL PUBLIC ART IN NEW DEAL PUBLIC BUILDINGS

CLAYTON PUBLIC SCHOOL ART COLLECTION
Hersztein Museum
Second and Walnut Street
Clayton, NM 88415
(575) 374-2977

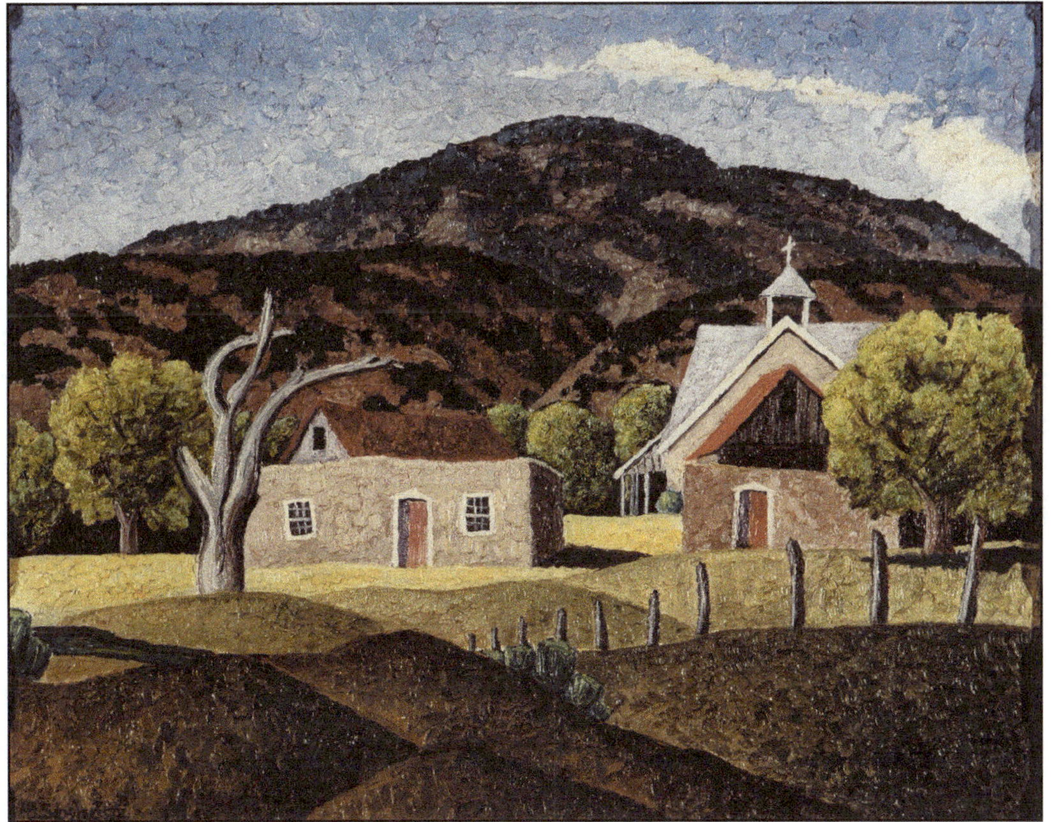

"The Dead Tree" by Howard Behling Schleeter once in the Clayton High School. Photograph by Pat Berrett from *A More Abundant Life, New Deal Artists and Public Art in New Mexico*, courtesy of Sunstone Press.

Clayton, in the direct path of the Dust Bowl of the Great Depression, survived primarily by the ability of School Superintendent Raymond Huff to come up with numerous programs funded by the Federal New Deal monies and also the State's heavy participation. School buildings including Kiser Elementary School in 1940 and the Junior High and High School are still in use. Local citizens were hired to build and make furniture, mattresses, ironwork, ceramic dishes and other items, colcha embroidered drapes, rugs, and to teach home management. Taking donated old copper stills from the ranches and making them into copper bookends and waste baskets was one of the first public recycling projects.

Frequent trips by Huff to Santa Fe to seek New Deal funds also included his acquiring paintings from the WPA-Federal Art Project done by a variety of New Mexico artists. The school system has thirty-six paintings in its WPA Museum which is the largest collection of New Deal public art in a New Mexico public facility that is not exclusively an art museum or gallery.

This collection, now at the Hersztein Museum, can be enjoyed thanks to the foresight of Raymond Huff and later the Home Economics teacher, Joanne Butt, and her students. There are those who say the whole town of Clayton was saved thanks to the WPA. Many of the paintings have been conserved by the New Mexico Chapter of the NNDPA.

They include the following:

Bakos
"Blue Shadow on the Hill"
(This painting was done by Jozef or his wife, Teresa)
Bybee, First name unknown
"Windblown"
Chapman, Manville
"Indian Man"
"Indian Woman"
"Woodland Scene"
Cooke, Rejina Tatum
"Blue Gate"
"Still Life"
"Well by the House"
"Street in Taos"
"Christmas Eve-Taos Pueblo"
"Arrival of Spring"
Jones, D. Paul
"Zinnias"
"In Chamita"
Kloss, Gene
"Penitente Good Friday"
"Christmas Eve—Taos Pueblo"
"New Mexico Indian Village"
"Acoma"
"The Sanctuary—Chimayo"
"Ranchito, New Mexico"
"New Mexico Mountain Town"
Morris, Jim
"Cerro Gordo Road"
Naumer, Helmuth
"Cottonwood Tree"
"Sangre de Cristo"
"Wagon Trail"
"Mount Taylor"
"Upper Pecos"
"Canoncito"
Nordfeldt, B.J.O.
"Street Scene"
"Church & Cemetery"
Pillin, Polia
"Santa Fe Fiesta Booth"
Schannon, G.
"Portrait"
Schleeter, Howard Behling
"The Dead Tree"
"Red Church"
West, Harold
"Get Down, Come In"
"Oklahoma Storm"
Will, Blanca
"My Garden Gourds"
Willis, Brooks
"Still Life"

NEW DEAL BUILDINGS, STRUCTURES and PROGRAMS

CITY HALL

CITY PARK

MUNROE BUILDING
State Register for Cultural Properties #1814

This is the old Public Library. Some of its original furniture is now in the local hotel which is owned by a member of the Munroe family and other investors. At this writing in early 2011, the hotel is closed and is for sale.

RURAL ELECTRIC ADMINISTRATION (REA)
Southwestern Electric Cooperative
216 Main Street
(575) 374-2451

This New Deal program continues today to keep 897 rural consumers electrified in this northeastern portion of the state of New Mexico and Las Animas, Colorado.

OTHER STRUCTURES AND IMPROVEMENTS included roads, drainage systems, moving a bridge from Watrous, well drilling, curbs, gutters, water and sewer lines, dam over Perico Creek, storm sewers/repairs, Mansker school teacherage, County Courthouse improvements and utility plant improvements.

MYSTERY ARTWORK

Possibly one more painting is known of in the community.

CLOVIS

"I learned a tremendous amount in the WPA project. Young, unknown artists and well-known artists were all having big problems. The WPA actually accomplished more than any other program that the government had previously backed. The money went directly to the people who needed it the most."

—James Ridgley Whiteman in an interview with Sandra D'Emilio

NEW DEAL PUBLIC ART IN PUBLIC BUILDINGS

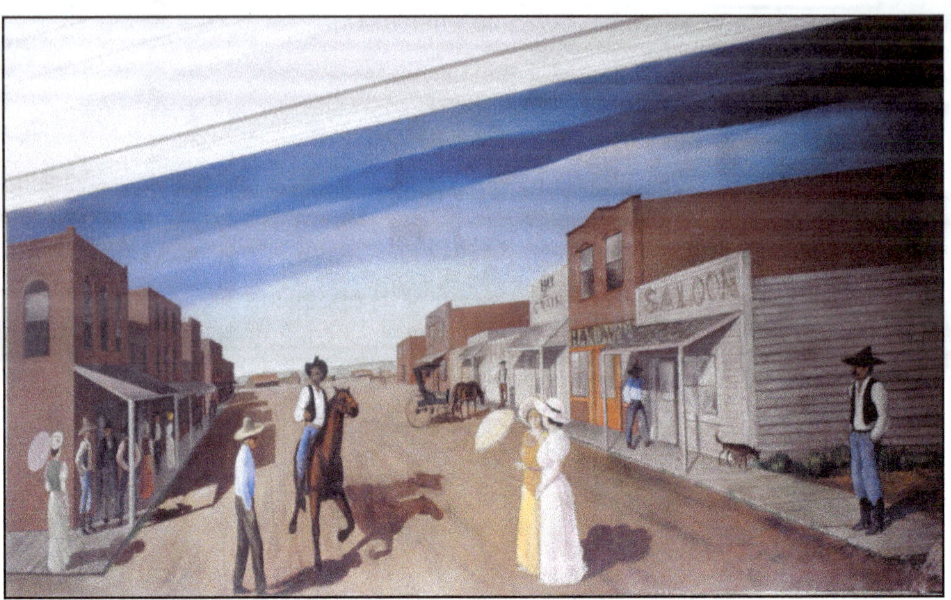

Paul Lantz's mural of Main Street in Clovis is still on view in the town's former post office which is now an architect's office. He was commissioned to paint this by the Section of the Treasury Art Program, a lesser known New Deal program, that provided public art in all the new post offices built during that era. Photograph by Pat Berrett from *A More Abundant Life, New Deal Artists and Public Art in New Mexico*, courtesy of Sunstone Press.

CLOVIS COMMUNITY COLLEGE
417 Schepps Boulevard
(575) 769-2811

Two Howard Schleeter (1903–1976) paintings are on display at this institution. They were both created in 1937 and are titled "Aspen and Oak" and "Ochre Hills." They were originally located in one of the public schools.

FORMER OLD POST OFFICE BUILDING
122 West Fourth Street
(575) 762-2968

This structure was built in 1931 but now provides office space for its current owner, a private architect since the mid-1990s. After its postal days, it served as the Regional Service Center from 1965 to 1974 for the public schools and then it was converted to the Carver-Clovis Public Library in 1974.

The two-story sandstone and brick building with a tiled roof combined Spanish-Colonial revival and Neo-classical styles to create a dignified federal building that was still consistent with its Southwest location. The building was part of the Hoover Administration's efforts to respond to the Depression within its existing programs. Although it predated the New Deal programs, the intention and effects were the same—employment for local workers and business for local suppliers.

NEW DEAL BUILDINGS, STRUCTURES and PROGRAMS

CURRY COUNTY COURTHOUSE on State Register #1274

HILLCREST PARK is on the State Register and includes a swimming pool which records indicate had three sculptures done for the pool by a New York artist. What happened to the sculptures, once in shell-like niches, is a mystery.

MARSHALL JUNIOR HIGH is still in use.

MEMORIAL HOSPITAL is now office space.

MUNICIPAL AUDITORIUM

NATIONAL GUARD ARMORY

RURAL ELECTRIFICATION ADMINISTRATION (REA)
Farmers' Electric Cooperative
3701 Thornton Street
(575) 769-2116

This New Deal program is still serving approximately 7,169 consumers in the rural areas surrounding this town and in DeBaca and Guadalupe counties.

OTHER STRUCTURES AND IMPROVEMENTS include demolishing TWA hangar and salvaging materials, Unemployment office, roads, sewer, lines, sidewalks, sewing room improvements, paving, baseball park construction, library and book repairs, incinerator installation, camp for transients, sewing room operation and indexing real estate records.

MYSTERY ARTWORK, see Chapter 4 (Kloss and Nordfeldt)

COLUMBUS

NEW DEAL BUILDNGS, STRUCTURES and PROGRAMS

OLD SCHOOL

TOWN HALL and Roads

RURAL ELECTRIC ADMINISTRATION (REA)

Columbus Electric Cooperative continues to provide electricity for this area of the state thanks to the New Deal. Its main office is in Deming.

CONCHAS DAM

"The men who worked on the WPA projects were not leaning on a shovel. They earned the $18.75 a week that they were paid by the government as opposed to just being placed on a welfare role. That payment amount was determined by the federal government."

—Mildred Constantine, New Deal staff in New York.
Telephone interview in 1993 with Kathryn A. Flynn

NEW DEAL PUBLIC ART IN NEW DEAL PUBLIC BUILDINGS

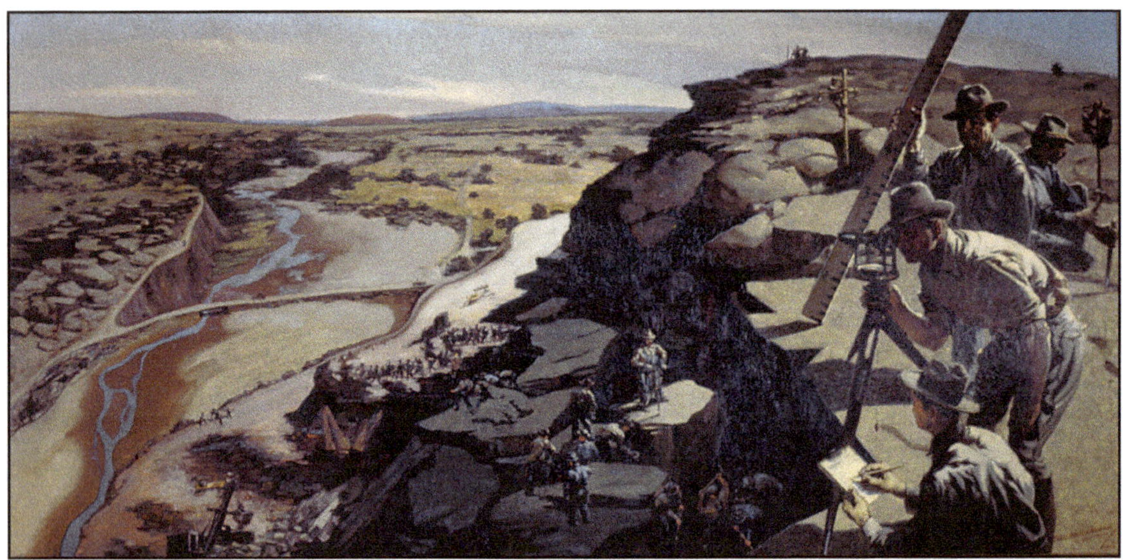

"Conchas Dam Construction" mural size oil painting by Odon Hullenkremer is in the Conchas Dam Visitor Center. Both WPA and CCC participants were involved in the construction pictured here. Photograph by Pat Berrett from *A More Abundant Life, New Deal Artists and Public Art in New Mexico*, courtesy of Sunstone Press.

CONCHAS DAM AND VISITOR CENTER

Conchas Dam is the oldest and one of the largest water projects of the U.S. Army Corps of Engineers in New Mexico. Begun under the New Deal's Emergency Relief Act of 1935, this project included the construction of the dam, associated facilities near the dam and a small community to house the workers and their families. This provided employment for nearly 2,400 people in both the CCC and WPA. The WPA supported school teachers for the children of the work crews and after the dam was completed, the small community was torn down and the adobes were used to build more structures at the dam site. Today the headquarters building is still in use, and five other units provide housing for public use. The Conchas Dam Historic District is part of the State Register SCRP #1791.

Odon Hullenkremer, a Santa Fe New Deal artist, created two mural size oil paintings of the CCC men at the beginning of the construction of Conchas Dam and the other a landscape featuring the small community where the workers lived. Both paintings are approximately 6' x 4' and were painted in 1937. They are now hanging in the Visitor's Center.

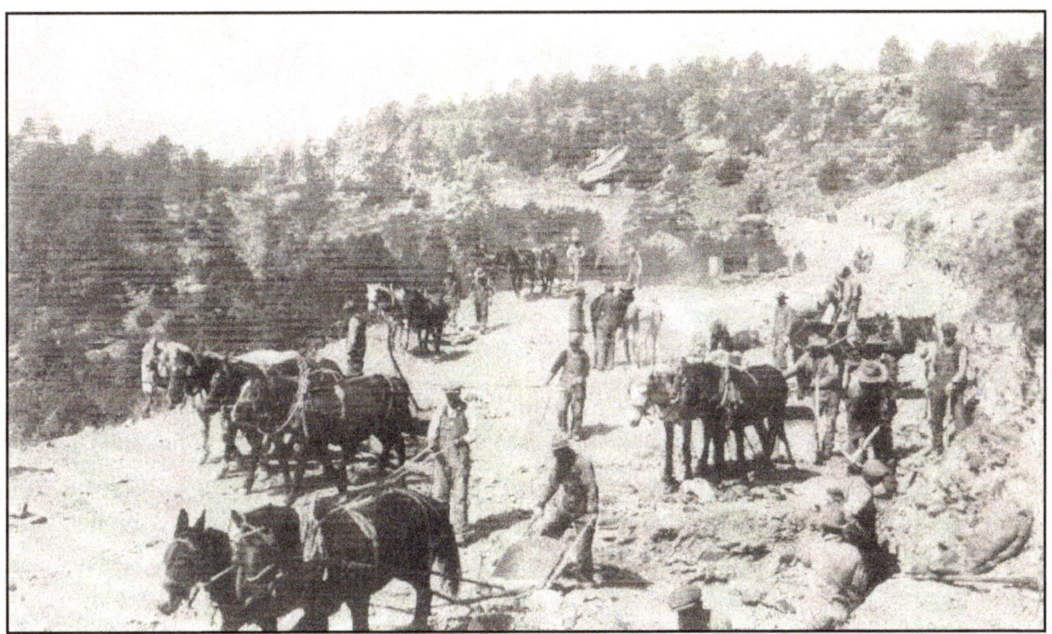

WPA workmen in Trujillo Canyon east of Las Vegas obtaining rocks for construction of Conchas Dam in 1935.

NEW DEAL BUILDINGS, STRUCTURES and PROGRAMS

RURAL ELECTRIC ADMINISTRATION (REA) Mora-San Miguel Electric Cooperative still serves this rural area of the state and the main office is based in Mora.

CORONA

NEW DEAL BUILDINGS, STRUCTURES and PROGRAMS

RURAL ELECTRIC ADMINISTRATION (REA) Central New Mexico Electric Cooperative continues to provide electricity to this rural area of New Mexico. Their office is based in Mountainair.

SCHOOL A New Deal school building has been remodeled to serve as the school cafeteria.

DEMING

"Government programs did much to eliminate the idea that the artist was an odd guy . . . [He] was accepted by the community from that time on, just as was the doctor, the baker, the carpenter. He was no longer an odd-ball."

—Interview with Kenneth M. Adams conducted by Sylvia Loomis, April 23, 1969 from the Oral History Collections of the Archives of American Art microfilms

NEW DEAL PUBLIC ART IN PUBLIC BUILDINGS

DEMING POST OFFICE
Postmaster
210 West Spruce Street
(575) 544-2721
State Register of Cultural Properties SRCP 42

This building was constructed in 1937 by the Treasury Relief Administration Program (TRAP) and was nominated to be included in the National Register for Historic Places on February 23, 1990 because of its architecture and association with the history of federal projects in Deming, and also because of the fine Kenneth Adams mural in the lobby. It is a red brick, single story building with limestone belt courses, lintels, sills and decorative bas relief panels. It was built at a bid cost of $62,400.

Originally Andrew Dasburg, a Taos artist, was selected to do a mural for this post office, but his poor health made it impossible. He recommended Kenneth M. Adams. His recommendation was accepted and a landscape was done by Adams in 1937. Yucca and other local vegetation can be seen in the foreground, while the local familiar landmark, Cook's Peak, dominated the background. The choice of palette used in this work comes from the soft greens, blues, violets and yellows found in the nearby landscape.

NEW DEAL PUBLIC BUILDINGS, STRUCTURES and PROGRAMS

COLUMBUS SCHOOL

COUNTY COURTHOUSE IMPROVEMENTS

DEMING JUNIOR HIGH (1935)

FORMER DEMING PUBLIC LIBRARY

HOSPITAL ADDITION

MORGAN HALL was formerly the City Hall and Fire Station. Now it is a Community

Center and the stage is frequently used to put on community theater productions.

NATIONAL GUARD ARMORY

RURAL ELECTRIC COOPERATIVE
Columbus Electric Cooperative
900 North Gold
(575) 546-8838

This New Deal program based in Deming continues to provide electricity to approximately 2,978 rural consumers in this portion of New Mexico.

SUNSHINE SCHOOL Out of town and may now be closed.

WELFARE OFFICE

OTHER IMPROVEMENTS include roads, cemetery improvements, bridges, dikes, parks, playground improvements, athletic field, sewing and school lunch programs, golf course landscaping, sewer construction sidewalks, curbs, airport improvements, fencing of pastures, waterworks and a gas distribution system.

MYSTERY ARWORK, see Chapter 4 (Kloss and Nordfeldt)

DES MOINES

A WPA rock wall still surrounds the new school complex which replaced the New Deal building that earlier served many children in this Union County community and area.

DEXTER

"Future historians writing of today perhaps will call this era the A.B.C. Period of the Alphabetical Decade, one of the most significant decades in the history of our country. More thought is being given by our national government to the betterment of mankind than ever before."

—Ina Sizer Cassidy, *New Mexico Magazine*, June 1935

NEW DEAL PUBLIC ART IN NEW DEAL PUBLIC BUILDINGS

DEXTER PUBLIC SCHOOLS

The original school complex was built in 1936 by the WPA and the original documents are framed in the school halls to review. There are two oil paintings in the school complex one done by E. Martin Hennings titled "Across the Valley" and the other by Eliseo Rodriguez titled "San Ontonio."

NEW DEAL PUBLIC BUILDINGS, STRUCTURES and PROGRAMS

OTHER STRUCTURES AND IMPROVEMENTS include roads, fish hatchery improvements, and sewer systems.

RURAL ELECTRIC ADMINISTRATION (REA) Central New Mexico Electric Cooperative provides electricity thanks to the New Deal for this rural area. Their main office is in Mountainair.

MYSTERY ARTWORK, see Chapter 4

ELIDA

NEW DEAL PUBLIC BUILDINGS, STRUCTURES and PROGRAM

COMMUNITY CENTER

HIGH SCHOOL HOME ECONOMICS BUILDING

RURAL ELECTRIC ADMINISTRATION (REA) Roosevelt County Electric Cooperative continues to serve this rural area from the main office in Portales.

OTHER STRUCTURES AND IMPROVEMENTS include roads and water system construction.

MYSTERY ARTWORK, see Chapter2

EL RITO

NEW DEAL ART IN PUBLIC BUILDINGS

NORTHERN NEW MEXICO COMMUNITY COLLEGE
Administration Building
(575) 584-4501

This small community is near San Juan Pueblo now called by its original name Ohkay Owingeh. A tryptch by D. Paul Jones was conserved by Luis Neri Zagal in the mid-1990s as funded by the New Mexico Chapter of the NNDPA. It is in Bronson Cutting Hall.

A black framed picture with the WPA/FAP bronze plaque in the lower center of the frame was found in the Director's Office which indicates that there was once a New Deal painting, most likely a Gene Kloss, there but currently enclosed in that frame is a more current print.

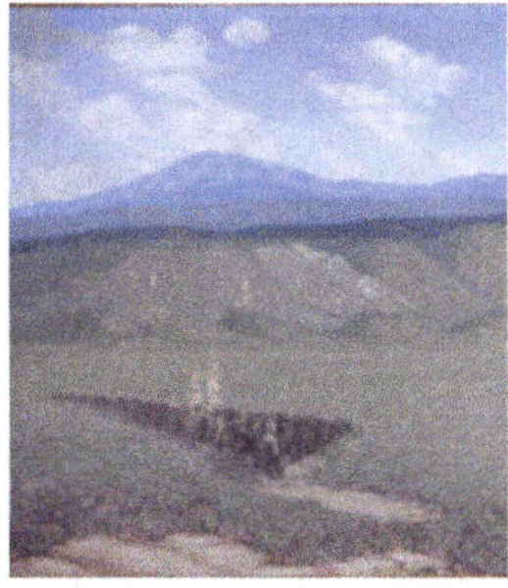 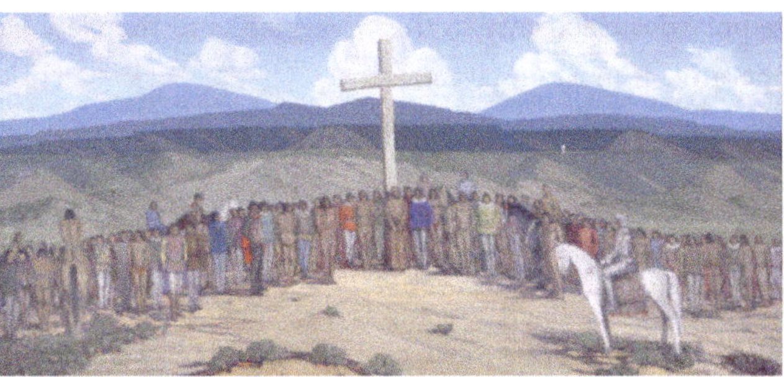 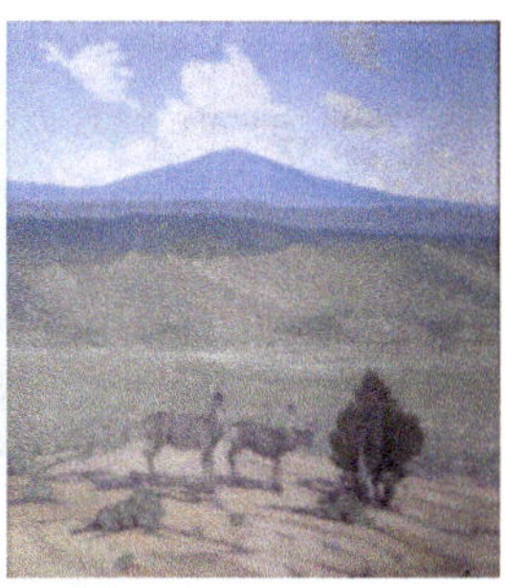

This large oil triptych by D. Paul Jones titled, "The Founding of San Juan, the Capitol of New Spain," depicts the Spanish explorers laying claim to this land to become New Spain. It is placed at the back of the stage in Cutting Hall where the community and Northern New Mexico Community College students come together to watch movies and have programs. Photograph by Pat Berrett from *A More Abundant Life, New Deal Artists and Public Art in New Mexico*, courtesy of Sunstone Press.

NEW DEAL BUILDINGS, STRUCTURES and PROGRAM

A CCC CAMP was located just outside the community and the young men did forestry and soil conservation in the area as well as the rock structures on the community college campus grounds. Buildings including dormitories, the laundry and bakery at the school were also created by the WPA. Original New Deal furniture is still in use in the cafeteria.

RURAL ELECTRIC ADMINISTRATION (REA) The Jemez Mountain Cooperative continues to provide electricity as a result of this New Deal project. Their main office is in Espanola.

OTHER IMPROVEMENTS include roads and a water and sewer system.

MYSTERY ARTWORK, see Chapter 4

As noted above, a black frame with the WPA-FAP bronze plaque on lower center frame was located in the Administrator's Office at Northern New Mexico College, but the artwork inside it was not New Deal art. Based on the size of the frame one might guess that it may have originally held a Gene Kloss etching or a B.J.O. Nordfeldt lithograph. Where is it now?

ENCINO

NEW DEAL BUILDINGS and STRUCTURES

RURAL ELECTRIC ADMINISTRATION (REA) Central New Mexico Electric

Cooperative provides electricity to this area thanks to the New Deal. The main office for this cooperative is in Mountainair.

SCHOOL GYMNASIUM.

This New Deal structure, which looks like all the other New Deal gymnasiums in the state, is in bad condition. There are crumbling murals in its interior but signs below each mural indicate that the murals were gifts of the Senior Classes in the 1940s so one can assume they were not done as part of the state's New Deal public art program. They were believed to have been done by a local woman. Other school buildings were also built during this period.

OTHER STRUCTURES and IMPROVEMENTS include a water system and sidewalks, curbs and gutters.

ESPANOLA

NEW DEAL PUBLIC ART IN PUBLIC BUILDINGS

BOND HOUSE MUSEUM

Three oil paintings, formerly in the public schools but rescued privately from being thrown away, now are housed at the Bond House Museum in downtown Espanola. They include two that are unsigned, "The Orchard" and "Santa Cruz #11," but Howard Schleeter painted the third but left it as "Untitled."

NEW DEAL BUILDINGS, STRUCTURES and PROGRAM

CITY HALL/ FIRE STATION BUILDING

JAIL

HIGH SCHOOL/GYMNASIUM

RURAL ELECTRIC ADMINISTRATION (REA)
Jemez Mountains Electric Cooperative
Chama Highway
(575) 753-2105

This New Deal program based in Espanola serves approximately 30,875 rural consumers of electricity in northern New Mexico thanks to the New Deal.

WELFARE OFFICE

OTHER STRUCTURES and IMPROVEMENTS include bridge over Chamita Creek and other sites, sewer and water line extensions, roads, water and sewer line extensions, river bank protection, and flood protection. In the county three New Deal sites are on the State Register of Cultural Properties: Los Ojos Fish Hatchery and Burns Lake Bungalow in Los Ojos SCRP #1599 and El Vado Dam in Tierra Amarilla SCRP #550.

MYSTERY ARTWORK, see Chapter 4

ESTANCIA

NEW DEAL BUILDINGS and STRUCTURES

BALLFIELD AND PARK

COMMUNITY CENTER Built in 1934 and renovated in 1992–1993.

COURTHOUSE-JAIL ADDITION

RODEO GROUNDS

RURAL ELECTRIC ADMNISTRATION (REA) Central New Mexico Electric Cooperative continues to provide electricity to this rural area of the state thanks to the New Deal. Their main office is based in Mountainair.

SCHOOLS, GYMNASIUM and STADIUM

OTHER STRUCTURES and IMPROVEMENTS include Arthur Park, swimming pool, bathing beach, sidewalks, roads, sewer system, lake widening, dikes, water works, ditch construction and demolition of pump house and building new one.

EUNICE

The Mellie Jordan Elementary school was built in 1939 and the Middle School was built in 1939. Both are reportedly still in use.

FARMINGTON

NEW DEAL BUILDINGS and STRUCTURES

CHACO CANYON's PUEBLO BONITO RUINS and MUSEUM Survey, excavation and stabilization work was done here by the HABS program. CCC also built roads and other structures.

FARMINGTON CHILDRENS' MUSEUM The Southwest Room in the present building was the original library built by the WPA in 1937.

"FLY-PROOF INTERIOR SANITATION UNITS"

This was the federal terminology for outhouses. Many were done in this county around Kirkland and many other rural areas around the state. They were quite an improvement over privately built ones since they had concrete bases.

TIBBETTS JUNIOR HIGH SCHOOL (1940) is known to still be in use as a school. A high school and gymnasium and other elementary schools were also used but may no longer be in use. New Deal art by Kloss and Nordfeldt was sent to this school district but has never been located. See note below in Mystery Art.

WELFARE OFFICE

OTHER STRUCTURES AND IMPROVEMENTS include dam and ditches, roads, sidewalks, airport improvements, land reclamation and a sewing room operation.

MYSTERY ARTWORK

In a telephone interview with a well remembered former high school art teacher in the late 1990s, this author was informed that the school received some paintings from the WPA/FAP office in Santa Fe but couldn't afford to purchase them so she indicated that she would buy them personally for the school but the Superintendent went ahead and bought them since he knew she didn't have much money. What they were or their whereabouts are unknown, but we suspect they were part of the Kloss and/or Nordfleldt creations.

FOLSOM

The New Deal school and gymnasium are still standing and serving as an area community center in this part of Union County. They are now privately owned. Most of the county farm roads are also from the New Deal era and still in use today. The Springer REA services this small community and its environs.

FORT BAYARD

Various buildings (theater, motor transport, greenhouse, recreational gateway, guardhouse, storm sewers and phone lines) were all constructed or improved with New Deal funds. Streets and landscaping were also done. The Columbus REA services this rural facility just out of Silver City.

FORT STANTON

"Both the Depression and ill health—the latter of which brought many artists to New Mexico—made the employment problem of Southwestern artists a particularly urgent one. Many artists had been forced to give up painting entirely and find other work."

—*New Mexico Art, 1930 WPA New Mexico*, University of Arizona Press

NEW DEAL PUBLIC ART IN OTHER BUILDINGS

FORT STANTON MUSEUM

Nineteen watercolors are on display here that were found in a closet some years after the hospital was closed as a Marine Hospital. Originally, a record indicates there were eighty paintings by eastern American artists sent to the hospital from the Section of Fine Arts Program in Washington, DC. According to those records, they were sent there to, "cheer up the sailors in that Marine Hospital." The remaining nineteen paintings, primarily watercolor scenes from "back East," have been restored by the New Mexico Chapter of the NNDPA and Dale Kronkright. The museum and NNDPA both would love to find the other sixty-one missing paintings or have them returned to the collection. No penalty would be applied on any returned paintings.

NEW DEAL BUILDINGS, STRUCTURES and PROGRAM

BUILDINGS

According to Nancy Owen Lewis' article in *El Palacio* (Winter 2010), "Roosevelt's New Deal programs provided funds for the repair of old buildings, the construction of new ones and the labor for many other improvements. In 1935 a new power plant and laundry building were added. In 1936 a ninety-two bed hospital—the first in the state with an electric elevator—was completed. The tent houses for the tuberculosis patients were replaced with wooden cottages. The Works Progress Administration (WPA) funded the construction of two silos at the farm, a concrete bridge over the Rio Bonito, and a new road. The Civilian Conservation Corps (CCC) workers, housed in a camp on the fort, repaired roads, dug ditches, planted trees and drilled wells. In 1940 a new nurses' residence, built in the Spanish-Pueblo Revival style was completed."

CCC CAMP

The master plan for Fort Stanton notes that there was a CCC camp across the Rio Bonito from the fort. Research indicates that the role of the CCC in construction of some of the later buildings at the fort were to be a priority. Records indicate that some buildings still in use were built in 1935 by the CCC. They include a boiler plant as mentioned above and some residences and Hidalgo Cottage.

Later this same general area was the location of a German POW camp. These German POWs were not actually German soldiers but rather the staff of a German luxury cruise ship, SS Columbus, that couldn't get all the way back to Germany when World War II broke out. They were able to deposit their passengers off safely in Havana and the ship went on to Mexico and then attempted to make it back to Germany. That attempt was unsuccessful since they were captured by a British destroyer in December 1939. Rather than surrender the ship, the captain ordered the crew to sink the ship and five hundred seventy-six crew members were taken on board the British vessel while watching the cruise ship go down with three crew members still on board. The female crew members were allowed to return home but the men were retained and shipped to Ellis Island and then Angel Island in San Francisco.

In August of 1940 the United States elected to send the remaining 400 men to Fort Stanton, New Mexico. This site was selected "because of the abandoned CCC camp, the hospital was near by and the area was so remote that any pro-Nazi activists would be isolated," according to Tomas Jaehn is his article in the Spring 2011 edition of *El Palacio*. Jaehn notes that "this then became America's first civilian internment camp of WW II." A small group of the crewmen were sent out in January 1941 to prepare the area for the whole contingent and by March all were "on board" in this wide open land. They were later joined by Japanese civilian internees. While there for about four years, they were housed in old CCC barracks or built themselves other facilities in the camp with materials from the torn down CCC buildings. They also built themselves a large swimming pool, rock bathhouse and gymnasium basically with their bare hands and shovels. These were all later enjoyed by the employees of the hospital facility and their children. At the end of World War II, the last of the internees left Fort Stanton on August 27, 1945 and returned to their homes in Germany except for four who died while at Fort Stanton and are buried in the Marine military cemetery there. The camp was officially closed on October 10, 1945.

RURAL ELECTRIC ADMINISTRATION (REA) Otero County Electric Cooperative based in Cloudcroft serves this area's 13,480 consumers in Chaves, Lincoln, Otero and Socorro counties.

OTHER STRUCTURES and PROGRAMS In addition to all of the above structures, the Kammer/Rose WPA report includes the creation by the WPA of a golf course, water and sewer improvements and landscaping at the U.S. Marine Hospital, now Fort Stanton State Facility and Museum.

MYSTERY ARTWORK

The Fort Stanton Museum and New Mexico Chapter of the NNDPA would like to locate the sixty-one missing watercolors. All the scenes in the existing watercolors are of scenes from the Midwest or East Coast areas—nothing from the Southwest.

FORT SUMNER

"These murals will become in future years a possession which Fort Sumner will cherish as a community asset and thousands will visit there to see them."

—R. Vernon Hunter, "Historic Murals," *Curry County Times*, June 21, 1934

NEW DEAL PUBLIC ART IN PUBLIC BUILDINGS

DE BACA COUNTY COURTHOUSE
Fort Sumner, New Mexico
State Register #1270, 5-9-86, National Register 12-7-87

Though architecturally interesting this courthouse is unusual for New Mexico because of its Georgian Revival style and was built too early (1930) to be a New Deal public building. However, the murals on three walls of the second floor of this building were done by Russell Vernon Hunter (1900–1955). Mr. Hunter was the statewide coordinator of the WPA's Federal Art Project from 1933–1943 and grew up in this eastern part of the state in a homestead community six miles north of Texico.

The murals, titled "The Last Frontier" were painted in 1934 but not until Hunter had done a vast amount of research regarding the history in addition to what he already knew before picking up his brush. Obviously many scenes come from that personal knowledge. Shown are events in the history of Fort Sumner and eastern New Mexico including subjects covering the adventures of Billy the Kid's beginnings, early days in Texico, where Texas and New Mexico cowboys worked and entertained themselves. The Long Walk that the Navajos were put through ending up in this area is also included as well as the final panel portraying the railroad and industrialization coming to the area.

One Texas newspaper noted about Hunter's work, "One is struck with the amount of research required. Hunter's preparation has been life-long and his residences in Farwell and Texico have qualified him to interpret the Panhandle-Plains of New Mexico as few can. But a deeper understanding than mere research makes this mural a sort of unchangeable pageant of the men and women who fought their lives away in taming America's last badlands."[1]

1. "Vernon Hunter Completes His Frontier Mural at Fort Sumner," *Dallas Morning News*, Saturday, September 8, 1934.

NEW DEAL BUILDINGS, STRUCTURES and PROGRAMS

FORT SUMNER WOMAN'S CLUB State Register SRCP 1832

HIGHWAY/RAILROAD UNDERPASS

OTHER STRUCTURES AND PROGRAMS include sidewalks, roads, cemetery improvements, water system, waste disposal system, library projects, irrigation improvements, and building of a swimming pool and bath house.

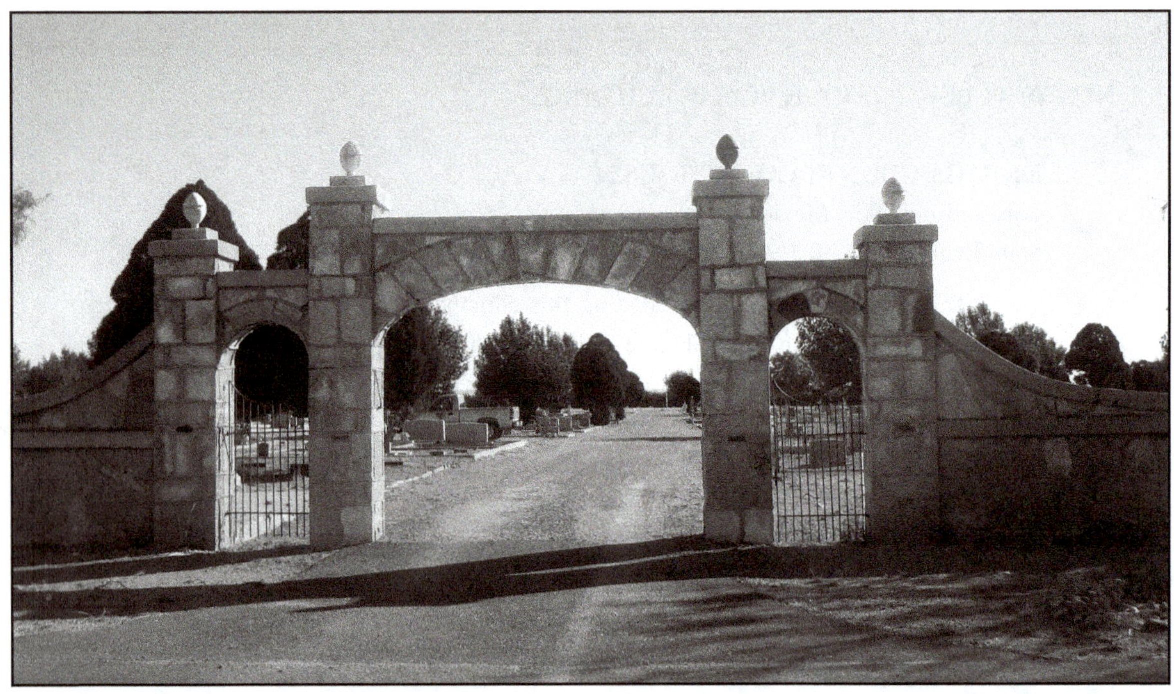

Rock walls can be found surrounding many old cemeteries in the state but none quite like this one in Fort Sumner thanks to the WPA worker's ingenuity. The decorations on top of parts of the wall and entry way are unique and were created with the help of old car headlights plastered over and added here and there. Better go see for yourself.

PUBLIC SCHOOL COMPLEX The Fort Sumner Combined school was built in 1935 and some of the buildings may still be in use. Constructional changes were made in 2011.

RURAL ELECTRIC ADMINISTRATION (REA) Central New Mexico Electric Cooperative continues to provide electricity to 3,753 consumers for this predominantly rural county and three others thanks to the New Deal.

GALLUP

"The mural (in the courthouse) portrays a powerful, all encompassing saga: the struggles of man against man and man's technological progress . . ."

—Patricia Locke, "Gallup Mural a Long Look Back," *Albuquerque Journal*, August 16, 1987

Gallup was one of the four New Mexico towns with New Deal Federal Art Centers. That center was located in a building that was once the old courthouse and has since been demolished. The City Hall is now located on that site. Art classes, exhibits of local art and traveling art exhibits from national and regional New Deal offices were held here.

NEW DEAL PUBLIC ART IN NEW DEAL PUBLIC BUILDINGS

MCKINLEY COUNTY COURTHOUSE
P. O. Box 1268 (Center of town)
(575) 722-3868 County Manager
State Register #1191, 9-20-85, National Register 2-15-89

The original courthouse was razed and is now the site of the Gallup City Hall. The WPA, as noted above, held their Federal Art Center program in that building prior to its being razed. The next courthouse, built in 1939, was partially funded by the Public Works Administration (PWA) of the New Deal. The four-story Spanish-Pueblo Revival style building was designed by the regionally renowned architectural firm of Trost and Trost. The interior is embellished with tin work, wood beams, posts and corbels, and the original main entry area has Indian motif tiles incised into the stucco. Furniture was also created for the building as well as tin chandeliers and one of those are missing. At the building's opening there was a blessing done by local Native American elders.

The building is eligible for the National Register both for its architectural qualities as well as for its association with the political history of New Mexico and the State Register includes the murals in the courtroom. Since its construction, a large addition was completed in 2006–07 with a more modern architecture and is attached to the original structure.

In the original building is one of the state's most spectacular murals which was painted by Lloyd Moylan in 1940. This mural entitled "The History of McKinley County" covers 2,000 square feet of the entire courtroom walls above a six foot wooden panel. The history of this northwestern section of New Mexico includes pre-historic to modern times. Included are scenes of Indian life in pre-conquest days, the arrival of the Conquistadors, the Pueblo Revolt of 1680, the Gold Rush and the Atchison, Topeka and Santa Fe Railway. The mural was conserved in 2006–07 by Steve Prins and

Associates of Santa Fe and paid for by the New Mexico Chapter of the NNDPA and McKinley County.

Another mural can be found in the District Attorney's Office. This one was done in 1942 by Anna Keener Wilton (1895–1982). It is called, "Zuni Indian Pottery Women." Wilton was one of the staff at the Federal Art Center and later became the head of the Art Department at Eastern New Mexico University in Portales. Another painting by Brooks Willis (1903–1981) is also hanging in one of the judge's offices.

Originally thirty-two New Deal paintings were hung in the earlier building. Today only twelve are in the county's inventory and hang in various locations in the newer structure. One wonders what happened to the others and would like to find them and have them returned. The remaining ones include:

Bakos, Josef
"Cottonwoods"
Jones, Paul
"Spring Landscape"
Kloss, Gene
"Grazing Horses"
Lantz, Paul
"Church in the Rio Grande Villa"
Moylan, Lloyd
"Dinner"
"Breadwinner"
"Storage Barn"
Nye, Virginia
"The Engineer"
Parsons, Sheldon
"Nambe Valley Summer"
"Casa on the Hill"
Willis, Brooks
"Desert"
"Trees"

As of 2011, a County Fine Arts Committee is working to have the various paintings conserved and additional new art work acquired. They are now also responsible for overseeing the care and handling of paintings from the Red Rock Museum including eight works on paper by Lloyd Moylan. Some of these have been conserved by the New Mexico Chapter of the NNDPA. They include:

"Wagon on the Campfire"
"Prelude to Dust"
"Squaw Dance"
"Rural Rococo"
"The Rio Grande Valley"
"Dance at San Felipe"
"Mother-in-Law"
"Rooster Pull"

They also acquired "Room on the Reservation" by Hal West and "Portrait of an Indian" by John Jellicoe.

NEW DEAL PUBLIC ART IN PUBLIC BUILDINGS

GALLUP PUBLIC SCHOOLS

There are four paintings by Edgar Payne in the school district's Board Room. They are not thought to be New Deal creations but rather private gifts to the school. However, the new High School has seven mural size oil paintings by J. R. Willis done in 1935 that hang in the library and depict New Mexico's settlement history by others. Events covered included:

- Early Caveman Explorers
- Franciscan Missionary with Armed Indians
- Conquistadors at El Morro Rock
- Conquistadors Attacking an Indian Pueblo
- Kit Carson Leading a Group of Indians Out of Canyon de Chelly
- Wagon Train at Red Rocks and Church
- World Map Indicating Travel Lines from Spain to Haiti to Mexico City to Zuni, Santa Fe to Gran Quivira.

Also one oil painting by D. Paul Jones is at the Roosevelt Elementary school and is untitled but features six horses in a valley.

OCTAVIA FELLIN PUBLIC LIBRARY

115 West Hill
Contact Person: Librarian
(575) 863-1291

Some of this collection has been conserved thanks to the New Mexico Chapter of the NNDPA.

Barger, Erik
"Shiprock"
Begay (possibly Timothy)
"Navajo Girl with Lamb"
Begay, Harrison
"Yeibachai" (Navajo Dance)
"Navajo Rug and Weaver"
Burbank, E. A.
"A Lincoln Log Post Office"
"Hopi Indian House"
"Redwood Trees"
Detwiller, Frederick
"Dutch Harbor"
Fleck, Joseph
"Westwind" (Pueblo Maiden)
Groll, A. L.
"Enchanted Mesa"
"Kit Carson House"
"Inscription Rock"
"Red Rocks"
"Under Western Skies"

Houser, Allan
"Apache Devil Dance"
Huntington, Anna
"Mule" bronze sculpture
Leigh, William R.
"Horses and Whiskey Don't Mix"
Moylan, Lloyd
"Enroute to Ceremonial"
"Approaching Storm"
"Household Duties"
"Journey through Long Horse Valley"
"Pueblo Indians"
"Rain on the Reservations"
"Rolling One"

Naumer, Helmuth
"Dead Cottonwood"
Smith, A. D.
"Chief Deer, Sioux Indian"
Tshudy, H. B.
"Cedar Tree"
WPA Crafts person
Trastero
WPA Crafts person
Carved Trastero

CITY HALL Early in 2011 workers found a New Deal painting by Eliseo Rodriguez up in the rafters. No one knows how it got there but it is in fairly good condition.

NEW DEAL BUILDINGS, STRUCTURES and PROGRAMS

COMCAST TV OFFICE (Originally the Gallup Post Office)
201 South First
#1189 State Register 9-20-85, National Register 5-16-88

This building was formerly the Gallup Post Office and was constructed as part of the New Deal projects and still has the original carved beam ceilings that are quite unique with carved animal head corbels.

This building is also unique in that it exhibits a mix of several architectural styles, including Mediterranean, Decorative Brick Commercial and Spanish Pueblo Revival. This eclectic approach works very well, however, and as such the blond brick building is listed in the National Register as being significant architecturally as well as for its association with the civic history of Gallup.

Warren Rollins created three large paintings of Indian scenes which hung up high in this building. When the Postal Service sold the building, the paintings were removed and stored elsewhere by GSA. In 2008 they were restored and hung on the second floor of the U. S. Federal Courthouse in Santa Fe which is next to Santa Fe's Main Post Office downtown. Members of Rollins family were present for the unveiling in their new location.

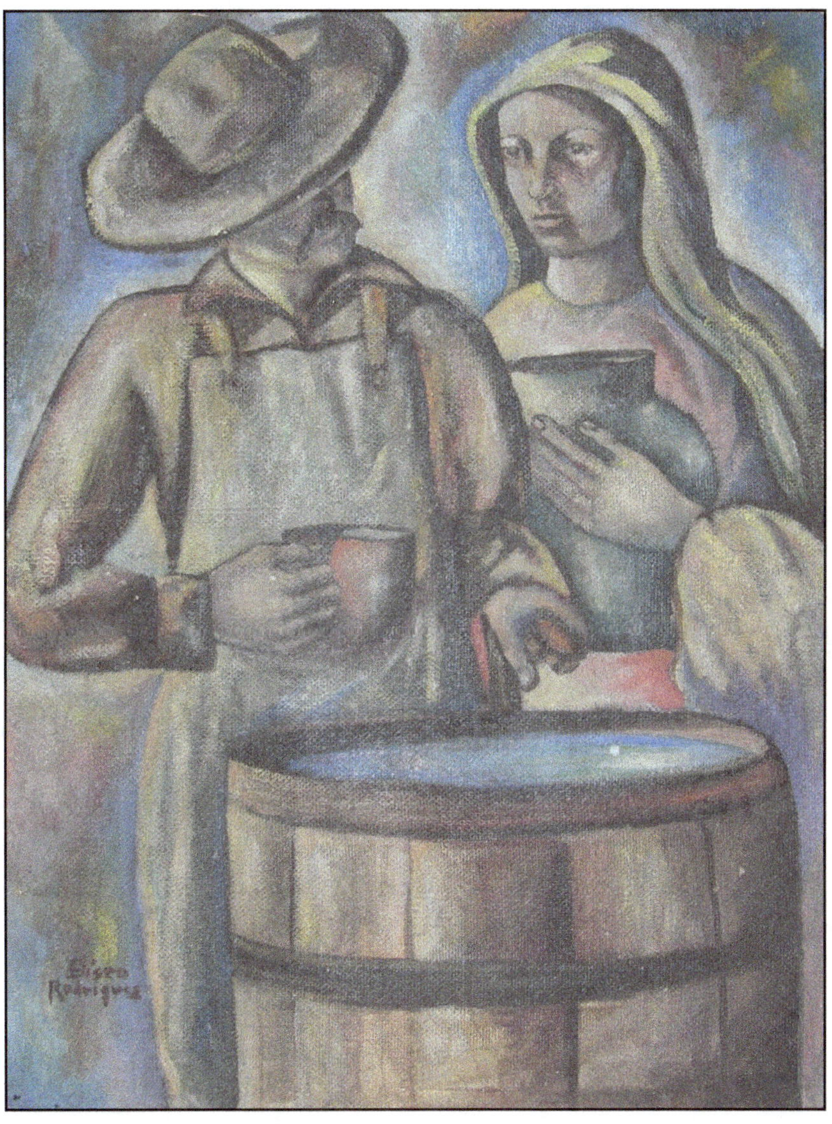

Hidden New Deal public art treasures are still being found as of 2011. This time the treasure was found up in the rafters of this Gallup's City Hall. Santa Fe artist, Eliseo Rodriguez, now deceased, would be smiling proudly to see one of his paintings, "Quenching Their Thirst," again surfacing now that it has been brought down out of the attic rafters and in good shape but covered with a lot of dust. No one knows, or is saying, how it ended up there but when staff went up to examine bad weather damage to the roof, the treasure was found. Photograph provided by Gallup City Hall staff.

RURAL ELECTRIC ADMINISTRATION (REA) Continental Divide Electric Coop, with its main office in Grants, New Mexico, continues to provide electricity to the vast rural areas of this county most of which is Native American land.

OTHER KNOWN BUILDINGS/STRUCTURES

New Mexico National Guard Armory is now the L.B. Mitchell Recreation Center
State Police office
Some of the local school buildings
Lyons Memorial Park
In nearby Fort Wingate there is the Southwestern Sheep Breeding Station which is on the State Register for Cultural Properties # 1815.

OTHER STRUCTURES AND PROGRAMS include roads, curbs, gutters, sidewalks, sewers, privies, cemetery project, athletic field, high school tennis courts, park improvements, Sheriff's office garage, vault in courthouse, demolition of Central grade school for junior high school and sewing of garments, sheets and towels.

MYSTERY ARTWORK, see Chapter 4

(Kloss and Nordfeldt but the reader is encouraged to help locate the other missing art originally located in this courthouse.)

GLENWOOD

There was a CCC camp in this rural area and some remains (foundations and steps) can still be found in place. A portion of the barrack housing the kitchen is located on a private ranch in the area and a marker identifies where the original CCC catwalk was constructed across some rocky precipices. It has since been replaced by a newer walkway.

A fish hatchery was also constructed in Glenwood in 1937–1938.

GLORIETA

A CCC camp full of young men conserved forest areas including trails and built the Baldy Lookout Tower which is on the State's Historic Register of Cultural Properties #SR 1451.

GOODSON

GOODSON SCHOOL

This 1935 WPA structure is on Highway 456 in the Cimarron Valley near Clayton and Kenton Oklahoma. It is on the State Register #1806. You can't miss it since it is sitting out in a field all by itself surrounded by the WPA rock wall. Unfortunately it is on the road to deterioration.

GRANTS

NEW DEAL BUILDINGS, STRUCTURES and PROGRAMS

FURNITURE A conference table, chairs and benches done by the WPA are still in use at the local Chamber of Commerce office.

RURAL ELECTRIC COOPERATIVE
Continental Divide Electric Cooperative
200 East High Street
Grants, New Mexico
(575) 285-6656

This New Deal rural electric cooperative serves approximately 23,408 rural consumers in this portion of New Mexico and even into Arizona.

SCHOOLS School additions were done including a vocational building at the High School. According to state records, the San Rafael Elementary School (1930) and the current Desert Pride Alternative School (1939) are still in use.

OTHER STRUCTURES include sidewalks, sewers and road improvements.

MYSTERY ARTWORK, see Chapter 4 (three Nordfeldt lithographs)

HAGERMAN

NEW DEAL BUILDINGS, STRUCTURES and PROGRAMS

CITY PARK and BUILDING

HIGH SCHOOL BUILDINGS (2)

WATERWORKS

MYSTERY ARTWORK

A Fremont Ellis painting was known to be at this school for a number of years but may have inadvertently been thrown away later because the frame was broken.

HATCH

NEW DEAL BUILDINGS, STRUCTURES and PROGRAMS

HOME ECONOMICS BUILDING

JAIL

OTHER PROJECTS included waterworks, sewer system, sidewalks, curbs and gutters levees, tennis courts and landscaping at the High School, and ten miles of drainpipes to Hockett, which were all constructed during the New Deal era in this small community.

MYSTERY ARTWORK

An oil painting by Carl Redin titled "Superstition Mountain" is missing from the schools. See Chapter 4

HAYDEN

One can still see the WPA School and rock wall surrounding it in a rural area west of Amistad.

HOBBS

NEW DEAL BUILDINGS, STRUCTURES and PROGRAMS

AIRPORT

CITY HALL

FORMER HIGH SCHOOL, now Junior High School Shop building. Also Will Rogers Elementary School (1939) is still in use.

HOUSTON ELEMENTARY SCHOOL

LIBRARY

PORT OF ENTRY

UNEMPLOYMENT OFFICE

OTHER STRUCTURES and PROGRAMS include roads, a sidewalk on Dunham Street and others in the town

HOPE

The New Deal school gym and auditorium complex is still being used by this community as a Community Center. It was included in of President George H. Bush's "100 Points of Light" program.

HOUSE

It is our understanding that the original old gymnasium was moved to McAlister, New Mexico.

JAL

NEW DEAL BUILDINGS and STRUCTURES

JUNIOR/SENIOR HIGH BUILDING (1938) is reportedly still in use.

HIGH SCHOOL STADIUM

PORT OF ENTRY

JEMEZ SPRINGS

NEW DEAL BUILDINGS, STRUCTURES and PROGRAMS

CHECK DAMS These were built by CCC and are known to exist on the Villa Grande property near Jemez.

FISH HATCHERY

JEMEZ PUEBLO MISSION RUINS EXCAVATION

RURAL ELECTRIC ADMINISTRATION (REA) Jemez Mountain Electric Cooperative with its main office in Espanola continues to provide electricity to 30,875 consumers in five counties in the north as a result of the New Deal.

SCHOOL Jemez Mountain's Lindrith Heritage Charter school building was built in 1933. The Jemez Valley's San Diego Riverside Charter School was built in 1935 and both are still in use.

STATE PARK

KINGSTON

NEW DEAL BUILDINGS and STRUCTURES

CAMP SHILOW

This CCC campground was built in the 1930s and includes two acres with five cabins, dining hall, dispensary and lodge. The camp is currently owned by the Boy Scouts of America. In the 1950s the then owner built an Olympic pool on the side of the mountain and it is still available for swimming in the summer. Write to HC 2 Box 120, Hillsboro, New Mexico 88042 for more information or visit with June Ander at the Black Range Museum, former owner.

KIRTLAND

NEW DEAL BUILDINGS, STRUCTURES and PROGRAMS

According to the San Juan County Historical Society there are at least two remaining WPA Sanitation Units as discussed in the following article from the *Farmington Times Hustler*, April 17, 1936:

> COMPLETE 388 SANITATION UNITS
>
> Floyd D. Painton in charge of the county's WPA Sanitation program, reports that work is progressing steadily with 388 units complete to date out of a possible 800 in the county. Twenty men are engaged in this project, with sufficient order piled up to keep them busy until June 1. The sanitation project consists of replacing all outdoor toilets in the town and in the county with modern fly proof buildings.
>
> Mr. Painton states his department has received fine cooperation from the citizens and especially from two officials of Farmington who have rendered every possible assistance in encouraging the installation of these sanitary buildings within the city limits.

Note: Although similar projects have not been identified by other communities during the research period of this book, the author is aware of one or two in other communities including Santa Fe and Bosque Farms and feels confident that they are remnants of similar county (and possibly national) projects that erected these governmental "fly-proof interior sanitation units," as referenced by the federal government. One of their unique and valuable features was the concrete base, sometimes stamped with WPA and the year installed.

LA LUZ

NEW DEAL BUILDINGS, STRUCTURES and PROGRAMS

LANDSCAPING IN THE PLAZA
RURAL ELECTRIC ADMINISTRATION (REA) Otero County Electric Cooperative continues to provide electricity to this rural area thanks to the New Deal.
SENIOR CITIZEN CENTER

LAS CRUCES

"Federally sponsored art programs were a great thing for me since they allowed me to do what I wanted to do."

—Telephone interview with Tom Lea in El Paso, Texas conducted by Sandra D'Emilio, November 11, 1988.

NEW DEAL PUBLIC ART IN PUBLIC BUILDINGS

BRANIGAN CULTURAL CENTER
106 West Hadley
(575) 524-1422

On view at the Cultural Center is the existing mural, "First Book about New Mexico—1610" which was done by Tom Lea (1907–2001) in 1935. In reality some have indicated that it may have been privately commissioned by Mrs. Alice Montgomery Branigan to be placed in this building which previously was the public library. In the WPA report, a library was built in 1935 and was identified as Brennan Library (possibly a misspelling) along with warehouse improvements. Library personnel were also funded by the WPA. The building is on the State and National Historic Register. The library program later moved into a new location as noted under "Branigan Public Library" and the earlier building became a museum and cultural center. Next door to Branigan Cultural Center is now the new Las Cruces Museum of Art.

BRANIGAN PUBLIC LIBRARY
200 East Picacho Avenue
(575) 526-1045

It is possible to view upon request if not on exhibit the "Navajo Blankets Portfolio" by Louie Ewing and Eliseo Rodriguez and a small watercolor by Ramos Sanchez of San Ildefonso Pueblo. On request one can also study the *Portfolio of Spanish-Colonial Design* designed by E. Boyd and painted by others referred to as "copyists."

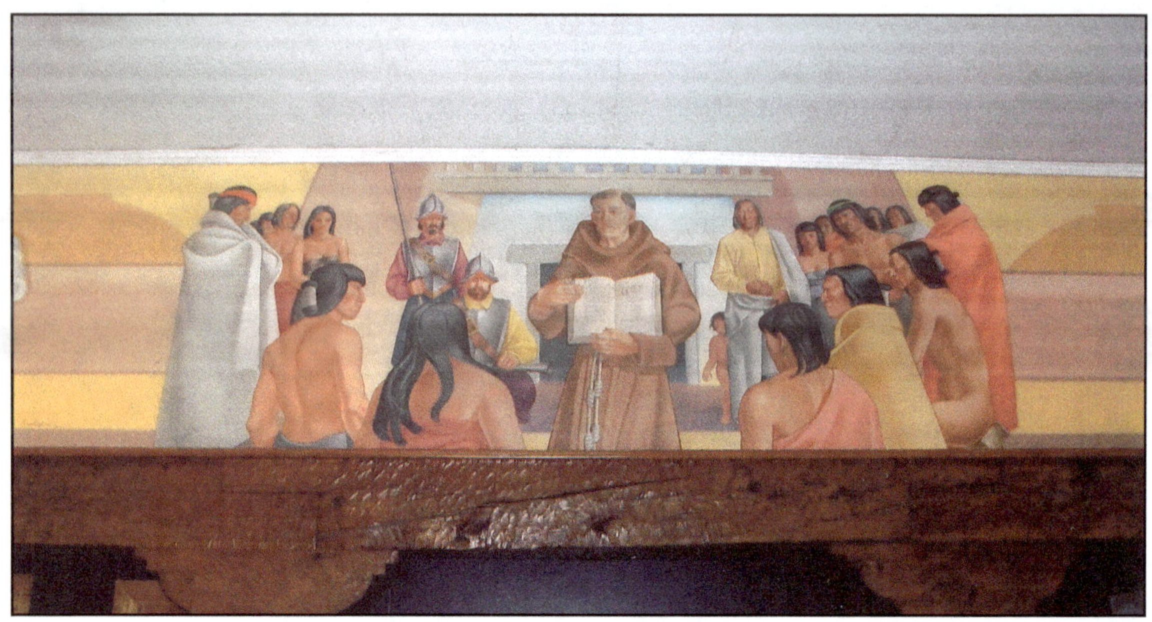

This mural by Tom Lea in The Branigan Cultural Center illustrates Franciscan friars bringing the first books to New Mexico in the 17th Century.

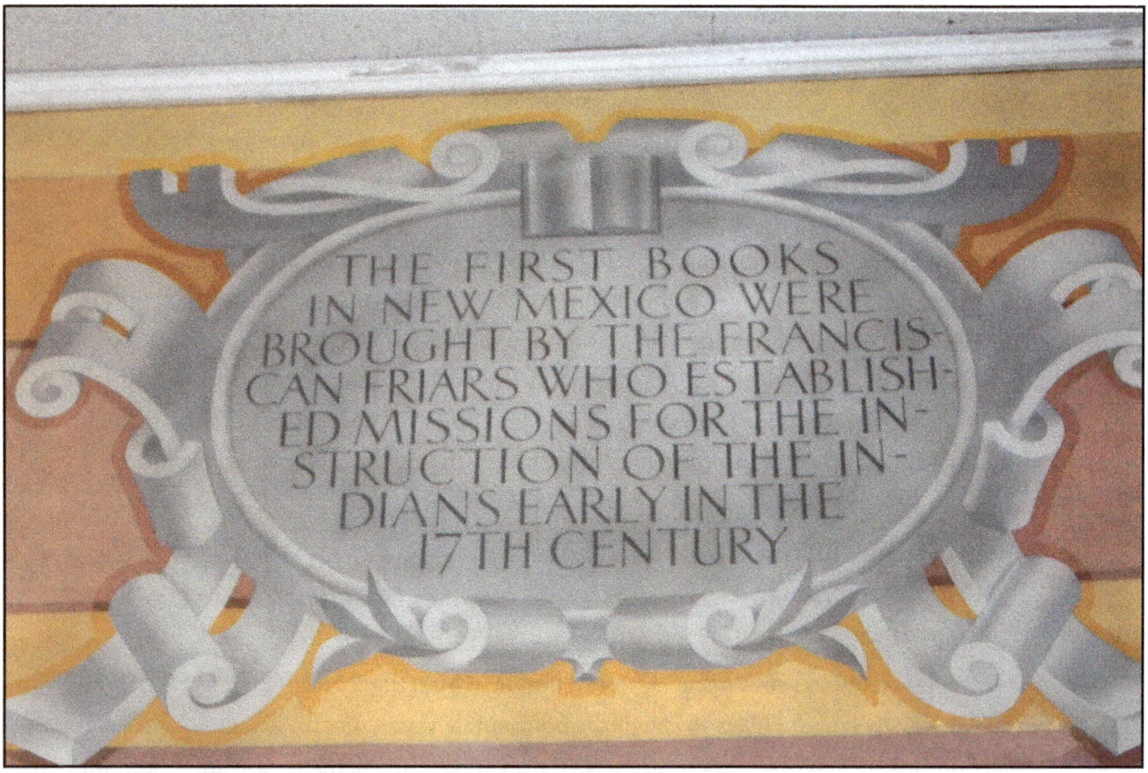

THE FIRST BOOKS
IN NEW MEXICO WERE
BROUGHT BY THE FRANCIS-
CAN FRIARS WHO ESTABLISH-
ED MISSIONS FOR THE IN-
STRUCTION OF THE IN-
DIANS EARLY IN THE
17TH CENTURY

One of the medallions on each side of the mural.

LAS CRUCES PUBLIC SCHOOLS

The administration has identified six paintings that were acquired by that school district as part of the New Deal work. They include:

Bakos
"Iris"*
Barton, Howard
"Still Life on Table"
Jones, Paul
"Untitled Landscape"*
Loeffler, Gisella
"Girl by the Fireplace"
Parsons, Sheldon
"Santa Fe Hills"
Willis, Brooks P.
"Liberty Café"

*These two paintings have been conserved by NNDPA funds after being surveyed and determined to be in poor condition.

NEW MEXICO FARM AND RANCH MUSEUM
P.O. Box 1898
(575) 522-4100
Website: www.frhm.org

Five New Deal paintings by Manville Chapman from Raton can be found in the Administrative Offices. It is understood that they were a gift from a woman who had owned a ranch in the northeastern portion of the state near Raton. They include:

"Lucien Maxwell Mansion"
"Stagecoach"
"Women with Pottery"
"Family at Taos Pueblo"
"Taos Art Gallery"

NEW MEXICO STATE UNIVERSITY (NMSU)

FOSTER HALL (Biology Building)

In 1934 Olive Rush, under WPA/FAP, decorated the dome-shaped entrance to the Biology Building, with a fresco. The themes are the history of the development of plant life on the walls and animal life from earliest beginnings in the ceiling. The more complicated life forms are also represented with special attention given to local flora and fauna. The cotton industry and farming, which flourished at the time, are also featured.

Unfortunately these frescoes were painted over some years later by two members of the school's maintenance staff who weren't artists following some water damage to the wall. The National New Deal Preservation Association has worked with the university to remove that overlay of paint that has covered over up the original fresco. This restoration project was finally completed in June 2008 by Luis Neri Zagal, Albuquerque conservator. However, it did not include the restoration of the ceiling also done by Rush.

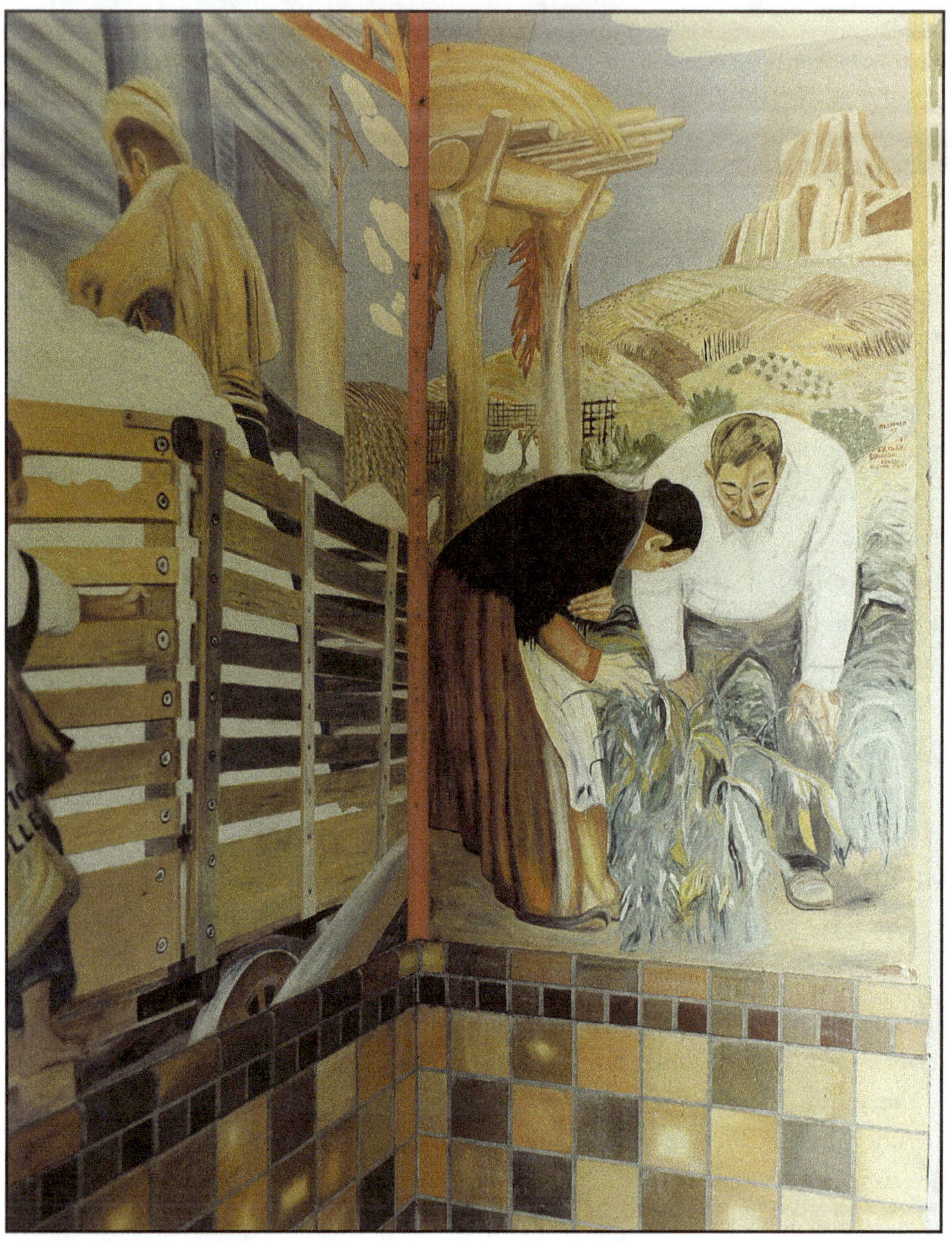

Untitled fresco by Olive Rush in Foster Hall at New Mexico State University. Photograph by Pat Berrett from *A More Abundant Life, New Deal Artists and Public Art in New Mexico*, courtesy of Sunstone Press.

LIBRARY

Tom Lea who lived in El Paso prior to his death, created two fifteen-foot panels which are housed in the entry area of this building. They depict scenes from New Mexico's colorful history from 1599 to 1870. "Conquistadors" presents the Spanish conquest and late historical developments in the area while "La Mesilla" deals with the two main industries at the time—agriculture and ranching. Also included are scenes from events in the Mexican War, Apache raids and the acquisition of La Mesilla as a part of the United States via the Gadsden Purchase. Lea researched his material in Santa Fe using documents from the Palace of the Governors as sources to ensure historical accuracy.

NEW DEAL BUILDINGS, STRUCTURES and PROGRAMS

FORMER COURT JUNIOR HIGH (1940) Now used as an alternative school building.
402 West Court Street
(575) 541-0140
State Register for Cultural Properties SRCP #1500

FORMER DONA ANA COUNTY COURTHOUSE
State Register SR #1276, 5-9-86

In 2009 this New Deal building was sold to a private individual who is remodeling it to be used for housing upstairs and businesses downstairs. In early 2012, the remodeling is still not completed.

This 1937 Spanish-Pueblo Style building is three stories high with flat roof and two towers. The U-shaped building, with its exposed vigas and projecting wooden balconies carved with Spanish motifs, was partially funded by the Public Works Administration (PWA). The interior of the building features red tile floors with tile and wood base moldings, covered plaster walls, and exposed viga ceilings bearing Pueblo Indian motifs. What the new owner will do with these features remains to be seen but it is expected to be made into office and commercial spaces with apartments available up on the upper floors.

HUMAN SYSTEMS RESEARCH BUILDING (1938)
(575) 524-9456
State Register SR #1912

This New Deal structure built in 1938 has quite a history. First it was built as part of CCC Camp BR-39 by the CCC to be an educational facility for that New Deal program. This was followed by the US Army during WW II using it as an administrative office when they were responsible for German and Italian POW camps across the street. A second building has since been torn down. After the war it also served as a Mental Health Clinic. Today it houses a private, non-profit program that focuses on archaeological work and they hope to use it in the future as a museum.

MacARTHUR ELEMENTARY SCHOOL was built in 1941 and is also still in use.

NEW MEXICO STATE UNIVERSITY

The following buildings and structures can be found on the New Mexico State University campus thanks to the New Deal's WPA program.

Dove Hall

This structure was originally the Home Economics building. The department occupied the top floor and the university administrative offices the bottom floor. Its cost ($43,000) and was achieved with a 45% grant from WPA and 55% from loans. It was finished in October, 1936. Much of the Spanish-Colonial Revival furniture that was originally in that building was built by the NYA students.

Goddard Hall

A wing to this Engineering building was done in 1937 at a cost of $41,000 from WPA funds.

Kent Hall, History Museum

New Deal furniture done by NYA youth can be found here along with archival documents.

Milton Hall

The Student Union was funded partially by a WPA grant of $105,000 with an additional $60,000 in bonds and was completed in 1941.

Neale Hall

The Dairy Department had a building constructed with $41,000 WPA funds and it is now incorporated as the center part of Neale Hall. This was most likely done in 1941–1942.

Rhodes and Garrett Halls
State Register for Cultural Properties #446

These make up the women's dormitories and were constructed with WPA funds ($150,000) in early 1940s. Fine New Deal furniture done by the NYA youth can be found on display in Rhodes Hall.

Science Hall

The Regulatory Building which was built with WPA monies ($65,000) may now be part of the Science Hall and that portion was completed October 1939.

Sidewalks in the older part of the campus were funded and built by WPA workmen.

Williams Hall

This building was not funded by the WPA but the plastering of the inside of the gym was done by WPA workmen.

OTHER IMPROVEMENTS AND PROGRAMS

Road improvements to Organ Mountain. US 80 landscaping for 21.5 miles and repairs, canning labor, child care, drainage ditches, sidewalks and bridges, storm inlets, index birth/death records, storm sewer system, park and recreation grounds, tennis courts, sewing room operation, day nursery, school lunch operation, book repair, sort tax assessments, Jornado Range improvements, vegetation and grazing analysis, sewer line construction, dike construction, irrigation and ditch improvements. A gas distribution system was also installed by the Public Works Administration (PWA) funds.

OTHER STRUCTURES

Addition on Union High School
City Hall
Demolition of earlier court house
Municipal Airport Improvements
Public Welfare Office
Remodel National Guard Armory
Repairs on six rural schools
Six room school house
Unemployment Compensation Office
Warehouse

MYSTERY ARTWORK, see Chapter 4 (Kloss and Nordfeldt)

LAS VEGAS

"Few dreamed there could ever be a national art movement. Regardless of the art quality or value of the work, the project has been successful in proving we do have and have had all along, an innate art consciousness...[,]a definite awakening to the enrichment which art brings to life has taken place all over the country."

—Ina Sizer Cassidy, "Art and Artists of New Mexico," *New Mexico Magazine*, June, 1935

NEW DEAL ART IN NEW DEAL BUILDINGS

NEW MEXICO HIGHLANDS UNIVERSITY

ROGERS HALL, Administration Building
#918 State Register 1-1-82, National Register 9-22-88

Designed by John Gaw Meem and constructed by the WPA, Rogers Hall was completed in 1937. It is currently the school's Administration Building but it was originally the school's library. The wall bases of the Spanish-Colonial Revival building are of rusticated ashlar sandstone capped with a finished molding. The upper walls are of stuccoed brick and framed by sandstone quoins and a frieze below the eaves. Stone scroll brackets join the overhanging eaves and the walls and the sloped roof is covered with clay tiles. The walls of the main staircase and the second floor foyer are covered with murals by Lloyd Moylan.

"The Dissemination of Education in New Mexico" is the title of the mural by Moylan done under the WPA/FAP in 1937. The fresco covers walls around a double stairway from first to second floor and continues in the second floor foyer in light green tones with two areas on the second floor that are now enclosed into office areas and are in yellow tones. These differences in color are a curiosity. As the title suggests, the educational theme traces the evolution from the Creation to New Mexicans being engaged in ranching, weaving, pottery-making, dentistry, the sciences and modern technology.

NEW DEAL PUBLIC ART IN PUBLIC BUILDINGS

ILFELD AUDITORIUM

Brooks Willis painted eight oil paintings on canvas over the exterior and interior doors of the lobby of this building. This was done in the 1930s but for some unknown reason they were all later painted over five and some six times with white paint. In 2007 the NNDPA-New Mexico Chapter and the university partnered to have Steve Prins, a Santa Fe art conservator, to professionally remove the paint thereby restoring these unusual depictions of figures that are symbolic of the different colleges/departments of the university. After uncovering the half-moon shaped murals over each door, there was enough money left to conserve two of the seven. In 2012 more funds were obtained to finish the conservation of the other five works on canvas. Unfortunately the eighth canvas is missing—the one depicting the English Department and its whereabouts are unknown.

LIBRARY

Paintings by Fremont Ellis, Howard Schleeter and Sheldon Parsons have also hung in the President's Office in Rogers Hall. However, they may have been moved to the Library. The Library also has a copy of Louis Ewing and Eliseo Rodriguez's "Navajo Rug Portfolio" displaying some of the rugs that can be found in the Laboratory of Anthropology in Santa Fe.

NEW DEAL BUILDINGS and STRUCTURES

COMMUNITY CENTER (on the west side of Las Vegas)

HIGHLANDS UNIVERSITY OTHER STRUCTURES and PROGRAMS

The football stadium was completed by the National Youth Administration (NYA) youth. Other structures at this institution worked on by New Deal programs include dormitories (Kennedy and others), dining and kitchen facilities, playing field, warehouse, shops, landscaping, book repairs and various repairs.

HIGHWAY DEPARTMENT

LUNA VOCATIONAL SCHOOL Improvements of the then Camp Luna were made by the WPA and possibly CCC.

NATIONAL GUARD ARMORY REMODELED

NORMAN L. KING MEMORIAL STADIUM
State Register #1780

The CCC constructed this horse pavilion with flagstone bleachers outside of Las Vegas near Luna Vocational Technical campus. A private organization continues to attempt to get monies from the legislature in order to restore the structures so they can be used for multiple purposes. Such a public pavilion space is needed for entertainment activities today.

REHABILITATION FACILITY Originally this facility was built to provide hospital care for people with orthopedic conditions but later was the town's main hospital, St. Anthony's Hospital.

ROUGH RIDER MUSEUM This stone building housing the Rough Riders memorabilia originally was the City Hall and was created by the WPA.

RURAL ELECTRIC ADMINSTRATION (REA) Mora/San Miguel Electric Cooperative continues to serve this county.

SAN MIGUEL COUNTY COURTHOUSE (built 1940)
700 West National Avenue
(575) 425-9331

STATE MENTAL HOSPITAL Some additions were completed on existing buildings and landscaping and other improvements were also done.

OTHER MUNICIPAL BUILDINGS

Fire Station, Airport additions, landscaping of recreational facilities and Sewage Plant.

Las Vegas Municipal Building is on the State Register SR #1915.

Robertson High School (1936) is still in use. West Las Vegas's Don Cecilio Martinez Elementary School was built in 1939.

OTHER STRUCTURES and PROJECTS include roads, sewage plant, dam diversion, tree planting, wall construction playground, park landscaping, wall construction salvaging a ten room school, high school tennis courts and track, sidewalks and curbs, reconstruct dam, improvements at the following sites: playing field schools, airport, Storie Lake, City Hall, Camp Luna, and a ranger station. In the county (San Miguel) there is the Glorieta Baldy Lookout Tower SCRP # 1451 most likely built by the CCC and the Sheridan Schoolhouse in Sheridan, New Mexico SR #1732.

MYSTERY ARTWORK, see Chapter 4

LINCOLN

NEW DEAL PUBLIC ART IN NEW DEAL PUBLIC BUILDINGS, See below

NEW DEAL BUILDINGS, STRUCTURES and PROGRAMS

BACA CAMPGROUND

This camp was built by the New Deal and for some time was a CCC camp then a National Youth Corps (NYA) facility for young women. They were taught homemaking skills and did sewing projects for Carrie Tingley Hospital children over in nearby Hot Springs, New Mexico now Truth or Consequences New Mexico.

During the time it was a CCC Camp or adjacent camps, three lookout towers were built in this area by the CCC. They are Mesa Ranger Station in Nogal was built (SCRP 1743), Montjeau Lookout in Alto (SCRP 1445) and Ruidoso Lookout Tower (SRCP 1447). Other CCC activities have received State Register designation (SCRP 1737) as the Public Works of the CCC in the Lincoln National Forest.

EL TORREON

This three-story tower was built by early Hispanic settlers for defense against Indian depredations. WPA funds and the Chaves County Historical Society of Roswell restored it in 1935.

OLD LINCOLN COUNTY COURTHOUSE

This was the famous building where Sheriff Pat Garrett shot Billy the Kid in a gun fight. It was built in 1874 but as the population declined in this area, the county seat was moved to Carrizozo in 1909. When New Deal funds became available the former courthouse received restoration work done as WPA Project # 465-85-2-150 in April 1938 in cooperation with the Museum of New Mexico. According to Foreman J. W. Hendron, the project's objective was to restore the former county seat of Lincoln County as designed by George Peppin as a big store for L. G. Murphy & Company, "as nearly as possible to the time Billy the Kid made his escape." The restoration was completed in 1939 at a complete cost of $8,190 and the building was dedicated by Governor John F. Miles on July 30, 1939. It now serves as a museum, part of the state's monument system, and is included in the village's status as a National Historic Landmark. This includes eleven buildings in that community. Archival New Deal photos of the restoration are on display in the museum.

OLD SCHOOL

In 1938 WPA funds enabled the building of a Pueblo Revival style adobe school containing four large classrooms, an auditorium, indoor restrooms and a kitchen. The school, closed in 1958, later housed a foundry but has now been renovated and made into a private home. It is located right next to the old courthouse.

RURAL ELECTRIC ADMINISTRATION (REA) Otero County Electric Cooperative provides electricity for this rural area thanks to the New Deal.

LORDSBURG

"There are throughout the nation murals in public buildings and works of art in museums and public collection which are now part of our cultural heritage that were created under government sponsorship."

—Milton W. Brown, "New Deal Art Projects—Boondoggle?" *Art News*, April 1982.

NEW DEAL PUBLIC ART IN NEW DEAL PUBLIC BUILDINGS

LORDSBURG-HIDALGO PUBLIC LIBRARY
208 East Third Street
Lordsburg, New Mexico 88045
State Register SR #1856

This WPA building built in 1937 houses an oil painting by Joseph Fleck titled, "Landscape from Talpa." The painting was restored in 2003 by Luis Neri Zagal with New Mexico Chapter of National New Deal Preservation funds. A very similar painting by the same artist is also in the Albuquerque Museum collection.

NEW DEAL BUILDINGS, STRUCTURES and PROGRAMS

HIDALGO COUNTY FAIRGROUNDS is still in use. There is a rock pillar entryway with WPA designation on it.

HIGH SCHOOL This became the Junior High, then the Enrichment Center. Now vacant but locals are considering rehabilitating it.

LORDSBURG CITY HALL Built for $10,971.89 in 1935. Now the Chamber of Commerce.

PORT OF ENTRY STATION has been replaced by newer structures

RURAL ELECTRIC ADMINISTRATION (REA) Columbus Electric Cooperative provides electricity to 2,978 in the three southern counties and one county in Arizona thanks to the New Deal.

SUNSET CANAL DAM (1936)

WILSON SCHOOL IMPROVEMENTS

OTHER STRUCTURES AND PROGRAMS include sidewalks, roads, tennis courts, concrete water tank and water mains, streets, utilities system extension, library cataloging and book repair, clean courthouse, football stadium (now gone), and sewing room operation. Work was done in the lower Gila River area near Verdon, New Mexico.

MYSTERY ARTWORK, See Chapter 4

LOS LUNAS

"Of the many illusions about the political nature of art during the Federal Art Project years, the art community came face to face with the realities of union, the government, and the autonomy of the individual artist (both employed and unemployed) between those institutional realism."

—Belisario P. Contreras, *Tradition and Innovation in New Deal Art*, 1983

NEW DEAL PUBLIC ART IN PUBLIC BUILDINGS

LOS LUNAS MUSEUM OF HERITAGE AND ART (former City Hall)

This former municipal building is now the local museum and art gallery. It is now the proud displayer of a fine New Deal painting by J. Charles Berninghaus entitled "Road to Santa Fe." The painting is officially owned by the Los Lunas Community Center which was formerly the home of Los Lunas Hospital and Training School, the state's institution for mentally retarded or developmentally disabled. The institution was later closed once the residents were moved into community based programs around the state. This large oil painting was restored in early 2000 by Luis Neri Zagal thanks to the New Mexico Chapter of the National New Deal Preservation Association.

NEW DEAL BUILDINGS, STRUCTURES and PROGRAMS

COURTHOUSE ANNEX and improvements, vault construction

RAYMOND GABALDON SCHOOL and other schools, High School remodeling

RESERVOIR, DAM CONSTRUCTION and WATERWORKS

RURAL ELECTRIC ADMINISTRATION (REA) The nearby rural areas are still being provided electricity thanks to the New Deal by the Socorro Electric Cooperative.

OLD SUPERINTENDENT'S HOUSE This building at the former hospital and training school is the only remaining building in this complex that was built with New Deal funding.

MYSTERY ARTWORK, see Chapter 4

LOS OJOS

There is a large mural on the front of an old adobe building thought to have been an old fort building in downtown Los Ojos (Rio Arriba County) that was done by Brooks Willis in 1938. It is a WPA mural and the building was most likely a public building at the time. It is currently an apartment building and is located close to the Tierra Wools store. The mural depicts various early settlers in the area including Native American and early Anglo ranching settlers. A WPA historic plaque identifies the creation of this mural.

LOVINGTON

NEW DEAL BUILDINGS, STRUCTURES and PROGRAMS

COURTHOUSE

The first Lea County Courthouse was built for $25,000 after the county was established in 1917. Around 1937 there was a group in Hobbs that focused on getting the county seat moved from Lovington to Hobbs and as a gesture of "good faith" they deposited with the County Treasurer $40,000 to construct a new courthouse in Hobbs. A petition was submitted to the county populace but was rejected when it was determined that state law required that a new courthouse would have to be at least twenty miles from the existing county building. According to Donald Whisenhunt's *New Mexico's Courthouses*, "a quick check revealed that the proposed site in Hobbs was eighty-nine feet short of twenty miles from the courthouse in Lovington. The donation was returned after another attempt failed to create a new town closer that was to be called New Hobbs." The county commissioners moved then to award a contract to construct a new courthouse in Lovington and this was accomplished at a cost of $179,000 in 1937. The source of those funds appears to not be New Deal funding but the architecture is similar to other New Deal courthouses on the east side of the state and west side of Texas. However, the county was experiencing a monumental oil boom and possibly could have financed the construction with incoming revenues from that source. A new addition was added later and it is quite a handsome and prominent building located on the city square—the biggest structure in the community.

FIRE STATION A combined City Hall and Fire Station was created in 1941 for $9,007 and is on the State Register.

RURAL ELECTRIC COOPERATIVE
Lea County Electric Cooperative
1300 West Avenue D
(575) 396-3631

This New Deal program continues to provide electric power to approximately 6,807 rural consumers in this portion of the state.

OTHER STRUCTURES AND PROGRAMS include road improvements, landscaping of school grounds, and map preparation.

MYSTERY ARTWORK, see Chapter 4

LYDEN

MYSTERY ARTWORK

Between Espanola and Velarde one can find a major basalt laden mesa as a result of volcanic eruption from an area near Questa centuries ago. These basalt boulders, both large and small, became the canvases for ancient petroglyphs created by the Native American inhabitants in this Rio Arriba county site. Among that ancient art one can also find more recent New Deal rock etchings primarily done in 1938. They identify a major New Deal program "WPA" which the etchers were obviously participants in. Since the original core of the school in that area is a WPA built school, maybe they wandered into the hills and left their marks. The marks include "WPA, JVJ, 1938" on various rocks while others have initials "V.V." and "WPA." Only one has a complete date—WPA, Marjo 17, 1938." So now the mystery is who were J.V.J. or V.V.?

On the other side of the highway there was a CCC Camp most likely the Soil Conservation Camp #SCS-5-N. Partial foundations of buildings still exist there.

The area is now being preserved by Mesa Prieta Petroglyph Project, a private non-profit organization. They provide opportunities for Native American youth and adults to survey and research the area.

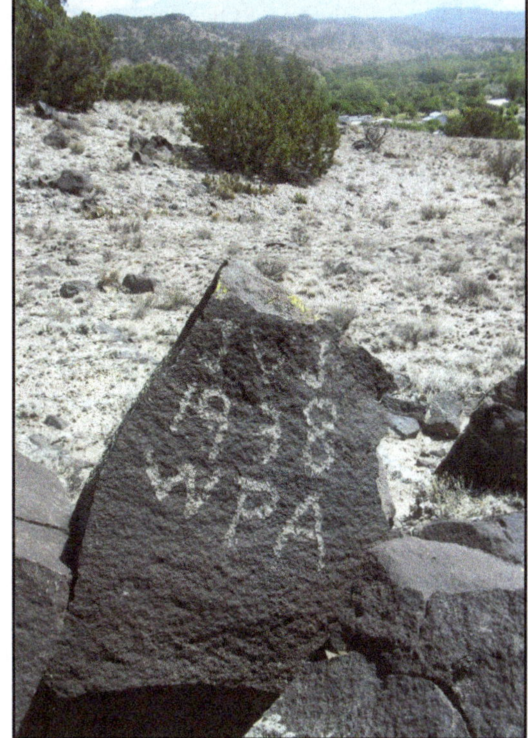

Unique petroglyphs in this area include various WPA markers with years and worker's initials.

MADRID

NEW DEAL BUILDINGS, STRUCTURES AND PROGRAM

COMMUNITY BALL PARK, PLAYGROUND and TENNIS COURTS The original BLEACHERS were also built then by New Deal workers but in the summer of 2010 they were replaced with new seating.

ROCK WALL around the ballpark and road work.

MADRID STONE SCHOOLHOUSE

RURAL ELECTRIC ADMINISTRATION (REA) Central New Mexico Electric Cooperative provides the electricity for this rural community.

MAGDALENA

NEW DEAL BUILDINGS, STRUCTURES and PROGRAMS

HIGH SCHOOL AND GYMNASIUM The gymnasium is now the home of the London Frontier Theater, a small, local performing arts group. Check their website.

RANGER STATION

RODEO GROUNDS

RURAL ELECTRIC ADMINISTRATION (REA) Socorro Electric Cooperative supplies electricity to this predominantly rural area thanks to the New Deal.

OTHER STRUCTURES AND PROGRAMS include roads, underground water storage, forest improvements.

MALAGA

NEW DEAL BUILDINGS, STRUCTURES and PROGRAMS

PORT OF ENTRY was built with WPA funds.

SCHOOL was built with PWA funds.

MAYHILL

To the best of our knowledge, the only New Deal treasure still in existence in this small community in Otero County is a former CCC camp built in 1940 that later housed a

German Prisoner of War camp. The prisoners were from North Africa and worked with the local farmers in the area and also helped restoring structures and landscapes after a major flood. Two buildings and a rock wall still stand and the U.S. Forest Service owns the property now. It is known as the Mayhill Administrative Site and is on the State Register for Cultural Properties SRCP 1504. The structure was saved during a forest fire in May 2011.

MAXWELL

NEW DEAL BUILDINGS, STRUCTURES and PROGRAMS

CITY HALL

DAM CONSTRUCTION, ROADS

RURAL ELECTRIC ADMINISTRATION (REA) Springer Electric Cooperative provides the needed electricity for this rural area of the state thanks to the New Deal.

SCHOOL GYM

TENNIS COURTS

MELROSE

"Art in Melrose benefited greatly under the Federal Arts Project of the WPA, as early as 1936. Art exhibits were regularly scheduled and several different projects got under way. Such things as the murals in the Library-Stud Hall, curtains in the Administrative Office windows and in the stage of the gymnasium-auditorium, furniture in offices, commercial rooms, and state, all were adjuncts to a scheduled training in the arts of painting, ceramics, carpentry, etc. The above had its highlight when a Dedicatory Service was held on June 22, 1938. A Federal Art Center was located on the lower floor of the Masonic Hall."

—Ray J. Lofton, former Melrose Superintendent of Schools, 1930–1940s.

During the 1930s Melrose, along with Las Vegas, Gallup, and Roswell was designated to have a New Deal Federal Art Center where art classes and traveling exhibits were held. These were well attended and women in the communities enjoyed providing refreshments for the art exhibit events. Unfortunately, the Center did not survive. However, the one in Roswell did survive and is the core structure of the existing Roswell Museum and Space Center and the basis of the institution's fine collections. It is one of two known WPA Federal Art Centers that have never closed its doors. The other one is the Southside Federal Art Center in Chicago.

NEW DEAL PUBLIC ART IN PUBLIC BUILDINGS

MELROSE PUBLIC SCHOOLS
100 E. Missouri
Contact Person: Superintendent
(575) 253-4267

Some of the current buildings in the public school complex were constructed during the WPA time. An outstanding collection of New Deal public art (second only in number to the Clayton school collection), is owned by this school district. The collection is on view in the newer buildings. The paintings with an asterisk (*) by the title have been conserved by the New Mexico Chapter of the NNDPA. The whole collection includes:

Bakos, Josef
"Autumn Flowers"
"Valley Scene"
Bakos, Teresa
"Peas"
Cervantez, Pedro
"The Wind Mill"
"Zinnias"
Claflin, Majel
"Hill Road"
Cooke, Regina Tatum
"Taos Chapel"
Jones, D. Paul
"Women Sweeping"
"The Women to Truchas"
Kloss, Gene*
"Mountains"
"Church at Trampas"
"Rio Grande Pueblo"
"Snow Scene"
Morang, Dorothy
"Mountains from East Garcia"
Naumer, Helmuth*
"Autumn in Aspens"
"Oaktree in Winter"
"Old Town—Pecos Plaza"
Ortiz, Max
"Mountain Church"
"Windmill and Water Tank"
Parsons, Sheldon
"Upper Canyon Road"
Pillin, Polia
"Snow on Atalaya Hill"
Schleeter, Howard
"Cowboy on Horseback"
"Family in Wagon"
"Farmer on Tractor"
"Indians on Horseback"
"Rain"*
"Surveyors"
Toledo, Jose Rey
"The Drum Makers"
West, Harold
"Bored Cowboys"
"River Baptism"
"Untitled"
Will, Blanca*
"In the Greenhouse"
Willis, Brooks*
"Tree"

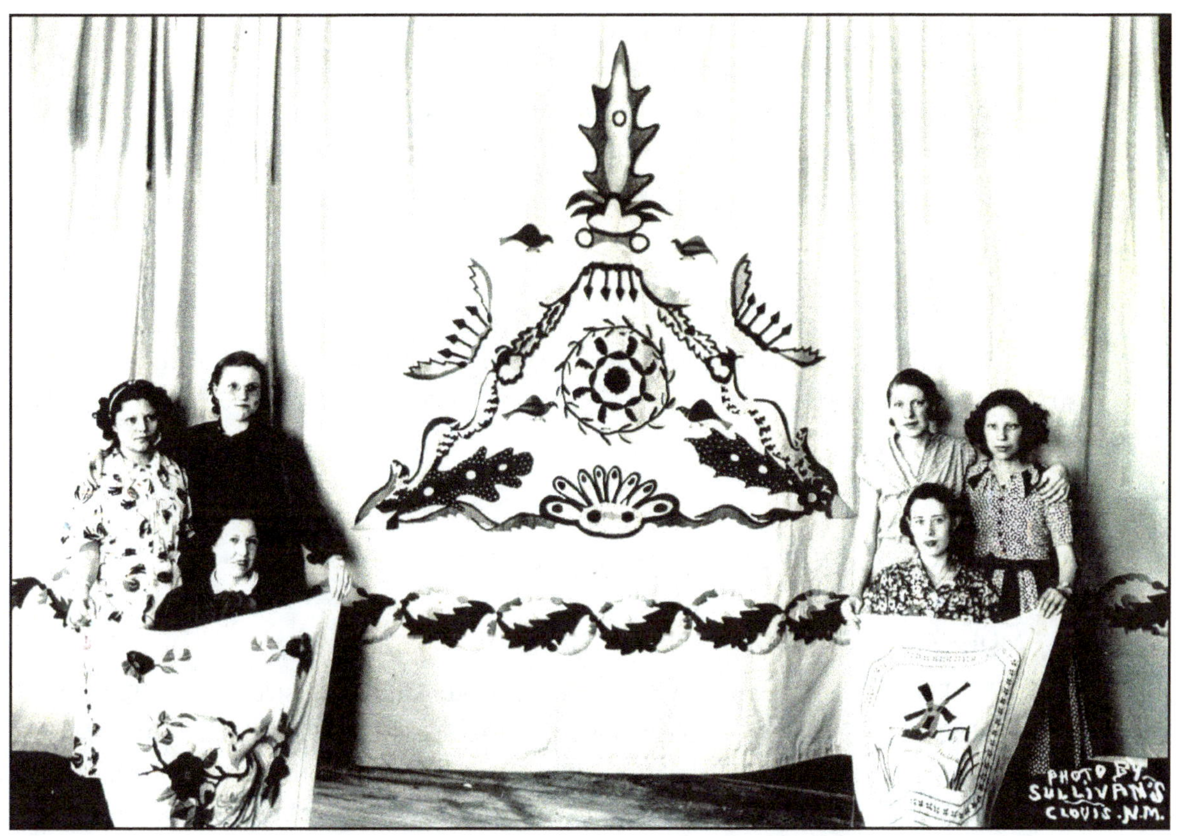

Young women were taught colcha embroidery in the WPA and NYA classes in many parts of the state. Large stage curtains with colcha embroidered designs were known to have been created for the Melrose School, the Roswell Art Center and Carrie Tingley Hospital in Truth of Consequences but all have disappeared. This one was destroyed in a fire but the whereabouts of the others are still unknown. Photograph from Roswell Federal Art Center archives.

NEW DEAL PUBLIC BUILDINGS, STRUCTURES and PROGRAMS

CITY HALL and JAIL

FARMERS ELECTRIC COOPERATIVE (REA) serves this community and its surrounding ranches.

RENOVATION OF SCHOOL ADDITION and some small support buildings

ROAD IMPROVEMENTS

SEWING ROOM OPERATION

It was likely that the sewing room operation was the site of the beautiful colcha embroidered stage curtain for the auditorium which was created with the skilled hands of the local women. The design for the curtain was done by James Ridgely Whiteman,

Clovis artist and son of the owner of the Whiteman Printing Co. that helped print some of the *Portfolios of Spanish-Colonial Design*. The curtain was later destroyed in a fire when the school building burned. They created another stage curtain for Carrie Tingley Hospital in Truth or Consequences but its whereabouts are unknown.

SCHOOL GYMNASIUM/AUDITORIUM, sidewalks and landscaping

MYSTERY ARTWORK

A set of the *Portfolio of Spanish-Colonial Design* was originally owned by the school district but has disappeared.

MORA

NEW DEAL BUILDINGS, STRUCTURES and PROGRAM

MORA COUNTY COURTHOUSE/JAIL

Public Works Administration (PWA) helped to build this structure in 1938 for $60,050 and WPA funds supplemented the total amount in 1939. Today it has been demolished and temporarily replaced with portable buildings until the new courthouse is completed. The new courthouse has been started but it has not been completed as of early 2012.

SCHOOL BUILDINGS (High School, Gym, Auditorium—demolished)

RURAL ELECTRIC ASSOCIATION (REA)
Mora-San Miguel Electric Cooperative
Main Street
(575) 387- 2205

This New Deal program continues to serve approximately 7,725 rural New Mexicans in the four counties in this area of the state.

WELFARE OFFICE (Then referred to as the Relief and Security Office)

OTHER STRUCTURES and PROGRAMS include roads, irrigation ditches, swamp drainage and bridges. The Tipton House and Barn on the Enoch Tipton Ranch were a Public Works Administration (PWA) in 1940. They are on the State Historic Register #SR 1982.

MYSTERY ARTWORK, see Chapter 4 (Kloss)

MOSQUERO

NEW DEAL BUILDINGS AND OTHER STRUCTURES

COMMUNITY BUILDING (adobe) in 1936.

COURTHOUSE VAULT

RURAL ELECTRIC ADMINISTRATION (REA) Still serving this area via the Mora-San Miguel Electric Cooperative, it meets the electrical needs of those in a four county area in the northern portion of the state. See contact information above.

SCHOOL (SIX ROOMS AND GYM) These are in very good shape.

WATER TOWER

OTHER STRUCTURES AND PROGRAMS include sewing rooms operation, school lunch preparation, sidewalks, index county records, water system, roads, and walls.

MOUNTAINAIR

"Our business is to put men to work, to do it quickly and to do it intelligently. To this end the PWA and the Procurement Division of the Treasury Department—responsible for Federal Buildings—had by 1937 allotted funds through grants and loans to over 34,500 projects and helped to bring into the economy nearly 7 billion dollars in new construction costs."

—Short, C. W. and Stanley-Brown, R. *Public Building Architecture Under the Public Works Administration, 1933–1939* Vol. I. De Capo Press, 1986

NEW DEAL BUILDINGS, STRUCTURES and PROGRAMS

JAIL

MOUNTAINAIR MUNICIPAL AUDITORIUM (Dr. Robert J. Saul Recreation Center) SR #1371 State Register 2-6-87, National Register 4-30-87

This auditorium was designed by local architect/builder, Everett Crist, and constructed between 1934 and 1936. Like most federal relief program sponsored construction, the auditorium was built with local materials. Rock and mortar for the rough-faced sandstone ashlar walls were quarried east of town near the site of Abo Mission. The style of the building has been described as a provincial version of Modernistic style. The interior is notable for the tree trunk pillars which support the balconies and the roof.

OTHER STRUCTURES AND PROGRAMS include roads, sidewalks, sewage plant, and home sewing project.

RURAL ELECTRIC ADMINISTRATION (REA)
Central New Mexico Electric Cooperative
Highway 55
Mountainair, New Mexico 87036

This Rural Electric Cooperative Association office that serves approximately 17,247 consumers in the rural areas near this community.

SCHOOL BUILDINGS (High School Shop, Gym, other school buildings, landscaping)

MYSTERY ARTWORK, see Chapter 4 (Kloss)

Note: One should not miss viewing the artwork in the Shaffer Hotel. It is believed to have been done by Marvin Shaffer, the son of the original owner of the hotel but the work is unsigned. It was not a New Deal project, but the young Shaffer lived and studied in Taos with many of the known Taos artists during the time and was obviously greatly influenced by them.

NARA VISA

This community on the northeast side of the state sits closely adjacent to Texas and was settled by the Rock Island Railroad in 1901. The school was built twenty years later and the adobe gymnasium was created in 1935 by WPA laborers. The buildings are listed on the National and State Registers and serve as a community center today.

ORO GRANDE

The current Community Center was originally the New Deal school in this Otero County community. Road improvements were also made throughout the village.

PECOS

NEW DEAL BUILDINGS, STRUCTURES and PROGRAMS

FISH HATCHERY

MORA /SAN MIGUEL REA provides electrical service to this community and its surrounding 7,725 consumers.

PECOS MONUMENT (MISSION)-improvements

ROAD TO LOOKOUT TOWER and LA QUEVA ROAD and most likely the Lookout Tower was done by the CCC.

SCHOOLS—The Middle School was built in 1935 and is still in use.

PLACITAS

NEW DEAL BUILDINGS AND STRUCTURES

A WPA school was built and is now houses a mission program for the Catholic Church. A road up to the mountain, rock walls, culverts, and bridges were all created by CCC and WPA and landscaping was done around the plaza.

PORTALES

NEW DEAL PUBLIC ART IN NEW DEAL BUILDINGS

EASTERN NEW MEXICO UNIVERSITY

Administration Building
(575) 562-2123
State Register SR #1468

Located in the center of this building which was built in 1934 is a mural painted under WPA/FAP in 1936 by Lloyd Moylan (1893–1963) titled, "The 12th Chapter of Ecclesiastes." It took Moylan and his assistant five months to complete what is considered his finest work and they were paid by the federal funds. It covers the walls, floor to ceiling, around the stairway from the first to the second floor. The mural's theme, unlike others in New Mexico is based on the scriptures of the Bible. Semi-cubist in style, the subjects are rendered with a cross-hatching technique. Funding for the paint and materials (approximately $160) used for the murals was donated anonymously, with two required conditions: (a) the artist, selected from the WPA/FAP list, must not paint on Sunday; and (b) the unknown donor would select the subject matter for the mural. This is most likely why the theme turned out to be religiously based.

As the *Clovis News Journal* described the mural in 1936, "Colors of the mural range from deep brown to lavender, pale green and reds combining to make one of the most beautiful and inspirational centers of interest in the whole college. The mural on the wall, extended from the floor of the first floor to the ceiling of the second floor has been practically completed. Many persons watch the artist work daily as the details of his sketches become clearer.

"The passage especially easy to identify as verses 5-8 in the mural now completed is 'Also when they shall be afraid of that which is high and fears shall be in the way and the almond tree shall flourish, and the grasshopper shall be a burden and desire shall fail; because man goeth to his long home and the mourners go about the streets; or ever the silver cord be loosed, or the golden bowl be broken, or the pitcher broken at the fountain, or the wheel broken at the cistern. Then shall the dust return to the earth as it was; and the spirit shall return unto God who gave it. Vanities of Vanities' saith the preacher, 'all is vanity.'"[1]

Also in this building and in the Golden Library across the street are two large abstract mural panels titled "Art" and "Science" by Raymond Jonson. They were planned as a pair, with the aim of serving as spiritual stimuli for the students. Regarding these panels, Jonson wrote in 1937: "My desire is to have a fine quality in these works based on, as a starting point, "Art" and "Science." One panel will place the emphasis on Art—the other on Science (note: my aim is to develop a series of rhythms and forms that can function as Abstract). These works will not be the usual or typical kind of decoration. Rather they will be powerful unusual ideas presented sincerely. As a result of my visit to the College, I have the conviction that there is a spirit of 'today' fully aware of what is occurring in the Art world. My hope is that these works will be a real stimulus to the students there and to all who may chance to see them."

On the second floor of this building is another mural that was not a New Deal project and was created by Bill White in 1941. White, at 25, was a member of Eastern New Mexico College's first four-year graduating class of forty-one members. This mural depicts the history of Portales and the plains country from the time of the Indians, the buffalo, the dozens of saloons in the town and the church dominated community as of 1941.

1. "Bible Passages Theme for Gigantic Mural Being Executed at College," *Clovis News Journal*, Jan. 12, 1939.

Roosevelt County Museum

This building was created in 1940 with WPA funding of $17,286.32. Visitors to this museum will find a variety of items including one of the Gene Kloss New Deal etchings, "Christmas Eve, Taos Pueblo" and the Kenneth Adams etching, "The Spring." These pieces were conserved by the New Mexico Chapter of the NNDPA in 2010.

PORTALES POST OFFICE
116 West First Street
Contact Person: Postmaster
State Register SRCP 106, National Register 2-23-90

Funded by the Public Works Administration (PWA), the Main Post Office in Portales was completed in 1937. This Classical Revival style building is a single story red brick structure on a raised basement. The relatively plain exterior is a common style for federal buildings in the West during this period. Two years after the building was completed, the interior was embellished with a mural by Theodore Van Soelen. The Post Office is part of a complex of New Deal administrative buildings in the downtown area which includes the WPA constructed courthouse across the street.

Regional subject matter is the theme for Theodore Van Soelen's 1938 "Buffalo Range," funded by the Section of the Treasury funds. Preliminary studies for the mural done by Van Soelen (1890–1964) were extensive by the local paper, *The Portales News* including the following: "The artists photographed sand hills and prairies and took back to his studio a cart load of bear grass and other flora to be sure that his painting would accurately portray the Roosevelt County landscape. He visited zoological gardens in Cincinnati and Chicago to study live buffaloes and sketched stuffed animals in the American Museum of Natural History."[1]

1. "Large Mural Placed at Post Office," *The Portales News*, July 18, 1938.

NEW DEAL PUBLIC ART IN PUBLIC BUILDINGS

EASTERN NEW MEXICO UNIVERSITY

Golden Library

The paintings in the library include one of the Jonson murals mentioned above, as well as the following:

Kloss, Gene
  "Penitente Friday"
  "Acoma"
Walker, Stuart
  "Black and White Sawmill"
  "Abstract"
Wells, Cady
  "Mesas" (may not be New Deal)
Willis, Brooks
  "Sawmill"

Music Building

Three oil paintings done around 1934 by Nils Hogner grace the walls of the staff lounge. They are colorful Navajo Indian scenes. We understand that one has disappeared. It is titled "Sanitation, Isleta Pueblo" and we hope someday it will be found and returned to this university to join with the three other Hogner paintings.

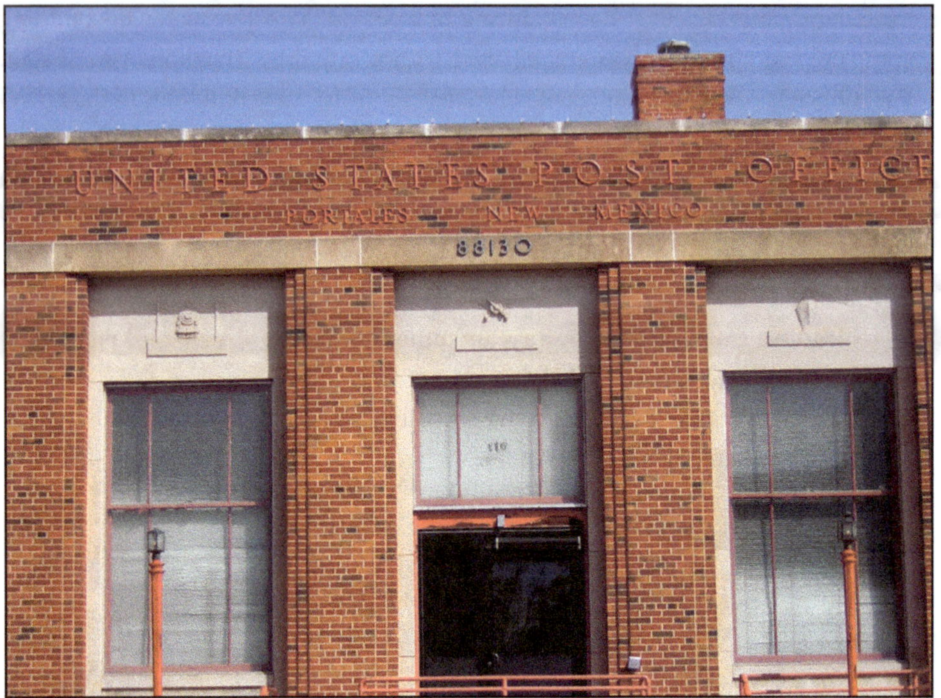

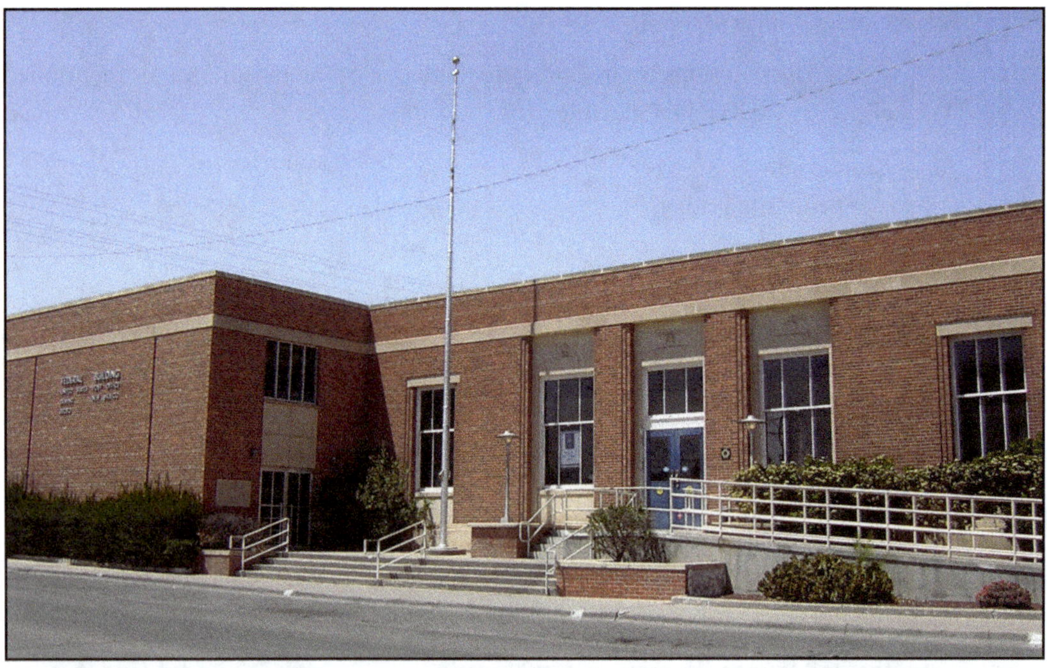

These two red brick post offices in New Mexico are typical of many post offices created around the country by the New Deal's PWA program. Frequently the bas reliefs on the front depict the mail delivery by land, air and water. Both of these structures also have murals over the Postmaster's door just like in other post offices as funded by The Section of Treasury Art. (Portales, above and Deming, below).

NEW DEAL PUBLIC BUILDINGS, STRUCTURES and PROGRAM

ATHLETIC FIELD FENCE

BLACKWATER DRAW PARK

This CCC built site was originally created to reforest 9,600 acres of that Dust Bowl area. Later the state government reduced the amount of acreage to 400. The CCC built a large bath house, other houses, camping areas and a lake. All but one lone house near the highway remains and was most likely the home for the park manager. In 1951 the state deeded the property to Eastern New Mexico University in Portales and they later built a large football stadium and the Blackwater Draw Museum which houses major archaeological findings from the area.

CEMETERY IMPROVEMENTS

EASTERN NEW MEXICO UNIVERSITY'S LEA HALL and QUAY HALL

FAIRGROUND BUILDINGS

FIRE STATION ADDITIONS Earlier fire station near Women's Club

GOLF COURSE

PORTALES WOMEN'S CLUB Some recall WPA paintings in this building that were later transferred to the university but no records have been located to determine which ones were transferred and where they now live on campus.

PUBLIC SCHOOLS

Junior High including gymnasium which is the only portion of that facility still in existence.

High School Home Economics and Industrial Arts buildings

East Ward (Steiner) and Lindsay Elementary schools—both buildings have been recently torn down and replaced with new buildings.

ROOSEVELT COUNTY COURTHOUSE/JAIL
SR #1278 State Register 5-9-86

The 1938 Art Deco Style Roosevelt County Courthouse is a four story structure of cast stone and blond brick with cast concrete and metal bas relief embellishments. It was designed by R. E. Merrell and partially funded through the Public Works Administration (PWA). The decorative exterior motifs include thunderbirds and bas relief medallion depicting three early settlers with an Indian guide walking across the prairie. The interior continues the Art Deco styling with terrazzo flooring and Deco style grills over the radiators.

It is interesting to note that when the money began to run out for the jail portion of the project, workers went to the wrecking yard and cut the tie rods off of old cars and used them for the bars in the jail. This building was constructed in 1939 for a cost of $18,756. Landscaping around the building was also carried out.

The structure was restored in the recent past with an elevator addition on the exterior. A statue of one of the town's early citizens, Washington Lindsay, has been recently placed on the grounds. He was New Mexico's third governor.

RURAL ELECTRIC ADMINISTRATION (REA)
Roosevelt County Electric Cooperative
121 North Main Street
(575) 350-4491

This New Deal cooperative has approximately 6,081 consumers that it continues today to provide electricity for on a daily basis in the rural areas of this county and surrounding counties.

SWIMMING POOL and ADJOINING PARK

OTHER STRUCTURES and PROGRAMS include cemetery improvements, roads, municipal water and sewer systems, sidewalks, demolition of old jail, and privy construction. The federal government referred to these outhouses as "Fly-proof Interior Sanitation Units."

MYSTERY ARTWORK, see Chapter 4 (Kloss and Nordfeldt)

QUEMADO

When passing through the Village of Quemado in southwestern New Mexico, don't miss the New Deal rock jail built in 1934 by the Federal Emergency Relief Administration (FERA). These letters are chiseled over the entry area and the building is located at #5 First Street in the center of town. Early in the 1930s there was a CCC camp in that area and they built the El Caso firetower, which has since been abandoned by the U.S. Forest Service, and many trails in that wilderness area near Quemado Lake. The New Deal school gym is gone but about ten miles west of Quemado, the old Red Hill school still stands some distance from the highway. For more information about the New Deal in this area, contact Craig Crissinger at the True Value Store in downtown Quemado.

RATON

"New Mexico post offices will have probably the best murals of any of the post offices throughout the nation because New Mexico has the best artists and it is difficult to find paintings of their equal."

—*Raton Range*, August 18, 1936.

NEW DEAL ART IN NEW DEAL BUILDING

ARTHUR JOHNSON MEMORIAL LIBRARY

This building was originally the Raton Post Office and was built during the PWA era. Paintings were funded by the WPA and done by well known New Mexico artists and four young boys in the public schools (Bill Warder, Mike Zunick and Trinidad Moses are the only three identified.) The library has also placed some of its collection on loan to the City Hall. An earlier library (Carnegie) also had 27 ceiling decorations done by John Jellico and Juanita Lantz but all were destroyed during the demolition of that building as a result of highway changes.

RATON MIDDLE SCHOOL (formerly the High School) was built in 1939. Boris Nordfeldt lithograph in a staff office has been conserved by NNDPA.

NEW DEAL ART IN PUBLIC BUILDINGS

EL PORTAL HOTEL

This private hotel, originally known as the Seaburg Hotel, once housed the local WPA office. Manville Chapman, the local coordinator, also taught art classes here to WPA supported individuals. He created WPA murals here in 1939, and later in 1950 one of his students, William Warder, painted six other murals for the building. In 2009 there was a fire in the building but the owner has indicated the murals were not destroyed but one could expect that there was possible smoke damage.

MINER'S HOSPITAL
Sixth Street

Howard Schleeter's oil and tempera of "Red Foothills," 3'1/2" x 4'1/2", is in the same building which is now a long term care facility. The date, March 1940, is written on the back as the date it was created. Structures created at this facility include a greenhouse, annex, and landscaping. The landscaping includes a rock wall and long trench on a hill side behind the building.

PUBLIC SCHOOL John Jellico created a mural for the junior high school but its whereabouts are unknown. Some feel it may have been painted over.

RATON POST OFFICE

In 1936, under the PWAP, Joseph A. Fleck (1893–1977) was commissioned to paint two murals titled "Butterfield Mail and "Unloading Mail at Raton" for the earlier post office. The first mural depicts Taos Indians and Raton miners in 1849 reading mail delivered by a scout on a white horse and can now be seen in the current lobby. The other mural focuses on the local mail system during the 1930s and is located in the staff conference room. When they were first adhered to the walls in the earlier post office one official commented, "Once placed they are durable and will last as long as the building." They indeed have outlasted that building and were later moved to the current post office and are still quite beautiful and durable. Fleck chose Raton as the site for these murals because he felt he could do his best work if he were familiar with the place. Raton was a site he visited often and liked."[1]

1. Lynette Hunnicutt, "New Deal PWAP Mural is Rendered for Local Post Office," *Raton Range*, Thursday, August 25, 1983.

SHULER THEATER FOYER
Second Street
State Register SRCP 470

Eight ceiling panel murals by Manville Chapman (1903–1978), created under PWAP, depict scenes from the history of Raton and surrounding communities; "Cheyenne Village, 1845" depicts the annual spring buffalo hunt; "Maxwell's Mansion, 1865" is a view of a local house given by the Spanish governor to two of his friends; "Wooten Toll-Gate, 1868" built by Richard Wooten, depicts the first passageway in the mountains for traders and trappers. "Willow Spring Ranch, 1870" is of an early ranch house which welcomed travelers; "Clifton Station, 1875" was where the early Barlow and Sanderson stage coaches stopped; "Elizabeth Town, 1885" was a former mining town on the Red River. Also included are "Raton's First Street, 1893" and "Blossburg Mine, 1895" an early coal mine in the area. The viewer will note that Chapman has one figure in each mural pointing on to the next mural with the left arm.

NEW DEAL BUILDINGS, STRUCTURES and PROGRAMS

COLFAX COUNTY COURTHOUSE/JAIL
Contact Person: County Clerk or County Manager
(575) 445-5551
SR #1273 State Register 5-9-86, National Register 6-18-87

The 1936 Art Deco style Colfax County Courthouse, a Public Works Administration (PWA) structure, is a five-story blond brick building with a hipped tile roof on the top story and flat roofs on the lower portions. The building is embellished with glazed tile cornices and bas relief metal panels. The larger bas reliefs depict farming, mining, and cattle raising, the main industries of Colfax County. Cattle brands from the region encircle the exterior doors. The interior continues the Art Deco styling with terrazzo floors, tile wainscoting, and deco light fixtures. A garage was also built.

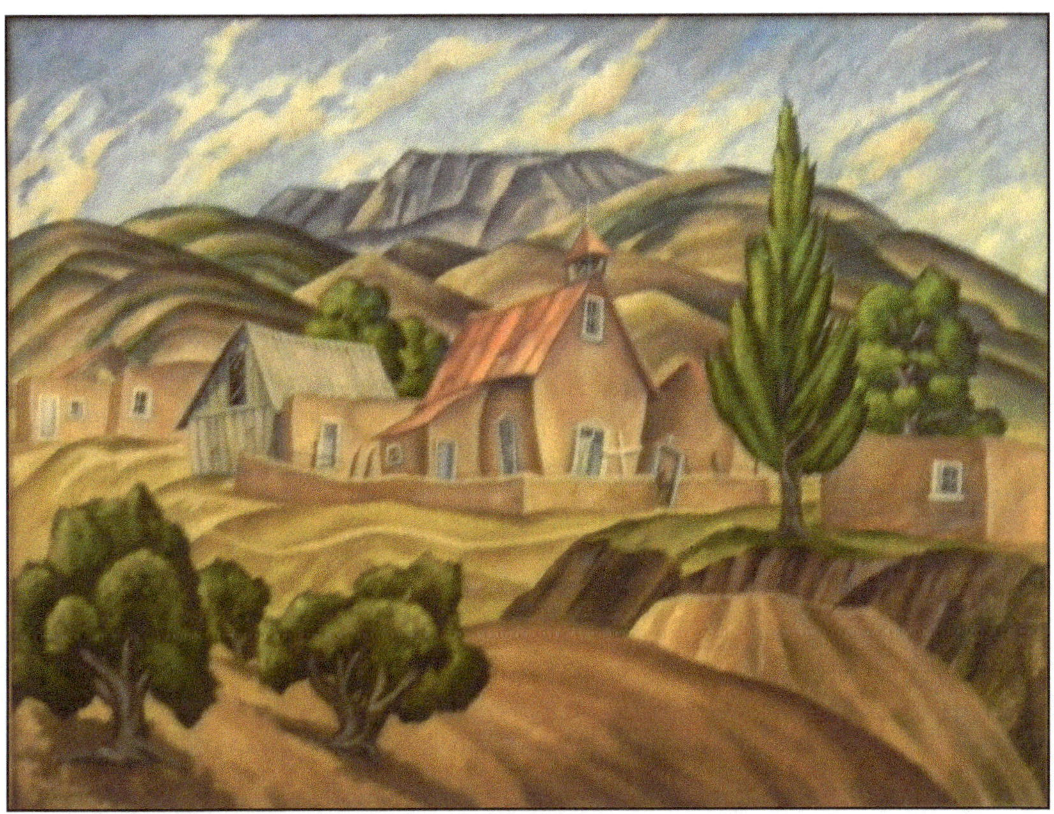

"Red Foothills" is a large oil painting done by Howard Schleeter and is still on view over a Nurse's Station at the Miner's Hospital. Photograph provided by the hospital.

COUNTY HIGHWAY DEPARTMENT BUILDING

MUNICIPAL STRUCTURES

Airport, golf course, sewer and water systems, rock drainage channels,* hand graded streets, sidewalks, work camp for transients, and Welfare Office. *This site as part of the Original Townsite Historic District is on the State Register SRCP 1919.

NATIONAL GUARD ARMORY State Register SCRP 1628. This facility is now the Raton Convention Center.

RURAL ELECTRIC ADMINISTRATION (REA) Springer Electric Cooperative continues to provide electricity to the rural areas surrounding the metropolis of Raton.

SCHOOLS

Columbian* (1940), Kearney* (1935), Longfellow* (1935) and the Middle School* (formerly the High School) 1939, tennis courts, football bleachers, and salvage the earlier gym.

*These schools are on the State Register. SRCP #1624, 1626, 1625, 1627.

OTHER STRUCTURES AND PROJECTS include Miami Dam, channel construction, erosion control dams, landscape 2nd Street underpass, log building, rock flood control, bridges, Port of Entry, and warehouse.

MYSTERY ARTWORK, see Chapter 4

RED RIVER

A New Deal public building? Yes, and rather an amazing story! The second Red River Schoolhouse was built in 1914 and was entered into the National Register of Historic Places on February 23, 1984 according to Jerry Rogers, the then "keeper" of the National Register in Washington, DC. Why is it included in this book about New Deal treasures? Because in 1939, amazingly, WPA funds paid workers to raise the building made with pressed metal siding that gives it a rusticated stone pattern in order to construct concrete living quarters for the teacher as well as a furnace and storage area. The building is currently owned by the Questa School District but has been maintained since 1942 by the Red River Women's Club when its use as a school was discontinued.

RESERVE

In September 1935 Catron County used $3,152 to remodel its courthouse and another $2,820 was used to landscape the area around the courthouse. Later in December 1938 another $1,007 was used to do more remodeling of the courthouse. WPA laborers also worked in Reserve to complete a rock High School in 1935 for $3,164.87. That courthouse has been torn down and a new one opened in 1969. Most of the high school is gone but what remains houses a Headstart program now. Roads were built and indexes of mining locations and tax rolls were also done. The creation of a textbook depository cost $924.27 in October 1938.

ROSWELL

"Community Art Center projects of the Federal Art Project were an attempt to expand participation in the arts, bringing art "to the people." Easel paintings, sculpture, and graphic arts were taught by Project teachers, giving the citizen the opportunity to comprehend aesthetic arts both as artists as well as spectators."

—Francis O'Connor, *Art for the Millions*
(from Holger Cahill's essay, "American Resources in the Arts").

NEW DEAL PUBLIC ART IN NEW DEAL PUBLIC BUILDINGS

ROSWELL MUSEUM AND ART CENTER
100 West Eleventh Street
Contact Person: Director or Registrar
(575) 624-6744

This facility came into being first as one of the state's four New Deal Federal Art Centers. Today it is one of the only remaining federal art centers in the nation that has never closed its doors and has continued to fulfill its original mission to this day. It is an outstanding museum and art center today. The Center and its furnishings were built during 1937–1939 at the cost of $10,338. A room has been set aside to exhibit the remaining pieces of furniture and other creations from that era.

On view are selections of WPA art from the permanent collection include: Olive Rush's "Weird Land," a watercolor which was the first art work accessioned in the museum's permanent collection; Manville Chapman's woodblock of the museum with contemporary restrike prints; pastels by Helmuth Naumer; bulto by Juan Sanchez; paintings by Regina Tatum Cooke and Sheldon Parsons; selected prints from the Louie Ewing/Eliseo Rodriguez *Portfolio of Navajo Blankets* and *Portfolio of Spanish-Colonial Design in New Mexico* which was part of the nationwide Index of American Design project; and a mural study by Emil Bisttram for a mural now in the old Federal Courthouse in Albuquerque. This mural was originally in the early Federal Courthouse in Roswell. Jan Marfyak, Juanita Lantz and Reiney Woolsey all worked in this early New Deal Art Center. Peter Hurd, Paul Horgan and Robert O. Anderson were also on the Board of Directors when Roland Dickey was the facility's second administrator.

NEW DEAL PUBLIC ART IN PUBLIC BUILDINGS

HISTORICAL CENTER FOR SOUTHEAST NEW MEXICO
200 North Lea
(575) 622-8333

Four bronze busts done by John Raymond Terken in 1937 are included in their collection. The busts, on loan from the Art Center, are of prominent eastern New Mexican citizens John S. Chisum, Joseph C. Lea, John J. Hagerman and Amelia Bolton Church.

NEW DEAL BUILDINGS, STRUCTURES and PROGRAM

BITTERLAKE REFUGE
Northeast of Roswell

BOTTOMLESS LAKES STATE PARK

This state park was created in 1934 by the CCC and is an outstanding recreational facility just a few miles east of Roswell. A tall rock torreon structure is a core architectural icon as part of the bathhouse and swim site.

CAHOON PARK

This local park was built in 1936 and includes within it a sunken garden all constructed as part of the federal programs. Today it is one of the best kept New Deal metropolitan parks done on the east side of the state.

NEW MEXICO MILITARY INSTITUTE
SR #1008 State Register 6-8-84, National Register 5-7-87

Several current structures, all reflecting the Gothic Revival style, in the New Mexico Military Institute (NMMI) were built with support from the Public Works Administration (PWA). The J. Ross Thomas Memorial Recreation Center was completed in 1933 and alumni and New Deal artist, Peter Hurd, began painting a series of murals in the lounge. The panels were painted in egg tempera on a base of gesso and his major goal in the painting was to depict the three great strains of human life that have reacted and blended to form the history of New Mexico and the Southwest. Unfortunately the valuable murals were destroyed in a fire of unknown origin in May 1938.

In 1934–1937 various other projects were financed with New Deal monies including oiling of the streets, a new artesian well, Lea Hall, three officers' houses, and new stables. The officer's quarters (commandant, dean of junior college, and high school principal) were built with PWA Project New Mexico 1059R ($45,425) and fine horse stables were built with PWA Project New Mexico 1059RS ($56,000). The Institute may have added matching funds for these structures. It is noteworthy that the stables were the finest in the country and could house 140 fine cavalry horses which were also used to play polo. In 1938 a building fund was set up and PWA funds were sought for a $250,000 project that was quite encompassing. A rifle range and landscaping were also included in New Deal funding activities.

RURAL ELECTRIC ADMINISTRATION (REA) The rural areas of this county are actually provided electricity by the Central New Mexico, Roosevelt County and Otero Electric Cooperatives.

OTHER MUNICIPAL STRUCTURES

Old Roswell Municipal Airport. This facility was built in 1940.

City Hall and Unemployment Office

DeBremond Stadium and Rock Wall. These are across from the Roswell Art Center.

Schools

High School addition and remodeling, auditorium, gym, and improvements in various schools were done by the WPA. Today the East Grand Plains Elementary School (1940) and the Sidney Gutierrez Charter Middle School are still providing educational services.

Fairgrounds

Highway Department Office and Machine Shop

OTHER STRUCTURES and PROGRAMS include sidewalks, water system extensions, warehouse, and cemetery improvements, indexing and repair of books, roads, sewing room operation, clothing relief project, and Rio Hondo channel improvements.

MYSTERY ART, see Chapter 4

Also a New Deal colcha embroidered stage curtain created by local young women has never been located and some of the New Deal furniture created for this building has disappeared from this collection.

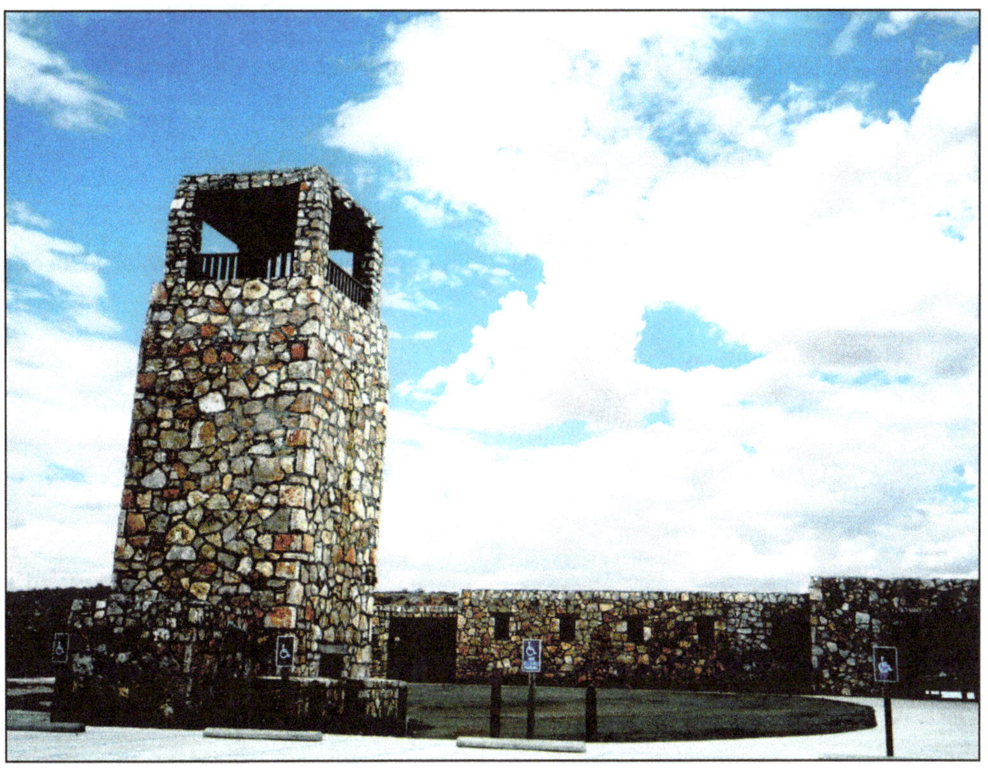

The CCC built this rock structure as well as the bathhouse and lake just out of Roswell at the Bottomless Lake State Park.

ROY

NEW DEAL BUILDINGS, STRUCTURES and PROGRAMS

MUNICIPAL City Hall, Baseball Park, sidewalks, curbs, gutters, water and sewer systems, and caliche roads.

RURAL ELECTRIC ASSOCIATION Springer Electrical Cooperative serves this area.

Note: One early resident, Mrs. Hugh Frazier, recalls, "my husband and other men were paid by the WPA to haul wheelbarrow loads of grasshoppers off the roads since the vast volumes of them made the roads very slick."

SCHOOLS Auditorium, Gym, four room school, rock shed.

RUIDOSO

NEW DEAL BUILDINGS and STRUCTURES

GYMNASIUM AND AUDITORIUM now the Ruidoso Athletic Club.

MONTJEAU LOOKOUT TOWER and mountain road. State Register SRCP 1445

REA-OTERO COOPERATIVE serves 13,480 consumers in a four county area including Lincoln County

RUIDOSO LOOKOUT TOWER State Register SRCP 1447

STETSON SCHOOL This is now the home and foundry of the family of deceased artist, Luis Jimenez.

SCHOOL A second school (possibly the one in Hollywood aka Ruidoso Downs) is a day care center.

MYSTERY ARTWORK, see Chapter 4

SAN MATEO

There is a dam and spillway construction done in this area in 1936, most likely by CCC since there was a CCC camp in Cibola National Forest and conservation work done by CCC in the forest.

SANTA FE

"It [Olive Rush's mural] will endure to carry its message to future generations. No one else could have caught the hunger for knowledge, or so sympathetically depicted the self-sacrificing spirit that prompts women's public works, as has Olive Rush in her splendid murals in our Santa Fe Library. Her work belongs not alone to this ancient city but the entire state."
—Ina Sizer Cassidy, "Art and Artists of New Mexico," *New Mexico Magazine*, April 1935.

NEW DEAL PUBLIC ART IN NEW DEAL PUBLIC BUILDINGS

NEW MEXICO SCHOOL FOR THE DEAF
1060 Cerrillos Road
(505) 827-6731
State Register 7-8-88, National Register 9-22-88

In the 1930s, six buildings were built at the New Mexico School for the Deaf utilizing WPA resources. The Hospital building is on the State Register SRCP 1472 was completed in 1937 and is still in use today. It is a single-story Spanish Pueblo Revival building. The School Building #2 is also on the State Register SRCP 1469, and on the National Register and is an excellent example of Spanish-Pueblo Revival style, with its stepped profile and projecting vigas. It was built as a multiple use classroom, administration and teachers' quarters and is still used as a classroom building. Currently, most of the school's New Deal art collection is in the Superintendent's Home. It includes:

Ellis, Fremont
"Untitled"
Hullenkremer, Odon
"Untitled"
Parsons, Sheldon
"Chupadero"
Pierce, Edma
Two murals in the school cafeteria.
Schleeter, Howard
"Untitled"

NEW MEXICO SUPREME COURT BUILDING
237 Don Gaspar
(505) 827-4860
State Register SRCP 1795

This hall of justice was erected by the New Deal in 1937 at a cost of $282,433. In order to reduce sound, the floors in the main reference library are made of cork. This agency's art collection is distributed throughout the building in the offices of the different justices. Included in the collection are works by:

Henning, E. Martin
"Indian Hunters"
Jones, D. Paul
"Hernandez Church" (Similar one at Carrie Tingley Hospital in Albuquerque)
Parsons, Sheldon
"Untitled"

OLD SANTA FE TRAIL BUILDING (National Park Service)
1100 Old Santa Fe Trail
(505) 988-6014
State Register SRCP 144, 1-20-70, National Register 10-6-70 NHL 5-28-87

This magnificent adobe building is a National Historic Landmark and was designed by the NPS and built and completed by the CCC in 1937. For many years it has housed National Park Service staff as the southwest regional headquarters of the NPS and other agencies. Located at a bend in the Old Santa Fe Trail, this Spanish-Colonial style adobe building comprises some 24,000 square feet. Built around a patio surrounded by flagstone floored portals, the buildings abound with beautiful architectural details—vigas, hand-hewn beams, wooden lintels, decorated corbels, and decorative buttresses. The interior features hammered tin light fixtures, hand-carved Spanish-Colonial style furniture, flagstone floors, and wooden grillwork as well as Southwestern pottery, rugs and art works. Many of the paintings, drawings and etchings were funded by the WPA and other Federal relief art programs.

This building is the largest known adobe office building and one of the largest secular adobe buildings in the United States. The timbers were cut and shaped from the forest nearby and the thousands of adobe bricks were molded from the dirt dug out at the site.

The art collection can be viewed during normal working hours in the conference room where a large conference table and chairs were also created within that same room. The collection includes:

Boyd, E.
"Hail Storm"
Fleck, Joseph
"Leisure Hour"
Gutierrez, Lela
Indian Pottery (6 pieces)
Higgins, Victor
"Untitled"
"Landscape"

Hullenkremer, Odon
"Stephen Mather" (The first National Park Service Superintendent.)
Kloss, Gene
"New Mexico Mountain Town"
"Winter Mass"
"Christmas Eve, Taos Pueblo"
"Penitente Good Friday"
"Santuario Chimayo"

Martinez, Maria
  Pottery
Matta, Santiago
  Pottery and paintings
Naranjo, E.
  Pottery
Nordfeldt, Boris
  "Canyon Road"
  "Morada Santa Cruz"
  "Tres Ritos"
Quintana, Agrapina
  Pottery

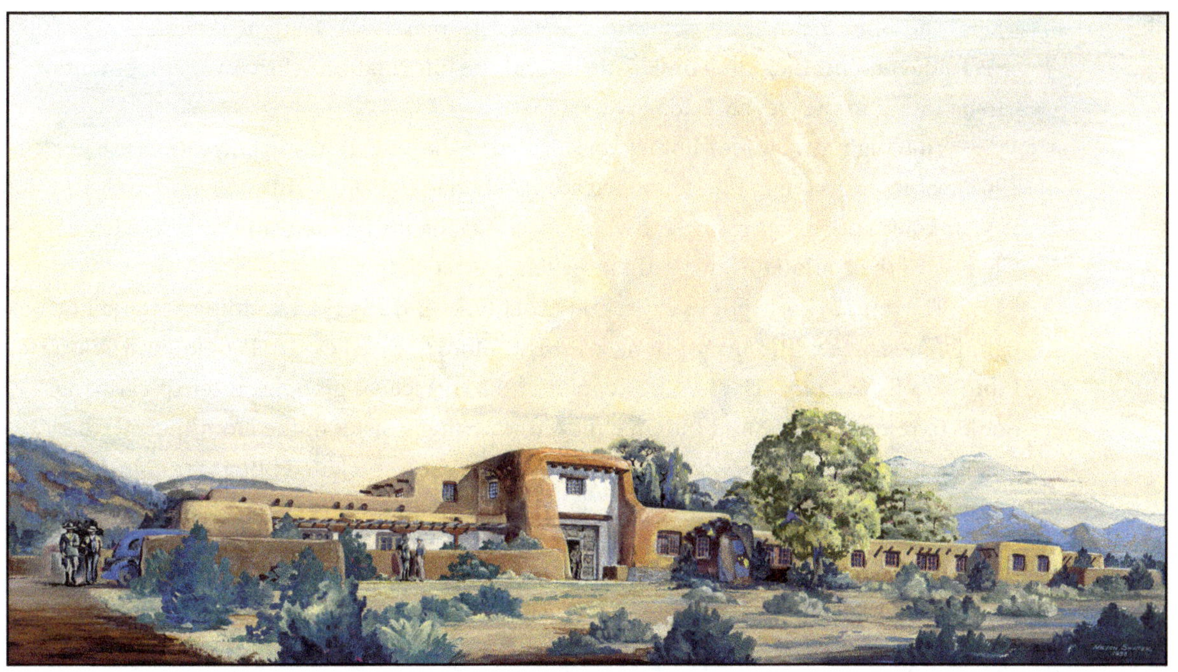

The National Park Service (NPS) had the CCC build this large, adobe office structure—the largest such adobe building known in the nation—to serve as its southwest regional office in 1937. It was constructed with 280,000 adobe bricks made on the site from the earth dug out to build the building. It continues in that capacity and houses New Deal artwork, furniture, and tinwork created by the WPA. Photograph provided by the National Park Service.

SANTA FE PUBLIC LIBRARY
143 Washington Avenue
(505) 984-6788

The library's WPA building was built in 1937 as the City Hall and Fire Station at a cost of $121,131. Later it became the city's Public Library and the two charming sculptures of children by Hannah Mecklem Small done during the WPA for the original library were transferred to their new location in the entry area. One can view one of the original sets of the *Portfolio of Spanish-Colonial Art*, a project of the Federal Art Project.

NEW DEAL PUBLIC ART IN PUBLIC BUILDINGS

FRAY ANGELICO CHAVEZ HISTORY LIBRARY
120 Washington Avenue
(505) 476-5090

This building was originally constructed by the Santa Fe Women's Board and was the community's early public library.

The library houses a collection of the original WPA Federal Writers Project (FWP) documents including oral histories and site information. More FWP documents can be found in the New Mexico State Archives.

The original children's library was located in the basement and Olive Rush (1873–1966) painted a fresco in the stairwell leading down to that area. This was funded by the PWAP and in 2006 was restored by Luis Neri Zagal with funds from the New Mexico Chapter of the National New Deal Preservation Association.

The mural's inscriptions express love of books and an understanding of the state's trilingual heritage. The inscriptions are "The Library Reaches the People" and "Con Libros no Estas Solo." The frescoes depict children receiving books; a burro carrying books to remote places; and Indian children watching a Sister of the Dominican Order open up a traveling library trunk. Some areas appear to be faded but are not, just her intention to be lighter.

LABORATORY OF ANTHROPOLOGY
708 Camino Lejo, Museum Hill
SR #890 State Register 12-1-82, National Register 7-12-83

This Carnegie Foundation funded institution was built in 1931 as designed by architect, John Gaw Meem. It is considered a masterpiece of the Pueblo Revival style. The interior features detailed work by local craftsmen in tin work, furniture, vigas, corbels and even such details as carved wooden radiator screens and hand-wrought door plates and pulls. Event the light switch plates were custom designed. The landscaping and early parking lot areas were created with New Deal funds.

The library was founded to conduct anthropological research, to further the welfare of Native Americans in the Southwest and to participate in public education and publication programs. The results of that early work are included in their archives.

Documents from the New Mexico Federal Art Project administrative offices are also housed here along with two portfolios of Indian Rugs—one by Louis Ewing and Eliseo Rodriguez and a lesser known one by Ruth Connely. In their library, one will find a comprehensive collection of a Native American New Deal monthly publication called, "Indians At Work."

MUSEUM OF INDIAN ARTS AND CULTURE (MIAC)
710 Camino Lejo, Museum Hill
(505) 476-1260

This museum acquired some of the New Deal art from the New Mexico Museum of Art. They include:

Goodbear, Paul
"Animal Dance"
"Buffal o Dance"
"Cheyenne Animal Dance"
"Cheyenne War Dance"
"Cheyenne Arrow Ceremony"
"Flying Eagle"
"Matachinas"
Herrera, Velino Shije
Four untitled pieces
Toledo, Jose Rey
"Pecos Bull at Jemez"
Velarde, Pablita
Various pieces and video about the artist

New Deal pottery and rugs by various Native American potters are also included in this museum's collection.

MUSEUM OF INTERNATIONAL FOLK ART (MOIFA)
706 Camino Lejo, Museum Hill
(505) 476-1200

This museum has examples of Patrocino Barela carvings as well as arts and crafts from other New Deal Hispanic artists.

NEW MEXICO HIGHWAY DEPARTMENT (now State Transportation Department)
1120 Cerrillos Road
(505) 827-5100

Odon Hullenkremer was the artist for a painting which hangs in this building. Another by Fremont Ellis was stolen from this department during a renovation of the building.

NEW MEXICO HISTORY MUSEUM
113 Lincoln Avenue

This is now the home of the vast historical collections that had been stored in the Palace of the Governors for many years. Various New Deal items exist in these collections. Some santos have been restored with NNDPA funds.

NEW MEXICO HUMAN SERVICES DEPARTMENT
37 Plaza La Prenza
(505) 827-7750

This building is south of Santa Fe on Frontage Road parallel to the Albuquerque Highway, south of *The Santa Fe New Mexican* building.

Sheldon Parsons' "View Near Espanola" was assigned to this agency and has been restored by Santa Fe art conservator, Steve Prins, as funded by NNDPA in 2006. Another Parsons' creation, "View Near Otowi," also known as "View Near San Ildefonso," for years was on view in the administrative offices of this department's predecessor agencies (New Mexico Welfare Department and later Health & Social Services Department). This large painting has not been located.

NEW MEXICO MUSEUM OF ART
107 West Palace Avenue, corner of Lincoln and Palace Avenues
(505) 476-5072

The interior courtyard features six fresco panels by Will Shuster depicting scenes from Pueblo Indian ceremonials and domestic life adorning the Museum's patio walls. Painted under PWAP, the frescoes are entitled "Voices of the Earth," "Voices of the Sky," "Voices of the Sipophe" and "Voices of the Water," and two identified as "Untitled." The text which is inscribed on a bronze plaque on the patio wall by ethnologist, Alice Cunningham Fletcher, inspired the subject for the frescoes. It reads:

> "Living with my Indian friends, I found I was a stranger in my native land. As time went on the outward aspect of nature remained the same, but a change was wrought in me. I learned to hear the echoes of a time when every living thing, even the sky had a voice. That voice devoutly heard by the ancient people of America I desired to make audible to others."[1]

Shuster's son, Don, recalls his father's preparation for the Museum project, "My Dad read everything he could about the fresco technique after he was asked to do the murals. In order to fix the pigments for the fresco, "Shus" decided to invent a machine to grind the pigments. He got a goldfish bowl and filled it with glass marbles driven by a motor. He then added pigment with water and ran the machine for days at a time until the pigment was ground very fine. He then stored that pigment and ground another color. He was always inventing things."[2]

A second larger fresco on the east wall in this courtyard was done more recently by Frederico Vigil.

1. "Murals for New Patio," *El Palacio*, Vol. XXXVI, No. 9-10 August-September, 1934, p. 74.
2. Interview with Don Shuster in Santa Fe conducted by Curator Sandra D'Emilio Sept. 29, 1988, Museum of Fine Arts.

The museum's art collection is likely the largest collection of the state's New Deal public art. They are reported to have a number of the pieces listed here, with some duplicate images.

Adams, Kenneth
- "Untitled" (Indian Woman)
- "Indian Woman"

Barela, Patrocinio
- "Ascension"
- "Holy Family"
- "Resurrection"
- "Untitled"

Bisttram, Emil
- "Two Indian Women"

Chapman, Manville
(Most are woodblocks)
- "Adobe Pond"—tempera
- "Cemetery" (2)
- "Chimayo Church" (2)
- "Church at Night" (2)
- "Church in Northern New Mexico" (2)
- "Cottonwoods in Autumn"
- "Cutting Vigas"—tempera
- "Drying 'Dobes"
- "Dry Trees" (2)
- "Eagle Dance" (2)
- "Falling Leaves" (2)
- "Farm House" (2)
- "Fishing" (2)
- "Indian Woman Sitting" (2)
- "Laying 'Dobes"—tempera
- "Laying Vigas"—tempera
- "Morning Sunlight" (2)
- "Night"
- "Our Lady of Guadalupe" (2)
- "Plastering"
- "Peonies and Indian Pots"
- "Reflections on Adobe"(2)
- "Rock Wall"
- "San Antonio de Padua"
- "Study in Brown and Gold"
- "Tamping the Roof" (2)
- "Taos Indian"
- "Taos Pueblo" (2)
- "The Virgin"
- "Winter"

Cooke, Regina T.
- "Abo"
- "Abo 1629"
- "Pecos"
- "Quarai"
- "San Miguel"

Ellis, Fremont
- "Street Scene, Galisteo"

Henderson, William P.
- Landscape—Oil

Herrera, Velino Shije
- "Untitled"
- "Untitled"

Kavin, Zena
- "Back Stage"
- "Gringo at Fiesta"
- "Santa Fe Plaza During Fiesta"
- "Mother and Child" Sculpture
- "Mother and Child" Sculpture

Kloss, Gene
- "Acoma"
- "Christmas Eve-Taos Pueblo"
- "Church at Trampas, New Mexico"
- "Penitente Good Friday"
- "Rio Grande Pueblo"
- "The Sanctuary, Chimayo"
- "Winter Mass"

Loeffler, Gisella
  "Chicken"
  "Church San Antonio"
  "Endurance"
  "Golden Threads"
  "King and Queen"
  "Orange Sweet"
  "The Little Blind Hen"
  "The Little Coyote"
Lumpkins, William
  "Anglo Village"
  "Hispanic Village"
  "Indian Village"
  "Red Hill"
Matta, Santiago
  "Crucifix"
  "Guadalupe"
  "Trinity"
Morris, James
  "Corn Huskers"
  "Cross of the Martyrs"
  "Lightning"
  "Penitente Procession at Truchas"
  "Santa Fe Rococo"
  "Saturday Night Jug"
  "Taxco"
  "Untitled"
  "Valorio"
Moylan, Lloyd
  "Hen and Rooster"
  "Untitled"
Nash, Willard
  "Movement"
Naumer, Helmuth
  "Untitled"
  "Winter in Tesuque"
Nordfeldt, Boris
  "Canyon Road"
  "Cerrillos"
  "Church at Trampas"
  "Morada, Santa Cruz"
  "Rio de Medio"
  "Tres Ritos"
  "Water Street"
Parsons, Sheldon
  "Summertide-Alcalde"
  "Winter in Tesuque"
Pillin, Polia
  "Snowscape"
Sanchez, Juan
  Five Santos (restored by NNDPA)
Saville, Bruce
  Six bronzes of Indian Dancers
Schleeter, Howard
  "Cottonwoods by the Church House"
  "Fall Pattern"
Shuster, Will
  "The Voice of the Earth"
  "The Voice of the Sipapu"
  "The Voice of the Sky"
  "The Voice of the Water"
  "Untitled"
  "Untitled"
Toledo, Jose Rey
  "Pecos Bull Dance at Jemez"
Willis, Brooks
  "Architectural Subjects in Santa Fe"
Wiswall, Edna
  "Fiesta Booth"

Also archived in the Educational Division of this facility are the New Deal's Farm Security Administration (FSA) photographs from Pie Town and Northern New Mexico as taken by Dorothea Lange, Russell Lee and John Collier, Jr.

NEW MEXICO STATE CAPITOL
491 Old Santa Fe Trail
Responsible Agency: Legislative Council Service
(505) 986-4600

Some art done for the State Capitol during the New Deal has not been located. See Chapter 4. The following New Deal art included in the fine current art collection established by the State Capitol Art Foundation includes:

Passageway between Capitol and Capitol Annex: A large Randall Davey triptych called "Polo Ponies" now hangs in the passageway between the Capitol and the Capitol Annex. These oil paintings are on a long term loan from the New Mexico Military Department who has had them for a number of years. Their first placement was in the state's early Horse Calvary Unit which was in an area possibly now part of the University of New Mexico campus. Since then the paintings have been in three other National Guard sites. Davey was an avid polo player thus the subject selected by the artist and the assignment to the agency of state government that had horses. The paintings were restored and conserved by art conservator Steve Prins in 2007 as funded by the New Mexico Chapter of the NNDPA prior to their placement in the State Capitol Passageway between the Capitol and Capitol Annex.

Second Floor: Joseph Fleck did an oil painting as a mural study or "cartoon" which the original owner was told was to be the prototype for a New Deal mural. To the best of our knowledge, that mural was never completed, at least not in New Mexico. The untitled cartoon was purchased by a woman from Texas and was later donated by her family to the State Capitol upon her death. It hangs on the second floor of the Capitol.

Third Floor: A lithograph by B.J.O. Nordfeldt, titled "Canyon Road," is on a long term loan to the State Capitol by a donor who purchased the piece at a garage sale for $5.00. It hangs on the third floor and still has its original brass plaque identifying it as a piece done for the Public Works of Art Project (PWAP). It has been conserved recently by the New Mexico Chapter of the NNDPA.

Bronze Bust on the east promenade leading up to the State Capitol that faces Old Santa Fe Trail. The bust is of U. S. Senator Bronson Cutting who was an early owner of *The Santa Fe New Mexican*. Although not a piece of New Deal artwork, it is of the period and the sculptor, Bruce Saville, did New Deal creations elsewhere. Records indicate that he did a New Deal sculpture for the Santa Fe National Cemetery, but it has never been located. Cutting, also an early owner of the Sena Plaza complex, was very active in the beginning of President Franklin Roosevelt's first term and supportive of his New Deal programs for New Mexico. During his attempt at a second term as Senator, he was killed in a plane crash on a flight from Santa Fe to Washington. Dennis Chavez, his opponent, was appointed to fill out his term of office and he became one of our state's longest serving senators.

Cutting was well known as a patron to many New Mexico families and individuals. They were responsible for having this bronze bust created as a memorial and the New Mexico Chapter of the NNDPA had it restored in 2006 by Santa Fe conservator Dale Kronkright. After many years outside, its original patina was almost gone and the plan was to put it inside the Capitol but the solid marble pedestal prevented the move because of its weight.

On the west side of the Capitol is a life-size bronze statue of a Civilian Conservation Corps (CCC) Worker that was installed in 2009 across from the Bataan Veterans' Eternal Flame memorial—an appropriate and closely related setting. It was financed by legislative funding and personal memorial donations. The coordination of the project was carried out by the New Mexico Chapter of the NNDPA and the Legislative Council staff. This bronze is a memorial commemoration of all the conservation and construction work done during 1933–1943 by the young 56,000 CCC "boys," who were assigned to work in this program in New Mexico. Most of them all went into WWII and provided, according to various generals, the "backbone" of our military due to the training they received in the CCC.

NEW MEXICO STATE LIBRARY (SOUTHWEST COLLECTION) and also the STATE ARCHIVES
1205 Camino Carlos Rey (West Capitol Complex)
(505) 476-9700

Two copies of the *Portfolio of Spanish-Colonial Design of New Mexico* are included with other WPA reference materials. The original artwork for this collection was done by E. Boyd. Possible engravers were Fritz Boeske and later Manville Chapman. There were 200 sets of 50 renderings printed on Gustave Baumann's printing press at El Rito and R. Whiteman Printing Co. in Clovis, New Mexico. These 200 sets were distributed to various people, some known artists and others not known but qualified to be on the WPA Federal Art Project. They were given watercolors and instructions on how to paint the printed images. These individuals were called "copyists" and one might think their assignment was much like doing a "paint by number" project.

This project was planned to become part of the Index of American Design, a national project of the Federal Art Program with the goal of collecting folk art designs typically found in every state. New Mexico submitted its unique project which was criticized as being too primitive since the works were not seriographed. The state didn't have enough money to pay for that process. The Library of Congress today has all the original portfolios that were submitted by the various states including New Mexico's and the New Mexico pieces were included in a show in Washington.

NEW MEXICO TAXATION AND REVENUE DEPARTMENT
1100 South St. Francis Drive (South Capitol Complex)
(505) 827-0700

Helmuth Naumer created seven New Deal pastels of New Mexico scenes and they have been in the New Mexico Taxation and Revenue offices in Santa Fe since that time. They have all been preserved by Santa Fe art conservator, Patricia Morris, as funded by the New Mexico Chapter of the NNDPA and can now be seen in the lobby of this agency and in other rooms within the central office. They are titled:

"Pines"
"San Ildefonso Kiva"
"Evening at Lamy"
"Taos Pueblo"
"Copper Mine at Silver City"
"Mount Taylor"
"White Sands"

SANTA FE INDIAN SCHOOL
1501 Cerrillos Road
(505) 989-6300

This school was created over 100 years ago (as of 2011) along with many other such schools around the country. During the New Deal era most of the buildings' exteriors were refurbished with the New Mexico adobe architecture style as designed by John Gaw Meem. The focus at all the schools was to educate the students and much was done to shape them to become more like "the White Man." The students were not allowed to speak their native language or wear the clothes that were most familiar to them. Most children were there from their early youth on to late teens and rarely got to go home. A military atmosphere prevailed which was very harsh, particularly for the younger children. Today that style of administration and education is not the case and new and modern buildings have mostly replaced the older structures.

All the early buildings and their art work were demolished in July 2009 much to the horror of the community. It created a community outcry of outrage and sadness over the loss of the beauty and historical significance. This action was taken by the nineteen pueblo governors that administer this school program. They took this action after supposedly determining they could not afford to remove the existing asbestos and lead in the buildings as required by federal mandates. These buildings had been redesigned by John Gaw Meem thanks to New Deal funding and remodeled with New Deal funds. There is still one Meem designed structure on the campus.

These older buildings had been decorated with murals and paintings created by the art students of the teacher, Dorothea Dunn. There were a number of murals in the Dining Hall and Social Science building. Each mural in the Social Science building portrayed scenes of the young artists' own pueblos. They were quite special to the students as reminders of home and also special because of their unique quality and beauty. Some of these young students went on to become New Deal artists. Furniture and craft items were also destroyed during the demolition.

Two large New Deal paintings remain and can be found in the school's new library. Both are believed to have been done by Velino Shije Herrera. However, only one is signed by him. They were originally in the Albuquerque Indian School and transferred to this school when that school was torn down.

There is also a collection of posters hanging in the library. In addition, this space holds some children's books that were illustrated by New Deal Native American artists in that period and are beautiful insights into Native American lives of children. There are many reference books on the subject of the Indian New Deal program. Other crafts were also created during that period on campus.

SANTA FE MAIN POST OFFICE
120 South Federal Place

Santa Fe's Main Post Office on Federal Place contains two large murals in the lobby, which many think were done during the New Deal. Actually they were done privately prior to that in 1929 by Gerald Cassidy who did some New Deal work. Another large mural was never finished because he died of carbon monoxide poisoning during its creation due to the poor ventilation in the warehouse in which he was painting. Because of this, his wife, Ina Sizer Cassidy, who was the director of the Federal Writer's Project, always said "her husband gave his life for the WPA."

These two Cassidy murals on canvas were originally created for the Onate Theater on the Santa Fe Plaza. (That building houses The First National Bank.) After the theater was closed, the murals were purchased by John J. Hardin of Oklahoma City and transferred to one of his hotels or a theater in Hobbs. Later they were transferred to another of his hotels in Acapulco. In 1948 he donated them to the State of New Mexico with the hope that they would be placed in the State Capitol. This did not happen and they were stored in the Museum of New Mexico collection until 1962 when they were given to the federal government to go in the new post office with the proviso that they would never leave the state again. Conservator John Pogzeba restored them prior to their placement in the post office.

UNITED STATES FEDERAL COURTHOUSE
106 South Federal Place (next to Downtown Main Post Office)
Contact Person: GSA Regional Administrator
(505) 766-8834
SR #260 State Register 3-20-72, National Register 5-25-73

Federal funds for a "capitol" building in Santa Fe were appropriated by Congress in 1851, 1860, and 1886, but the building was not actually completed until 1889. It was never used as a capitol; instead it has housed various federal courts and offices of the United States Land Office. The three-story Greek Revival style courthouse was built of rough stone quarried in the Hyde Park area near Santa Fe. The door lintels, window frames, and ornamental trim are of dressed stone quarried at Cerrillos.

New Deal Public Art in this building is on the main floor. Six large brilliantly painted murals by William Penhallow Henderson were started with funding in 1933 from the Public Works of Art Project (PWAP) but later completed with funding from the Treasury Relief Art Project (TRAP) and installed in 1938. They can be viewed in the lobby during normal working hours but being a federal building therefore visitors must go through a security check including metal detection and showing personal identification.

The themes for the murals are different landscape areas located in New Mexico because Henderson chose not to use typical courthouse themes but rather wanted to bring some of New Mexico's fabulous landscapes in to the building's interior. To quote the artist, "After all it is best out here," so why not use it!"[1] All were restored by Santa Fe conservator, Steve Prins, in the late 1990s. They are titled:

"The Old Santa Fe Trail"
"The Old Cuba Road"
"Monument Rock-Canon de Chelly"
"Taos Mountain"
"Cabezon Puerco Valley"
"Sand Trail Up Acoma Rock"

"In these large canvasses, he had masterfully combined reality with imagination... critics pronounced these murals outstanding works of art."

—Ina Sizer Cassidy, "Art and Artists of New Mexico,"
New Mexico Magazine, December 1943.

On the second floor of the building Warren Rollins created three paintings of Indian scenes which originally hung in the former post office in Gallup. When that building was sold to a private source, the federal government's General Services Administration (GSA) removed the paintings and stored them possibly in Fort Worth. They were in storage for a number of years but late in 2007 they were restored and transferred to this building.

1. "Henderson Murals Installed at Federal Building by Art Project Chief—All Landscapes," *The Santa Fe New Mexican*, May 11, 1938, WPA Files, Folder 155, New Mexico. State Records Center and Archives.

NEW DEAL PUBLIC BUILDINGS and STRUCTURES

FORMER STATE POLICE HEADQUARTERS
1350 Alta Vista

Located at the corner of Cerrillos Road and Alta Vista, this WPA structure built in 1935 now provides space for the Planning Division of the State Transportation Department (formerly the State Highway Department). Their main building, a newer structure, is adjacent to this building.

FORT MARCY PARK

HYDE PARK STATE PARK HEADQUARTERS
740 Hyde Park Road

This log structure was built by the CCC as were most of the campsite areas throughout the forest and park areas. Small check dams can be also found throughout the forests done by the CCC. This building has been also known earlier as the Girl Scout Building and the Evergreen Restaurant.

NATIONAL GUARD ARMORY
1050 Old Pecos Trail
Now a New Mexico Military Museum
State Register SRCP 1908

PUBLIC SCHOOLS

Agua Fria, Acequia Madre, Alvord, Carlos Gilbert,* Gonzales, Kaune, Larragoite, Leah Harvey, Salazar and Wood Gormley were designed by renowned New Deal architect, John Gaw Meem and built by the WPA. Manderfield Elementary might also have been done by the WPA. Also the old high school athletic field (Magers Field) where Zozobra is burned every September as the opening event of Santa Fe's Fiesta celebrations was a New Deal project as well as some of school gymnasiums.

*This building is on the State Register SRCP 1904 and has recently been remodeled and enlarged thanks to Federal Stimulus funds. Leah Harvey Junior High School is now a U.S. District Courthouse.

RURAL ELECTRIC ADMINISTRATION (REA)

The Central New Mexico Electric Cooperative provides electricity primarily to the southern part of this county. The Statewide REA or Central office is also located in Santa Fe on Don Gaspar Street near the State Capitol.

SANTA FE COUNTY COURTHOUSE/JAIL
102 Grant Avenue (in Santa Fe historic district)
(505) 986-6200
State Register 5-9-86, National Register 7-23-73

The 1939 Spanish-Pueblo Revival style Santa Fe County Courthouse is a two story masonry structure with wooden details, including lintels, door frames, and a post and corbel portal with a beam and split cedar ceiling. The interior features brick floors, carved beams with Indian motifs and tin work light fixtures. The building was designed by John Gaw Meem and funded by the Public Works Administration (PWA). The murals in the building were done more recently by Frederico Vigil.

SANTA FE BOYS CLUB
730 Alto Street

SANTA FE RIVER PARK

The river area running through downtown Santa Fe along Alameda Street with rock embankments was done by the WPA and CCC.

STEVE HERRERA FIRST DISTRICT COURTHOUSE
100 Catron Street

This building across from the Main Post Office was formerly Harvey Junior High School, which was constructed for a total cost of $132,874 in 1938.

VILLAGRA BUILDING
408 Galisteo Street
State Register SRCP 1821

This building designed by John Gaw Meem housed the WPA and CCC offices as well as the Welfare Department. Now it has the New Mexico Parks and Recreation program in it. A new addition to the building called the Paul Bardacke Attorney General Complex obviously now provides space for the State Attorney General's Office.

OTHER

Don Gaspar Bridge*, other bridges, streets, roads, sidewalks, sewers, acequias, early airport runways, walls, demolition of National Guard camp stables, golf course, National Cemetery landscaping and improvements, privies (federally referenced as fly-proof interior sanitation units).

*This bridge is on the State Register SRCP 1820.

MYSTERY ARTWORK, see Chapter 4 plus the missing art from the State Transportation Department and the State Human Services Department.

SANTA ROSA

"In the Public Works Administration (PWA) Region 5 (which included New Mexico) climate has been the controlling factor in the development of plans for buildings—small windows and thick or well-insulated walls must provide protection against the heat of the sun in summer and extreme cold of winter."

—Short, C. W. and Stanley-Brown, R. *Public Building Architecture Under the Public Works Administration 1933–39.* Vol 1.

NEW DEAL BUILDINGS, STRUCTURES and PROGRAMS

BLUE HOLE LAKE AND PARK IMPROVEMENTS
The Park Lake District is on the State Register SRCP 1620.

CITY HALL

GUADALUPE COUNTY COURTHOUSE ANNEX and landscaping

HIGH SCHOOL—Now a City Administration facility.

MIDDLE SCHOOL

PARK CARETAKER QUARTERS—Reportedly no longer there.

RELIEF AND SECURITY BUILDING

RURAL ELECTRIC ADMINISTRATION (REA)
Central New Mexico Electric Cooperative provides electricity to 3,753 consumers in a goodly portion of this rural county.

OTHER STRUCTURES AND PROGRAMS include fish hatchery, fish pond construction, sidewalks, roads, sewers, dam and ditch reconstruction, quarrying, lake improvements, canning food, pre and post natal training

MYSTERY ARTWORK, see Chapter 4 (Nordfeldt)

SHIPROCK

The only known New Deal structure in this area is the San Juan River Bridge which is on the State Register of Cultural Properties SRCP 1666.

SILVER CITY

"Grant County has the best courthouse in the state and I decided this building was the one that should have the murals."

—Theodore Van Soelen, "Van Soelen Murals at the Courthouse Formally Accepted," *Silver City Enterprise*, July 20, 1934.

NEW DEAL PUBLIC ART IN PUBLIC BUILDINGS

GRANT COUNTY COURTHOUSE
Contact Person: County Manager (in the Silver City historic district)
(575) 574-0001
SR #197 State Register 5-9-86, WPA Murals SRCP 1271, National Register 5-23-76

The Art Deco Style Grant County Courthouse was built in 1929–30 prior to the New Deal funding but was the first county courthouse in New Mexico to use New Deal funds for decorative murals. The three-story flat-roofed building is an excellent example of monumental use of the Deco style, which was carried over into the interior design.

Theodore Van Soelen, N.A. (1890-1964) painted two murals titled "Chino Mines" and "The Round Up" under PWAP in 1933 and 1934 for the entry area of this building. Both visuals are very appropriate since mining and ranching are the county's main industries. Van Soelen researched his subjects thoroughly and spent six months on the two murals. For "Chino Mines" he spent time in the pits making sketches. For "Round Up" he drew on his own experiences as a cowboy in Nevada and New Mexico.

In 1934, the *Silver City Enterprise* newspaper reported the artist's satisfaction with the project: "I have given you the best I had and you in turn have given me whatever I asked for and I hope everyone is as well satisfied as I am with the results of our team work."

"The Round Up" was exhibited, along with one of Velino Shije Herrera's murals, at the Corcoran Gallery in Washington, DC during the National Exhibition of Art by the Public Works of Art Project (PWAP) from April until May 1934.

These two mural size paintings were restored and conserved in 2009 by Santa Fe conservator Steve Prins, and paid for by the New Mexico Chapter of the NNDPA. Also it should be noted that a number of the county offices have moved from this building to newer quarters at a different location in town. The jail and court activities remain in this building.

WESTERN NEW MEXICO UNIVERSITY A painting by Carl Redin entitled "Progress" is known to be on this campus but yet to be located.

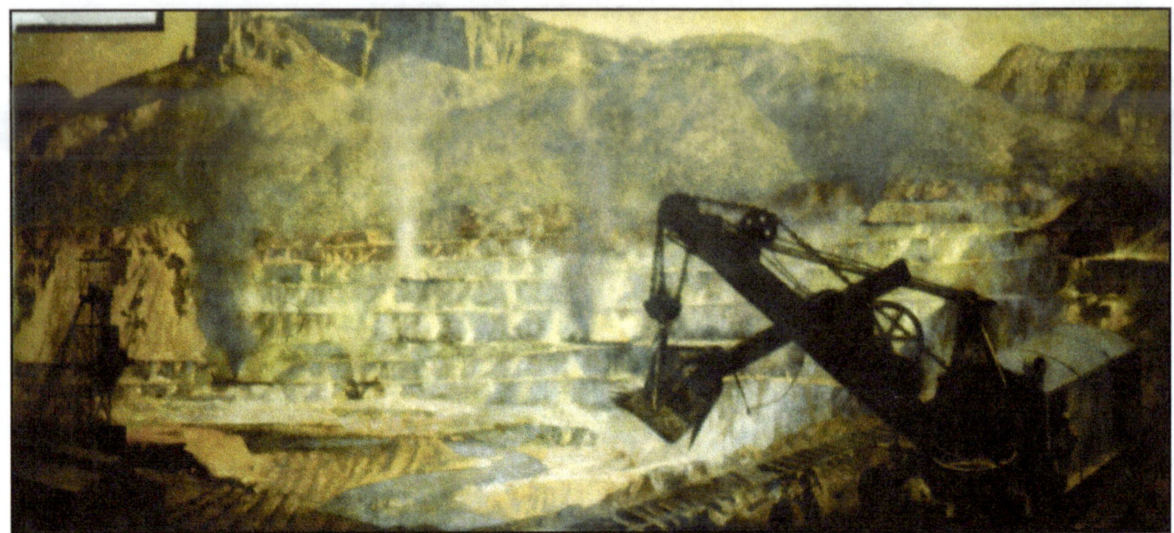

The older Grant County Courthouse was enhanced with two large murals created by Santa Fe's Theodore Van Soelen in 1934. They portray the two major industries of this part of the state—ranching and mining. They were originally placed in the building's entry way but now the building's entry area has been reversed and they are not as readily seen. Photograph provided by Steve Prins.

NEW DEAL BUILDINGS and STRUCTURES

COUNTRY CLUB HOUSE AND GOLF COURSE may have had some funding from WPA.

DOWNTOWN

The well known Riverwalk Park Area was done with New Deal funds following a severe flood. The main purpose for the project was flood protection. There are also WPA sidewalks in this area and water and sewer lines were put in throughout the city. On one building in the downtown area, there is a contemporary mural that has a sidewalk included in it with the highly visible "WPA" stamp painted on it.

HOSPITAL

This building was created on a prominent hillside in the community and served the area well for many years. The landscaping around it was also done at that time by WPA. It later was abandoned after a newer hospital was constructed and has now been demolished.

NATIONAL YOUTH ADMINISTRATION (NYA) HOUSING

The NYA was a branch of the WPA that funded programs that were used to provide high school age students from needy homes assistance which helped them to stay in school. They were provided part time employment in the schools, supervised recreational activities and vocational guidance. This program was statewide and nationwide. A building was remodeled and repaired and made available to house the NYA programs and became the Community Center. A similar program exists today in New Mexico called the Youth Conservation Corps (YCC) and is administered by the Department of Energy, Minerals and Natural Resources.

NEW MEXICO TEACHERS COLLEGE CAMPUS (now Western New Mexico University)

GRAHAM GYMNASIUM
New Mexico Western University
State Register #1464, 10-31-81, National Register 9-22-88

During the 1930s, the New Mexico State Teachers College now New Mexico Western University, took advantage of the availability of PWA funds to improve and enlarge the campus. They engaged the services of architect, John Gaw Meem, and under his direction many structures were remodeled using these funds. The architecture of this structure was Pueblo Revival style incorporating Indian motifs in its design.

Additionally, a stadium at the then New Mexico Teachers College was built and named the James Stadium after the resident of the institution at the time. It was a concrete structure two hundred feet long and ten seats high and cost at least $27,000. Plus they built a six foot stone wall around it. The athletic field was sodded for the first time making it possible to have more games with other schools that previously were unwilling to play there because the field was unsodded. A warehouse, recreation building improvements and shop building were built on campus.

The WPA shop building on the campus gave the school opportunities to train students in various mechanical and technical fields in order to be better equipped to provide skilled labor employment.

REMODELING of Ritch Hall and a former music building which then allowed for an office of the college newspaper, a stage property room, a practice room, and a room for student organizations to meet.

STUDENT ACTIVITY BUILDING and parking area

POST OFFICE

RECREATION CENTER Former National Guard Armory's Vehicle Maintenance Building (1940).

REMODEL OF 111TH CALVARY ARMORY AND NEW STABLES by FERA

The stables were built with adobe but have since burned down. A Hippodrome was also built by the CCC on their days off. For this donation of time and effort, the CCC group were rewarded with a five day long trip to El Paso, staying at Fort Bliss, and were guests at the annual army horse show.

RURAL ELECTRIC ADMINISTRATION (REA) Columbus REA serves 2,978 consumers in this area and on into Cochise, Arizona.

SCHOOLS

A newer building is part of the Sixth Street Elementary School built in 1938 in Silver City. The elementary school in Cliff just out of Silver City was built in 1936 and is still educating students in that part of the county. Various town schools also had improvements made and landscaping done and a school lunch program was developed.

The old Silver City High School built with PWA funds is now gone. Other school buildings were built in the rural areas with Public Works Administration (PWA) funds. They included Central, Pinos Altos, Redrock, San Lorenzo, Dwyer, San Juan and Cliff.

WOMENS CLUB On State Register SRCP #1830 built with FERA (Federal Emergency Relief Administration funds) in Silver Heights area continues to be used.

OTHER STRUCTURES and PROGRAMS provided by WPA

Airport runway which is still in use
Warehouse still standing
Rifle Range built
Work camp for transients
City Park
Reconstruction of highway building
Telephone lines were strung
Canning labor jobs provided
Restoration of an Indian Kiva
Roads and rock walls throughout the city and county
Dismantled twelve miles of bridges
Planted many trees
Improvements on irrigation systems
Sewing room operation and day nursery
Indexing and book repair

Soil erosion improvements and flood control projects in the city's watershed
Pit privy project throughout the county

MYSTERY ARTWORK, see Chapter 4 (Kloss and Nordfeldt)

SOCORRO

NEW DEAL ART IN PUBLIC BUILDINGS

NEW MEXICO INSTITUTE OF MINING AND TECHNOLOGY-SKEEN LIBRARY

New Deal furniture (small table, cabinet and a set of carved chairs) can be found in this building along with a fine collection of New Deal public art. Included are the following works:

Bakos, Joseph
"Hill Near Chama"
Chapman, Manville
Four Watercolor Prints of Indian Heads
Ellis, Fremont
"Landscape in Autumn"
Grant, Blanche
"Mine"
Jones, D. Paul
"Cottonwood Trees"
Kloss, Gene
"Winter Mass"
"Sanctuary Chimayo"
Loeffler, Gisella
"Two Mexican Dancers" *
Nordfeldt, B. J. O.
"Canyon Road"
Parsons, Sheldon
"Untitled"—oil landscape

*While this piece was being restored by Luis Neri Zagal and the New Mexico Chapter of the NNDPA, an unfinished painting was found on the back of the canvas. The one on the back of the canvas is a vertical and the other painting is horizontal so it is hard to display both at the same time but a photograph is on display of the second painting which could be entitled "Rooster Pull."

A recently located 1982 inventory list indicates that some other paintings did exist at one time at the school. The pieces have not been located as of 2011:

Chief Flying Eagle
"Indian Dance"
Ellis, Fremont
"Adobe House"
Gerring, Marguerite
"Rocks"
Grant, Blanche
"Old Prospector"
Jones, D. Paul
"Still Life"
"Landscape"
"Locust Tree"
Kloss, Gene
"Sanctuary Chimayo"
"Winter Mass"
Parsons, Sheldon
"Landscape 2"
"Winter Scene"
"Autumn Morning"

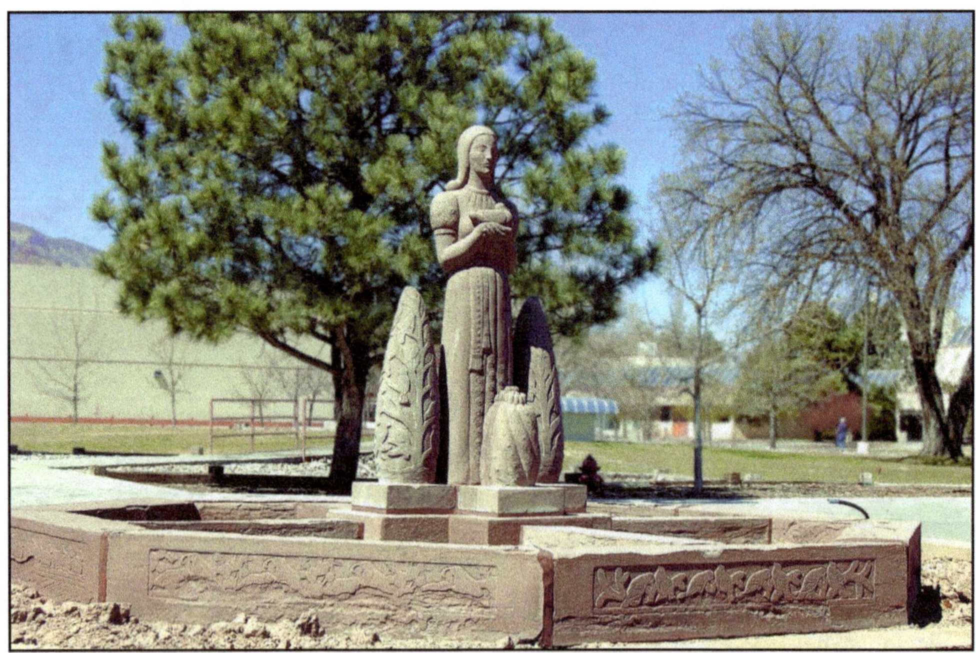

The "Desert Maiden" sits firmly on the campus of New Mexico Institute of Mining and Technology in Socorro. Photograph by Paul Harden.

A sandstone sculpture called the "Desert Maiden" or sometimes "The Maiden of the Desert" was made by Eugenie Shonnard, a New Deal era artist, who was commissioned in 1935 by Ruth Hanna McCormick Simms, a former Congresswoman from Illinois, to create this piece. McCormick, who later married Albert Simms, a prominent Albuquerque business executive, was the founder of the Sandia Girls School in Albuquerque and had the sculpture done for that institution. Since then it has had quite a traveling history.

When that school's original location was closed in 1946 to make room for the building of the airbase, some of the buildings were leased with an option to buy by New Mexico Tech, then called the New Mexico. School of Mines. The statue, first known as "The Youth in the Desert" by the artist, was excluded from the lease but when the Atomic Energy Commission took over the Sandia School site, the family that had owned the school, the Albert Simms family, gave the sculpture to the New Mexico School of Mines as a memorial to his deceased wife, Ruth Simms. The President of this institution at the time was E.J. Workman and he was responsible for changing the school's name to the New Mexico Institute of Mining and Technology to better express the role of the college.

He also had the Research and Development Building constructed around 1949 and placed the statue in front of that building. The statue consisted of the female figure with a dove in her arms, juniper trees to either side, a cactus in front and Southwestern animals around the base...symbolic of the Southwest. She then became known on campus as "Saint Rita, The Saint of the Impossible" but interestingly does not look like the usual depictions of the Catholic Saint Rita. Santa Rita of Cascia, Italy was born in 1386, died in 1456 and canonized in 1900 because of the many miracles that seemed to come about based on her intercession.

In 1968 the piece was stolen but later returned. Then in 1997, the piece returned to Albuquerque to Sandia Prep School which had been revived as a co-educational private school. It was sent there on a long term loan from New Mexico Tech and was in great need of repair since it had "been tarred and feathered, painted green, and used for target practice." The central figures were restored by funds from Save Our Sculpture (federal funding), alumni donations, the Sandia student "penny fund" and the New Mexico Chapter of the NNDPA. In 2005 the university requested the return of the Desert Maiden including the border pieces with delightfully carved animals. Upon its return, it remained in storage until 2008. At that time, it was finally placed again near its original site in front of a newer building, the Workman Center, which replaced the earlier structure and was named after President Workman upon his retirement. Other new buildings are in that area. The statue's border pieces, with some damaged areas due to all its traveling, still include most of the charming animal figures.

NEW DEAL BUILDINGS, STRUCTURES and PROGRAMS

AIM HIGH SCHOOL Torres Alternative School is housed in a school building created in 1936.

BOSQUE DEL APACHE BIRD REFUGE (north of Socorro)

NEW MEXICO INSTITUTE OF MINING AND TECHNOLOGY
SR #1461 State Register 7-8-88, National Register 5-16-89

Like many institutions of higher learning in New Mexico, the New Mexico School of Mines, as NMIMT was known then, took advantage of the New Deal federal assistance programs (PWA and WPA) to add new buildings and remodel existing buildings on campus. One of the new buildings from that period, Fitch Hall, is a two and one-half story, masonry and stucco, California Mission Revival style building which was completed in 1937. It has been placed on the New Mexico State Register of Historic Buildings, #1461 State Register 3-4-83.

Other WPA structures on campus include:

Gymnasium built by PWA in 1936
Fitch Hall dormitory built by PWA in 1937, on the State Historical Register #146 as 1989.
Brown Hall remodeled by PWA in 1938
Cramer Hall remodeled by PWA in 1938
Wells Hall built by PWA in 1938
Assay Laboratory was built by PWA in 1938
Weir Hall built by WPA in 1939
President's Hall buit by PWA in 1939
Golf course developed by WPA
Athletic field developed by WPA
Carpentry shop developed by WPA
Socorro CCC Camp buildings built by WPA were moved to campus in 1939 for temporary Bureau of Mines Offices

OFFICES OF ERNIE MOORE This building was originally a CCC building in Escondido but was moved to Socorro at a later date and a new facade added.

RURAL ELECTRIC ADMINISTRATION (REA)
Socorro Electric Cooperative
215 Manzanares Avenue
(575) 835-9560

This New Deal program continues to provide electricity today to approximately 12,972 rural consumers in this portion of New Mexico.

SOCORRO COUNTY COURTHOUSE
SR #920 State Register 3-4-83

The Spanish-Pueblo Revival style Socorro County Courthouse was built in 1940 for $60,414.06 by WPA.

OTHER STRUCTURES and PROGRAMS include:

National Guard Armory improvements
City Hall and Jail—now Department of Transportation
Infirmary Improvements, Tuberculosis Wards
Relief & Security Office
Public Welfare Office
Fire Station addition
Demolished old high school and built new high school (1940) which is now a community center
Sewer and water systems, ditch control/repairs, dikes, canals, sidewalks (1936–1937), curb and gutter completion, trestle improvements and many privies throughout the county. Some of the programs carried out included prairie and porcupine eradication, rodent control, book repairs, sewing projects, surplus commodities handling, home wool production, maintaining a work camp for transients, school lunch distribution, canning projects, cleaning schools and archaelogical surveys.

MYSTERY ARTWORK, see Chapter 4 (Kloss and Nordfeldt)

Along with the paintings mentioned above with whereabouts unknown, there has also been a reference to this author of sixteen panels (16" x 22") with tin frames that have not been located to date.

SOFIA (near Grenville)

NEW DEAL BUILDINGS, STRUCTURES and PROGRAMS

A number of years ago the town of Sofia was developed by a group of immigrants from Sophia, Bulgaria, however there is little remaining of that community now. The old school complex included the main building, a gym and teacherage (housing for the teachers) building and was built between 1937–1939 for $60,842 and served the area until 1963. Since then it has been in private ownership, first as a possible home, then a hunting lodge and now is being used by a private facility to help troubled teens. The WPA 1939 designation is part of the rock sidewalk up to the building and the sign that was on the front of the building has been plastered over.

RURAL ELECTRIC ADMINISTRATION (REA) Southwestern Electric Cooperative serves 897 consumers that include customers in this area. Its base office is located in Clayton.

SPRINGER

"Italy had its Renaissance, and thanks to President Roosevelt, we had ours in the 1930s: Paintings, music, theater and literature. That period will never be equaled."

—John Jellico, New Deal artist, July 27, 1992
letter to the Secretary of State of New Mexico.

NEW DEAL PUBLIC ART IN OTHER BUILDINGS

SPRINGER PUBLIC LIBRARY A Carl Redin oil painting titled "Placita Wash Day" still hangs in this library.

NEW DEAL BUILDINGS, STRUCTURES and PROGRAMS

NEW MEXICO BOYS' SCHOOL

This reformatory had various improvements including a gym and dormitory. A total of $97,709 was spent here by the WPA between 1939–1941.

PUBLIC SCHOOL BUILDINGS

High School Addition
Agriculture and Shop Buildings
Miranda Gym and Football Field improvements
Stadium construction
A combined school was built later in 1945.

RURAL ELECTRIC ADMINISTRATION (REA)
Springer Electric Cooperative
408 Maxwell Avenue
(575) 483-2421

This New Deal program continues today to provide electricity to approximately 1,952 rural consumers of New Mexico making their lives more productive and comfortable than before the 1930s.

OTHER STRUCTURES and PROGRAMS include water tank base and water lines, sewers, bridge SR 58, roads, cemetery road, fairgrounds demolition of a school and landscaping of the school.

MYSTERY ARTWORK, see Chapter 4

NEW MEXICO BOYS SCHOOL An oil painting, "El Puerton" 22" x 30" by Fremont Ellis has disappeared and if found, should be returned to that institution or some other public site in Springer.

STANLEY

NEW DEAL BUILDINGS and PROGRAMS

SCHOOL

The former school house and gymnasium where former Governor Bruce King and other members of his family were educated were built for $38,000 between 1938–1940. It has since been razed.

RURAL ELECTRIC ADMINISTRATION (REA) Central New Mexico Electric Cooperative provides the electricity to 13,382 consumers in this very rural area of Santa Fe County thanks to the New Deal.

TAOS

"They (Americans) have seen, across these last few years, rooms full of paintings by Americans . . . all of it native, eager and alive—all of it painted about things they know and look at often and have touched and loved."

—President Franklin D. Roosevelt in *Democratic Vistas: Post Offices and Public Art in the New Deal.* Marlene Park and Gerald E. Markowitz. Temple University Press, Philadelphia. 1984.

NEW DEAL PUBLIC ART IN NEW DEAL PUBLIC BULDINGS

FORMER TAOS COUNTY COURTHOUSE
On the north side of the Plaza (in Taos downtown historic district)
(575) 758-9016
SR #860 State Register 5-9-86, National Register 7-8-82

The 1932 Spanish-Pueblo Revival style Taos County Courthouse was built with partial funding from the PWAP in the heart of the downtown plaza. This two-story, flat-roofed building has a curvilinear parapet, exposed vigas and an added portal with carved beams and corbels and wooden posts. Unfortunately, it has been determined that the floor is weak and therefore it is next to impossible to easily view all the murals on the second floor. The County is responsible for the building.

The second floor courtroom was decorated with ten frescoes on law related subjects. They are some of New Mexico's finest New Deal art treasures. The frescoes were painted by the Taos Fresco Quartet including Emil Bisttram, Ward Lockwood, Victor Higgins and Bert Phillips. Work started in the fall of 1933 and was completed in the summer of 1934 and the artists were paid $56.00 a month. Ila McAfee also shared that she was allowed to help with the mixing of the sand but not to paint.

The general subject in all ten relates to the use and misuse of law. Inscribed above and under each painting are the titles in English and Spanish. The largest one (4' x 8') is "Moses, the Law Giver" executed by Victor Higgins, originally placed above the judge's bench. Some of the other topics include, "Avarice Breeds Crime/Avaricia Engedra Crimen," "Justice Begets Content/Justica Causa Felicidad," and "The Shadow of Crime/La Sombra del Crimen."

Work on these ten frescoes did not always go smoothly, a local paper reported. "What with additional carloads of sand having to be brought all the way from Rinconada and washed in the river at Placita, Bisttram painting six fingered ladies and Higgins having suddenly to go back to bed with milk and toast, the artists are wondering what jinx is working against them and what will happen next week."[1]

An eleventh mural was done more recently by Frederico Vigil after he conserved the ten original murals.

1. "What's Wrong with This Picture? Artist Produces Freak in Courthouse," *Taos Valley News*, 1934.

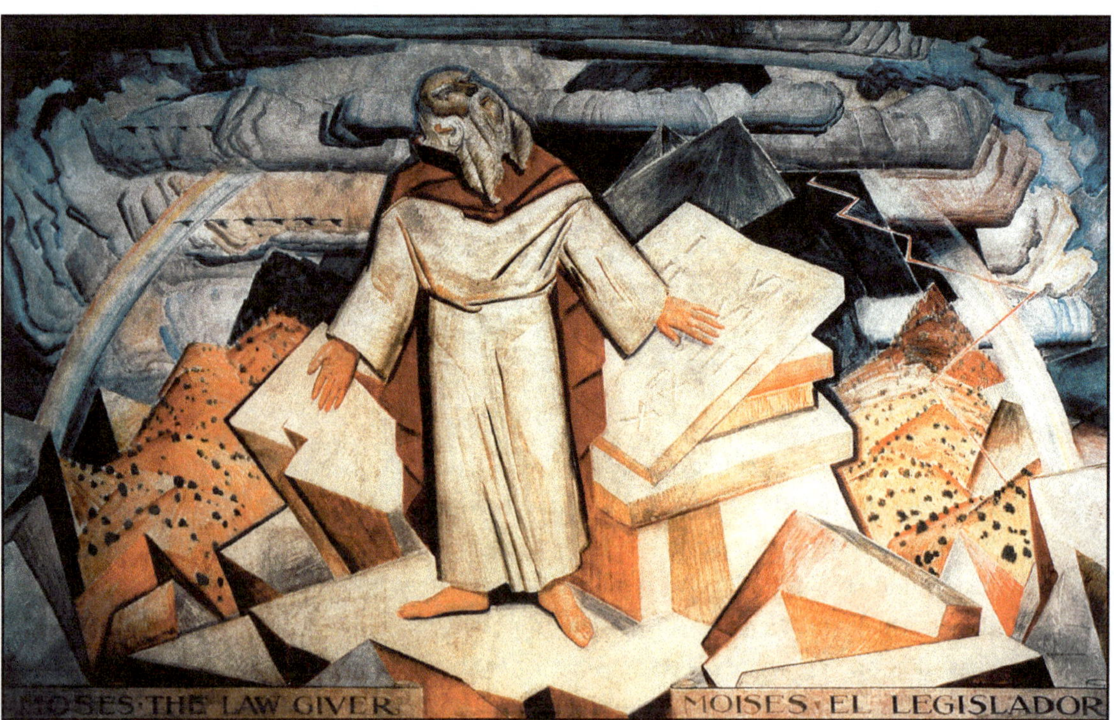

Victor Higgins was one of the four Taos artists who were hired by the Public Works of Art (PWAP) program to paint ten large murals for the new New Deal courthouse. This one by Higgins with Moses in the foreground was placed right behind the judge's bench and had to be a very effective placement. Photograph by Pat Berrett.

HARWOOD MUSEUM and TAOS PUBLIC SCHOOL ART COLLECTION
238 Ledoux Street
(575) 758-3069
State Register #362

In October 2012 the Taos Public School Art Collection was transferred to the Harwood Museum in Taos. This collection includes 18 New Deal public art pieces.

Prior to this transfer, the Harwood Museum Collection included numerous pieces of New Mexico's New Deal public art by well-known Taos artists and others. This includes approximately 40 wood carvings by Patrocinio Barela—most done during his WPA period when he was "discovered" by the New Mexico Federal Art Project Director, Russell Vernon Hunter.

Decorations done by New Deal artist, Gisella Loeffler, can be found in various locations in the building as well as some of her unusual folk art pieces. Two artists who did New Deal public artwork elsewhere but later resided in Taos were Ted Egri and Bea Mandelman.

The New Mexico New Deal funding sources also provided some improvements ($30,300) in 1936 on this building itself and tin work light fixtures and furniture enhance the ambiance of the museum. A collection of materials on the art and artists is available to researchers.

NEW DEAL BUILDINGS, STRUCTURES and PROGRAMS

CARSON NATIONAL FOREST OFFICE In 1937, $22,406 was spent and another $17,865 for a warehouse in 1938.

CITY HALL and JAIL In 1939 $14,006 helped to get this important structure in place.

EYE INFIRMARY In 1935 $10,302 was sent by the federal government for this service.

FAIRGROUND In 1935, the New Deal issued $15,231 for this facility.

FIRE STATION

In 1935 $20,078 was used to build and landscape this municipal building and it is still in use. A special "must see" art exhibit is on view here in the station's Community Room that easily is the largest collection of fine art in a public building in Taos. This art has been donated by local artists for a number of years and was initiated as a means of raising funds to help cover civic needs. One will find paintings done by almost any artist that ever lived in Taos including various New Deal artists who made donations to this cause.

FISH HATCHERY $38,113 was spent between 1936–1940 to create and improve this facility.

FORMER POST OFFICE

Now a city building, it is near Armory Road. New Deal furniture is still in use.

FORMER TAOS HIGH SCHOOL

This building was finished in November 1935 and was built for a total of $71,377 WPA funds. It included a gymnasium and auditorium all of which were designed by Wilfred Stedman. It is still being used as one of the town's schools and is located near the plaza.

RURAL ELECTRIC COOPERATIVE
Kit Carson Cooperatives
118 Cruz Alta Road
(575) 758-2258

This New Deal program continues to provide electricity to approximately 27,892 rural consumers in this area of the state.

TAOS VALLEY SCHOOL Located on Randall Street, this is now a private school.

TAOS and TAOS COUNTY ELEMENTARY SCHOOLS

Enos Garcia Elementary School built in 1942 is still functioning. Arroyo Hondo, Arroyo Seco, Canon, El Prado, Llano Quemado, Questa (now Day Care Center, San Cristobal and Talpa (now Community Center) were WPA built schools.

OTHER MISCELLANOUS STRUCTURES AND PROGRAMS include roads, privies, demolition of old privies, sidewalks, sewer system, ditch improvements, water works, curbs and gutters, viga preparation, plaza landscaping, reservoir improvements, food for relief families, indexing of county records, and furniture construction.

MYSTERY ARTWORK, see Chapter 4 (Adams, Kloss, and Nordfeldt)

TATUM

NEW DEAL PUBLIC BUILDINGS, STRUCTURES and PROGRAMS

JAIL and CITY HALL

The LEA COUNTY COOPERATIVE serves 6,807 consumers in the rural area around Tatum.

ROAD REPAIRS

RURAL ELECTRIC ASSOCIATION

SCHOOL GYM and AUDITORIUM

TEXICO

Texico was the early home of Russell Vernon Hunter, who was the director of the Federal Art Project for New Mexico.

NEW DEAL ART IN NEW DEAL BUILDINGS

TEXICO PUBLIC SCHOOLS
520 North Griffin
Contact Person: Superintendent
(575) 482-3801

An oil painting by Howard Schleeter called, "The Old Blue Well," hangs in the superintendent's office.

NEW DEAL BUILDINGS and STRUCTURES

CITY HALL AND FIRE STATION REMODELING

HIGH SCHOOL Improvements and an addition on another school.

PORT OF ENTRY

Between 1936–1938 WPA paid for the construction of this facility at a cost of $5,966. Others were also built at other entry locations into the state likely for the same amount.

RURAL ELECTRIC ADMINISTRATION (REA) Farmers' Electric Cooperative continues to provide electricity to the northern portion of Curry County which is predominately rural.

OTHER Roads, sidewalks, water line extensions, and drains made improvements in this village.

MYSTERY ARTWORK, see Chapter 4 (Kloss and Nordfeldt)

A local artist, Pedro Cervantez, may have done a number of paintings that could have originally been in the schools. Their status is unknown. One of his paintings is known to belong to the San Francisco Museum of Modern Art and another piece in the Melrose school collection.

TRUCHAS

NEW DEAL BUILDINGS, STRUCTURES and PROGRAMS

EARLY SCHOOL

MATTRESS FACTORY (now gone)

RETAINING WALLS AND LITTLE CHECK DAMS

ROADS

RURAL ELECTRIC Jemez Mountains Electric Cooperative serves 30,875 consumers in this northern rural area with its main office in Espanola.

TRUTH OR CONSEQUENCES

"The New Deal sought to make the national governments' presence felt in even the smallest, most remote communities ...The means for realizing this vision were eleven hundred new post offices ...The post office was "the one concrete link between every community of individuals and the Federal government" that functioned importantly in the human structure of the community."

—Marlene Park and Gerald Markowitz. *Democratic Vistas: Post Offices and Public Art in the New Deal.* Temple University Press, Philadelphia. 1984.

NEW DEAL PUBLIC ART IN NEW DEAL PUBLIC BUILDINGS

TRUTH OR CONSEQUENCES POST OFFICE
200 Main (no longer the Main Post Office Building)
Contact Person: Postmaster
State Register #242 National Register 2-23-90

This town's original name was Hot Springs so named because of the number of hot mineral springs found in this area and throughout the village. In 1950 the town elected to change the town's name after winning a challenge made by Ralph Edwards and his NBC television show called "Truth or Consequences." He offered to support and promote and feature any town that would change their name to Truth or Consequences. As a result of this, Edwards or his family and television stars have continued to come to Truth or Consequences (TorC) every year for an annual celebration. Periodically there has been a proposal to return to the original name since than is the main economic feature of the area.

This building was completed in 1940, prior to the name change (see below), and was built according to the same standardized plan used for the Deming, Portales, and others, but with even less ornamentation. This simplified Classical style building is of poured-in-place concrete with a flat roof and very plain window and door treatments. In 1990 it was designated as part of the National Register of Historic Places, most likely along with many others that are similar (examples can be found all over the nation, for example in Ponca City, Oklahoma, Des Plaines, Illinois and Walsenburg, Colorado). In the early 2000s the building was refurbished with new windows and exterior treatments; the renovation cost more than the cost of constructing the building.

The lobby of the building contains a mural by Boris Deutsch (1892–1978) which was the New Mexico winner of a 48 state competition in the Section of Fine Arts of the Treasury. This expressive and stylized mural was also created in 1940, not for the purpose of recording the authenticity of any Native American dance in detail, but to represent the spirit and color of an Indian Bear Dance. One art critic describes the mural by noting, "the artist gave his dancers a bizarre touch of surrealist angst muddled by leaden humor. . . . The inspiration behind the design was the indigenous art of the Southwestern Indian—large and small figures without regard to spatial positions, as though the Indians were decorative patterns on pottery."[2] Another source notes the muralist's sense of humor by referencing that Deutsch's original sketch for the national competition for post office mural designs cleverly showed an Indian Chief dancing out of the path of an Atchison, Topeka & Santa Fe Super Chief train. The actual mural, apparently redesigned, does not show the train but instead features mountains in the background.

1, 2. Karal Ann Marling, *Wall-to-Wall America: A Cultural History of Post Office Murals in the Great Depression.* University of Minnesota Press, Minneapolis, 1982, p. 81-82, 223.

NEW MEXICO VETERANS CENTER
Formerly Carrie Tingley Hospital for Crippled Children
992 South Broadway
(575) 894-9081
State Register #1835

In 1936, $158,390 WPA funds came in to this community to build a poliomyelitis hospital for the state's children afflicted with this paralyzing disease. Another $98,955 came in 1937 and the state allocated approximately $296,000 to complete the hospital. The location was selected because of the existence of hot mineral springs which had been determined as a therapeutic resource for treatment of polio including in the treatment of one of the nation's most prominent polio victims, President Franklin D. Roosevelt. Within the hospital, a hot mineral pool was included and the hospital was named for the then governor's wife. In the 1980s the hospital program was transferred to Albuquerque and the University of New Mexico medical school. A few years later, the state converted the facility into a care facility for its veterans that need long term assisted living care.

Included in the inner courtyard is a large round turtle fountain created by Eugenie Shonnard, WPA sculptor. It is made of stone and has carved frogs which face in four directions. It is an imaginatively designed fountain and one which reflects the artist's love for animal life. Records indicate that it was created at a cost of $700. Eliseo Rodriguez, Santa Fe New Deal artist, recalled that he and his neighbor, Louie Ewing, created and painted blue tiles which were to surround the base of the fountain, however, the current base is brick and no one is sure about the whereabouts of the tiles. They are most likely behind the bricks. Today the fountain has been cleaned up and can be enjoyed by the veterans either in the courtyard or from the glassed in hallway that encircles the courtyard.

An outstanding collection of New Deal paintings were placed in the hospital to cheer up the children and staff. When the hospital program was transferred to Albuquerque, the paintings went along also and can now be viewed in various locations throughout the new hospital still cheering up the patients and staff. Most of them have been restored or conserved either by the New Mexico Chapter of the NNDPA or the Carrie Tingley Hospital Foundation.

Some will also remember the statue of a mother caring for her small child that was created by Oliver LaGrone for the original hospital clinic lobby. He called it "Mercy" that depicts his memory of his mother nursing him through malaria as a little boy. La Grone grew up in Albuquerque and was the first African American to graduate from University of New Mexico's Art Department. He continued his studies and became a university professor in North Carolina until his death.

The statue was also brought to Albuquerque and again placed in the clinic lobby. Children continued to play around and on this life size plaster statue and finally the statue received its long awaited bronze patina in the 1980s thanks to Albuquerque's 1% for Public Art funds. At that time a second casting was done and the second statue was placed in the Sculpture Garden at the Albuquerque Museum. The first statue has now been transferred to the inpatient unit of Carrie Tingley Hospital in the Bill and Barbara Richardson Pediatric Unit of University of New Mexico Hospital on Lomas.

NEW DEAL PUBLIC ART IN PUBLIC BUILDINGS

WPA furniture has been found in the Truth or Consequences Chamber of Commerce office and the City Offices and Senior Recreation Center.

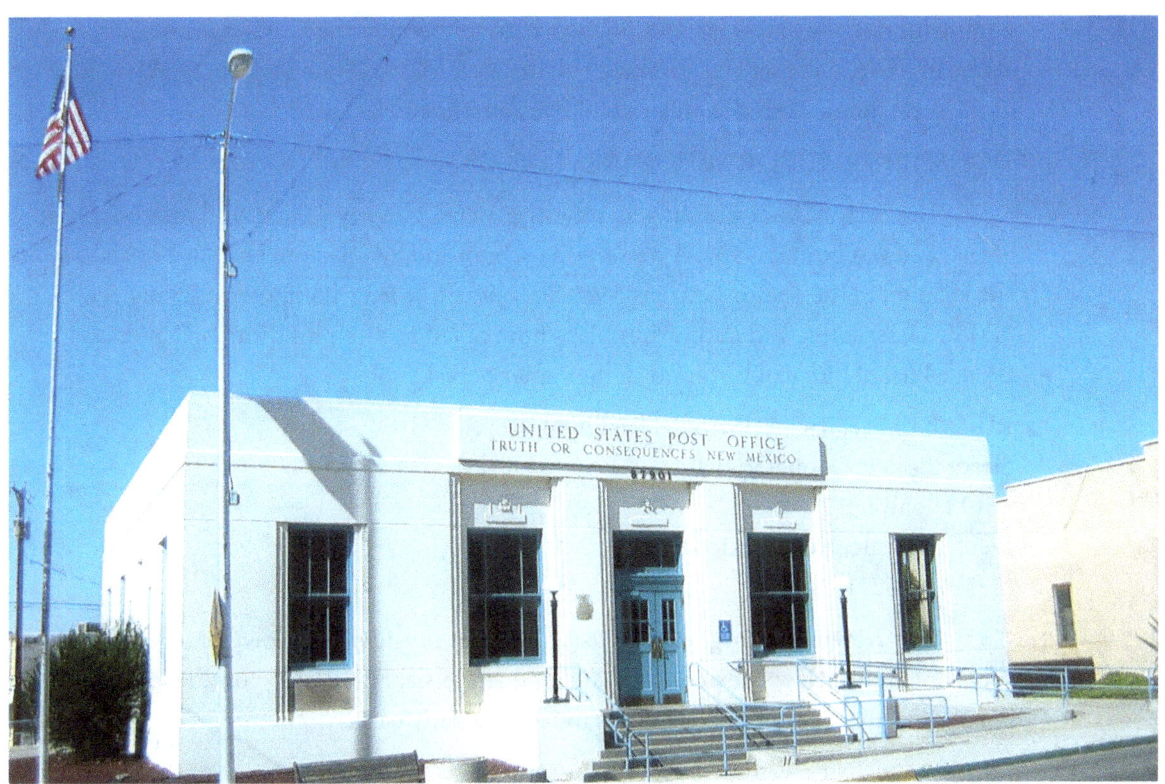

During Roosevelt's New Deal era, many post offices were built and a large number of them also had murals painted in the area right over the Postmaster's door. The downtown post office is still in use and was refurbished early in 2000.

NEW DEAL BUILDINGS, STRUCTURES and PROGRAMS

CIVIC CENTER/AUDITORIUM/LIBRARY

State Register #1876

This building is still being used by the many retirees in this community. The library program has been moved nearby but the facility is quite busy still with various activities. Built in 1938 for $22,326, the interior has its original New Deal furniture, tin light fixtures and carved doors.

ELEPHANT BUTTE RECREATIONAL AREA/RESORT

State Register #1642

The main building, now a lodge and restaurant, and a number of individual cabins are still providing recreations spaces for tourists vacationing at Elephant Butte Lake. The buildings were primarily built by the Civilian Conservation Corps (CCC) in 1940. The site of the CCC camp is now the site of the park's maintenance yard. To commemorate the extensive and fine work done there by the CCC, a life size bronze statue of a CCC Worker was dedicated by the New Mexico State Parks in October 2008 at the recreational dam site area near the restaurant and lodge.

HOT SPRINGS PUBLIC SCHOOL BUILDINGS

The early school building is now the Sierra County Office Building on Date Street, and was built in 1937. A newer high school and gymnasium built in 1938 is now the location of the Senior Citizens Meal Site, a thrift store, a computer learning center, NMSU classrooms, and auditorium. It is now called the Ralph Edwards Center and a bronze bust of him can be found in the center portal.

RURAL ELECTRIC ADMINISTRATION (REA)
Sierra Electric Cooperative
#610 Highway 195
Elephant Butte, New Mexico 87935
(575) 744-5231

This New Deal program has its offices just outside Truth or Consequences in Elephant Butte, New Mexico. This area, which is near the lake, continues to serve approximately 3,996 rural consumers today on a daily basis.

SIERRA COUNTY COURTHOUSE

A one-story Territorial style building was constructed in 1937–38 with $58,372 WPA funds to house the county courthouse activities when the county seat was moved from Hillsboro to Hot Springs. A newer addition was added to the exterior of the building in the early 2000s.

OTHER STRUCTURES

Bath house repairs
City park (later named the Ralph Edwards Park)
Salcido Stadium built in 1938 was torn down in 1986 with the exception of the front wall and the site is now city tennis courts.
School landscaping, sidewalks and curbs, roads, cemetery improvements, water system extensions and airport improvements were all some of the ways this community used their WPA funds.
Nearby Hillsboro Peak Lookout Tower and Cabin are on the State Register #1443.

MYSTERY ARTWORK, see Chapter 4 (Kloss etchings)

Also a sculptured bas relief of birds in flight was most likely in a former state bathhouse located where the Oro Grande Hotel is now. We have yet to find it in this community.

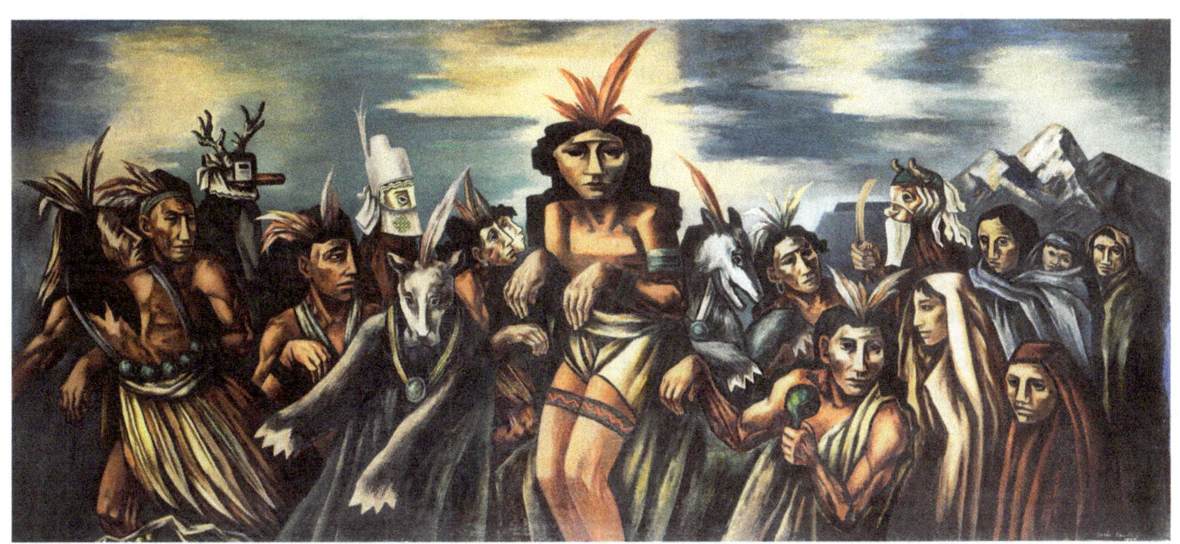

In 1939 a contest was conducted by the Section of the Treasury Fine Art program to determine which mural in each state would make their "48 State Best Murals." The Director, Edward Bruce, wanted these murals to capture "the same feeling I get when I smell a sound, fresh ear of corn—to make me feel comfortable about America." According to Karal Ann Marling in her book, "Wall to Wall America," she indicated that the Section suggested subjects like "The Post; Local History, Past or Present; Local Industries; Local Flora and Fauna; Local Pursuits, Hunting, Fishing, recreational activities; Themes of Agriculture or pure landscapes."[1] The one selected from New Mexico was done by Boris Deutsch for Hot Springs (now TorC). His surrealist representation of the Indian Bear Dance is quite different and must have fallen in the Local History category. Photograph by Pat Berrett.

TUCUMCARI

"Those that lived through it still wear scars like a well-earned badge of experience. Some lament the excess of governments it spawned; others remember this fondly as a creative response to a desperate situation."

—Peter Bermingham, *The New Deal in the Southwest—Arizona and New Mexico*, The University of Arizona Press, Tucson, 1980.

NEW DEAL PUBLIC ART IN NEW DEAL PUBLIC BUILDINGS

QUAY COUNTY COURTHOUSE
(575) 461-0510
SR #1280 State Register 5-9-86

The New Deal Quay County Courthouse has a mural on the inside but these bas reliefs on the exterior of the building share about the economics of the county if the viewers or passers by should happen to look up near the top of the building. Bas reliefs with Colfax County representative motifs can also be seen on the Colfax County Courthouse but no one knows who designed these exquisite bas reliefs on either site.

The 1939 Art Deco style courthouse is a four-story concrete, granite, and cast stone building with stone bas relief embellishments depicting farming, cowboys and the railroad—significant symbols of the community's economic base. The interior exhibits terrazzo floors, plaster ceilings, marble walls in the lobby, and Art Deco details, such as hand rails, grilles, and light fixtures. The landscaping expenses were covered by WPA but the Public Works Administration (PWA) paid for the structure which resembles other courthouses on the east side of the state (Clovis, Portales, Lovington, and Raton) and nearby West Texas.

The second floor courtroom doors have aluminum bas relief embellishments with justice themes and above the doors is a large mural of Coronado created by Ben Carlton Mead. It is entitled "I, Francisco Vasquez de Coronado, Have Passed This Way and Left My Mark." Coronado is seated on a rock in front of a tall tree and yucca plants. Nearby, Indians and Spanish soldiers surround Coronado as a large wooden cross is placed in the ground. The palette is of the Southwest and quite colorful and in good condition.

Landscaping around this building was also carried out by New Deal funds.

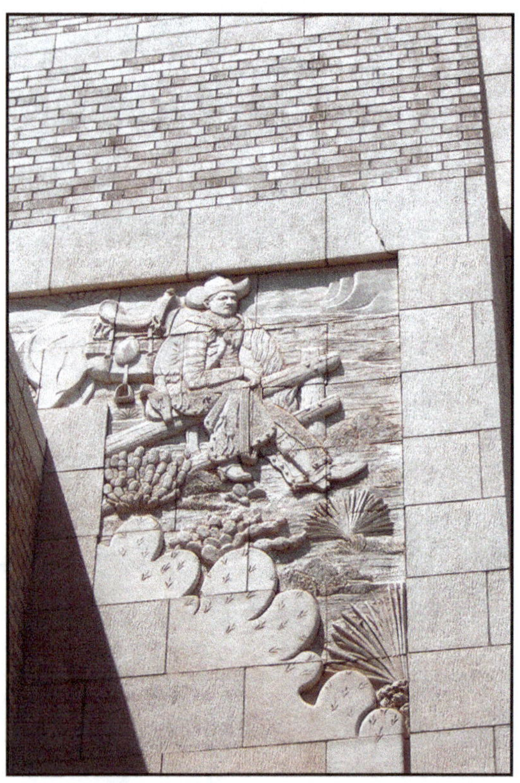

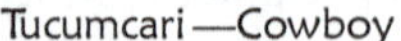
Tucumcari—Cowboy

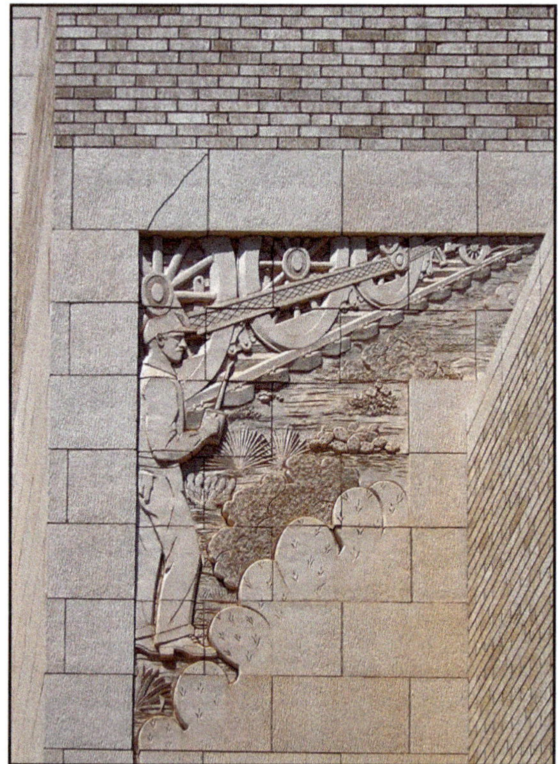

Train Engineer

NEW DEAL BUIILDINGS and STRUCTURES

ARCH HURLEY CONSERVANCY DISTRICT OFFICE
State Register #1599

AUDITORIUM AND GYM

CHAPEL at CEMETERY and improvements

CITY HALL and its landscaping

FAIRGROUNDS and improvements

HOSPITAL

METROPOLITAN PARK aka FIVE MILE PARK
State Register # 1618

Including a large swimming pool and bathhouse, this once popular community center is in great need of restoration and preservation due to a poorly installed roof sometime after the building was built. Many have great memories of family gatherings here and are disappointed that this damage has not been repaired and the facility is no longer available for use.

NATIONAL GUARD ARMORY and GARAGE

PUBLIC WELFARE OFFICE improvements.

RURAL ELECTRIC ADMINISTRATION (REA)
Farmers Electric Cooperative
PO Box 550 or 3701 Thornton Street
Clovis, New Mexico 88102
(575) 769-2116

Provides electricity to 7,169 consumers in the rural areas surrounding this community.

SCHOOL BUILDINGS

OTHER STRUCTURES and PROGRAMS

Incinerator, city park including masonry wall around park, roads, sewers and plant, irrigation, water system design and system, sidewalks, curbs, gutters, tennis courts, bridge extensions, warehouse, hospital landscaping, sewing project, clerical school aid, school lunch preparation.

MYSTERY ARTWORK, see Chapter 4

TULAROSA

NEW DEAL BUILDINGS and STRUCTURES

CITY HALL—remodeled

COMMUNITY CENTER

MUNICIPAL BUILDING (Possibly, the existing Police Station and jail are still in use)

TOWN MUSEUM was the former Police Station

RED BRICK SCHOOL This former school is rehabilitated.

RURAL ELECTRIC ADMINISTRATION (REA) Otero County Electric Cooperative serves the rural area of this part of Otero County.

TULAROSA PUBLIC SCHOOLS

Administration Building—originally this was the high school
Small adobe building—now used for storage
Football field and landscaping at school buildings
School Gym is now used as city storage.

OTHER STRUCTURES and PROGRAMS

WPA outhouses (the supervisor of this project was the father of war correspondent, Bill Mauldin), roads, water system, sidewalks, improvements, irrigation system improvements, ditch system improvements, water system, reservoir construction, plaza landscaping, school cleaning, clothing project, and library cataloging and operation.

WAGON MOUND

"Escape into the refuge of history marked nearly all the work of New Deal project artists doing murals ...This paved the most direct route to contact with the general public. Occasionally widened in succeeding decades, that road has remained open ever since."

—Peter Bermingham, *The New Deal in the Southwest-Arizona and New Mexico*, University of Arizona Press, Tucson, 1980.

NEW DEAL PUBLIC ART IN NEW DEAL PUBLIC BUILDINGS

The Public Schools of this village received monies for their school buildings and gymnasium and also had two B.J.O. Nordfeldt lithographs—"Morada" and "Canyon Road." Also in their collection were two large Native American pots. The lithographs have disappeared and the two pots are daily guarded by the Superintendent in his office. He understands at one time the school owned eighteen pots but this is all that remains. The WPA furniture in the cafeteria and library are still being used now by the third and fourth generations of students since the 1930s.

NEW DEAL BUILDNGS, STRUCTURES and PROGRAMS

CITY HALL

COMMUNITY CENTER

RURAL ELECTRIC ADMINISTRATION (REA) This New Deal program continues to provide electricity to this rural area of the state through the Springer Electric Cooperative.

SCHOOLS, GYM and Landscaping created in 1935 still in use

OTHER STRUCTURES AND PROGRAMS include roads, cobblestone gutters, water supply construction and sewer line construction.

MYSTERY ARTWORK If indeed the Nordfeldt lithographs are gone, where are they?

WEED

NEW DEAL BUIILDINGS, STRUCTURES and PROGRAMS:

COMMUNITY CENTER

This small mountain village in the Lincoln National Forest is proud of its WPA built gymnasium built in 1939. It continues to play a critical role in the area as the Weed Community Center despite the closure of the school in 1991. It is the home of the Weed Annual Reunion and the Blue Grass Festival but its very active role in the village began when the REA brought electricity to the area in 1948. Some say that getting electricity brought the greatest change in their lives. Sports, movies, roller skating, box supper socials, plays, carnivals, music performances, proms and graduations were all held in it. A former student who attended the 2010 annual reunion recently reported that "the hardwood floor still dances pretty darned well after all that use." While there he met the family of the man who laid that floor and another fellow remembered his father worked on the gym throughout its entire construction.

LOOKOUTS

The Carissa Lookout Complex in this area is also a CCC product that is on the State Register of Cultural Properties SHR#1450 and the Bluewater Lookout Complex is SHR#1448.

ROADS

Building this structure and the CCC constructed roads and bridges during this time of long drought and the Depression brought badly needed employment to the folks in the area. Getting new roads was also helpful to the sawmill in the area since it provided better transportation for the lumber. It was expected the roads would open up the mountain farms to the outside market but the reverse happened since it meant families could more easily drive into town for groceries than to grow their own. The roads did open up this isolated region to campers and hunters.

There was a CCC "fly station or side camp" near Weed and some of the boys may have been sent to work on the new Army Air Force base in Alamogordo in 1941. That base was intended at the time for training British-Canadian flyers. Once the war came on many of the families left to go into wartime jobs elsewhere but the annual reunions bring many back on those roads to that building to share their memories.

NOTE: Other New Deal properties listed on the State Register of Cultural Properties include all New Mexico Federation of Women's Club Buildings, SRCP 1834; New Mexico Campus Buildings built between 1909 and 1938, SRCP 1707; National Forest Fire Lookouts in the Southwestern Region, SRCP 1708 and David Kammer's Survey Report on "Architectural and Historic Resources of the New Deal in New Mexico," SRCP 1617.

2

NEW MEXICO SCHOOLS BUILT BY PUBLIC WORKS ADMINISTRATION (PWA) OR WORKS PROGRESS ADMINISTRATION (WPA) FUNDING

Far more small communities, not identified in the previous chapter, were also recipients of WPA public school buildings of varying sizes—one room and larger. Many towns also got an accompanying gymnasium. These continued in use until after 1953 when New Mexico disbanded the Rural School system and the rural students were transferred to the nearest larger community.

The information provided below came from individuals and from a list provided by the New Mexico Legislative Council of Public Schools built in the 1930s–1945s and still on their insurance coverage list. The other major source was from a project done for the State Historic Preservation Division of the Department of Cultural Affairs in 1994 by Dr. David Kammer and Jeff Rose, a graduate student in History at University of New Mexico. They used microfilm prepared by the National Archives. The title of that document is "WPA Projects Funded in New Mexico." This document is on file with the New Mexico State Historic Preservation office and also on their website. There are 361 schools identified in this project as being built by the WPA. Some of them and even their towns no longer exist. Other buildings are no longer schools but now meet other community needs.

Santa Fe County received the most WPA schools (43) while this funding source built only one school in McKinley County town—Gallup. However schools were built on the reservation in that county but with primarily federal funding from a different funding source.

Reference is made below regarding the current status of these buildings where known. Some of the villages or settlements themselves have been abandoned and many are "unkown" so one can assume the schools have disappeared with the towns. *The Place Names of New Mexico* by Robert Julyan was also used to try to identify possible historical village information. The author would be delighted to learn anything regarding the status/condition of those schools where no information was obtained at the time of publication.

Bernalillo County

Albuquerque (public schools)
- Albuquerque High School—now private residences and commercial
- Atrisco—still an elementary school
- Bandelier—(1939) still in use
- Coronado—now used as Administrative Offices
- Duranes—(1940) still an elementary school
- Five Points
- Griegos—(1940) still an elementary school
- La Mesa—still in use and has had improvements
- Las Candelarias
- Lew Wallace—(1934) still in use
- Lincoln—APS Maintenance Offices
- Monte Vista—(1931) still in use
- Pajarito—still in use and has had improvements
- Santa Barbara—owned by the City, possibly a Community Center and elder apartments
- Stronghurst—demolished

University of New Mexico—various buildings still in use, see Albuquerque in Chapter 1

Catron County

Apache Creek—building gone
Aragon—community center
Cruzville—private ownership, home
Greens Gap—abandoned settlement, status of building unknown
Horse Springs—still standing, vacant
Lower Frisco—private ownership
Luna—community center
Middle Frisco—school closed, status of building unknown
Mogollon—building burned
Pie Town—may be a home
Pipe Springs—school closed (may be Greens Gap)
Quemado—old Red Hill School down the road, not in use
Reserve—portion of building now Headstart program
Tres Lagunas—demolished

Chaves County

Acme—abandoned village, school closed, status of building unknown
Dexter—(1936) still in use
Elkins—virtually abandoned, school closed, status of building unknown
Frazier—stone ruins of school only remains of settlement
Hagerman—may still be in use
Lake Arthur—still in use as museum

Ripley—unknown community
Roswell—(1940) S. Gutierrez Charter Middle School, still in use on Industrial Air Center and East Grand Plains Elementary, (1940) possibly still in use

Cibola County (previously part of Valencia County)

Alarque—abandoned after dam broke and washed out the town
De Vargas—abandoned settlement, status of building unknown
El Cerro—unknown community
Fence Lake—town still survives, school unknown
Grants-San Rafael Elementary—still in use
San Rafael—remodeled, still in use
Seboyeta—community still exists, school unknown
Tingle—abandoned settlement

Colfax County

Bernal—community no longer exists, status of building unknown
Cimarron—most of the buildings destroyed but the bricks from those buildings now form a wall around a private home in town, gym still in use
Eagle Nest—no longer in use, condition unknown
Elizabethtown—demolished
Farley—village virtually gone—school closed
Kiowa—village virtually gone—school closed
Lynn—an abandoned railroad settlement—school closed
Maxwell—building may be gone
Miami—deteriorated shell
Moreno Valley—no longer in use (Eagle's Nest)
Newton—school closed, status of building unknown
Raton—high school now a junior high, three elementary schools still in use
Springer—still in use
Tafoya—abandoned community, assume building gone

Curry County

Bellview—school closed, status of building unknown
Center—now consolidated with Clovis
Claud—abandoned village, school closed, status of building unknown
Clovis—Marshall Junior High still in use
Field—school closed, status of building unknown
Grady—(1934) still in use
Melrose—still in use as school
Pleasant Hill—school closed, status of building unknown
Ranchvale—school building may still be there, not in use
Rosedale—an abandoned town, status of building unknown
St.Vrain—school closed, status of building unknown
Texico—still in use

De Baca County

Dunlap—settlement gone, church only surviving building
Fort Sumner—(1935) some parts still in use
Taiban—closed, shell may still exist
Yeso—closed, shell may still exist

Dona Ana County

Anthony—(1934) elementary school still in use, on State Historic Register
Garfield
Hatch—demolished in recent past
Las Cruces
- McArthur Elementary still in use
- Court Jr. High, now charter school and public alternative high school

Mesilla Park—currently a recreation center
Mesquite—status unknown
New Mexico State University—various buildings (see Las Cruces)
Radium Springs
Rincon—brick building, still in use
Salem—school closed, status of building unknown
Tortugas—most likely deteriorated

Eddy County

Artesia—old high school gym still in use, Annex in use, was junior high, Central Grade still in use
Atoka—deteriorated but still used as a barn. Playground now an animal grazing area
Carlsbad
- P.R. Leyba Midddle School, still in use
- Edison Elementary school
- West School (middle school)

Hope—community center
Lake Arthur—(1931) combined school still in use
Lakewood—possibly a church
Otis—former school may now be a community center, sometime church
West School—has been vacant but recently used temporarily

Grant County

Bayard—new buildings, believe old building demolished
Central—new buildings, believe old building demolished
Cliff—(1936) school still in use
Dwyer—abandoned village, status of building unknown
Fierro—mostly gone
Gila—school closed, students go to Cliff, status of building unknown
Hachita—may still be open

Hanover—nearly abandoned settlement, building now empty, was a Catholic Center then restaurant
Mimbres—now private home
New Mexico Western University—Graham Gym in use, see Silver City in chapter 1
Pierre—community no longer exists
Pinos Altos—remodeled building
Red Rock—building gone
San Juan—building gone
San Lorenzo—may still be in use
Swarts—building might still be there
Silver City—new building on that site
Siopar—school closed. status of building unknown
White Signal—school closed, status of building unknown

Guadalupe County

Anton Chico—may still be in use
Arabella—still standing
Barica—school closed, status of building unknown
Colonias—only church still there in the area
Cuervo—school building privately owned by former student
Dilia—school closed, status of building unknown
El Valle—school closed, status of building unknown
Los Ojitos—abandoned village, school closed, status of building unknown
Pastura—school closed, status of building unknown
Puerto de Luna—school building gone
Santa Rosa—high school now city offices
Vaughn—(1933) school burned but portion may have remained as part of new school

Harding County

Alamosa—no building standing
Bueyeros—community use, bad repair
Mills—no building standing
Mosquero—building in use
Quintana—school closed, status of building unknown
Rosebud—school now a community center
Roy—demolished for new school building
Solano—part of school still standing, gym now privately owned business

Hidalgo County

Animas—school and gym remodeled and in use
Lordsburg—high school, then junior high, then Enrichment Center. Now not in use but still standing
Virden—building badly deteriorated

Lea County

Eunice—(1937) M. Jordan Elementary School and middle school, Catron (1939) still in use
Hobbs—(1939) Will Rogers Elementary School still in use
Jal—(1938) junior/high in use
Lovington—school open but may not be WPA building
Tatum—none still there, all newer buildings

Lincoln County

Capitan—high school now junior high
Carrizozo—gym now a grocery store
Corona—one building now school cafeteria
Hollywood (now Ruidoso Downs)—may be day care center
Hondo—may currently be a church
Ruidoso—not sure any existing buildings are WPA built
Stetson—private foundry and/or residence

Luna County

Columbus—may still be in use
Deming—(1935) elementary School still in use
Sunshine—school closed, status of building unknown
Waterloo—abandoned village, assume building gone

McKinley County

Gallup—none still there

Mora County

Buena Vista—deteriorated
Cleveland—deteriorated
El Abuelo—unknown community
Golondrina
Guadalupita—building (Kennedy school) demolished
Holman—still in use
Las Borregas
Las Cacas
Llanaclel Coyato—unknown community
Lucero—most buildings here have been abandoned
Mora—building demolished
Ocate—almost abandoned community
Ojo Feliz—small community, school building status unknown
Rainesville
Velasquez—unknown community
Wagon Mound—(1935) still in use
Watrous

Otero County

Alamogordo—(1939) North Elementary School still in use
Cloudcroft—Old Red School House now a Library
Mayhill—Forest Service Administrative Site area
New Mexico School for the Blind—some still in use
Tularosa—Administration Building still in use as a museum. The red brick schoolhouse in bad condition, but has new roof. May become a museum
Weed—Community Center

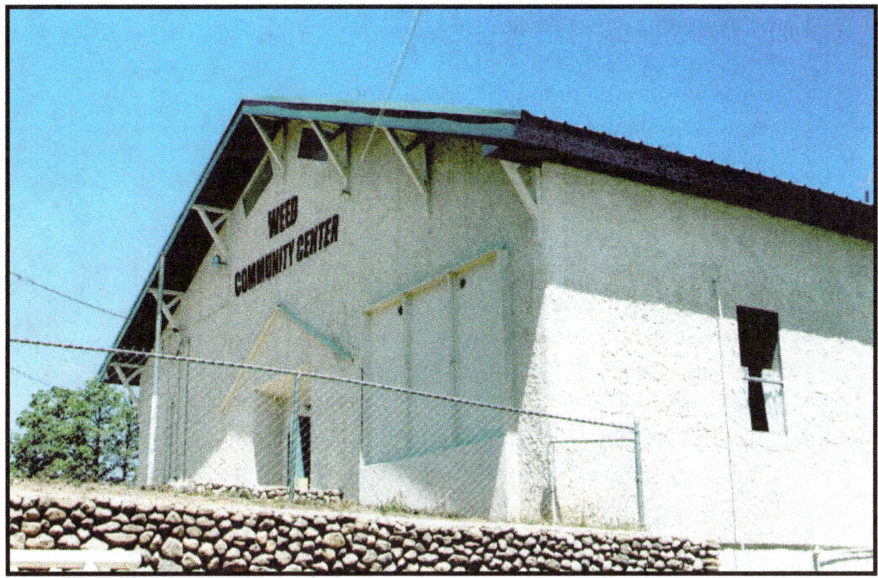

This former school building in Weed continues to serve the rural area as a community center. Photograph by Kermit Hill.

Quay County

Endee—private residence
Forrest—deteriorating
House—old gym now a barn on ranch nearby McAlister
Ima—community center
Logan—demolished
McAlister—demolished
Nara Visa—community center
Norton—demolished
Porter—demolished
San Jon—(1936) San Jon Combined still in use
Tucumcari—Zia School now houses a private business
Wheatland—rock school building demolished

Rio Arriba County

Great difficulty finding anyone who knew about most of these small places. Assume there is little or nothing left in small places.

Abiquiu—replaced by school paid for by Georgia O'Keeffe
Alcalde—classroom building closed due to mold, gymnasium still in use
Alire—abandoned community
Burns Canyon—abandoned community
Canjilon—school closed, status of building unknown
Canones—community center
Canova—community center
Capulin—unknown community in this county
Chama—school now senior center (possibly only the gym)
Chamita—school closed, status of building unknown
Chili
Chimayo—now senior center
Cibolla—school house now the County Complex building
Coral de Piedra—unknown community
Cordova—school open but status of building unknown
Coyote—still there
Dixon—school open but status of building unknown
Dulce—demolished
El Guigue—unknown community
El Rito—some buildings at the college still in use, public school now Mesa Vista
Ensenada—school closed, status of building unknown
Espanola—high school now charter school, elementary school now administration
Gallina—elementary school building possible used for storage
Governador—school gone
Haynes—abandoned settlement
Hernandez—school open, status of building unknown
La Ventana—still in use
Lindrith—school restored, now the Lindrith Area Heritage Charter School
North Agua—school gone
Nutrias
Ojo Caliente—high school building still there
Rinconada
Rio Puerco
San Juan—(1932) elementary school still in use
San Pedro—gone
Tierra Amarilla—still there
Truchas—school now library, preschool and community center
Velarde—school open, status of building unknown
Youngsville—no school

Roosevelt County

Arch—only four walls standing
Causey—intact but danger of it falling in
Dora—some structures still in use
Eastern New Mexico University—administration and museum building still in use
Elida—status of WPA building unknown
Hiway—closed, building gone
Lingo—school gone
Portales—junior high gym is all that remains of the WPA school buildings
Rogers—school closed, building still standing but in bad condition, gym has stamped ceiling

Sandoval County

Algodones—building demolished
Bernalillo—Roosevelt Elementary School still in use
Copper City—abandoned village, status of building unknown
Corrales—earlier school no longer standing
Domingo—abandoned village, status of building unknown
El Ranchitos—school closed, status of building unknown
Gonzalitas—demolished
Jemez Canyon—(1935) private home
Jemez Springs—(1933) elementary now Lindrith Heritage Charter School
La Jara—school closed, now community center
La Ventana—school closed, status of building unknown
Mesa Portales—unknown community
Penistaja—possibly abandoned village, school no longer there
Placitas—now owned by St. Antonio Catholic Church used as the Little Mission Parish Hall
Regina—status of building unknown
San Isidro—school closed, status of building unknown
San Luis—school closed, building deteriorated
Sile
Vallecitos—school closed, replaced with new school called Ponderosa

San Juan County

Aztec—school open, status of WPA building unknown
Blanco—school open, status of WPA building unknown
Farmington—(1940) Tibbetts Middle School still in use
Kirtland—school open, status of WPA building unknown

San Miguel County

Great difficulty in finding anyone who knew about these small villages and their schools.

Bernal
Chaparito—school closed, status of building unknown
Cherryville
East Pecos
El Chorro—unknown community
El Macho—unknown community
El Pueblo—unknown community
El Toloso—unknown community
Garita—unknown community
Laguna Seca
Lagunita
Las Gallinas—elementary school closed
Las Vegas—Robertson High & W. Las Vegas' Don Cecilio Martinez Elementary still in use
Los Montoyas—now a private home
Los Vigiles
Lower Rociada
New Mexico Highlands University—Rogers Hall (administration building), Douglas School
Newt—unknown community
Ojo del Chapello—unknown community
Ojo del Medio—unknown community
Pecos—(1935) middle school still in use
Rio de Mora
San Isidro
San Jose
Sena
Sheridan—building still in place and on State Register #1732
Tremetina—school gone
Upper Tewa—unknown community
Ventanas—also known as Trujillo
Villanueva—community desirous of making school into a community center

Santa Fe County

Barton—abandoned community, status of school building unknown
Cedar Grove
Cerrillos—closed, privately owned, has been a gallery
Chimayo—now an interfaith community center
Cienega—now community center and fire department, a vocational school now demolished
Cow Springs—only the cemetery remains
Cundiyo—now fire station and community center
Edgewood—still a school
El Rancho—senior center

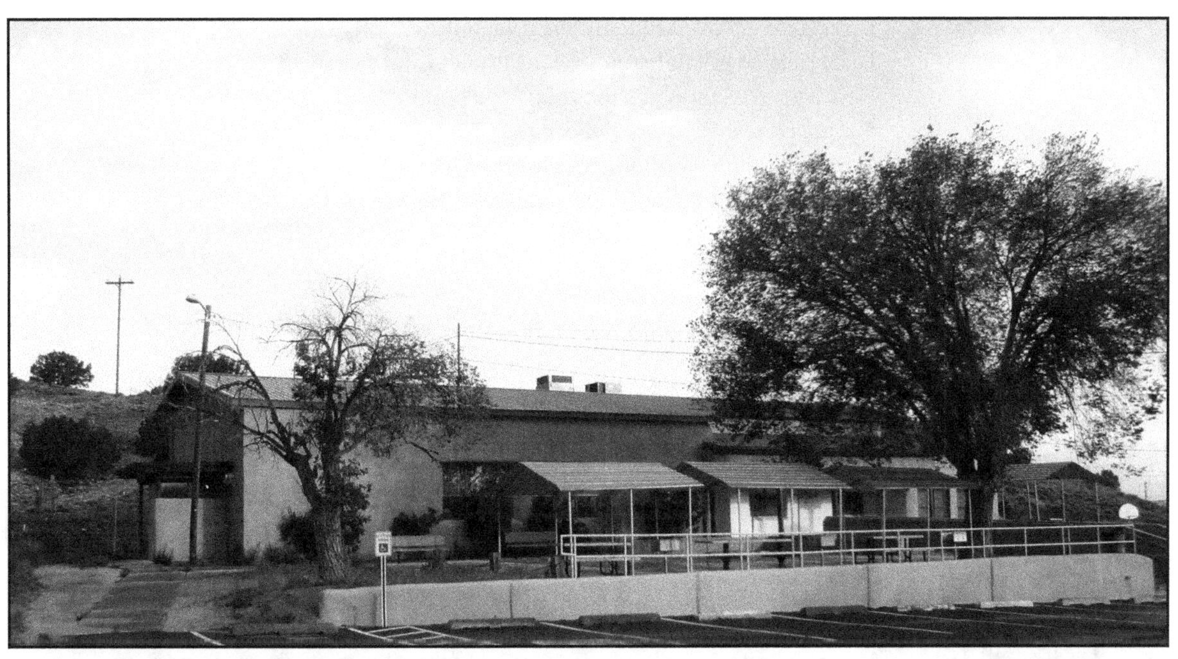

Senior citizens are well served in this remodeled WPA school in Santa Fe County. Some may have attended school in this building in their younger years. Photograph provided by the center.

Galisteo—school closed, status of building unknown
Gauhman—village unknown
Glorieta—private home
Golden
Hyer—building no longer standing
Kennedy—appears not building still standing
Lamy—private home
Los Cuertelas
Madrid—community center and private home
Nambe—community center for Pojoaque
Pojoaque—same as Nambe above
Puye
Rio en Medio—may be a senior center
Santa Cruz—may be a senior center
Santa Fe:

- Acequia Madre—still in use
- Agua Fria—still in use but may be demolished and new school built
- Alvord—charter school
- Carlos Gilbert—recently remodeled and expanded
- Gonzales—still in use
- Kaune—still in use and scheduled to become home of Desert Academy (charter)

Larragoite—Now Academy at Larragoite School
Leah Harvey Jr. High—now U.S. District Courthouse
New Mexico School for the Deaf—six buildings still in use including hospital and school building #2, on the State Registry
Salazar—original building demolished, new school built
Santa Fe Indian School—old remodeled buildings demolished
Wood Gormley—still in use

Stanley—demolished
Tesuque—still in use, expanded
Venus—abandoned trading post

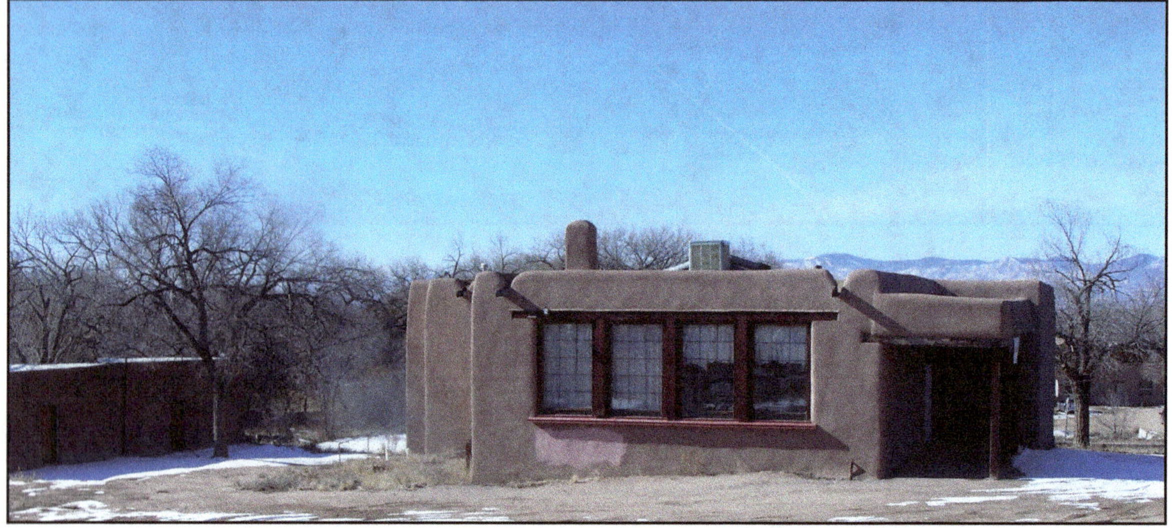

This WPA school continues to serve the residents of this northern portion of Santa Fe County which helps the folks in Pojoaque also. Photograph provided by the center.

Sierra County

Arrey—(1936) elementary school still in use
Caballo—community center (may have been a CCC building)
Cuchillo—school gone
Derry—school gone
Hillsboro—former high school now community center, on National Register
Hot Springs (now Truth or Consequences):

Early Public School with WPA addition, County Office, Date Street
Former High School, Second Street
Expanded High School/Gym—Civic Center

Kingston—still in use, Community Center
Lake Valley—Bureau of Reclamation Museum/Office
Monticello—still standing, badly deteriorated
San Miguel—school gone

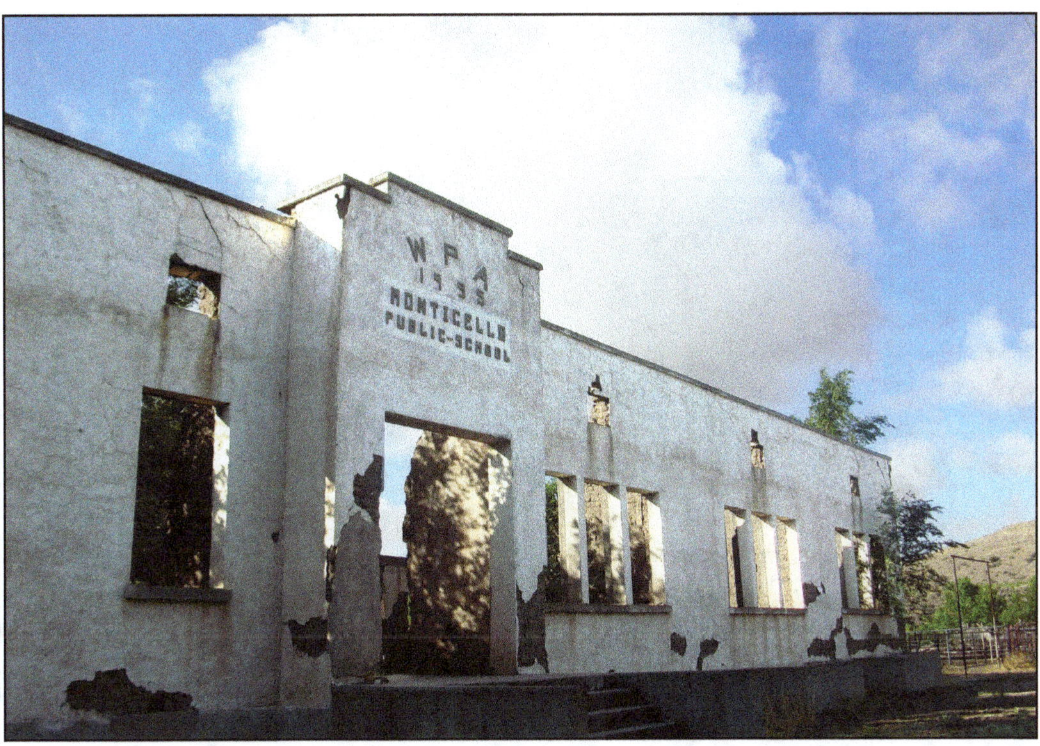

Monticello's adobe school in rural Sierra County no longer has a roof and tall trees have grown up inside the four walls. The playground area surrounding it is now a corral for livestock and hay. Photograph by Kathryn A. Flynn.

Socorro County

Alamillo—private residence
Bingham—abandoned, school now private property
Claunch—school still standing, deteriorating
Contreras—school closed, status of building unknown
Escondida—abandoned community
Las Nutrias
Lemitar—new fire station on that site now
Magdalena—gym now owned by local theater group
New Mexico Technical University—various buildings
Polvadera—private residence
Sabinal
San Acacio—private residence
San Antonio—still in use
San Antonito—flooded out
San Pedro—abandoned 1953
Scholle—abandoned community, status of school building unknown
Socorro
- Grade School no longer used.
- High School now municipal offices, police department and alternative school

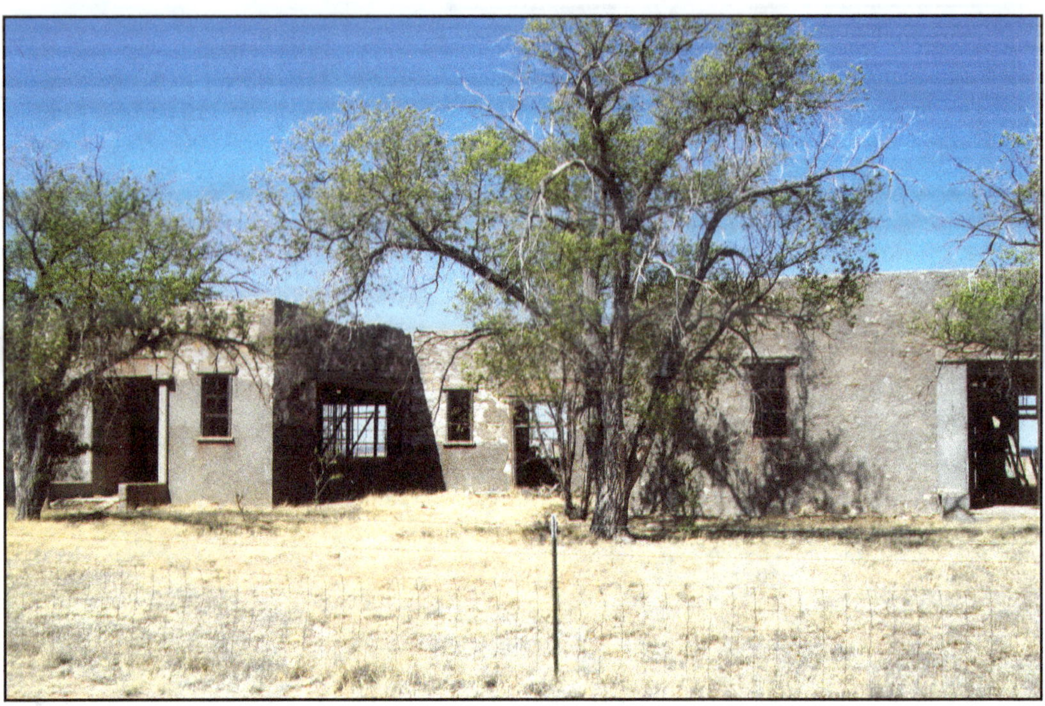

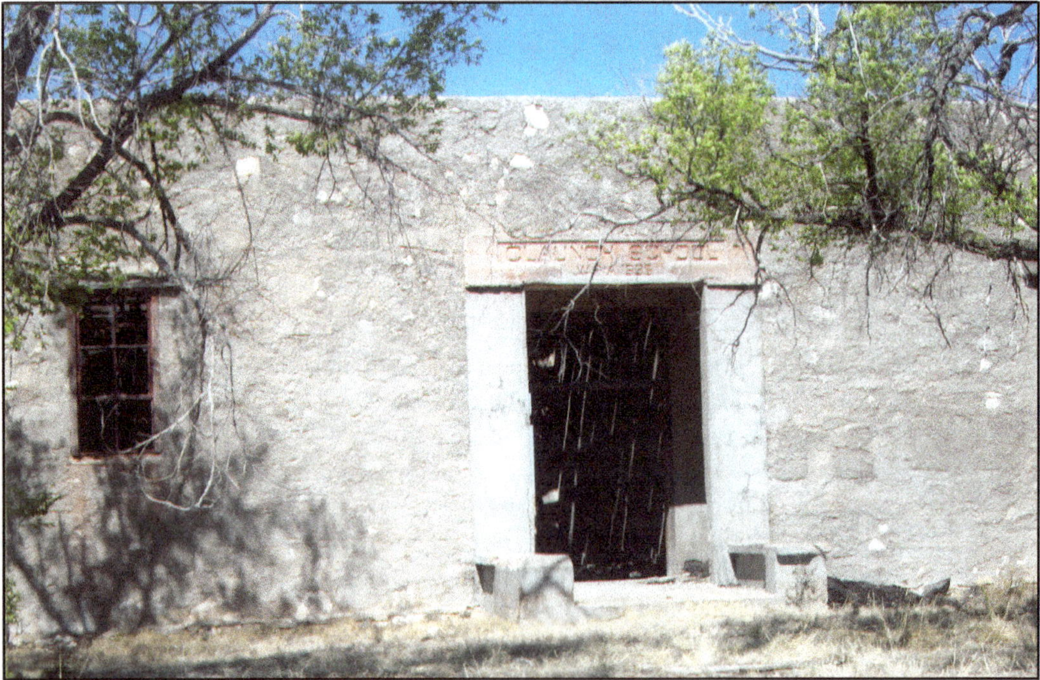

These buildings in Claunch now crumbling are identified as a tribute to all those school houses in New Mexico that were built out on its prairies.

Taos County

Amalia—still standing and community is considering making it a community center
Arroyo Hondo—community center
Arroyo Seco—community center
Canon—Chrysalis Alternative School
Cerro
Chamisal—still standing
Costilla—closed except gymnasium still in use
Llano Quemado—Headstart Program
Ojo Caliente
Pilar
Questa—day care center
Ranchos de Taos
Rodarte—still standing
San Cristobal—community center
Skarda—abandoned community
Talpa—community center
Taos—junior high still in use, Enos Garcia Elementary School (1940) still in use
Vadito—still in use, possibly Headstart Program

Torrance County

Cedarvale—deteriorating badly, on State Historic Register
Center Point
Derramoderro
Encino—gym falling down
Estancia—may be open, status of building unknown
Gran Quivera—school closed, status of building unknown
Lincoln—private residence
Lucero
Manzano
Moriarty
Mountainair
Old Abo—school closed, status of building unknown
Palma—abandoned community, status of building unknown
Pedernal—community virtually abandoned, status of school building unknown
Pinos Wells—community virtually disappeared during drought of 1917–20
Punta de Agua—little known about this earlier settlement
Roundtop—school closed, status of building unknown
Torreon—school closed, status of building unknown
Tres Piedras
Willard—school closed, status of building unknown

Union County

Amistad—community center
Atencio—demolished
Capulin—demolished
Clapham—private residence, also restoring teacherage
Clayton—high, junior schools and Kiser Elementary still in use
Des Moines—demolished, rock wall still exists
Folsom—privately owned but used as community center
Goodson—deteriorating
Grenville—deteriorating
Hayden—rock fence around abandoned school area
Lakeview—nothing left
Miera—walls still standing
Mt. Dora—only rock wall left
Otto—some walls still standing
Pacheco—nothing left of building
Pasamonte—nothing left of building
Pennington—nothing left of building
Perico—nothing left of building
Sedan—demolished
Seneca—demolished
Sofia—private dentention facility
Spring Creek—nothing left of building
Sutton—nothing left of building
Thomason—nothing left of building

Valencia County (In 1981 the county was divided into Cibola and Valencia counties)

Adelino—gym still in use
Belen—still in use
Bosque Farms—(1936), still in use, New Deal resettlement town
El Cerro—community unknown
Jarales—community center, on State Registry
Los Lentes—annexed to Los Lunas in 1970s, status of building unknown
Los Lunas—(1938) Raymond Gabaldon Elementary, still in use
Peralta—a private home, on State Historic Register
Tome—community exists, school unknown

VOCATIONAL SCHOOL LOCATIONS

Abiquiú
Agua Fria
Albuquerque
Antón Chico
Atarque
Cerrillos
Cerro
Chupadero
La Ciénega
Clayton
Costilla
Coyote
Las Cruces
Cundiyó
Delia
El Rito
Española
Galisteo

Gallup
Glorieta
Grants
Hot Springs
Las Trampas
Las Vegas
Lemitar
Los Lunas
Mesilla
Monticello
Mora
Peñasco
Pojoaque
Puerto de Luna
Questa
El Rito
San José
San Gerónimo
Santa Cruz
Santa Rosa
Seboyeta
Socorro
Stanley
Taos

3

NEW MEXICO'S NEW DEAL ART WORK CONSERVED BY THE NEW MEXICO CHAPTER of the NATIONAL NEW DEAL PRESERVATION ASSOCIATION

The following pieces of art were determined to be in poor or fair condition and have been conserved by the New Mexico chapter of the National New Deal Preservation Association. They are all in our public buildings.

Alamogordo—3 paintings
Albuquerque—5 paintings
Carrie Tingley Hospital—14 paintings and 1 sculpture were conserved through other funds.
Conchas Dam—1 mural
Clayton—20 paintings
El Rito—1 tryptych mural
Fort Stanton—19 paintings
Gallup—16 paintings, 4 murals
Las Cruces—1 painting, 4 murals (New Mexico State University)
Enamel paint had covered the 4 murals but was removed and the murals were conserved in 2011.
Las Vegas—7 murals (New Mexico Highlands University)
All 7 had coats of white paint covering them. The white paint was removed and all 7 were conserved in 2011. An eighth one is missing.
Lordsburg—1 painting
Los Lunas—1 painting
Melrose—7 paintings, 3 etchings
Portales—3 murals, 2 paintings, 3 etchings
Raton—8 paintings, 4 etchings
Roswell—1 painting, 1 pastel
Santa Fe—5 Santos, 5 murals, 9 paintings, 1 etching, 2 pencil drawings, 1 bronze bust
Silver City—2 murals
Socorro—1 painting, 3 etchings
Taos—17 paintings, 5 etchings

4

WHAT PUBLIC ART IS STILL MISSING IN WHAT TOWNS?

The New Mexico Chapter of the National New Deal Preservation has made numerous attempts to find all the following art works but with minimal success. Nine etchings were done by Gene Kloss and six lithographs were created by B.J.O. Nordfeldt. The group plans to continue their search and hope you will join us. Please let them know if you have information regarding the disposition and/or whereabouts of the following art or any other pieces that were created originally as a result of the New Deal federally funded programs for the visual arts. These programs took place between 1933 and 1943. The art was supposed to be hung or be placed in public buildings or ones that were tax supported. Most artwork started out there but some moved elsewhere. These "moves" may have been planned or otherwise. Some art works were in schools that burned down and others may have been destroyed for some unknown reason. Poor record keeping of these situations has left us with these "Unsolved Mysteries of Art."

Identifying their whereabouts doesn't mean that the owner will be fined or punished. They will be encouraged to return them either to the original public facility or some other public building of their choice. Identification of the art work is the prime goal and the old brass plaques on the lower center frame will help with that identification. If there is no plaque there may be two small nail holes where the plaque was originally. Please share any discovery information by writing to:

The National New Deal Preservation Association
P. O. Box 602
Santa Fe New Mexico 87504

or call:

Kathryn A. Flynn, (505) 473-3985 or email to: newdeal@cybermesa.com with any information that you might have or find.

GENE KLOSS MISSING ARTWORK IN FOLLOWING SCHOOLS

These etchings were done in groups but may have been separated when distributed around the state. They are all black and white etchings, 20"x26" in size.

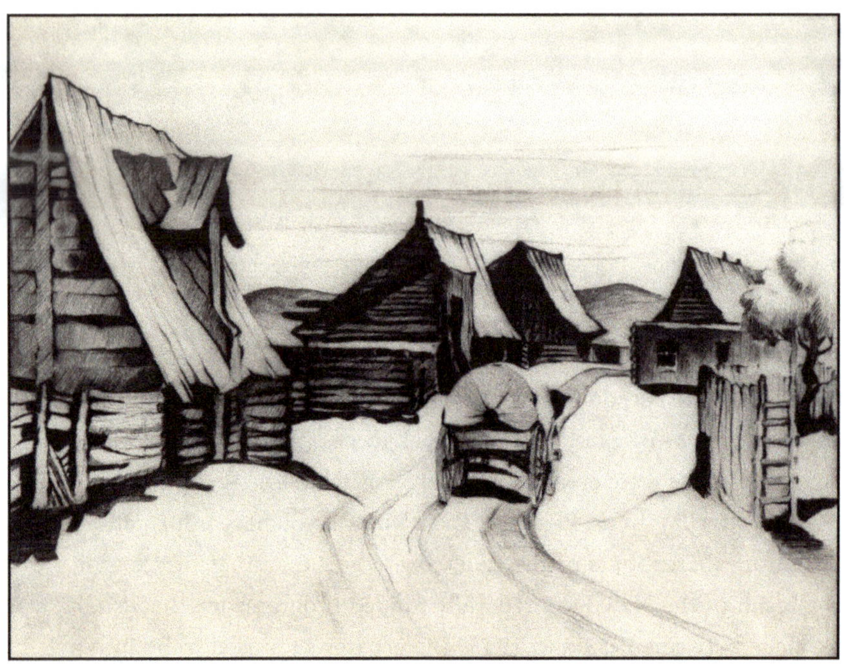

"New Mexico Mountain Town"*

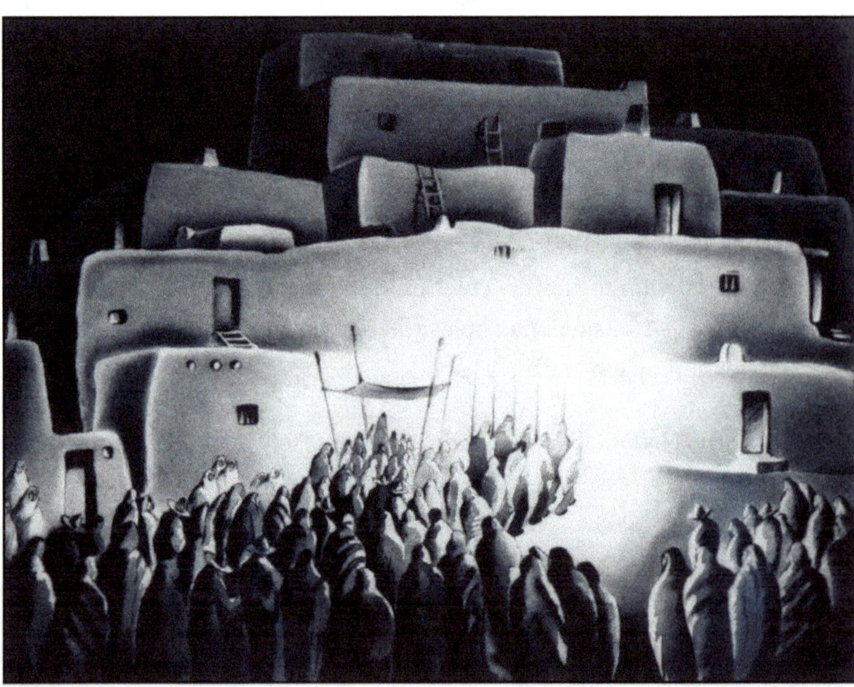

"Christmas Eve, Taos Pueblo"*

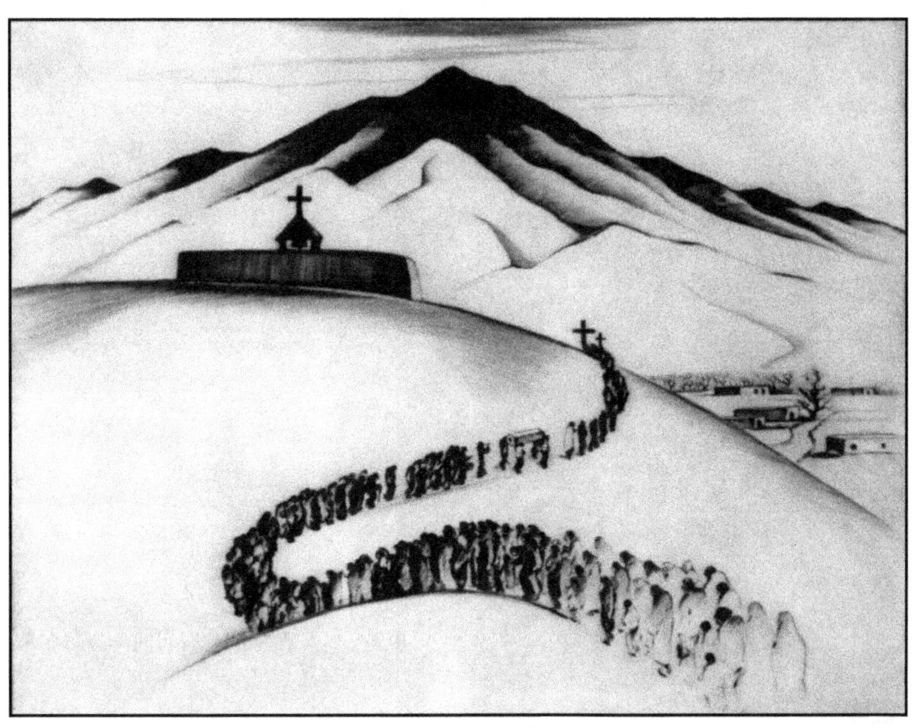

"Penitente Good Friday"*

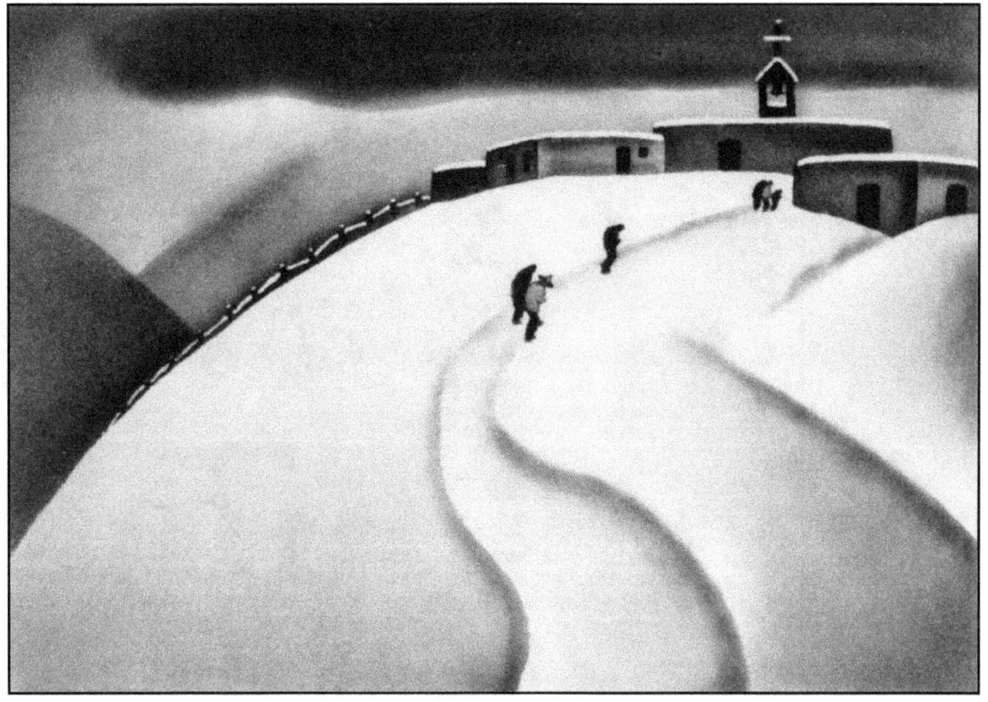

"Winter Mass"*

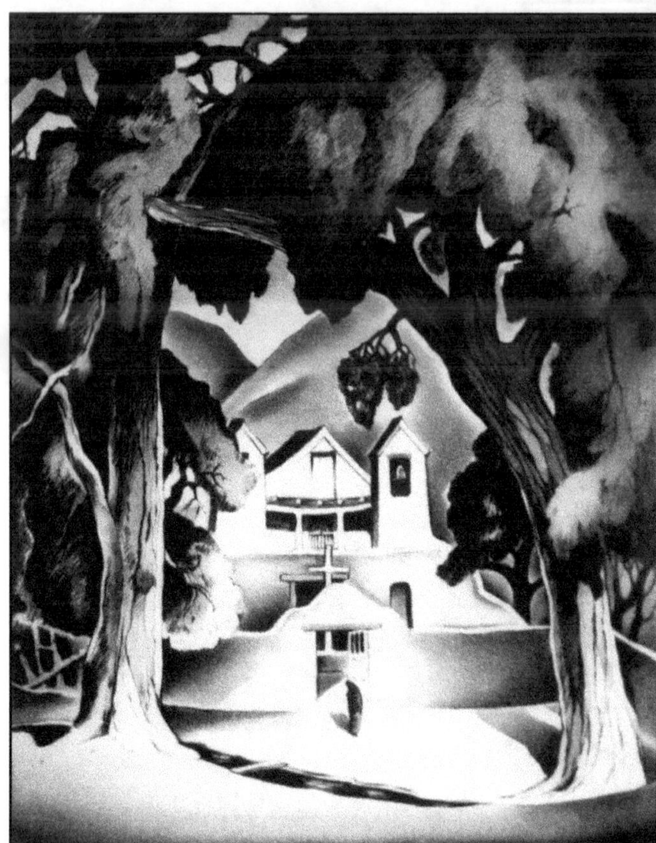

"The Sanctuary, Chimayo"*

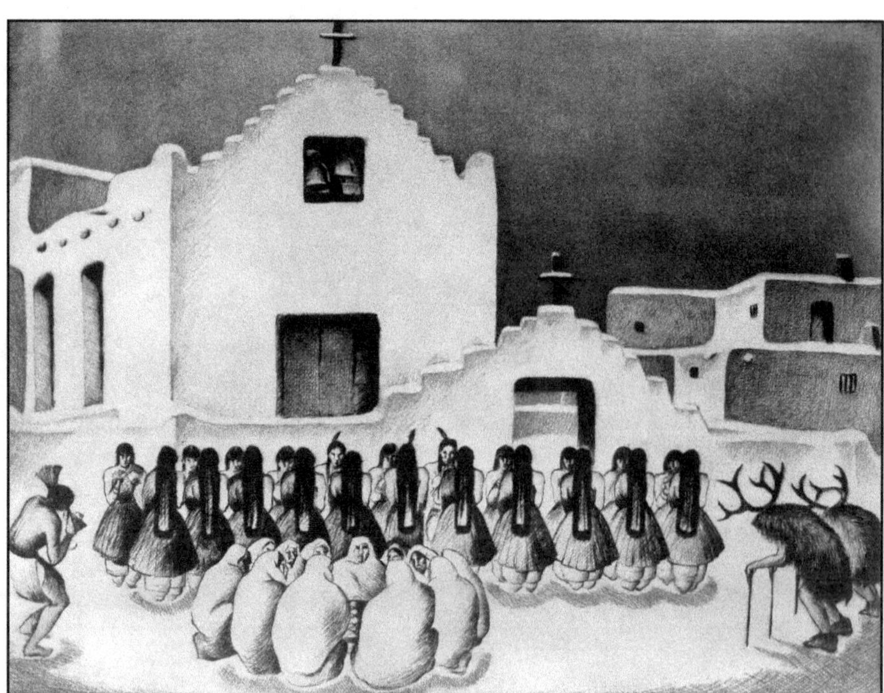

"Indian Ceremony"*

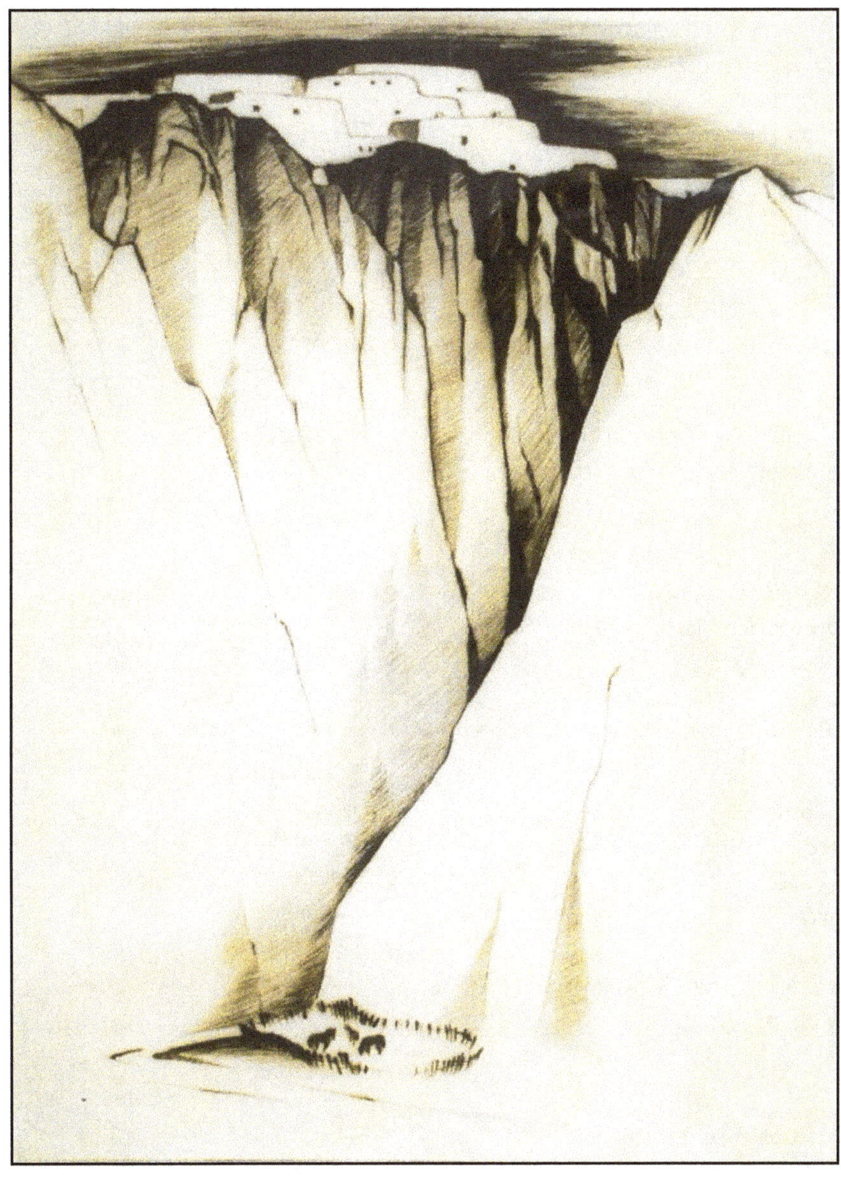

Acoma"

Photographs by Pat Berrett from *A More Abundant Life, New Deal Artists and Public Art in New Mexico*, courtesy of Sunstone Press.

GROUP A:

"Indian Ceremony"
"Indian Pueblo"
"Indian Harvest"

LOCATIONS where Group A was distributed:

Albuquerque public schools, University of New Mexico
Artesia
Carlsbad
Deming
Gallup
Las Vegas, "New" or Old Town schools and Highlands University
Lordsburg
Mountainair
Raton
Roswell
Santa Fe
Silver City
Tucumcari

GROUP B:

"Sanctuary Chimayo"
"New Mexico Mountain Town"
"Winter Mass"

LOCATIONS where Group B was distributed:

Alamogordo
Anthony
Aztec
Carlsbad
Clovis
Cuba
Las Vegas, "New" Town or "East" School
Lovington
Magdalena
Mora
Portales
Raton
Santa Fe
Tularosa
Tucumcari

GROUP C:

"Christmas Eve, Taos Pueblo"
"Penitente Good Friday"
"Acoma"

LOCATIONS where Group C was distributed:

Belen
Elida
El Rito–Northern New Mexico College
Farmington
Hurley
Las Cruces
Santa Fe
Taos
Tierra Amarilla
Truth or Consequences

B.J.O. NORDFELDT MISSING ARTWORK

These black and white lithographs were 10"x13" in size and were also distributed primarily to the public schools.

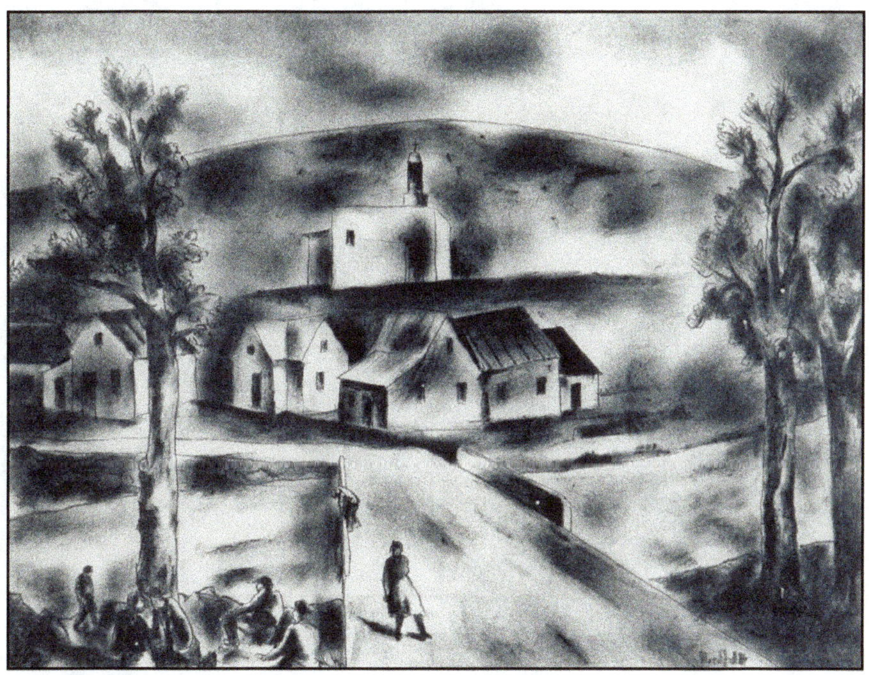

"Tres Ritos"

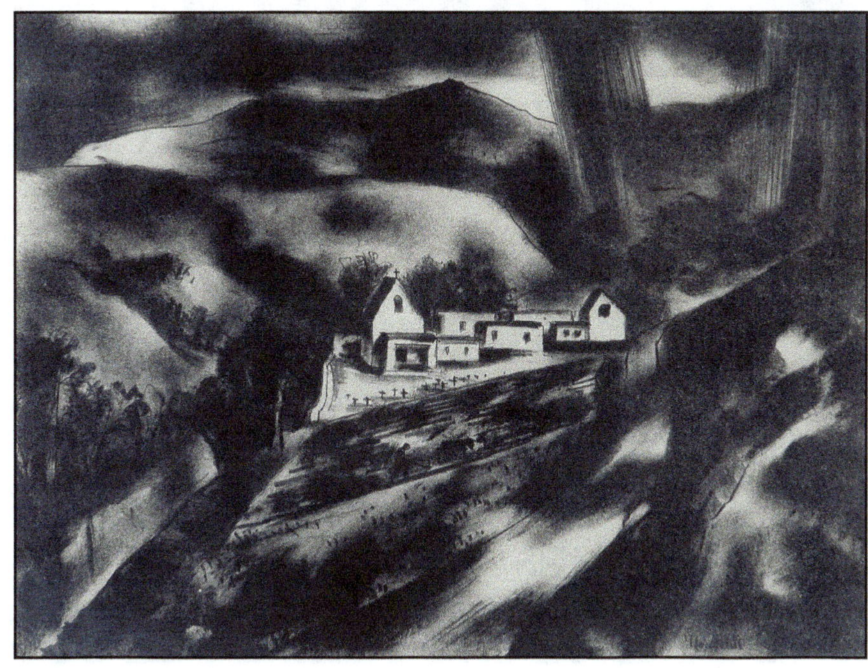

"Rio en Medio"

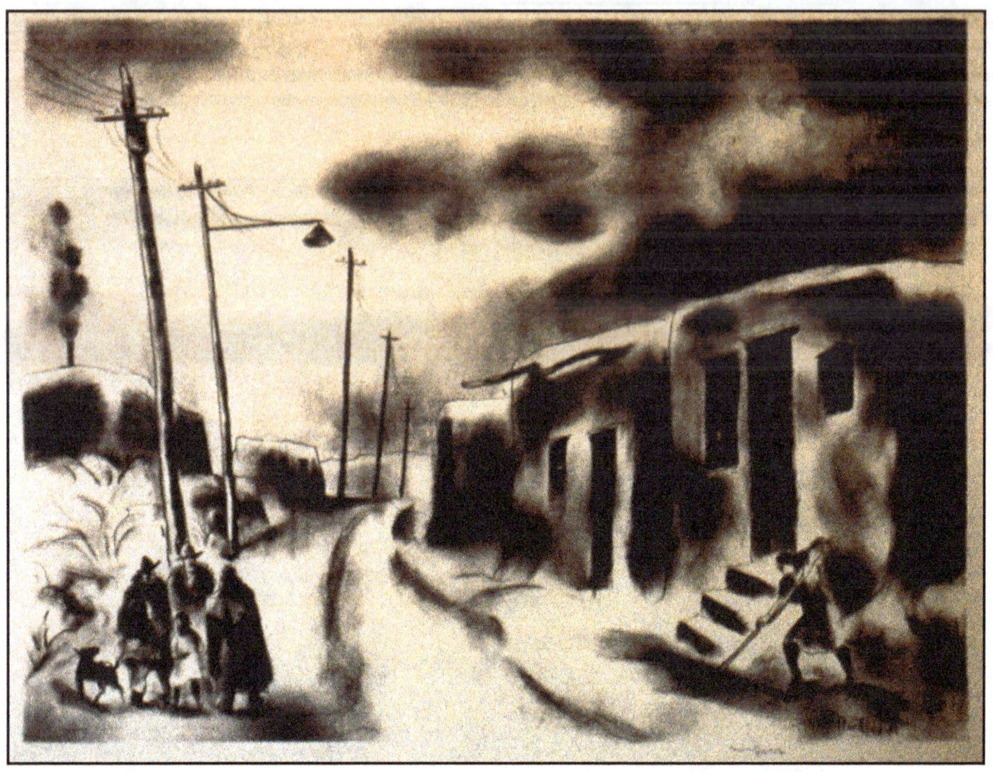

"Canyon Road"

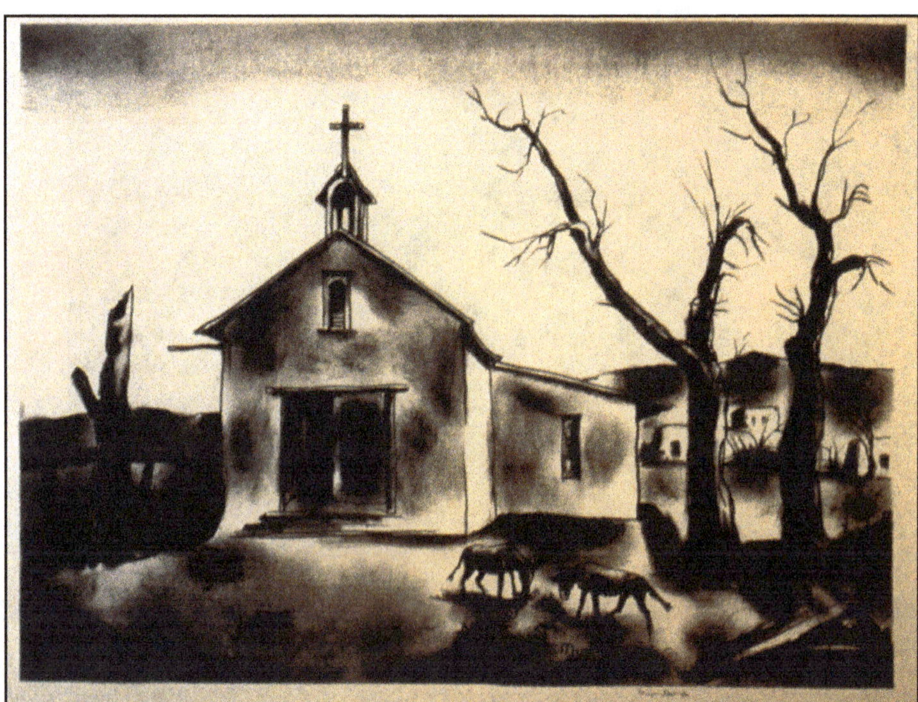

"Morada,
Santa Cruz"

Photographs by Pat Berrett from *A More Abundant Life, New Deal Artists and Public Art in New Mexico*, courtesy of Sunstone Press.

GROUP A:

"Tres Ritos"
"Morada Santa Cruz"
"Canyon Road"

LOCATIONS where Group A was distributed:

Alamogordo
Albuquerque
Gallup
Grants
Las Cruces
Mosquero
Roswell
Santa Rosa
Silver City–Western New Mexico University
Springer
Taos
Tres Ritos
Vaughn

GROUP B:

1. "Rio in Media"
2. "Cerrillos"
3. "Water Street"

LOCATIONS where Group B was distributed:

Albuquerque
Artesia
Belen
Capitan
Carlsbad
Clovis
Deming
Hurley
Las Cruces
Las Vegas, "New Town" School
Portales
Raton
Socorro
Tucumcari
Wagon Mound

OTHER MISSING NEW DEAL ART IN NEW MEXICO

Albuquerque:
Old Post Office (2 Martin Hennings paintings, 6 Stuart Walker watercolor paintings)
Old Bernalillo County Courthouse (1 Stuart Walker mural, 1 Brooks Willis mural)
Former Girls Welfare Facility (1 Carl Redin painting)

Deming:
Unknown location (1 Millard Everingham painting)

El Rito:
Northern New Mexico College (1 mural by Charles Barrows and James Morris)

Fort Stanton:
U.S. Hospital (71 watercolors, various artists)

Las Cruces:
New Mexico State University (1 Howard Schleeter painting)

Las Vegas:
Former Veeder Museum (1 Omar Hearn painting)

Portales:
Eastern New Mexico University (1 Nils Hogner painting)

Raton:
Raton Middle School (1 John Jellicoe mural)

Santa Fe:
State Capitol (1 La Verne Nelson Black painting)
State Capitol or Governor's Mansion (1 Fremont Ellis painting)
Department of Transportation (1 Fremont Ellis painting)

Silver City:
New Mexico Western University (1 Sheldon Parsons painting)

Socorro:
New Mexico Tech University (10 panels in tin frames)

Springer:
New Mexico Boys School (1 Fremont Ellis painting)

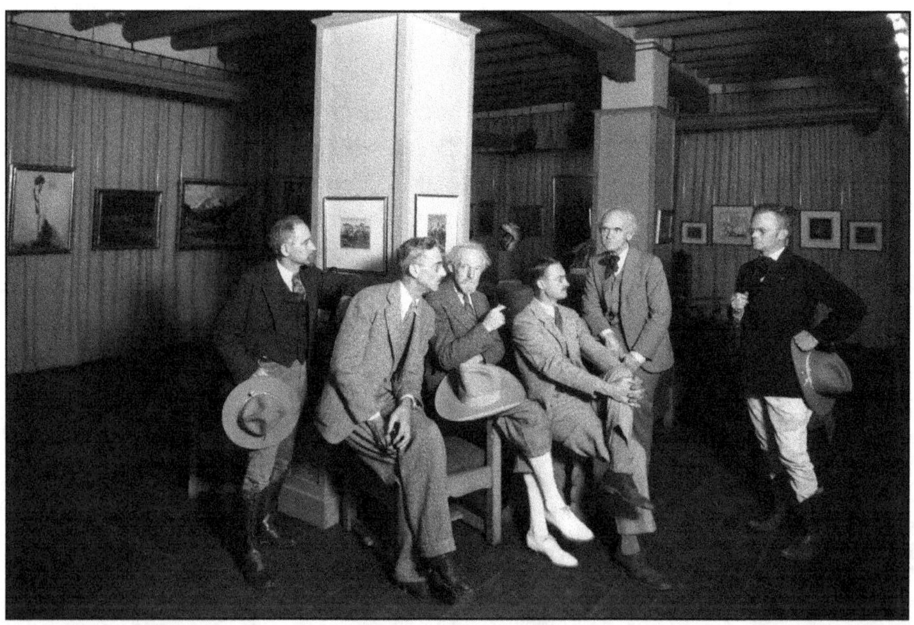

Santa Fe artists including three New Dealers "cleaned up" for a public exhibit of their art at La Fonda Hotel in 1933. From left to right: Carlos Vierra, Datus Myers, Sheldon Parsons, Theodore Van Soelen, Gerald Cassidy and Will Shuster. Myers was a supervisor of the New Deal Indian art projects. Cassidy died while working on his New Deal mural. Photograph by T. Harmon Parkhurst #20787 in State Photo Archives.

5

WHAT DID THE NEW DEAL DO FOR NEW MEXICO'S ANGLO ARTISTS?

I Create To Survive And I Survive To Create

Louise Turner / Sandra D'Emilio

Letter from Will Shuster in Santa Fe to John Sloan in New York:

> November 11, 1933
>
> Dear Sloan,
>
> "...I have been able to make all told since I returned from the homestead only $75....
>
> "The merchants here...are now beginning to feel the pinch and are consequently beginning to pinch the other fellow...I am trying my damndest to meet all my current bills and letting the old ones ride until such time as I get the cash to pay them. Yesterday I had to tell the light company to turn the godam (sic) electricity off if they wouldn't play on those terms and that I would use kerosene lamps. However, they didn't turn it off notice.
>
> "All of them are getting tough as hell. Except might say, Kaune's [local grocery store(s), in existence since late 1800s].
>
> "The etching business is non-existent...
>
> "I started to paint but had lousy luck and then I realized I had to do something to make a little money..."[1]

Thus it was late in the year 1933 that Santa Fe artist Will Shuster expressed his financial woes to his good friend, New York artist John Sloan, renowned as one of "The Eight" or "The Ashcan School," who annually spent time in Santa Fe.

The hardships of painter Shuster were replicated thousands of times over among artists country-wide, and his plight bespoke those of construction workers, clerical personnel, engineers, teachers, merchants—America's working class as well. Shuster's words admitted the reality of a bleak and frightening future for the US community at large.

Across the country, fifteen million people were unemployed. Franklin Delano Roosevelt, who had been President of the United States for only a few months, faced potential economic, social and political disasters for his country, generated by the stock market crash of 1929.

For the artist, the collapse of the stock market equated the collapse of the art market: art collectors and patrons, now without stock dividend income that provided the means for the acquisition of "luxury" items, could not purchase art. The romance of the timeless sobriquet "starving artist" took on urgent and less than romantic connotation and warning.

But on December 7, 1933, "Shus" wrote once more to Sloan. This letter is one of ebullience and optimism, a far cry from his missive of the previous month.

> "The most important thing which has happened to the Shuster family is this Federal Art Project. (Shuster's wording is not to be confused with Federal Arts Project, implemented in August 1936). Forty-two fifty a week from the Government for painting. My God it doesn't seem real. The day after I landed the job I had to go to bed. That's a big help. I suggested three projects for myself: 1. to paint a series of portraits of the distinguished Indian artists of this region. 2. To redesign the currency and stamps of the United States using Indian design elements. 3. To do a series of large paintings of the Carlsbad Caverns for distribution in public buildings.
>
> "Number three was handed to me as a job of work. Gosh, John, I think this is a tremendous opportunity for us to put something over in a big way ...I think it would be a good thing for all organizations of artists all over the country to write every one connected with the inauguration of this movement an appreciatory note to help us keep the ball a-rolling."[2]

Ultimately, Shuster created a number of paintings of the Carlsbad Caverns. One group of four large pieces was done in 1934 for the PWAP program but they have never been found. Black and white photos of them can be found in Lois Manno's recent book, *Visions Underground: Carlsbad Caverns Through the Artist's Eye*. However some done later were acquired by the National Park Service and have been stored in the Western Archaeological Conference Center in Tucson, Arizona. He was awarded a second Public Works of Art Project (PWAP) project: to paint fresco murals on the walls enclosing the patio of the Museum of Fine Arts in Santa Fe.

It is interesting to note that a weekly wage of $42.50 in 1933 was the equivalent of $472.00 per week in 1992. Today its relative difference would be even greater.

What exactly was the cause for Shuster's elation scarcely a month after his expressions of despair and near hopelessness? What was the "Federal Art Project" of which he spoke with such fervor, indeed, that necessitated his taking to his bed, nearly sick, one might assume, with relief and joy over the assurance of income for doing what he did best—creating art?

Specifically, it was the PWAP, the first federally funded art program under the Civil

Works Administration (CWA)—a New Deal work-relief program created by President Roosevelt to alleviate the economic job crisis in this country. In time, all the federal art projects have come to be generically referred to as "WPA Art," WPA the acronym for Works Progress Administration.

The CWA was administered by socially conscious Harry Hopkins whose heartfelt belief was that "artists have to eat like other people." The PWAP started in December 1933 and continued until June 1934, and was the brainchild of artist George Biddle, a former schoolmate of Roosevelt at Groton and Harvard.

An advocate of mural art in America, Biddle had studied with the Mexican muralist, Diego Rivera, and it was his belief that Rivera, with Mexican muralists Jose Clemente Orozco and David Alfaro Siquieros, gave voice to the social ideals of the Mexican Revolution of 1910 through their vivid, colorful murals. It would follow, he believed, that murals painted by American artists in the United States would be appropriate vehicles for the expression of the ideals of President Roosevelt's New Deal. He perceived the achievements of the Mexican muralists as "grand", and believed that young American artists would be eager to express the ideals of a Roosevelt-guided social revolution on the public walls of America where they would help achieve Roosevelt's social ideals, and remain as lasting monuments to them. The artistic community would welcome and embrace the government's cooperation.

As well, in this country, the work of American muralist, Thomas Hart Benton, had virtually exploded across the milieu of the private sector, and his popular motifs seemed to open a door to the feasibility of creating popular mural art under a federal umbrella.

The time was right, and Biddle expressed the thought that "a little impetus" was all that was needed to generate national expression and national excitement in the possibility of mural art that depicted social consciousness.

A little impetus! New Mexico artists benefited significantly from Biddle's little impetus. In the early days of January, 1934, an article in the *Albuquerque Journal* noted that 100 New Mexico artists had been assigned CWA art projects which would beautify selected New Mexico public buildings, and that the projects would be funded with federal money.

For nearly a decade these New Mexico artists worked under various federally funded programs which included Public Works of Art Project (PWAP), 1933–1934; the Works Progress and later Projects Administration/Federal Arts Projects (WPA/FAP), 1935–1943; the Treasury Relief Art Project (TRAP), 1935–1939; and The Section, 1934–1943. New Mexico was, with Arizona, number 13 of sixteen regional districts across the nation.

The administrative team for Region 13 was a distinguished one. New Mexico anthropologist Jesse Nusbaum was the director, another anthropologist, Kenneth Chapman, served as secretary and Gustave Baumann, a woodblock printer and one of Santa Fe's favorite artists, was regional coordinator. They were assisted in selecting public sites, obtaining public funds for materials, and in deciding on themes for works to be commissioned by an equally distinguished and capable volunteer committee: United States Senator Bronson

Cutting, esteemed Santa Fe architect John Gaw Meem, and social activist writer Mary Austin of Santa Fe.

Collectively and individually, they recognized the existence of potential difficulties. For example, mural painting would be a first for most New Mexico artists and fitting a painting into a predetermined architectural space would present a unique problem. Narrow hallways, stairwells and areas surrounding elevators presented challenges in terms of the utilization of color, composition, scale, and most of all, the artists would be working with new and unfamiliar materials and techniques particular to mural painting. While such problems were given appropriate attention and concern, they were not perceived as insurmountable.

Fired with verve generated by—at long last—optimism for a productive and economically more stable future for a significant number of gifted New Mexico artists, the administrative and volunteer teams, with the help of project-designated artists, launched the monumental task of selecting towns and sites for consideration for artwork.

For instance, Gus Baumann and artist Theodore Van Soelen trekked from northern to southern New Mexico in a less-than-reliable vintage Ford in the cold winter months of 1934 to inspect federal courthouses, post offices, universities and libraries as potential sites for murals as well as for easel paintings. Their journeys were often impeded by snow and vehicular breakdowns, necessitating that the artists momentarily turn their attention to mechanical matters! Other team members went to theaters, hospitals, office buildings, trading posts, auditoriums, high schools, national parks, federal offices and museums. In this book we have identified approximately 110 buildings.

Initially, sites were inspected in Albuquerque, Las Vegas, Raton, Taos, Santa Fe, Roswell, Carlsbad and Artesia, and indeed "WPA Art," appears today at all these sites except Artesia. That community has a rock wall around its New Deal football field that has artistic rock formations (flowers, a cross, etc.) embedded in this vast structure. Ultimately and incredibly, over 40 communities in New Mexico boast approximately 1000 pieces of New Deal public art, including murals, easel paintings, pottery, sculpture, and furniture and craft items.

The projects, under their various federal titles, were not in place simultaneously. As artists, administrators, mural sites and plans for specific works of art in towns and cities were determined for each given project over periods of time, the quintessential component was finally addressed creating a picture.

Yes, a vast, historical picture. Mural painters, sculptors, easel painters, potters, furniture makers, embroiderers, tinsmiths, woodcarvers faced the exhilarating job of creating a visual history of New Mexico, an arts and crafts "picture book" of the hand of Enchantment. If the murals might be considered the front piece for New Mexico's picto-biography, then the other arts and crafts forms could be viewed as the intimate portraits and sketches of the New Mexico memoir.

But nearly a half century after their completion, the magnitude and brilliance of the enormous body of work produced cannot ultimately be confined by the simplicity of an analogy to a picture book. Rather, the deep ebony of the black-on-black pottery coiled by Tewa artists, the long, elegant lines of the trasteros crafted by Hispanic craftsmen, the drama, color, poignancy, anguish or triumph conceived by the mural and easel painters, and the vivid detail defined by the sculptors are more than a story in pictures. They are a rich, patterned, textured mosaic, each art form a vibrant tile in the finished work.

Energized by creative challenge and the welcome assurance of financial remuneration for work done (recall that Shuster's letter to Sloan revealed elation and raw incredulity), the artists began preparations for their work. Decisions as to themes and subject matter were the first order of business to be dealt with for this exhilarating creative endeavor.

The "American Scene," as advocated by American muralists, Thomas Hart Benton, Grant Wood and John Steuart Curry, depicted local and regional American themes, or "Democrat art"—art for the people. American Scene painting, the earlier Mexican mural movement, and the Depression phenomena all combined to inspire New Deal art.

In the case of the New Mexico artists and craftsmen, an additional source of inspiration and subject matter was at hand: the rich multi-cultural heritage of a state scarcely out of territorialism. New Mexico was the 47th state to be admitted to the Union, and in 1933, at 21 years of age, had barely achieved "adulthood." Many of the artists selected by the WPA were older by many years than the fledgling state, and could draw upon personal or family memories and knowledge of a land and a diverse people struggling for rights, recognition and a measure of reward.

The ancient Anasazi, the coming of the Spanish "conquistadors" and their impact on the lives of the Pueblo Indians, the frontier towns and their colorful, violent histories, the Pueblo rebellions, Mountain Men, Indian dances and ceremonials, the wildlife—buffalo, bighorn sheep, and grizzlies, the opening of the frontier, the dramatic, ever-changing topography of the huge state, the coming of the railroad, ranchers, farmers, trappers, cowboys, the Pentitentes, Apache and Comanche raids, and outlaws were but a sampling of the myriad of possible subjects for artwork. As well, philosophical and political themes came under consideration, as did those dealing with law and order, science, medicine, and obedience.

It is not difficult to imagine the frenzied excitement, the fervor of creativity, the challenges, the attention to detail, and dedication of the artists and administrators associated with the WPA project. Each surely must have had a special experience, a unique or difficult or absorbing one, in creating their work. Of the many anecdotes that bespeak the enthusiasm and creativity of the artists and the tireless work of the administrators involved in the WPA project in New Mexico, the following profiles reveal certain individual characteristics of the WPA participants which are at once personal, professional, devoted, inventive, often amusing, and always human.

Virginia Hunter Ewing, widow of Russell Vernon Hunter, recalled that her husband, himself a muralist and one of the significant creators of WPA art, was appointed State Director for the project in 1935. Although the Director's job was not conducive to "relaxed nights of peaceful sleep,"[3] and that the Director was constantly on demand to "juggle requirements, needs, objections,"[4] Vernon Hunter, and one other State Director were the only two in the United States who neither resigned nor were replaced."[5]

Hunter, unlike many of his muralist contemporaries who were transplants to New Mexico from the East (some for reasons of health), grew up six miles northwest of Texico, where his parents had homesteaded. He therefore had a lifelong, comprehensive perspective of "his" New Mexico. He researched his subject matter thoroughly. The combination resulted in three American realism murals titled "The Last Frontier" located at the De Baca County Courthouse in Fort Sumner. To prepare for the work, Hunter interviewed hundreds of pioneers of the area, studied legends and photos for the work, and collected historical facts. Various reporters, in reviewing the work for their periodicals, noted that one figure in one of the murals, Billy the Kid, had his left hand on his gun (Hunter's research had turned up the fact that the gunslinger was left-handed), and that an image of Billy's mother in the mural had a ribbon on top of her head to hide a wound in her skull caused at an earlier time by an Indian tomahawk. Hunter had found an old tintype of the mother's image, which he studied at length, and found documentation that supported the tomahawk story. And, it was noted, the mother's right eyebrow drew upward, as did that of her notorious son!

Another descendant of a pioneering family, Manville Chapman, had graduated from Raton High School, attended the Art Institute of Chicago, and returned to New Mexico where he painted in Raton and Taos. When awarded a commission to paint WPA murals, he boldly advertised in his hometown newspaper, the Raton Range, for old photographs to study, particularly those of old buildings, old trails, old railroad engines, old costumes, old famous characters, and emphasized that scenic photos would be of no help to him at all! Evidently the community responded, and with these images, in combination with his own lively imagination and spirit of creativity, he produced at least eight murals depicting a wealth of early New Mexico history. He painted Indian villages and mansions of the era, a stage coach line station and early coal mines. Today, these murals are located in the foyer of the Shuler Theater in Raton.

The "Fresco Quartette" of Taos executed, not without mishap, 10 of the most stunning frescoes of the WPA era. At the Old Federal Taos County Courthouse in Taos are the combined works of Emil Bisttram, Ward Lockwood, Victor Higgins and Bert Phillips. They are "American Scene" in subject matter and moralistic in tone and emphasis, as revealed in some of the mottoes: "Avarice Breeds Crime," "Justice Begets Content," "The Shadow of Crime." It is believed that Bisttram taught the others fresco technique, and the murals depict, according to Alexandre Hogue, who wrote about the work upon its completion, "the use and misuse of law.[6] While the artistic progress was of interest to Taosenos, of equal interest was an assortment of "jinxes" which befell the artists personally, and often hindered the execution of the project: Victor Higgins frequently took to his bed, sustaining himself on a diet of milk toast; Bert Phillips fell off a scaffold, and Emil Bisttram painted six-fingered ladies. Despite these difficulties, the murals were completed and the works are regarded as outstanding examples of WPA frescoes anywhere in the United States.

William Penhallow "Whippy" Henderson had a long association with the Southwestern culture, which he loved. A native of Massachusetts, Henderson spent his very early youth with his family in Texas. When he was eight years old, he returned to Massachusetts, and in 1904, at 27, he came once again to the Southwest, specifically Arizona. In 1916, as a family man, he moved to Santa Fe with his wife, poet Alice Corbin Henderson, and "Little Alice," their young daughter. Alice, ill with tuberculosis, as was true of many of the members of the artistic community, regained her health and the Henderson family settled in as popular and respected members of the fledgling art colony. "Whippy" and "Little Alice" took long horseback rides to the various pueblos of the area or to Taos, and that on every trip, his daughter recalled years later, he observed minute details of the landscape, sometimes stopping to sketch during their horseback journeys.

"Whippy" was a Renaissance man. Painter, furniture maker, architectural designer, illustrator, scenic and costume designer, and ultimately muralist, his work—furniture, homes, renovated buildings, paintings, a museum, and murals—endure in Santa Fe today as testimony to his vast talent. When commissioned to paint murals for the WPA art project in the Federal Court House in Santa Fe, "Whippy" elected to use valleys, mountains, trails and rock monuments as his subject matter, a clear indication of his long love affair with the Southwestern landscape. He summarily dismissed the idea of painting "courthouse" scenes. The Federal Court House remains today a favorite place for visitors and locals alike to pause in a day's activity for a look at the magnificent work of William Penhallow "Whippy" Henderson.

One of the young modernists who came to the forefront of the art scene in Santa Fe in the 1920s, Willard Nash painted canvases characterized by forceful line and the use of bold color—the latter a trait he shared with his fellow Santa Fe modernists, "Los Cinco Pintores." In some of the canvases depicting sports scenes that hang in the Zimmerman Library in Albuquerque, there is a hint, too, of John Sloan's influence—groups of men and women participating in ordinary, everyday activities, such as, in this case, athletic events.

By July 22, 1992, Chiricahua Apache artist, Allan Houser, now deceased, was a long-time resident of Santa Fe. On that date he was presented with the National Medal of Arts, the nation's highest art award. This medal, awarded under the auspices of the National Endowment for the Arts, was presented to Houser by President George Bush. Back in the late 1930s, Houser painted murals for the WPA in Washington, DC with Picuris Pueblo artist, Gerald Nailor, Woodrow Crumbo, and Zia Pueblo artist, Velino Herrera. Incredibly, the self-effacing Houser believed later that the murals weren't very good, but was pleased with their later restoration. Although the bulk of Houser's work—spanning more than 50 years—is in the sculpture medium, he began as a student of painting under the tutelage of Dorothy Dunn at the Santa Fe Indian School. In 1991, the world-renowned sculptor was honored with a retrospective of his work on the occasion of his 77th birthday. A small Houser (oil) executed by the artist for the

New Mexico WPA Art Project features a Native American youth seated on a horse. The work hangs in the Raton Public Library. Another casein creation is also in the Gallup Public Library.

Although his name was not a household word among Southwestern art aficionados as were those of many other popular New Mexico artists, Lloyd Moylan's artistic output for the WPA was not only impressive creatively speaking, but prodigious in scope. Murals covering the walls of the Administration Building at New Mexico Highlands University in Las Vegas are of near titanic proportion, and address the theme of education; watercolors and oils, many of which depict Native American themes are on display in the Octavia Fellin Public Library in Gallup, and in the McKinley County Courthouse. Another colossal Moylan mural covers 2,000 square feet of the McKinley County Courthouse, and depicts centuries of New Mexico history. In the Administration Building at Eastern New Mexico University is yet another Moylan work, a religious mural, the theme for which is taken from the Scriptures. This mural might be regarded as Moylan's most ambitious work, and ultimately, may be recognized as his finest. In any case, no WPA artist utilized a greater range of subject matter, media and style (some, but not all, distinctly late cubist) than Lloyd Moylan.

Influenced by her teacher Auguste Rodin, Eugenie Shonnard brought her talent as a sculptor to New Mexico when she moved to Santa Fe in 1927. She became a close friend of Maria Martinez, the renowned potter of San Ildefonso. Shonnard's lifelong love of animals, in combination with the knowledge of animal symbolism she acquired from her Native American friends was undoubtedly another influence in her work. She sculpted a stone fountain which features a turtle and frogs (respectively, Mother Earth and cleansing symbols in the Native American culture) for the WPA art project. The fountain exists today at the New Mexico Veterans Center in Truth or Consequences.

There is irony in the fact that the various WPA art projects are often referred to as "Depression Art." If ever anything lifted spirits out of a state of depression for creator and viewer alike, it was the WPA art project. The real significance is that these works of art came into being at all—that a bold and far-seeing federal administration created something called the New Deal, a program for survival. Grateful artists and craftsmen worked and survived at the time, producing magnificent treasures that might well survive for all time.

The New Deal? A good deal! "A job of work" one artist said . . . "and a job well done."

1 From unpublished correspondence of Will Shuster and John Sloan, Courtesy Museum of New Mexico

2 Ibid.

3 From unpublished manuscript, Virginia Hunter Ewing, "*Some Memories Concerning New Mexico's WPA-Federal Arts Projects*," Santa Fe, 1988.

4 Ibid.

5 Ibid.

6 Ibid.

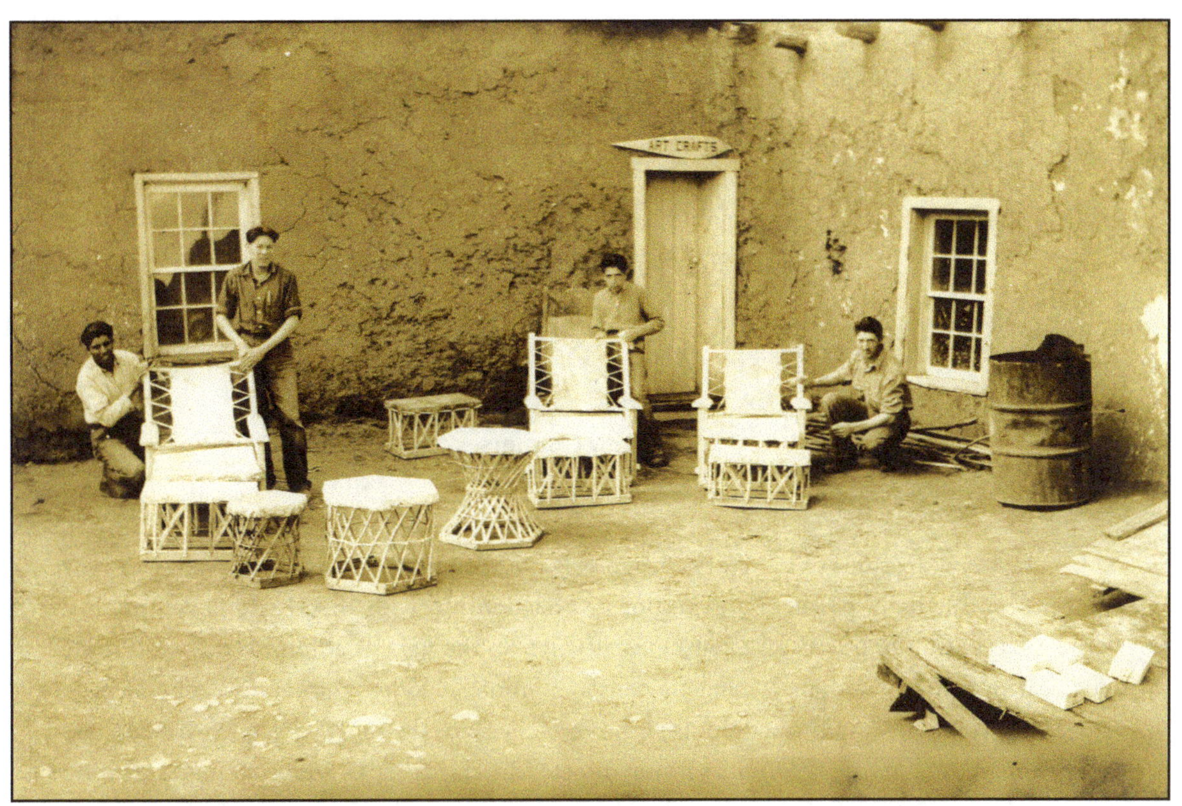

WPA, National Youth Administration (NYA) and Vocational Training programs provided opportunities to employ many Anglos and Hispanics (both young and older, male and female), to learn about how to make furniture like these in Chupadero. Tinwork, weaving, embroidery, artwork, religious art, pottery and other interior enhancements of public buildings were taught. Cooking, sewing and other crafts classes were also made available for the women all over the state. All these opportunities provided one of the first chances to bring the cultural arts and crafts of this ethnic group out for the public to view, appreciate and acquire. Photograph provided with permission from the Acequia Madre House, Curtin-Paloheimo Collection, Santa Fe, New Mexico.

6

HISPANIC ARTISTS AND ARTISANS GET MORE EXPOSURE

Andrew Connors

Several divisions of the Works Progress Administration succeeded in creating in New Mexico an intensely personal and responsive relationship with the Hispanic community. This success can be traced to a conscious attempt on the part of administrators and some dedicated staff to maintain a tangible sense of ethnic identity, community cohesiveness, and responsive training throughout their projects. Perhaps the most successful division was the Federal Art Project (FAP) which was directed by the artist R. Vernon Hunter. Hunter believed in a broad definition of "Art" which included both the fine arts and craft arts. He was dedicated to his task and encouraged his associates to imbue their wage labor creativity with an individuality and spirit in all media, from oil paintings to carved wooden religious statues and tinwork chandeliers. His personal interest in his artist colleagues was especially noteworthy with Hispanic artists and craftsmen. His diligence on their behalf, with the support of the Washington office, brought to a national audience, through exhibitions and published illustrations, the best work of the remote towns of his state.

This chapter focuses on the administrative correspondence found in the Federal Art Project records in the National Archives. These papers pertain primarily to the administrative management of the art program in New Mexico. Because of the presumably biased nature of this material, this paper will present the program as it saw itself. Because little critical analysis has been done on the art program in New Mexico, to commence such a study here would far exceed the scope of this paper. While a critical view from an exterior perspective would be helpful to place the New Mexico local program in a national context, this paper will serve as an introduction to that assessment.

As it was nationally, this period was crucial in the history of Hispanic villages in New Mexico where environmental degradation, land grant dissolution, and a lack of wage labor opportunities created social problems of monumental proportion. Long term neglect by government agencies in the form of social and economic injustices and state and federal governmental insensitivities threatened the existence of traditional, primarily pre-industrial, Hispanic communities through external cultural pressures. Various New Deal programs mandated by President Roosevelt literally saved these villages from starvation.[1] Programs for economic and social modernization led to improved standards of living, health, and nutrition.

While some local, state, and federal authorities were trying to eliminate symptoms of poverty and social inequality by destroying historical characteristics of the non-industrial Hispanic way of life, others were working with great enthusiasm and little budget to record and preserve these same traditions and life ways. Much of this preservation activity was sponsored by a series of work relief projects designed to employ artists, writers, and musicians. The idea was first tested in the Federal Works of Art Project and in New Mexico, achieved greatest success in preserving traditional arts under administration of Federal Project One of the Works Progress Administration (later renamed the Works Projects Administration). Federal Project One included the Federal Art Project, the Federal Writers' Project, the Federal Music Project, and the Federal Theater Project, though the latter was never instigated in New Mexico.

Holger Cahill, a writer, critic, authority on American folk art, and past director of exhibitions at the New York's Museum of Modern Art, was the FAP's first and only national director. The project was centrally controlled from Washington with regional advisors and state directors handling direct administration. New Mexico, with Arizona, Colorado, Utah, and Wyoming, comprised Region Five, which was administered by Donald Bear, the director for Colorado. Bear coordinated artistic activities in each of the five states and served as the liaison with Washington. R. Vernon Hunter, a respected New Mexican artist, served as first and only state director. Hunter's job consisted of the administrative direction and technical supervision of all projects under the FAP and coordination of personnel classification, placement, and assignments.

The FAP proposed, primarily, to employ artists certified for relief by their state or local relief agencies. At least ninety percent of employed staff had to have been listed on the relief register, and never was the total of non-relief workers to exceed ten percent of the total artists employed. In contrast to earlier New Deal programs which sought out the best art available for federal buildings, the FAP goal was to employ financially needy artists regardless of artistic consequences. Cahill wished to obtain for the public examples of outstanding contemporary American art, to integrate the concept of art into the daily life of the community, and to expand not only the skills of the artist but also the art consciousness of the nation. In an attempt to integrate art into the daily life of the community, educational programs, community art centers and galleries (called federal art centers), and traveling exhibitions of art produced with project support were presented to communities of all sizes which would otherwise not have been exposed to first-hand artistic activity.

The FAP in New Mexico promoted, initiated, and supervised all relief art activities in the state. In addition to commissioning easel work, prints, sculpture, and murals in fresco and oil for public buildings, the FAP supported programs for reviving craft work of Spanish-Colonial origin (woodworking, embroidery, weaving, and metalwork), teaching of arts and crafts in community art centers, researching native arts for the Index of American Design (IAD), and compiling a project unique to New Mexico, the *Portfolio of Spanish-Colonial Design*. This portfolio reproduced illustrations of arts with significant regional historical and artistic value. These and other projects were officially sponsored by the New Mexico Department of Education and the Office of the Governor. Frequently, local sponsors funded projects, either cultural or social organizations or commercial ventures interested in promoting and furthering cultural work in the state. (See Editor's Notes at the end of this section for more specifics about the *Portfolio*.)

The easel painting division was the largest single unit of the Federal Art Project. The project furnished all art supplies to the artists. The number of workers depended upon the number of artists qualified for relief and in need of work. The artists freely selected subject matter and worked in their own studios. Depending upon the size of the project, the artist had from four to eight weeks to submit a work, and every work completed by a project artist was accepted for allocation to a tax-supported organization requesting the work.

In the eyes of some critics, the art accepted by the FAP fell short of the quality of art deemed appropriate by the previous non relief projects. This may be attributed, in part, to little restriction on acceptability of products and, primarily, to the requisite that ninety percent of the employed artists be certified for relief. To a large degree, this criticism is applicable to the easel painters and those who had moved to the state from the East,[2] but is entirely incorrect in consideration of the contribution Hispanic artists and craftsmen made to the FAP.[3]

Of all the art programs in New Mexico, the FAP most benefited Hispanics by supporting and promoting arts through direct employment of artists, such as easel painter, Pedro Cervantez, saint carvers Juan Sanchez (traditional) and Patrocinio Barela (more untraditional), Jake Trujillo, weaver, and Carmen Espinoza, colcha and tin work, and others.

State Supported Projects

In addition to directing the FAP programs controlled from Washington, states established vocational training centers with federal funds. The New Mexico centers included arts and crafts instruction within the general vocational training programs which were directed by Brice H. Sewell, Supervisor of Trade and Industrial Education for the state.

(Note: According to Sarah Nestor's book, *The Native Market*, published by Sunstone Press in a new edition, the crafts program funding came about after Brice Sewell and Leonora Frances Curtin went to Washington and persuaded program directors to give New Mexico funds for this different approach to vocational training. New Mexico was the first state to receive funding for this and Sewell hired one of his former art students from the University of New Mexico Art Department, Bill Lumpkins, to teach the furniture making classes and develop the mimeographed Bluebook on Spanish woodworking and furniture making. Others hired were Henry Gonzales, a woodcarver; Dolores Perrault, a weaver and teacher; and Carmen Espinoza, a Spanish teacher and an authority on Spanish culture. They also created other Bluebooks on each craft area. Espinoza did the one on tinwork, Sewell, Perrault and Espinoza did painted chests, colcha embroidery was done by Espinoza and Perrault, vegetable dyeing by Perrault, and tanning by Sewell.)

Sewell had previously worked in New Mexico's state bureaucracy and was able to manipulate local, state, and federal funds to the advantage of Hispanic people. By combining resources, he was able to pay Hispanic men to build vocational schools that provided training for adults in a variety of traditional Hispanic crafts, including carpentry and furniture making, weaving, and black-and white-smithing. After the training programs had been completed, these schools functioned as community workshops for the use of all local craftspeople. At their heyday in 1936, there were twenty-eight vocational centers in New Mexico alone. These schools encouraged trained artists to pass their skills on to novitiates, thus contributing significantly to the revival and marketing of Hispanic crafts.

The Disposition of the Federal Art Project Toward Minorities

Holger Cahill encouraged R. Vernon Hunter, along with all the other state and regional administrators, in his sensitivity towards artists and the promotion of those with no public voice. In a letter to Taos artist, Ernest L. Blumenschein, in the early months of the FAP, Cahill wrote: "...I believe that we are helping many of the highly developed artists in these difficult times, and that we are getting some really vital work from them, especially from the young and almost unknown artists who are getting their first opportunities under our program."[4]

Programs within the WPA made several conscious attempts to address the needs of minority groups, most notably African-Americans. In 1938 a national survey was conducted to assess "the creative contribution of the Negro . . . (and) the nature and value of their work."[5] Although the Hispanic population, or "Spanish-Americans" as they were identified in correspondence, was not specifically targeted by the WPA, in New Mexico they were the largest ethnic group. The size of the population alone made them an important issue for consideration. The Native American population was assisted in economic and health issues by the less innovative United States Bureau of Indian Affairs and was not officially assisted through the WPA. Hunter, however, was able to hire a few Native Americans under his program and was sensitive to Native-American issues demonstrated in his selection of exhibitions for the local art centers.[6]

Crafts Programs in FAP

During the early planning stages of the FAP, both Donald Bear and R. Vernon Hunter recognized the importance of traditional craft work to New Mexico's Hispanic population. In January 1936, Bear wrote to Cahill that the state program had the capability of employing more than one hundred people in wood carving and native crafts. He explained that "the native wood carvers are capable of making some very excellent furniture" which could be used to supply government buildings, and that there were "one or two wood carvers in New Mexico who do very interesting and amusing wood sculpture." Such a development in crafts was dependent upon what Bear described as Hunter's ability to "work very closely" with these artisans.[7]

Cahill expressed concern over the "art quality" of such wood carving and advised serious consideration of the artistic nature of proposed projects.[8] Bear countered Cahill's position by explaining his perception of these "native craft projects" as important to the local communities, providing crucial support for public works of any sort, and relatively inexpensive in this region. Cahill had suggested that Hunter consider hiring artists who in East Coast art circles would have been called "folk artists." Hunter doubted that Cahill's proposal to feature such "peasant sculpture" at the expense of decorative arts would employ more than three artists in the entire state.[9] "He used the argument of low cost to propose that New Mexico be allowed to embark on an ambitious crafts program, "because their need is rather great."[10]

Bear followed this letter with another one two days later detailing seven crafts projects for the state for which he had already provided his authorization. These projects were all defended as legitimate under Federal Project Number One and as a most expeditious method of employing a large group of artisans certified for relief.[11] Thus he allowed Cahill no simple forum for rebuttal, and all seven projects were completed as originally intended and with enthusiastic local public support. Hunter then sent his own letter of support for the programs and included photographs of the type of high-quality workmanship he hoped to encourage through his programs. He explained the recent history of this type of work and its encouragement by the Anglo artists of Taos and Santa Fe.

> "... This phase of craft work was started some years ago by the artists in New Mexico who did the work themselves. Gradually, through encouragement, the Spanish-Americans began their own revival of this kind of work, typical of the region. It is they who should rightfully do (the craft work). This is another expression which the art colonies of the State has spawned; at least the artists were first to enthuse over this kind of handcraft.
>
> "... If I felt that the furniture item was in class with Grand Rapids stuff, or even considerably better, I would not think of entertaining such in connection with art projects. There seems to be a general attitude in the state that this work would come

under art projects. The Relief Certifying Officers have considered it so, and almost daily I receive applications and inquiries. I certainly would not be one to encourage the production of unattractive gadgets of the souvenir type."[12]

A marginal annotation in Cahill's hand expresses agreement with the statement that the Hispanic population themselves should carry on this sort of work. Cahill conceded authority to Bear and Hunter to make judgments on the appropriateness of crafts to New Mexico, where he saw them as perhaps more important than in other states, but expressed concern that crafts production remains proportion with the fine arts programs. Cahill believed crafts to be essential to the creative nature of New Mexicans because a vital craft tradition had existed in the state for several centuries, while the fine arts of painting and sculpture had been historically limited to small numbers of religious images. Cahill also expressed an interest in promoting weaving and embroidery as alternatives to an overly large furniture section.[13]

In May 1936, Hunter sent to Cahill a sample of Colcha embroidery, a type of wool embroidery unique to the region, which had been produced as requested by the exhibitions division of the FAP (in Washington) for inclusion in an exhibition of FAP work at the Phillips Memorial Gallery in Washington, DC. This embroidery pattern had been designed and produced by women employed by Hunter only three months earlier, a testament to the speed which he was able to enact his projects.[14] The sixteen yards of embroidered fabric was completed for the stage curtain for the Albuquerque Community Playhouse, a building which was completely furnished with objects made by Hispanic artists.

(Note: Another location where this craft was used was in the Office of Governor Clyde Tingley in the state capitol. "He furnished his office with the WPA furniture and the chairs had colcha embroidered seat cushions in them. Unfortunately, these cushions didn't last long since the metal brads on the levis pockets of the cowboys that came to visit frequently got caught in the beautiful stitchery," according to Joy Fincke McWilliams, Hunter's secretary.)

Hunter also wished to maintain traditional art forms which were in danger of extinction from pressures for wage labor jobs in a non-Hispanic dominated culture. He intended to revive the craft of straw inlay work on wood for use in the Albuquerque Playhouse. In a letter to the director of research for the IAD, Hunter wrote:

"This craft is one of the old mediums particularly appealing to me. I know of but one person in the state who has done it recently, a boy of twelve or fourteen years. Examples of this work are extremely rare. I have been of the opinion that it was done in imitation of marquetry.[15]

"There is no indication from the written record that straw inlay work was significantly revived by the FAP although at least a few examples were produced and included in a traveling exhibition."[16]

(Note: That young boy may have been Eliseo Rodriguez of Santa Fe who was active in the program and became known internationally for his outstanding straw inlay creations. He shared with this editor that he was the only artist at the time willing to learn how to do it as part of the WPA Federal Art program. A large cross is on display in the State Capitol, which was done by his wife, Paula, and now at least eleven family members have continued producing this form of art having learned it from their parents prior to their deaths. Other non-family members also took it up and such creations are now quite popular, admired and appreciated for the patience it must take to make such art.)

Classes in traditional crafts were offered through the Federal Art Centers in Melrose, Las Vegas, Roswell, and Gallup. Woodworking was the most regularly taught craft and the instructors, such as Domingo Tejada and Abad Lucero, frequently furnished the art center with their handmade furniture. Many developed talents which became important sources of income to otherwise unskilled laborers. In a few instances, the students attending such classes were later hired by the Project as craftsmen or artists' assistants. By Hunter's estimation, more than half of the instructors for the state vocational training centers received at least some of their experience through the WPA adult education program.[17]

The exhibition programs of the FAP actively included New Mexican Hispanic craft work in both regularly scheduled touring exhibitions and in large-scale retrospective shows highlighting the production of the FAP. Large exhibitions which included New Mexican Hispanic crafts were held at the Museum of Modern Art, New York, the New York World's Fair, the Art Institute of Chicago, and the National Museum (Smithsonian Institution) in Washington, DC. An exhibition of FAP work organized for the Museum of Modern Art in Washington, DC (no longer in existence) included three tin light sconces by Eddie Delgado, a carved mirror frame by Felix Guara, historic religious paintings reproduced by Pedro Cervantez, and a Colcha embroidery panel by Ida Parsons.[18]

Exhibitions organized by the state administrators in conjunction with the national touring exhibition program included shows featuring paintings of landscapes and domestic settings by Pedro Cervantez, figurative carvings by Patrocinio Barela, genre scene paintings by Johnnie Candelario (a non-project artist), and a survey exhibition of the FAP's Spanish-Colonial crafts. This exhibition of crafts included photographs of installed works such as a large reredos (carved and painted altar screen), embroidered stage curtains, and other decorations for the Spanish-American Normal School auditorium in El Rito. Also included were many examples of historic reproductions made by craftsmen such as a trastero (standing cabinet), chairs with embroidered seats, tin and glass candlesticks, and several carvings of saints by Juan Sanchez, some in metal work niches. The exhibition was augmented with New Mexican illustrations from the Index of American Design which provided an historical context for the new objects. The exhibited objects, therefore, served two functions: first, to demonstrate the high quality of work produced in modern times, and second, to illustrate the continuity of cultural expression encouraged by the FAP.

The somewhat conservative selection of art types for these exhibitions mirrors the tendency throughout the WPA programs away from abstraction and the avant garde in both style and subject matter. While there was no official censorship within the program, the avoidance of the new and unusual was expected, given Cahill's goals for the project. Certainly the Hispanic community was not used to viewing art of a modernist aesthetic, and the artists and craftsmen had no experience creating it. Had the program or its artists tried to introduce such art into these communities, it would have been acting against the wishes of its audience.[19] Such action also would have countered Cahill's wish to provide art for the masses rather than art for individual artists or an elite art establishment.

The traditional art forms chosen by most of the New Mexico artists, and certainly by the craftspeople, reflected a general feeling during this fiscally conservative period in American history that only utilitarian objects could be considered truly pleasing. Abstraction in both style and purpose was interpreted as self-indulgent and wasteful. The only exposure most New Mexicans had to non practical art was through commercially produced religious prints and locally created religious paintings and sculptures, where the art served a profoundly important spiritual purpose for the society.[20] Thus, without any external censorship, the artists and craftsmen (with the notable exception of Barela) imposed upon themselves limitations consistent with historic, communal precedents. The exhibitions of crafts and arts reflected these self-imposed guidelines, and the objects were received favorably nationwide.

Children's art and craft classes were probably the most oversubscribed service of the Federal Art Centers, and Hunter and the art center directors took great care to insure that instructors were competent, sensitive to the community, and, most important, able to communicate with their students. In a national artist loan program, several artist/teachers from the New York City FAP program worked in New Mexico for a period of months. One of these, Helena Herald, spoke fluent Spanish and was assigned to teach children's craft classes in Las Vegas. While there, Miss Herald helped to institute an innovative arrangement of public and private sponsorship to help buy class supplies for which students and the community were unable to pay. Roland Dickey, Director of the Roswell Museum and Federal Art Center, wrote to the Washington office, "The Children's Workshops in the Spanish district of Roswell has presented material of great charm and color interest. The teachers were Jan Marfyak, Juanita Lantz and Reiney Woolsey. The classes were held in the educational wing of the local Catholic church."[21] Children's issues were also taken into consideration in the Art Center's exhibition schedules to ensure that shows such as "Paintings by Mexican Children" were exhibited at times convenient for classes from the art centers and the local school system.[22]

These Federal Art Program craft classes and sponsorship could have, in theory, meshed well with the programs of the state-sponsored vocational training schools. The staff of the FAP felt the state vocational program, under the direction of Brice H. Sewell, was uncooperative to mutually beneficial programming. While Sewell's program was extremely effective within the state, both through direct training and publication of detailed technical bulletins on such topics as "New Mexico Colonial Embroidery" and "Spanish-Colonial Furniture," he was unwilling to distribute these publications and share these skills nationally. Hunter interpreted Sewell's reluctance as fear that the strong native designs would be copied by furniture manufacturers in the East, pulling business away from the currently productive local communities which had originated the style.[23] Perhaps with similar justifications, Sewell was unwilling to cooperate in lending to the illustrators and researchers working on the Index of American Design antique objects which his staff had collected for reproduction by vocational craftsmen. Objects included in the Index of American Design were to be published and circulated throughout the country as examples of the best of American design and perhaps Sewell was concerned about this publicity. Hunter also commented that more than half of the teachers for the State Vocational Department were employed by the WPA Adult Education Program, and they were perhaps wary or even jealous of the attention earned by the similar craft programs of the FAP.[24]

Clearly Hunter viewed his programs as providing more than just crucial financial reward to the artists. For him, the national exposure which he consistently sought for the artists was a method of raising ethnic respect both within the state's Hispanic communities and throughout the nation. He was sensitive to the importance of maintaining communal traditions as a way to establish a context for individuality, and he understood self-worth as a direct factor in pride of ethnic identity. By exhibiting these works to a national audience, and returning the favorable response to the community, Hunter was able both to strengthen local support for his programs and to encourage high quality in production. Cahill's personal interest in these exhibitions only added to their effectiveness as propaganda and contributed to national support for the state's ethnic diversity.

Throughout Hunter's administration he considered the needs and interests of his Spanish speaking constituents. Rarely was he contacted directly by members of the community, and he was required to rely on his own experiences with the population and those of acquaintances and members of his advisory panel. Hunter chose not to publicize the opening of the San Miguel Federal Art Center in Las Vegas, a racially and intellectually divided town. By avoiding all manner of official town attention, he provided no forum for partisan politics. The exhibition at the gallery's opening featured work from the state's crafts programs including reproductions of bultos (three-dimensional images of religious figures) by Juan Sanchez. The exhibition was a great success with the Hispanic population and gossip provided a steady flow of visitors. The Las Vegas community had been particularly reluctant to share their family treasures with illustrators for the Index of American Design because they had suffered such great losses of their material cultural heritage at the hands of unscrupulous collectors. Hunter requested permission from Washington to lend some of Sanchez' religious carvings to interested individuals as an indication of the project's good intentions. This request ran counter to FAP regulations regarding loans of government art. Although Cahill supported the idea, his administrative assistant, Thomas Parker, advised against such loans and the request was denied in favor of a uniform national policy.[25]

The Index of American Design and New Mexico's *Portfolio of Spanish-Colonial Design* projects initiated significant research in order to establish the history or heritage of illustrated objects from each state. The original intention of the projects, especially the IAD, was to record not only the visual appearance of each object but a brief history and context of the piece or type. More than thirty years after the completion of her illustration and research work for the IAD. E. Boyd, who was to become the foremost authority on Hispanic New Mexican "popular arts," was highly critical of the research done on Index objects. It is not clear whether she was critical of the research methodology of the period or if she simply felt that subsequent research had disproved earlier findings. It is clear, however, that research was not a strong point of the Index nationwide.[26]

Because Hunter encouraged and personally conducted research on the local arts, Bear, relying on his impressive knowledge of the subject, wrote an informed and impassioned essay to introduce the *Portfolio of Spanish-Colonial Design*. Hunter, in addition to administering the program and continuing to produce his own paintings, wrote several articles on his program and the artists within it. His essay on Patrocinio Barela, originally written in 1939 for the FAP's planned publication *Art for the Millions*, by Francis O'Connor, was based on his working relationship and close friendship with the artist and expresses a thorough understanding of the artist's environment and creative motivation.

Hunter's fascination with the subject led him into thorough investigations of topics pertaining to the arts projects under his control. He never entered into a new project without first discovering the history of the type, style, or medium. In several instances such intensive research led to proposals for additional projects. One such project which was never realized was similar in organization and purpose to the *Portfolio of Spanish-Colonial Design* but focused on the colcha embroidery traditions of the region.[27]

Most projects proposed by the New Mexico office were received enthusiastically by the Washington office. The Washington officials were continuously asking for more information, more background stories, more human interest items, all of which were frequently absorbed into the extensive exhibition ephemera, promotional material, published reports, and funding justifications published by the office of both the FAP and the WPA in general.[28]

Folklore in the form of beliefs, stories, and legends was perhaps the most enthusiastically received type of information sent to Washington. Hunter explained the battered appearance of some of the saint carvings illustrated for the Index of American Design by relating the 'theory' that rain could be brought by breaking a small sliver of wood from the saint figure and burning it in the fireplace. He also reported that lightning could be diverted from a house by throwing the saint carvings out into the rain for the duration of the storm.[29] He received this information from fieldworkers on the Federal Writers' Project who were gathering such material from older members of communities throughout the state. Cultural context clearly enhanced Hunter's understanding of the works, their makers, and the community he served.

This sense that Hunter had in dealing with artistic personalities and also, even more importantly, with Hispanic cultural traits enabled him to instill throughout the Federal Art Project a respect for variation of cultural expression within a communal tradition. The FAP succeeded where other Works Progress Administration programs could not in both hiring Spanish-speaking peoples for other than blue-collar jobs and in directing their productivity toward the Hispanic population as audience. The artists on the FAP were not expected to abandon their culture's visual or communal heritage in order to enter into a labor system established by a foreign set of bureaucrats, rather the system molded itself to suit the needs most appropriate to this cultural region.

The sensitivity of capable administrators forced a huge organization to accept the non-conformist within the American system. Artists, by nature, tend to be non conforming, fringe members of society, but in New Mexico the case of Hispanic artists was slightly different. The population which did not conform to expected roles within the WPA was exactly the same population which had existed for more than two hundred years in the state simply by following set traditions. The Federal Art Project in New Mexico provided a great service to the community by instilling a sense of self-respect and expressing national approval for community-based aesthetics and local, communally-conservative modes of life. Here the artists were individuals, but individuals with a culture and a long past, and the FAP, through R. Vernon Hunter and his staff encouraged them to show it.

(Note: More about the *Portfolio.* As presented in O'Connor's paper, the original intention of the Index of American Design and the *Portfolio* projects related to researching and visually recording historical art forms around the country and recording a brief history of the identified pieces and/or types of work. The goal was to have this happen in every state and reportedly twenty-four states got underway with the project. Unfortunately inadequate funds were the main deterrent to this goal being accomplished. New Mexico was among the few states that did create their own unique portfolio since it had earlier started such a project focusing on Spanish-Colonial art. Other states known to have participated included California, Pennsylvania, Arizona and possibly Ohio.)

The New Mexico *Portfolio* included 50 renderings of objects of art typical of our Spanish-Colonial heritage. Two hundred portfolio sets were completed thanks to the talents and energies of various people. It is our understanding that despite all the efforts put forth, the New Mexico *Portfolio* was not accepted by the people in Washington to be included in the Index of American Design.

This rejection was a great disappointment to Vernon Hunter and others who had worked so hard on it. Various reasons have been presented regarding this rejection. Exclusive of the original sets done by E. Boyd, there was inconsistent quality in the original work produced. Holger Cahill was not happy with the final results and the varied quality but there were no funds available to redo them. He had wanted them to be serigraphed originally to avoid this problem. It is important to note that the restrictions on the expending of money as established by the federal government did not allow for printing costs. Federal money could only be expended for labor costs. It is therefore projected that the costs of printing was covered by donations from supporters of the project and they may be the entities listed in the credit portion of the book.

Also, New Mexico's selection of typical Spanish-Colonial art featured subject material that was predominantly religious and there were some who were possibly overly sensitive to the requirement of separation of church and state. However, what they were not sensitive to was the fact that this material was indeed highly representative of the most common art known to the predominant culture of New Mexico for many years and at that time.

Despite that rejection, today the *Portfolio* is valued highly and a complete set will bring a substantial price. Individual renderings are occasionally found on the market and also have value, though lesser. Seventeen complete and numbered sets have been identified in predominantly public ownership such as libraries and museums. The New Mexico State Library has two complete sets in their vault and the Santa Fe Public Library has a bound set.

In 2009, various pieces of the New Mexico *Portfolio* were included in a national show at the National Museum of American Art.

Fourteen Hispanics were among the forty-six artists and copyists who painted the watercolor duplicated illustrations. E. Boyd prepared the original text and watercolor studies for the plates. She gathered the material from various New Mexico churches and homes. She also is known to have hand-colored in watercolor one set of prints, which is still in existence today. Roland Dickey, then at the University of New Mexico, assisted in the research and edited the text. The woodblock engravings were made by six engravers listed below. The text and woodblocks were composed and created for use in the printing with equipment of Rydal Press (Santa Fe), Whiteman Printing (Clovis) and Gus Baumann's press at the Spanish American Normal School (El Rito). The school also provided production assistance. The frontpiece indicates that it was published in Santa Fe in 1938 by the Federal Art Project of New Mexico of the Division of Women's and Professional Projects, Works Progress Administration.

PARTICIPANTS WHO CREATED THE *PORTFOLIO OF SPANISH COLONIAL DESIGN IN NEW MEXICO*

The following credits are in the front of the text of the *Portfolio:*

Thanks to:
Archbishop R. A. Gerken
Historical Society of New Mexico
Laboratory of Anthropology
School of American Research
Museum of New Mexico
Paul Horgan
Ruth Laughlin
John Gaw Meem
Sheldon Parsons
James Seligman
B. Sweringen
Carlos Vierra
Cady Wells
Rydal Press—printing equipment
Whiteman Printing Company—printing equipment
El Rito School—use of Gustave Baumann printing press there

Contributors:

Holger Cahill, Director, FAP-Washington
Donald Bear, Regional Advisor
R. Vernon Hunter, New Mexico Coordinator
E. Boyd Hall—Text and Renderings
Roland Dickey—Research

Engravers:

Fritz Broeske
Louie Ewing
Donald Cole
Frank Stevens
Manville Chapman
Stuart Walker

Composition:
Bruce Gentry
Ridgley Whiteman

Artists:

Mary Baca
Nash Bachicha
Jean Barka
Maye Barris
Charles Barrows
Mae Brown
Stanley Carson
Dale Case
Carlos Cervantez
Majel Claflin
Regina T. Cooke
Lucius Cummings
R. L. Day
J. V. Delgado
John Dorman
Evelyn Dryer
Chester Faris
Florencio Flores
Juan Garcia
Felix Gutierrez
Odon Hullenkremer
Lucino Huerta
William Hughes
D. Paul Jones
J. Henry Marley
Charles Mattox
Alfonso Mirabel
Sam Moreno
James Morris
Helmuth Naumer

Virginia Nye
Isauro Padilla
Edma Pierce
Loda Ralston
Lois Roberson
Eliseo Rodriguez
Lumina Rodriguez
Ernesto Roybal
Juan Sanchez
Howard Schleeter
Franz Trevor
Charles Wesley
Margery Wilson
Ardyce Wynn

Some observers considered the New Deal in New Mexico to have been only a qualified success. What they fail to take into account is that some complex human endeavors, like socioeconomic development, require a longer gestation period than others. Today one is able to see the powerful impact upon this state that has been sustained over time through these projects.

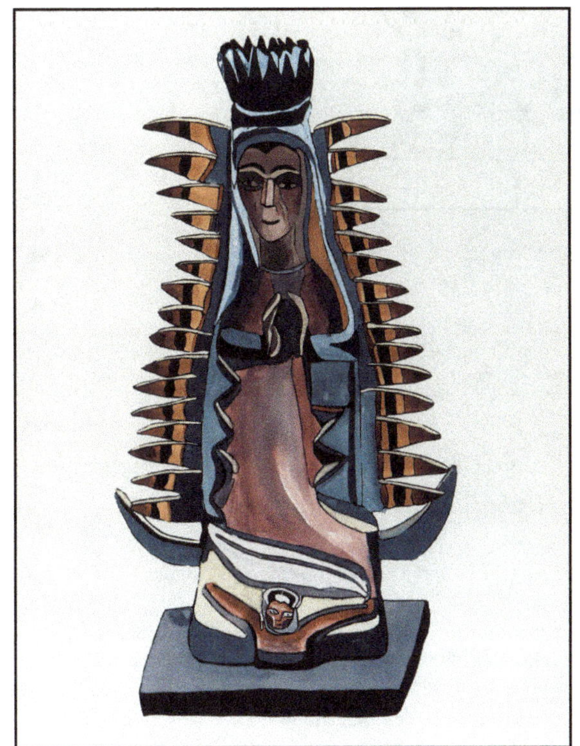

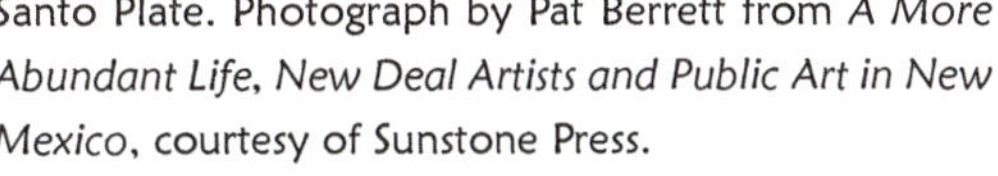

Santo Plate. Photograph by Pat Berrett from *A More Abundant Life, New Deal Artists and Public Art in New Mexico*, courtesy of Sunstone Press.

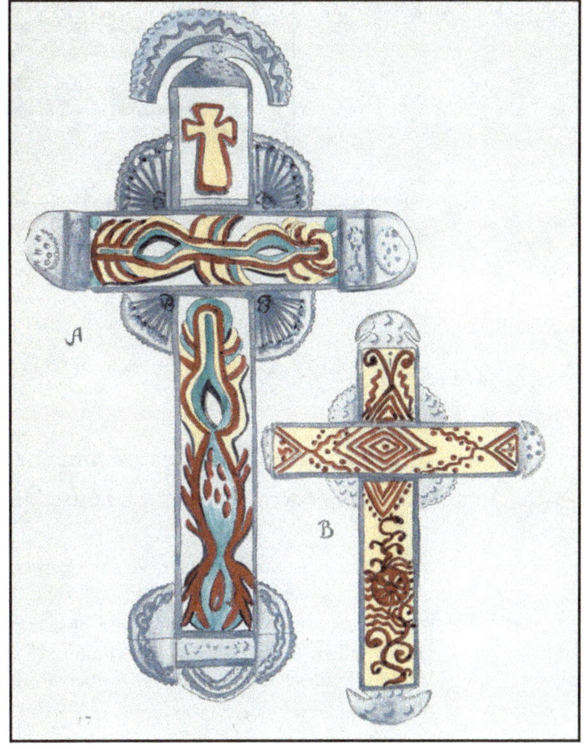

Crosses Plate. Photograph by Pat Berrett from *A More Abundant Life, New Deal Artists and Public Art in New Mexico*, courtesy of Sunstone Press.

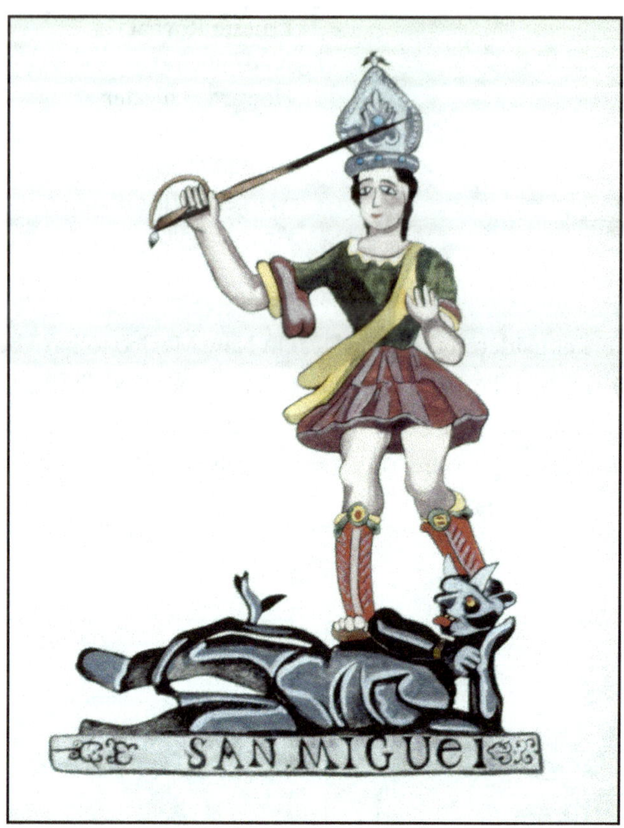

Santo Plate of San Miguel

NOTES

Unless otherwise noted, all papers are contained in Record Group 69, Papers of the Works Progress Administration, Federal Art Project, housed in the National Archives, Washington, DC.

1. John R. Van Ness introduction to Suzanne Forrest, *The Preservation of the Village: New Mexico's Hispanics and the New Deal.* (Albuquerque: University of New Mexico Press, 1989), vii.
2. These recent settlers to the region who primarily came from towns and cities in the Eastern United States are usually called "Anglo." This term is employed in the region to indicate persons of non-Native American, non-Hispanic heritage not-withstanding the person's true ethnic or national ancestry.
3. This sentiment is evident in modern criticism of the era such as Peter Bermingham in his *The New Deal in the Southwest: Arizona and New Mexico.* (Tucson: The University of Arizona Museum of Art, nd). It is perhaps more solidly stated through the administrative papers of the Federal Art Project. These papers indicated a strong bias from the Washington office towards the artwork produced by the Hispanic artists. While this may be viewed as an attempt toward cultural diversity, clearly Cahill, Mildred Holzhauer, Assistant Director for Exhibitions, and Edith Gregor Halpert, a New York art dealer who served for a time as Exhibition Coordinator, all preferred the work produced by the Hispanic artists to that of the Anglo artists.
4. Letter dated March 12, 1936 Central Files: State, New Mexico 1935–1944, (Box 1929 651.3112 to 651.315), File: N.M. 651.315.

5. Letter from Donald Bear to Vernon Hunter, August 25, 1938, Central Files: State, New Mexico 1935–1944, (Box1930 651.315), File: 651.315 N.M. July 1938.
6. Letter from Eckles by Hunter to Kiplinger attn. Holzhauer, Dec. 10, 1941. Central Files: State, N.M. 1935–1944, (Box 1931) 651.315 to 651.3159), file: N.M. 651.3152 April–Oct. 1940. "1 I have seen the Indian Ceremonial Dance pictures (Exhibit #602) now showing at Roswell, and I believe we would do well not to show them in Gallup. That town is very critical of such subject matter, with which this particular artist seems none too familiar."
7. Letter of Jan. 28, 1936. Regional and State Correspondence, 1935–1940, (Box 27) Minnesota-New Mexico, File: N.M. 1936.
8. Letter from Cahill to Bear, Feb. 4, 1936. Regional and State Correspondence, 1935–1940, (Box 27) Minnesota-New Mexico, File: New Mexico 1936.
9. By the end of the New Mexico's FAP, the number of "peasant sculptors." or as they would be identified today, traditional folk carvers, had increased significantly. This can be attributed, at least in part, to the national attention and encouragement this art form received from the activities of the FAP.
10. Letter from Bear to Cahill, Feb. 8, 1936. Central Files: State, New Mexico 1935–1944, (Box 1929 651.3112 to 651.315), File: N.M. 651.315.
11. Letter from Bear to Cahill, Feb. 10, 1936. Regional and State Correspondence, 1935–1940 (Box 27) Minnesota-New Mexico, File: New Mexico 1936.
12. Letter from Hunter to Cahill, Feb. 12, 1936. Central Files: State, N.M. 1935–1944, (Box 1929 651.3112 to 651. 315), File: N.M. 651.315.
13. Letter from Cahill to Bear, Feb. 13, 1936. Central Files: State, N.M. 1935–1944, (Box 1929 651.3112 to 651.315), File: N.M. 651.315. and Letter from Cahill to Bear, Feb. 15, 1936. Regional and State Correspondence, 1935–1940, (Box 27) Minnesota-New Mexico, File: N.M. 1936 and Letter from Cahill to Hunter, Feb. 21, 1936, (Box 1929 651.3112 to 651.315), File: N.M. 651.315.
14. Letter from Hunter to Exhibition Department, FAP, Washington, DC, May 15, 1936. Regional and State Correspondence, 1935–1940, (Box 27) Minnesota-New Mexico, File: N.M. 1936.
15. Letter from Lea Rowland by Hunter to Kathleen Calkins, Director of Research, Index of American Design, June 3, 1936. Central Files: State, New Mexico 1935–1944, (Box 1929 651.3112 to 651.315), File: N.M.651.315.
16. The loan of these works was discussed in a letter from Hunter to Mrs. Ruth Lawrence, Curator, The University Gallery, University of Minnesota, Minneapolis, Minnesota, and Feb. 1, 1940. Central Files: State, N.M. 1935–1944, (Box 1931) 651.315 to 651.3159), File: N.M. 651.3152 Nov. 1939–June 1940. The artist of the straw inlay work was not identified.
17. Letter from Lea Rowland by Hunter to Kathleen Calkins, Director of Research, Index of American Design, June 3, 1936. Central Files: State N.M. 1935–1944, (Box 1929 651.3112 to 651.315), file: N.M. 651.315.
18. A detailed objects list for the exhibition at the Museum of Modern Art in Washington was included in a letter from Hunter to Holzhauer, March 28, 1939. Central Files: State, New Mexico 1935–1944, (Box 1931) 651.315 to 651.3159), File: N.M. 651.3152 Jan.–Sept. 1939.
19. The FAP administration probably assumed more about its audience's expectations than it actually understood. They never instituted any methodical study of the intended audience for completed works of art. As a whole, the Program, probably understood the public it served better in a local context than it did on the national level. Members of the general public were quick to point out fault on the part of the federal government, and local administrators were occasionally called upon to defend actions taken by their programs.
20. For more information on the importance of religious art to the Catholic population of New Mexico see Thomas J. Steele, S. J.'s book referenced in the Bibliography.
21. Letter from Roland Dickey, Director, Roswell Museum to Parker, Jan. 27, 1939. Central Files: State, N.M. 1935–1944, And (Box 1930 651.315), File: N.M. 651.315 Jan.–Aug. 1939.
22. These sentiments were expressed in letters such as one from Hunter to Holzhauer, May 12, 1939. Central Files: State, New Mexico 1935–1944, And (Box 1931) 651.315 to 651.3159), File: N.M. 651.3152 Jan.–Sept. 1939. "The early fall would be a very good time to send the exhibition of paintings by Mexican children to Roswell. They should not be scheduled for Roswell before September as they should be seen by the Spanish children at the San Juan workshop, which is closed during the summer."
23. Letter from Lea Roland by Hunter to Kathleen Calkins, Director of Research, Index of American Design, June 3, 1936. Central Files: State, N.M. 1935–1944, (Box 1929 651.3112 to 651.315), File: N.M. 651.31.5.
24. Letter from Lea Rowland by Hunter to Kathleen Calkins, Director of Research, Index of American Design, June 3, 1936. Central Files: State, N.M. 1935–1944, (Box 1929 651.3112 to 651.315), File: N.M. 651.315.

25. Letter from R. Vernon Hunter to D.S. Defenbacher, Assistant Regional Adviser, FAP, Aug. 13, 1937. Central Files: State, N.M. 1935–1944, (Box 1930 651.315), File: 651.315 N.M. Jan. 19371 of 2. And Letter from R. Vernon Hunter to Mildred Holzhauer, Assistant Director for Exhibitions, FAP September 24, 1937. Central Files: State, N.M. 1935 to 1944, (Box 1930 651.315), File: 651.315 N.M. Jan. 19971 of 2. And Letter from R. Vernon Hunter to Mildred Holzhauer, Assistant Director for Exhibitions, FAP, and March 4, 1938. Central Files: State, N.M. 1935–1944, And (Box 1930 651.315), File: 651.315 N.M. Jan. 1938.
26. This statement is based on communication with John Michael Vlach, Department of American Studies, George Washington University, Washington, DC.
27. Initial research on the subject of Colchas, and preliminary discussions of a portfolio of Colcha design can be found in: Letter from Walter M. Kiplinger, Director, Public Activities Programs, attn. Benjamin Knotts, Assistant to Director to Connelly, Attn. Eckles, Feb. 5, 1941; and letter from Eckles by Hunter to Kiplinger attn. Knotts, March 6, 1941. Central Files: State, N.M. 1935–1944, (Box 1931) 651.315 to 651.3159, File: N.M. 651.3155 Jan. 1941.
28. Requests from Washington office for additional information, stories, and explanations, are found throughout the correspondence files.
29. Letter from R. Vernon Hunter to Glassgold, April 27, 1939. Central Files: State, N.M. 1935–1944, (Box 1931) 651.315 to 651.3159), File: N.M. 651.3155 Jan. 1941. And Letter from Florence Kerr by Glassgold to Connelly attn. R. Vernon Hunter, Oct. 14, 1939. Central Files: State, N.M. 1935–1944, And (Box 1931) 651.315 to 651.3159), File: N.M. 651.3155 Jan. 1941.

BIBLIOGRAPHY

Primary Sources

Administrative correspondence of Federal Art Project (FAP, August 1935–1943), in Record Group 69, Civil Records Section, National Archives, Washington, DC.

Papers of the Federal Writers Project (FWP, 1935–1939), Manuscripts Division, Library of Congress, Washington, DC.

Secondary Sources

Boyd, E. *Popular Arts of Spanish New Mexico*. Santa Fe: Museum of New Mexico Press, 1974.

Briggs, Charles L. *The Wood Carvers of Cordova, New Mexico: Social Dimensions of an Artistic Revival.* Knoxville: The University of Tennessee Press, 1980.

Forrest, Suzanne. *The Preservation of the Village: New Mexico's Hispanics and the New Deal.* Albuquerque: University of New Mexico Press, 1989.

Campa, Arthur L. *Hispanic Culture in the Southwest.* Norman: University of Oklahoma Press, 1979.

Nestor, Sarah. *The Native Market of the Spanish New Mexican Craftsmen: Santa Fe, 1933–1940.* Santa Fe: New Edition, Sunstone Press, 2009.

O'Connor, Francis V., ed. *Art for the Millions: Essays from the 1930s by Artists and Administrators of the WPA Federal Art Project.* Greenwich, Connecticut: New York Graphic Society, Ltd., 1973.

——— *Federal Art Patronage: 1933 to 1943.* College Park: University of Maryland, 1966.

Spurlock, William Henry, II. "Federal Support for the Visual Arts in the State of New Mexico: 1933–1943." Master's Thesis, University of New Mexico. 1974.

Steele, Thomas J., S.J. *Santos and Saints: The Religious Folk Art of Hispanic New Mexico.* Santa Fe: Ancient City Press, 1974.

Stoller, Marianne L. with Suzanne Martin and Kathryn Nelson. "Hispanic Folk Artists, Their Works, Their Words," *People and Policy: A Journal of Humanistic Perspectives on Colorado Issues.* (Summer 1980:26-49).

Vedder, Alan C. *Furniture of Spanish New Mexico.* Santa Fe: Sunstone Press 1976.

Weigle, Marta. *New Mexicans in Cameo and Camera: New Deal Documentation of Twentieth-Century Lives.* Albuquerque: University of New Mexico Press, 1985.

——— *Hispanic Villages of Northern New Mexico: A Reprint of Volume II of the 1935 Tewa Basin Study, with Supplementary Materials.* Santa Fe: The Lightning Tree, 1975.

——— with Kyle Fiore. *Santa Fe and Taos: The Writer's Era, 1916–1941.* Santa Fe: New Edition, Suntone Press. 2008.

——— with Claudia and Sam Larcombe. *Hispanic Arts and Ethnohistory in the Southwest.* Ancient City Press, 1983.

Wroth, William. "New Hope in Hard Times: Hispanic Crafts are Revived During the Troubled Years," *El Palacio.* 89 (Summer 1983:22-31).

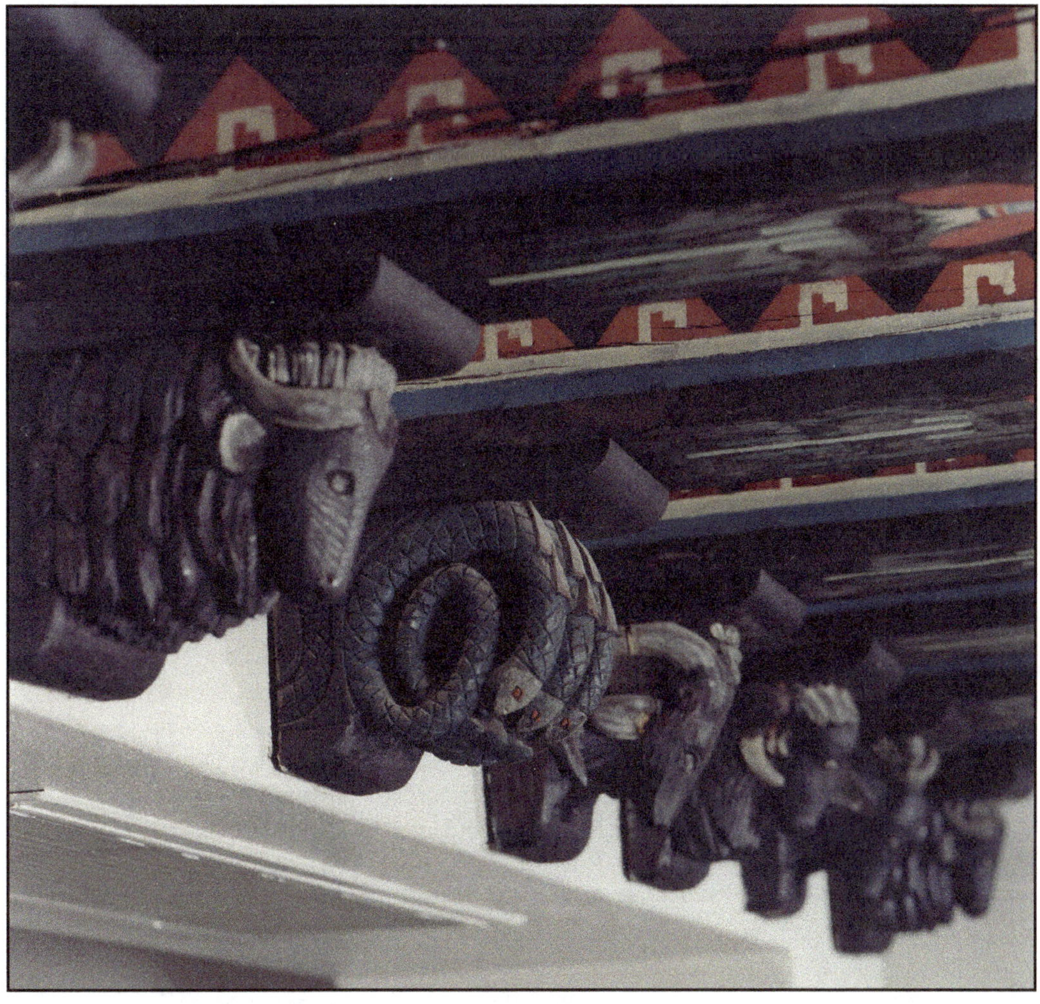

Exqusite animal head carvings are found on the corbels in the Psychology Building (Building 1) at the Vererans' Hospital in Albuquerque. The carver or carvers are unknown.

7

ADDITIONAL LISTS OF HISPANIC ARTISTS FROM THE NEW DEAL ERA

Tey Mariana Nunn

Research on locating New Mexico Hispanic artists was been done by Tey Mariana Nunn for her PhD and resulted in the publication by the University of New Mexico Press of the book, *Sin Nombre: Hispana and Hispano Artists of the New Deal Era*. In her book there are references to the following Hispanic individuals who participated in one or more of the New Deal programs in New Mexico or were possibly involved in the New Mexico Vocational School programs and/or the Native Market. These three programs were closely intertwined during that era with the artists moving from one to another.

Alvarado, Carmelita—student
Aragon, Moises
Archuleta, Antonio
Archuleta, Ernesto
Archuleta, Eugenia
Arellano, Eugenio
Baca Martinez, Amelia
Baca, Deolinda
Baca, Margaret
Barela, Josefa
Barela, Manuel
Caloca, Rafael
Campa, Arterio
Candelario, Jesusito
CdeBaca, David
CdeBaca, Elba
Cervantes, Carlos
Cervantes, Mary
Cervantes, Marie
Cervantes, Pedro
Chavez, Edward A.
Chavez, Eloy
Chavez, Eva Van Ryen
Cisneros, Elsie Martinez
Cobos, Lucy—student
Cordova, Gloria Lopez
Cordova, Lorenzo
Cordova, Rumaldo
Delgado, Epiminia
Delgado, Francisco
Delgado, Ildeberto "Eddie"
Dominguez, Benjamin
Emilio, Frank
Gabaldon Stark, Tillie
Garcia, Epifania—student
Garcia, Estela
Garcia, Pete
Gonzales, Edward
Gonzales, Elideo
Gonzales, Rudolfo
Guara, Felix
Gutierrez Rodriguez, Paula
Herrera, Belisandra
Herrera, Margaret
Lopez, Evangelina
Lopez, George
Lopez, Jose Dolores
Lopez, Maclovia
Lopez, Rose—student
Luna, Chris Herrera (Mrs. Max)
Luna, Max
Martinez, Amelia
Martinez, Atocha
Martinez, Dona Maria
Martinez, Ortilia
Martinez, Pascual
Martinez, Reyes Nicanor
Matta, Santiago
Mirabel, Alfonso
Montoya, Dolores P.
Moreno, Samuel
Ortiz, Max
Padilla, Emilio

Padilla, Martias
Padilla, Pablo
Perea, Beto
Perea, Edward
Perez, Esther—student
Perez, Filipo—student
Perez, Rudolfo—student
Quintana, Alejandro
Qunitana, Celso
Quintana, Pedro
Quintana, Ramoncita
Quintero, Maria
Rivera, Lorenzo
Rivera, Valentino
Rodriguez, Alice
Rodriguez, Eliseo
Rodriguez, Ernestine
Rodriguez, Gabriel
Rodriguez, Jessica
Rodriguez, Marcial
Rodriguez, Monica
Rodriguez, Teodicio
Rodriguez, Vickie
Rodriguez, Yolanda
Rodriguez, Romero de Romero
Romero, Robert—student
Roybal, Ernesto
Salazar, Arturo
Salazar, David
Sanchez, Juan Amado
Sandoval, Ben
Sedillo, Mary
Segura, George
Sena, Arlene Cisneros
Tamayo, Rufino
Tejada, Domingo
Tejada, Jose Moises
Trujillo, Alejandro
Trujillo, Esquipula
Trujillo, Joe
Trujillo, Rose
Trujillo y Vigil, Remedios
Josefa (Mrs. Patrocinio Barela)
Vierra, Carlos
Vigil, Fulgencio
Vigil, Juan
Vigil, Julian
Villalobos, Rafael
Younis, Rita
Zamora, Estevan

8

CREATIONS OF INDIAN ARTISTS AND THE ARCHITECTURAL STYLES IN PUELOS AND RESERVATIONS MOVE OUT INTO THE STATE

Sally Hyer

In his final report, Datus Myers, the field coordinator for the Indian Division of the Public Works of Art Project (PWAP), observed, "I think we artists in New Mexico were fortunate to work alongside of the Indian who was allowed to show his culture at the same time and make comparisons. There is no doubt in my mind that he has something which, to him, is just as important, though different, which might be worth our knowing." The significance of PWAP in the development of Indian arts in this century has been largely unrecognized. However, in spite of Myers' halfhearted opinion that native culture "might be worth knowing," the participants in the project are among the leading Indian painters, potters, and sculptors of this century. They created work of significant artistic and historical value under the federal sponsorship of this era. PWAP helped establish Santa Fe as a center of Indian art patronage and Santa Fe Indian School as an institution that fostered both traditional and innovative arts.1

At the same time that President Franklin Delano Roosevelt initiated "New Deal" emergency programs designed to boost the national economy and help bring the country out of the Great Depression, he appointed John Collier Commissioner of Indian affairs (1933–1945). Collier took full advantage of New Deal funds to promote Indian arts and crafts, increase employment, improve infrastructure on reservations, and construct schools. He was an idealist who struggled to reform federal Indian policy during his twelve year term. Years earlier, during a 1920 visit to his close friend, Taos resident and cultural arbiter, Mabel Dodge Luhan, he had embraced Pueblo Indian culture as offering nothing less than salvation from the ills of Western Civilization.[2]

Collier used New Deal funds to attempt to remedy the appalling federal neglect and underfunding of Indian health and education programs exposed in 1928 by private study of Indian affairs known as the Meriam Report. In 1933, the $19 million from Public Works Administration appropriations allotted to the Indian Service almost equaled the entire Indian

Bureau budget of $22 million.[3] Native Americans took part in the Civilian Conservation Corps (CCC), Public Works Administration (PWA), the Public Works of Art Project (PWAP), and the Treasury Section of Painting and Sculpture (TRAP), as well as in other federally supported programs for the visual arts and architecture.

Visual Arts

The Public Works of Art Project (PWAP), supervised by the Treasury Department, was funded from January to June, 1934. With over $1 million in funding, its aim was to put artists to work in the decoration of public buildings and also to provide emergency employment for artists. The Thirteenth Regional Committee of the PWAP consisted of New Mexico and Arizona. Its Indian Division aimed to give Indians an opportunity to create and display murals, watercolors, pottery, and weavings in Indian service buildings under construction through the Public Works Administration.

Indians were not involved in the administration of the program or selection of participants. Jesse Nusbaum, director of the newly-constructed Laboratory of Anthropology, was director and chairman of the Thirteenth Regional Committee. Laboratory curator and Indian arts specialist, Kenneth Chapman, was appointed secretary and graphic artist, and Gustave Baumann, area coordinator. Datus Myers, an artist who had studied art in Chicago, Los Angeles, and abroad and come to New Mexico with his wife Alice in 1923, was field coordinator for the Indian Division.

Commissioner Collier urged Southwestern traders on or near reservations to recommend Indian artists for the PWAP, but the final selection of artists was made on the basis of interviews with Datus Myers and his wife. Only a small percentage of the Indian artists in New Mexico participated in the project because many were unable to leave the reservation to come to Santa Fe. Others were ineligible because they had part-time employment and did not depend solely on their artwork for subsistence.[4]

Santa Fe Indian School

The headquarters of the Indian Division was at Santa Fe Indian School, where the artists took room and board. Since his arrival at the school in 1930, Superintendent Chester E. Faris had endeavored to hire Indian artists and craftsmen and promote Indian arts as a profession that would permit students to continue living at home if they desired. Myers selected about thirty painters and craftspeople from the Pueblos and the Navajo Reservation to paint murals and watercolors, weave rugs, and make pottery. They were to work under the direction of painting teacher Dorothy Dunn and crafts teacher Mabel Morrow. Geronima Montoya followed Dorothy Dunn as the instructor. The artists included SFIS students Pablita Velarde (Santa Clara) and Andy Tsihnajinnie (Navajo), both about 16 years old. They worked with established artists Velino Shije Herrera (Zia), Tonita Pena (San Ildefonso), Emiliano

Abeyta (San Juan), Tony Archuleta (Taos), Jack Hokeah (Kiowa), and Calvin Tyndall (Omaha). During the six-month project, 8 painters completed 13 panel murals and 46 watercolors. Two Pueblo copyists, Miriam Marmon (Laguna) and Alma Chosa (Jemez), along with several non-Indian artists, completed 200 Indian designs.

Velarde recalled that at SFIS, Tonita Pena became her mentor. "Tonita was really a help to me in my early years at the Indian school. She was staying at the girls' dorm. That's how we got acquainted. She talked Tewa, and she used to tease and laugh and joke in Indian, and that was fun. Then she would be sitting in her room in the evening, just painting for herself, and I'd watch her and talk to her." These conversations convinced Velarde that she could overcome the difficulties of being both a Pueblo woman and an artist.[5]

Six Navajo weavers came to the school, bringing their own wool and yarn. The school furnished additional wool, yarn, and dyes and paid each weaver a salary of $14.85 per person per week plus room and board. After Morrow and the weavers selected textiles from the Laboratory of Anthropology's collections to duplicate, Datus Myers copied the designs. The weavers prepared the wool and wove blankets based on Myers' copies.

Six Navajo weavers completed 12 rugs ranging in size from 3 ft. by 4 ft. to 4 ft. by 5 ft. 5 in. The weavers were Nellie Cowboy, Mrs. John Jim, Mrs. Elizabeth Pablo, Mary Phillips, Sallie Kinlichini, and Bah [Smith?]. The records indicate that speed of production was important: Nellie Cowboy completed three rugs in 101 days, while Mary Phillips only finished one. Pueblo potters Maria Martinez and Julian Martinez (San Ildefonso), Eulogio Naranjo (Santa Clara), Lela and Evangelio Gutierrez (Santa Clara) and Agrapina Quintana completed 62 pots.

A national exhibit of works done under the Public Works of Art Project was held at the Corcoran Gallery of Art in Washington, DC. In April and May, 1934. Two-thirds of the objects sent from New Mexico were Indian-made, featuring Navajo rugs; mural paintings by Andy Tshinajinnie, Pablita Velarde, Velino Herrera, and Tonita Pena; and pottery by Eulogia Naranjo, Maria and Julian Martinez, and Lela and Evangelio Gutierrez.[6]

Some of the works completed at SFIS are now in the collections of the Laboratory of Anthropology in Santa Fe, and may be seen upon request. These include Navajo blankets by Sally Kinlichini, Mrs. John Jim, Nellie Cowboy, and Bah; two polychrome jars by Lela and Evangelio Gutierrez of Santa Clara Pueblo; and three matte on black jars by Maria and Julian Martinez.[7]

Bandelier National Monument

In 1939, former PWAP participant Pablita Velarde, then 21, was hired to paint the ways of life, customs, and ceremonies of the Pueblo people for exhibition at Bandelier National Monument as part of a Works Progress Administration project. Velarde's work consists of 84 paintings in casein on masonite board and glass completed between 1939 and 1945. She interviewed Pueblo elders and did library research in order to describe the social, political, and economic life of her people in the early 1900s. The paintings document hunting and gathering, compare men's and women's activities, and describe daily events. Elements from different villages are often combined in single works. This exquisite series preserves a way of life that has changed irreversibly. Velarde believed that these paintings were among the most meaningful of all her work.[8]

The Velarde paintings are in the permanent collection of the National Park Service and are occasionally on exhibition. (Note: Remodeling of the Visitor Center in 2010 made it possible to have more of her work seen more frequently if not routinely.)

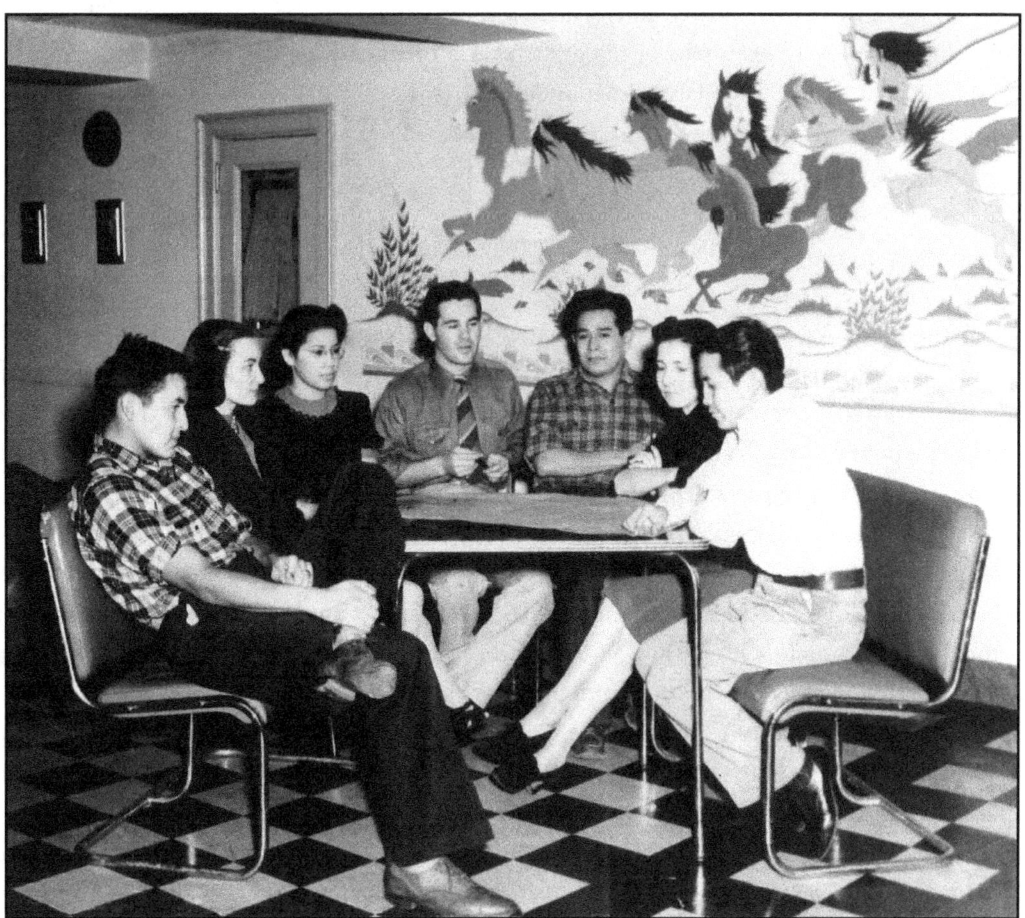

(Left to right) New Mexico's Native American young artists, Allan Houser, Woody Crumbo, Velino Shije Herrera, and Gerald Nailor, take a break with staff from their artwork in the Department of Interior penthouse/cafeteria. Interior female staff take a break with them in the top of this Washington, DC New Deal building. An oil painting, which is a reproduction of this photo, has been done by Gerald Nailor's son, Governor Gerald Nailor of Picuris Pueblo and hangs in the Picuris Art Shop of the Hotel Santa Fe. Photograph provided by the Velino Shije Herrera family. All four artists have sons who became artists.

Department of the Interior Building, Washington, DC.

The Interior Building in Washington, DC, constructed between 1935 and 1936, houses important murals by three of New Mexico's most notable Indian easel painters. The Treasury Section of Painting and Sculpture (1934–1938) and the Section of Fine Arts (1938–1943) commissioned Velino Shije Herrera (Zia), Allan Houser (Apache), and Gerald Nailor (Picuris), along with the Oklahoma artists Woodrow Crumbo (Creek/Potawatomi), James Auchiah (Kiowa), and Stephen Mopope (Kiowa), to decorate the building's arts and crafts shop, cafeteria, and employees' lounge. Each artist created vignettes of traditional tribal life in his own unique style. For example, Houser's "Apache Round Dance" and "Sacred Fire Dance" have a dynamic, linear vitality. Nailor's "Preparing Yarn for Weaving" and "Initiation Ceremony" are lovely examples of his graceful use of line and transparent color. Herrera's "Pueblo Woman and Child" and "Pueblo Symbol" show the artist's interest in pattern and geometric design. These restored murals may be seen only if one has a special security pass to enter or is accompanied by a tour guide.

Architecture

The Public Works Administration, Title II of the National Recovery Act of June, 1933, was set up to stimulate the economy through the construction of public buildings. PWA funds provided assistance for state, local, and federal projects ranging from schools and libraries to large-scale public works such as dams and highways. In the Southwest region alone, about $11 million in PWA funds was provided for Indian hospitals, day and high schools, employee quarters, dorms, shops, gyms, auditoriums, and other buildings.[9] Of this, $750,000 supported projects in Northern New Mexico such as a day school and hospital at Taos Pueblo; a school at Nambe Pueblo; roads at Taos, Nambe, and San Ildefonso; and comprehensive remodeling at the Santa Fe Indian School. (See Note at end of this chapter regarding the major changes that have taken place at the Santa Fe Indian School as of 2009.)

Nationwide, PWA architecture celebrated regional differences in culture and architecture. The goal of the building program was to provide work and to draw on indigenous building traditions and materials to create a new, distinctively American architecture. PWA architects did not simply copy old buildings, wrote a PWA advisor in 1939, they instilled new life into traditional styles.[10] The Spanish Pueblo Revival Style was by far the dominant architectural style used by PWA architects for Indian service buildings, both on the Navajo Reservation and among the Pueblos.

According to Collier, Indian Service architecture predating 1930 was "...a conglomeration of nondescript masses of wood, brick, stone, or other building materials, totally devoid of architectural feeling."[11] He recommended drawing on indigenous building traditions and using local materials and labor. For the first time, federal architects took into account the prevailing type of architecture in the area, the surrounding landscape, native building materials.[12] PWA funding made it possible to build carefully-designed schools drawing on regional architectural styles. Notwithstanding Collier's policy of sensitivity to cultural heritage, Indians were rarely involved in planning or designing buildings and were scarcely represented among laborers.

In Santa Fe, New Deal funding made it possible for regional architect, John Gaw Meem, to plan the remodeling in the Spanish Pueblo Revival style of 28 red brick school buildings constructed at Santa Fe Indian School between 1890 and 1928. Drawing on forms from Pueblo domestic architecture and mission churches, Meem made pitched roofs flat, stuccoed brick walls, altered window design and location, and added porches and buttresses. The campus became a showpiece of the Collier administration, but also showed the limitations of Collier's policy in that it emphasized exterior remodeling at the expense of students' needs for improved dorm and classroom space.

Visits to many of the surviving PWA buildings must be arranged through the Bureau of Indian Affairs, Pueblo Governors' offices, the Navajo Nation Historic Preservation Department, or individual schools.

Conclusion

The Interior Building's integration of Native American murals and the very creation of an Indian Division of New Deal programs show that, in spite of their shortcomings, Roosevelt's New Deal arts programs marked a transformation in Indian-White relations compared to the preceding decades. Indians did not take part in directing the programs or selecting artists who were hired. Fewer than one hundred benefited from jobs because of strict eligibility requirements and logistical problems. Nevertheless, they included individuals such as Maria and Julian Martinez, Tonita Pena and Velino Shije Herrera, recognized today as pioneers in the field of twentieth-century Indian art. Several, for example, Pablita Velarde and Allan Houser, have gone on to build international careers. PWAP was among the art programs at Santa Fe Indian School that contributed to that institution's tremendous impact on Indian easel painting, which continues today. The remodeling of Indian service buildings under the direction of John Gaw Meem influenced the striking revival of regional architectural styles in the Southwest. Much remains to be done to document Indian participation in New Deal programs in New Mexico, and this is just a beginning, but it shows that Datus Myers' hunch that Indian culture had value clearly understated what is apparent today.

Note: In 2009 all the Santa Fe Indian School buildings that John Gaw Meem redesigned during the New Deal were demolished. The early murals done in these buildings by the students were also destroyed rather than attempt to remove the asbestos and lead. The trees were also leveled to the ground. This action was taken by the nineteen Pueblo Governors, who are in charge of the school. It was devastating action upsetting most residents of Santa Fe and many pueblo members.

Those murals painted in the Social Studies Classroom were done by Belardo Nieto, Ted Suina, Ignatius Palme, Quincy Tahoma and Ben Quintana. Other artists, including Harrison Begay, did the larger murals in the cafeteria.

Behind the destroyed SFIS buildings were new educational and housing structures built just a year or so prior to the demolition activities. In the new library are two New Deal murals, one done by Velino Shije Herrera and the other is assumed to have been done by him. This art was originally in the Albuquerque Indian School prior to its demolition. The library has valuable New Deal research materials.

NOTES

1. For an overview of New Deal programs in New Mexico as well as an inventory of projects, see David Kammer, *The Historic and Architectural Resources of the New Deal in New Mexico*, unpublished report prepared for the New Mexico Historic Preservation Division, Santa Fe, New Mexico, June, 1994.
2. Kenneth R. Philp, *John Collier's Crusade for Indian Reform: 1920–1954*. Tucson: The University of Arizona Press, 1977, 1-25, 120-34.
3. Margaret Connell Szasz, *Education and the American Indian: The Road to Self-Determination Since 1928*, 2nd ed. Albuquerque: University of New Mexico Press, 1977, 42.
4. Mrs. Charles Collier, *The Indian Art Exhibit under the Public Works of Art Project*, Indians at Work 1 (May 1934): 28-9; Robert Fay Schrader, *The Indian Arts and Crafts Board: An Aspect of New Deal Indian Policy*, Albuquerque: University of New Mexico Press, 1983, 79-81.
5. Sally Hyer, *One House, One Voice, One Heart: Native American Education at the Santa Fe Indian School*, Santa Fe: Museum of New Mexico Press, 1990, 42.
6. William Henry Spurlock II, "Federal Support for the Visual Arts in the State of New Mexico: 1933–1943," (M.A. Thesis, University of New Mexico, 1974), 13.
7. Louise I. Stiver, "The Role of the Laboratory of Anthropology in Federally Supported New Deal Programs: 1933–1943," unpublished manuscript, 8.
8. Sally Hyer, "*Woman's Work*": *The Art of Pablita Velarde*. Santa Fe: The Wheelwright Museum of the American Indian, 1933, 8-9.
9. John Collier, "Indian Reservation Buildings in the Southwest," *American Architect and Architecture* 150 (June 1937), 36.
10. C.W. Short and R. Stanley-Brown, *Public Buildings: Architecture under the Public Works Administration, 1933–39*. Vol. 1 New York: Da Capo Press, 1986, II.
11. Ibid., 35.
12. Ibid., 38: Ellen Threinen, "The Navajos and the BIA: A Study of Government Buildings on the Navajo Reservation," unpublished document funded by the Bureau of Indian Affairs, Navajo Area Office, 1981, 1-2.

9

WHO CREATED OUR NEW DEAL TREASURES?

This information came from a variety of sources, books, personal interviews with living artists and family members of deceased artists. Another source was early interviews done by Sylvia Loomis which are at the Smithsonian and can be ordered on microfilm through a local library loan arrangement. Some of the biographies included in this chapter are available on either VHS tapes or DVDs. For further information contact Kathryn A. Flynn, the Executive Director of the National New Deal Preservation Association at: newdeal@cybermesa.com or call to (505) 690-5845 or write to P. O. Box 602, Santa Fe, NM 87504.

ABEYTA, EMILIANO

San Juan Pueblo. Native American name: Sa Pa

ABEYTA, NARCISCO "Cisco" PLATERO (1918–1998)

Navajo Name: HaSo-De (Fiercely Ascending)

Born in Canoncito December 18, 1918, Cisco began helping with shepherding at a very young age, and while out in the dry, western lands he would use charcoal or flint to draw or cut animal figures on the broad surfaces of the canyon walls. When he was six, he followed an older friend into a van that was from the Santa Fe Indian School (SFIS) and ended up in Santa Fe, where he was educated and forced to learn English and prevented from speaking his native language. He was one of Dorothy Dunn's students and painted a number of murals in the school buildings and also at Albuquerque at Maisel's Trading Post on Central. Before graduation in 1939, he was already a published artist for the 17th Annual Inter-Tribal Indian Ceremonial in Gallup, had won Second Prize for a Golden Gate Exposition poster and along with Quincy Tahoma, was selected to demonstrate his art at the 1939 Exposition. He received a scholarship to the Somerset Art Institute in Pennsylvania and attended there, prior to joining the United States Army for what he planned to be one year. Pearl Harbor changed that short stay, and he was involved in major fighting in the Pacific Theater, where he served as a Navajo Code Talker and suffered shell shock. Upon his return to New Mexico, he found the war injury had greatly impaired his ability to draw, so he took up silver smithing. Finally, in 1948, he enrolled at the University of New Mexico and began studying art with Raymond Jonson.

In 1953 his paintings were included in the Smithsonian's exhibit, "Contemporary American Indian Paintings," he made the semi-finals in the National Golden Gloves competition in Chicago, graduated from University of New Mexico with a Bachelors in Fine Arts, married Sylvia Shipley, who had three children, and settled down in Gallup to raise his new family. Four more children were born to this union, Pablita, Elizabeth, Rosemary and Tony, with all but Rosemary becoming artists and carrying on their father's legacy. He was employed for twenty-five years by the New Mexico State Employment Commission as a job placement interviewer and field representative, particularly for Native Americans, and did a lot of translating for the non-English speaking individuals. Abeyta's watercolors can be found in numerous museums in New Mexico and the country and feature Navajo mythology and creation myths, according to his artist son Tony Abeyta. He died in Presbyterian Hospital in Albuquerque, where he had been taken for a head injury.

LOCATIONS OF NEW DEAL ARTWORK: Murals were done at the Santa Fe Indian School but destroyed when buildings were demolished.

ADAMS, KENNETH MILLER (1897–1966)

Born in Topeka, Kansas, Adams was initially trained by George M. Stone, a Topeka artist. Later he attended the Art Institute of Chicago and the Art Students League in New York. In 1921, he went to Europe and studied in France and Italy for two years. Upon his return to America, he followed Andrew Dasburg, whom he had studied under in New York, to Taos. While there he was a member of the Taos Heptagon group that included Mozley, Dasburg and Lockwood. Adams, a resident of New Mexico since 1924, became the last member elected to the Taos Society of Artists before it dissolved in 1927. In 1938, a Carnegie grant brought him to the University of New Mexico in the early 1930s as an artist-in-residence, an association that ended some thirty years later as Professor Emeritus of Art.

Adams worked not only as a painter in both oil and watercolor, but also as a print maker in lithography. His style was considered realism that was simplified and unadorned, somewhat related to the Mexican art of Diego Rivera. In his University of New Mexico murals, he used a flat, linear technique to create a formal design suitable to the architectural enframement and the Indian theme of the work. Adams' representations are free of false sentiment and have a sturdy feeling for construction, linked with the premise that art's mission is to clarify inherent qualities of nature.

In 1935 Adams was invited to compete for mural decorations in the new post office in Washington, DC and as a result was awarded a commission to paint a mural "Rural Free Delivery" for the Goodland, Kansas Post Office. He also painted a mural for the Post Office in Deming in 1937. Some of his other works can be found in various locations around the state. For his work with the Treasury Department art program he was paid $42.50 a month which was greater than one could earn as a professor at the University. He also did a later mural privately for the Colorado Springs Fine Arts Center with Andrew Dasburg and Ward Lockwood.

Adams was married to Hilda Adams and Helen Osborne Hugrefe Adams. He died in Albuquerque three years after being honored with the Professor Emeritus status.

LOCATIONS OF NEW DEAL ARTWORK: Albuquerque, Carlsbad, Deming, Espanola, Las Vegas, Raton, Roswell, Taos, Santa Fe, New Mexico; Washington, DC; and Goodland, Kansas.

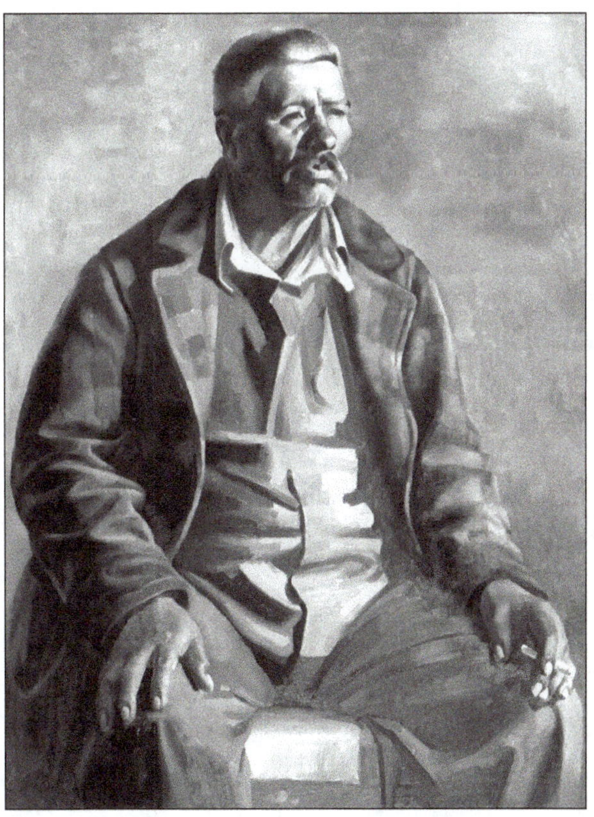

Kenneth Miller Adams, "Juan Duran," oil

ARCHULETA, ANTONIO (dates unknown)

Taos. His work is in the collection of the Museum of New Mexico.

AWAH TSIREH, see ROYBAL, ALFONSO (ca.1895–ca. 1955)

BAHE, STANLEY K. (dates unknown)

Navaho. Attended school in Phoenix.

BAKOS, JOZEF GABRYEL(1891–1977)

Bakos was born in Buffalo, New York on September 23, 1891 to a family of Polish ancestry which he never forgot nor neglected to acknowledge with pride. He also loved to share stories about his days as a street fighter in Buffalo. Bakos studied in the finest European schools and played as a child in the castles of kings. He studied at Albright Art School, Buffalo, Toronto, and in Denver with John E. Thompson along with Walter Mruk.

Bakos arrived in Santa Fe in 1921 and was the organizer of the original *Los Cinco Pintores* and the youngest member of another group called the New Mexico Painters. These groups were developed primarily to promote their work, having exhibitions throughout California and other places. In addition to painting, Bakos did carpentry work in order to pay his bills during the depression and over the years also taught at the University of Colorado in Boulder, where he was their first art instructor, the University of Denver, and Santa Fe High School. He was described in *Artists of the Canyons and Caminos* by Robertson and Nestor as "sociable, ebullient, an emotional and dramatic painter."

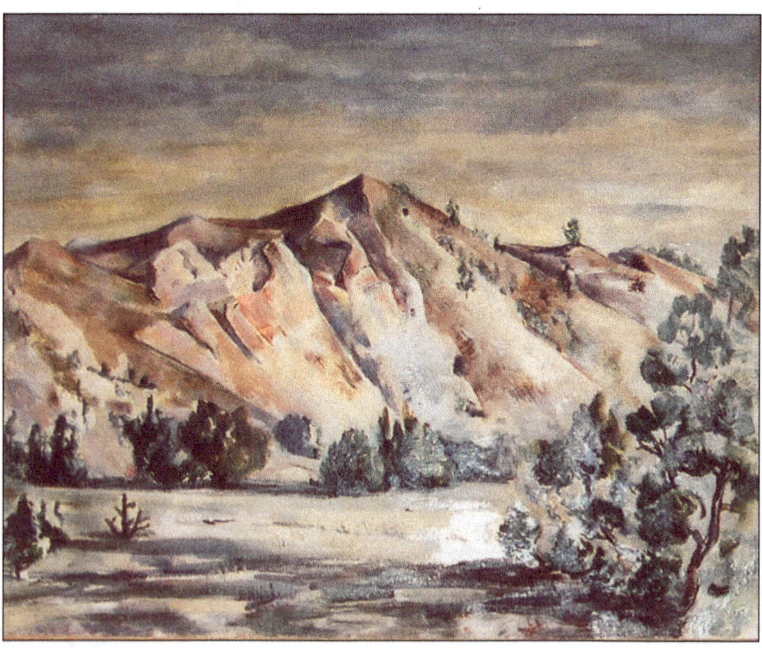

Josef Gabryel Bakos, "Hill Near Chama," oil, Socorro, New Mexico Technical University Library

He showed with other Santa Fe artists at the Los Angeles County Museum, 1923. Also in 1923 he married another artist, Teresa Dorman, an Italian woman with two small sons and they spent a good portion of their lives together, both loving the out of doors and painting their own interpretations of same. Jozef created easel paintings for the WPA Federal project. Bakos reported that he felt the project was valuable for a variety of reasons one being that it "was almost the last of the period of regional painting." In the late fifties he painted over thirty registered bulls over eight or nine years as a special commission. He once noted that he felt it was one of the best things he did in painting. He became "a Remington of bulls." After the owner of these creations died, the collection was given to the Hereford Association in Kansas City. He died in Santa Fe in 1977.

LOCATIONS OF POSSIBLE NEW DEAL ARTWORK: Clayton, Melrose, Raton, Socorro.

BAKOS, TERESA (1884 or 1888–1974)

Teresa Dorman Bakos is reported to have grown up in Trinidad, Colorado but was born in Nervi, Italy as the Countess Di Locci Di Lante. Another reference notes that her family was related to the Roman Catholic Pope at that time. She studied music in her early years but being also interested in art, she did in depth studies of the Italian Primitives for three years in churches, museums, galleries, and private collections. This research culminated in a book about her findings.

As a young woman she was married to Archibald B. Dorman from Kentucky and they lived in El Paso, Boston, and San Francisco. They were living in Berlin when son, John, was born in 1912. An exhibition in San Francisco of the work of a group of Santa Fe artists, including "My Garden" by Jozef Bakos, shown in Chicago attracted her to Santa Fe. In 1921 she brought her two young sons, Ralphael and John Dorman, to Santa Fe to see these artists and their work and two years later she was married to Bakos. They lived on the Camino de Monte Sol in a home he built and furnished with his own creations.

She never had any formal art training but noted that she belonged to no school of art since she felt there was only good painting and bad painting and she tried to follow the lead of only the "good" painters. She did not intend to give up her music for painting but enjoyed it so much she painted nearly all the time, finding no time for bridge and tea parties. She became best known for her imaginative still life creations of flowers with delicate colors and designs. Despite that she may have been on the FAP, she felt that the overall project "cheapened art and that the country never quite recovered from that." This related to the number of people who were paid to paint but knew nothing about painting. One clipping from the *Santa Fe New Mexican* provided us with the information that she taught art at the Sunmount School which may have been a private elementary school. She had exhibits of her art at the University of Denver in 1938 and in 1946 in Santa Barbara and the Museum of New Mexico.

Her son, John, later became an abstract and later a santos painter which may have come based on his early work as "a copyist" working on the New Deal art project that created the *Portfolio of Spanish-Colonial Art*. The other son, Raphel, became the vice president of Bechtel Corporation.

LOCATION OF NEW DEAL ARTWORK: Melrose

BARELA, PATROCINIO (1908–1964)

Barela was born in Bisbee, Arizona in 1908 and his mother died at his birth. When he was a small boy, he and his father moved to New Mexico. At age eleven he ran away from home to face the world. He had no schooling and spoke no English but lived in Colorado for a time with a black foster family who taught him English and "American Ways." In 1930 he returned to New Mexico, married and settled in a small village in Taos Canyon. He began carving bultos and worked under the Emergency Relief Administration as a teamster. His carving skills were brought to the attention of R. V. Hunter with the WPA/Federal Arts Project in 1935 and finally he was able to be employed to carry out his chosen vocation through that program. Barela and Vernon Hunter became close friends with Hunter serving also was his patron, promoter, and advisor. He helped him relocate his family to a pleasant town in the mountains and interested Holger Cahill and others in Washington to the simple beauty of Barela's folk art. They included him in every national exhibition for which his work was appropriate. For example, some of his works were displayed at the New York World's Fair in 1939. Today one can find his work in various museums including the Museum of Fine Art in Santa Fe and the Harwood Foundation collection in Taos. Unfortunately these unique creations are scarce since Barela died in a fire in his Canjon workshop October 24, 1964.

According to Charles L. Briggs in his book, *The Wood Carvers of Cordova, New Mexico: Social Dimensions of an Artistic "Revival,"* "Barela's work is acknowledged as some of the most important visionary art in the New Mexico folk tradition and the existence of much of his work can be directly credited to Hunter. His dedication to the man first and the employee/artist second encouraged Barela to carve many of his greatest works while in the employment of the FAP. Hunter had an ability to make suggestions in such a way that the artist immediately accepted them as his own and proceeded to impress his admirers with inspired work."

Patrocinio's son and two grandsons, Carlos and Luiz, have carried on his artistic talents with their own creations.

POSSIBLE LOCATIONS OF NEW DEAL ARTWORK: Bandelier, Santa Fe, Taos; Washington, DC.

BARGER, ERIK (dates unknown)

Barger lived in Albuquerque. He worked primarily in watercolors. He created replicas of the different military insignias to be displayed at Kirtland and in traveling tours of New Deal art.

LOCATION OF NEW DEAL ARTWORK: Gallup

BARROWS, CHARLES (1903–1988)

Charles Barrows was born in Washington, Pennsylvania on October 17, 1903 and started drawing at age five. After high school he spent three years working in a chemical laboratory, but abandoned that career in favor of attending Carnegie Technical Institute's College of Fine Arts night school for one year in order to learn more about painting. During the summer he took classes at the Pennsylvania Academy of Fine Arts. Then he took classes in New York City at the Art Student League where he attempted to study while trying to make a living. Finding this difficult, he chose to quit the art school and work by himself.

Barrows heard about Santa Fe from the Santa Fe cowboy and artist, Hal West, in a sandwich shop in Long Island where they worked side by side. Finally Barrows and a friend, Jim Morris, took off hitchhiking and arrived in Santa Fe in June 1928. Fortune smiled on these men once they arrived and they became active in the art colony. Charles or "Chuck" was included in the WPA Art Project and earned $74 a month for his watercolors. He was one of the artists that worked on the *Portfolio*. He married and moved to Chimayo, where, as his family increased, he was able to fish and hunt for the family's food. This mouth-to-mouth lifestyle finally became too difficult so Barrows went back to New York to learn the silk screen process. While there he became a charter member of the National Serigraph Society and found the medium that he enjoyed the most. When he returned to New Mexico, he made the first reproductions of the paintings of Navajo artist, Harrison Begay; and he and his second wife, Mary Habberley, developed a successful silk screen business, The Tewa Enterprises, which was later merged with the Artists Exchange on Canyon Road in the historic building known as the Borrego House. They worked with numerous artists in Santa Fe and New Mexico.

Barrows felt that painting should always present more than just a picture of something. They should be looked at as one listens to music—"an emotional rather than a mental process." Another love of this artist was collecting, identifying, painting, and writing about the numerous species of mushrooms. He became a recognized authority in the field of mycology. He died on May 28, 1988 at the age of 85.

POSSIBLE LOCATIONS OF NEW DEAL ARTWORK: Albuquerque—University of New Mexico, Raton; Washington, DC.

BARTON, HOWARD A. (1907–1992)

Born February 2, 1907 in Evansville, Indiana, Barton studied at the University of New Mexico from 1937–1939 with Raymond Jonson and in the summer of 1938 with Loren Mozley in Taos. According to Shirley Scanlon, his stepdaughter, he went into the Army prior to WWII and when he returned he was disabled but that didn't stop him from pursuing a variety of career opportunities to challenge his mind. He went to electronics school, photography classes, and dietetic classes and at 65 years graduated from chiropractic training and practiced for a period of time. "He was very intelligent and was always interested in learning something and then moving on to something else," she noted. Exhibited: "Art and the New Deal in the Southwest: Arizona and New Mexico," University of Arizona Art Museum on November 27, 1979 to June 30, 1980, at the Phoenix Museum. Most are not aware he was one of three brother-in-laws that were all in the New Deal art projects. The other two were Bill Lumpkins and Brooks Willis. He died in Albuquerque.

POSSIBLE LOCATIONS OF NEW DEAL ARTWORK: Albuquerque—University of New Mexico, Las Cruces.

BAUMANN, GUSTAVE (1881–1971)

Born in Magdeburg, Germany in 1881, the family immigrated to Chicago when Baumann was 10 years of age. He grew up there and studied at the Art Institute of Chicago as well as the Kunstgewerbe Schule, in Munich. In 1909 he went to Indiana and painted but began spending summers in Taos as of 1918. He ultimately moved to Santa Fe and in 1925 married Jane Devereux Henderson of Denver. They moved into their home at 409 Camino de las Animas where they lived for many years. The couple had one daughter, Ann. In 1939 he published a book of twenty six woodcuts which was selected as one of the "Fifty Books of the Year." A versatile artist, Baumann excelled as a painter, but also worked as a print maker and a carver of marionettes. In fact, he became internationally famous as the creator of color woodcuts depicting a wide range of Southwestern subjects. He was the New Mexico area coordinator of the initial PWAP program from December 1933–June 1934. In 1952 he was made a Fellow of the School of American Research.

Working closely with Will Shuster, they created the head of the first Santa Fe Fiesta's Zozobra, a giant sized puppet also known as "Old Man Gloom." Baumann reportedly made the head out of a "corrugated board box which was jammed on a pole draped with cheesecloth and stuffed to the shoulders with tumbleweeds." Bauman's normal size marionettes are in the New Mexico Museum of Art and are frequently exhibited at Christmas time. In a more serious vein, he created the beautiful altar screen in the Episcopal Church of the Holy Faith in Santa Fe. He died in 1971 in Santa Fe and a book about him and his creations was published in 1993 by the Museum of New Mexico Press.

LOCATION OF NEW DEAL ARTWORK: He served as a supervisor of the PWAP activity.

BEGAY, HARRISON (1917–2012)

Begay's Indian name was Haskay Yah Ne Yah (Warrior Who Walked Up to His Enemy) and he was born at White Cone, Arizona on November 15, 1917. After attending several reservation schools and graduating from the Santa Fe Indian School in 1939, he attended Black Mountain in North Carolina and Phoenix Junior College before WWII where he served for three years in the Army.

Begay became an internationally known artist and mural painter, noted for the fine, delicate lines and the softened colors of his paintings, often depicting scenes from the everyday life and work of his people. His work is distinguished by meticulous concern for detail, his ability to catch a moment of action, and can be characterized as "quiet and peaceful." He was able to work as a full-time artist and has had his paintings reproduced in quantity as silk screens. Since 1946, his work has been widely exhibited and has won numerous major awards. According to some sources, Begay's paintings have exerted greater influence on Navajo artists than those of any other painter.

In the recent past there was an exhibition of his paintings in Japan and a book published including many reproductions of his paintings with text in Japanese. In his last years he lived in the Chinle area with a niece and a friend.

LOCATION OF NEW DEAL ARTWORK: Gallup

BERNINGHAUS, JULIUS CHARLES (1905–1988)

Berninghuas was born at St Louis, Missouri in 1905 to artist Oscar Berninghaus and first wife, Emelia Miller. Charles first came to Taos at the age of three with his parents and sister where they lived in the summers. He attended public schools in St. Louis and studied at the St. Louis School of Fine Arts, the Art Institute of Chicago and the Arts Student League. The family moved to Taos permanently in his late teens and he lived there for the remainder of his life until his death in 1988. He was a Western landscape and still life painter and almost always worked outdoors. He assisted his father with the murals for the Missouri State Capitol and other commercial projects. He loved to fish and play tennis and was married twice, once to Mary Jane Woolsey, whose brothers, Carl, Wood, and Jean, were also engaged in art.

LOCATION OF NEW DEAL ARTWORK: Washington, DC.

BERNINGHAUS, OSCAR EDMUND (1874–1952)

Oscar Berninghaus was born in St. Louis, Missouri in 1874. The son of a lithograph salesman, he was educated in St. Louis and taught himself art. He did attend the St. Louis School of Fine Arts at night and later taught at Washington University in St. Louis. He became an excellent lithographer himself and the company for whom he worked, as a gesture of appreciation, gave him a month vacation in 1899 and he chose to travel out West. He did pencil sketching as he traveled and entered northern New Mexico tied in a chair that was tied on the top of a railroad car. This arrangement was worked out by the conductor so he could view and sketch the whole panorama of beauty. When he returned to St. Louis, he married Emelia Miller in 1900 and brought her to his beloved Taos in the summers. During that time he became one of the six original founding members of the Taos Society of Artists which was organized in 1912. He also became well known as an illustrator and frequently designed the elaborate floats for the annual "Veiled Prophet" parades in St. Louis.

After his wife's early death he moved himself and his two children to Taos permanently in 1925 but retained a studio in St. Louis which was next door to his friend, Charles Russell. During his early years, Berninghaus's paintings were of the Pueblo Indians, the Spanish Americans, the adobes, the mountains, generally with at least one horse. With his practice as a lithographic artist and illustrator, his approach was direct and objective, showing the Indians as they were rather than posed or nostalgic stereotypes. His technique was to work out of doors, painting on the scene. After he moved permanently to Taos, his style became more modern, his compositions more complex, and his colors richer. As a New Deal artist, he created murals in the main post offices of Phoenix, Arizona, Weatherford, Texas, and Fort Scott, Kansas. The latter mural was restored by a family friend in 1988. A second marriage to Winnie Shuler, the daughter of a prominent doctor in Raton, took place in 1932. Oscar died in 1952.

POSSIBLE LOCATIONS OF NEW DEAL ARTWORK: Los Lunas, Raton; Phoenix, Arizona (post office); Weatherford, Oklahoma (post office); Fort Scott, Kansas (post office).

BISTTRAM, EMIL JAMES (1895–1976)

Bisttram was born in Austria-Hungary on April 7, 1895. In 1906 he moved to New York where he began working early and developed a career as a commercial artist but also became an accomplished fine arts teacher. He studied successively at the National Academy of Design, Cooper Union, the Art Students League, and with Howard Giles at the New York School of Fine and Applied Art. He first traveled to New Mexico in 1930, for a three-month stay. Here he encountered the challenge as a painter in adjusting to the strong light and color typical of the region. He went on to Mexico to study true fresco techniques with Diego Rivera with the support of a Guggenheim grant which also afforded him the opportunity to return to Taos in 1931. At that time he opened the Heptagon Gallery which was the first commercial gallery in town. He also became known as the first teacher of modern art in Taos and opened the Taos School of Art with an avant-garde curriculum.

In 1938, Bisttram founded the New Mexico Transcendental Artists group. Bisttram's own style reflected the diverse range of his interests, from a 1930s classicism to cosmic abstractions. His work was influenced by Kandinsky, and by the theory of dynamic symmetry concerning the relationships of geometric forms.

Possibly because of this versatility and abilities as a teacher, his fellow artists selected him to be their supervisor during the first federal art project (PWAP) in New Mexico. In a 1963 interview, he recalled the artists got paid $56.00 a month and had to paint one painting a week which he collected and transferred on to Washington. Bisttram was one of the Taos "Fresco Quartet" who created the outstanding works in the Old Taos County Courthouse. He, along with Bert Phillips, Victor Higgins and Ward Lockwood, was commissioned in 1934 to execute a series of ten frescos in the courtroom. Here we see the true fresco technique and the interpretation of the subject matter in the full-bodied Marxist inspired manner of the Mexican muralists as adopted by the New Mexican artists. Now some sixty years later, those works are in the process of being restored.

He created another mural, "Justice Tempered With Mercy," for the Federal Courthouse in Roswell which is now in the lobby of the old Federal Courthouse in Albuquerque. The transfer occurred when the Roswell building was demolished. Another mural was done for the post office in Ranger, Texas. His most major work done during the project is in the

Department of Justice Building in Washington, DC. He called it "Justice" and was paid $2,500 for his nine months work on it. Bisttram lived in Taos until his death in 1976.

LOCATIONS OF NEW DEAL ARTWORK: Albuquerque, Raton, Taos; Washington, DC; Ranger, Texas.

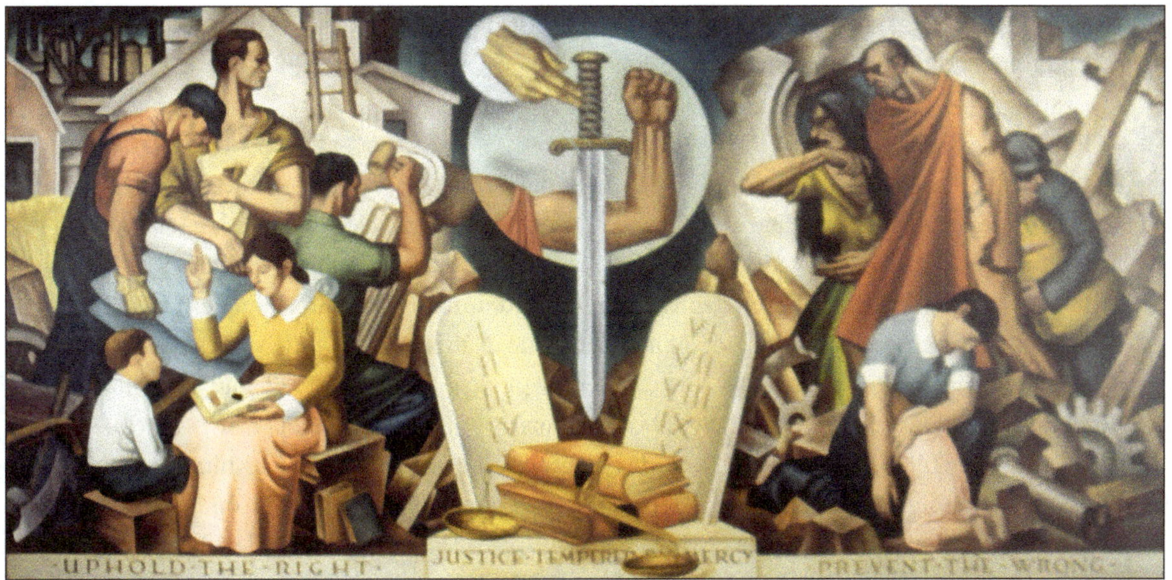

"Justice Tempered With Mercy: Uphold the Right, Prevent the Wrong" by Emil James Bisttram is in the old Federal courthouse in Albuquerque and another "Justice" mural is in the U.S. Department of Justice in Washington, DC. It emphasizes justice for women and children. Photograph by Pat Berrett.

BLACK, LAVERNE NELSON (1887–1938)

LaVerne Nelson Black was born at Viola, Wisconsin, in the Kickapoo Valley. This area was rich in Indian lore and as a boy, Black began drawing horses and Indians using vegetable juices and earth for his painting supplies. He once reported that he used "the red keel, a soft marking stone which the Indians used for painting their faces for their dances." In 1906 the family moved to Chicago and he enrolled in the Chicago Academy of Fine Arts. Because of his outstanding work he received a scholarship there the second year. Following his training he did artwork for newspapers in Chicago and New York City but continued painting. This included western pictures for the Santa Fe Railway. At some point he began sculpting in bronze and was the first to be shown at Tiffany's since Remington, an indication of his high quality work.

Ill health caused Black to take his wife and two children out West where they settled in Taos and once again in Indian country, he did some of his best work. Many in New Mexico remember well his snow scenes with Indians on horseback, the snow covered mountains and adobe buildings. One of his murals can be seen at the art museum in Carlsbad.

A warmer climate was required to improve his failing health so the family this time chose Phoenix. While in Arizona, he did four murals in post offices for the Public Works Administration including some in Phoenix. Friends believe he may have contracted a form of paint poisoning while doing the murals because not long after he required medical attention at Mayo Clinic and later died in a Chicago hospital at age 51.

POSSIBLE LOCATIONS OF NEW DEAL ARTWORK: Carlsbad, Roswell, Santa Fe; Washington, DC; Phoenix, Arizona.

BLUMENSCHEIN, ERNEST L. (1874–1960)

Blumenschein was born in Pittsburgh, Pennsylvania in 1874 and studied at Cincinnati Art Academy, Academie Julien and Ecole des Beaux Arts, Paris. He taught at the Art Students League, New York and first visited Taos in 1898 later spending summers there in 1910–1918. In 1919 he moved to Taos permanently and remained until his death in Albuquerque in 1960. Some of his achievements include being elected to National Academy of Design in 1927, receiving an Honorary Master of Arts, University of New Mexico in 1947, and being named Honorary Fellow in Fine Arts by the School of American Research, Santa Fe in 1948. No New Deal work by him is known of in New Mexico but a large mural was done by him for the post office in Walsenberg, Colorado. His Taos home was donated to the Kit Carson Museum and is open to the public on a regular basis.

POSSIBLE LOCATION OF NEW DEAL ARTWORK: Walsenberg, Colorado.

BOYD, ELIZABETH (E. Boyd) (1903–1974)

Elizabeth Boyd White was born in Philadelphia on September 23, 1903. She received training at the Academy of Fine Arts in Philadelphia and the Grande Chaumiere in Paris. Her studies were in both fine art and art history in her early years. She arrived in New Mexico in 1929 and began using a childhood nickname (E. Boyd) to sign her artwork. She returned to Philadelphia briefly but returned in 1930 to start a new life in New Mexico. Employment was hard to find so she worked along with other Santa Feans in the office of the Emergency Direct Relief Program. She joined several other artists in 1933 in forming the Rio Grande Painters with the common goal of displaying and selling their art since there were no galleries at that time. Unfortunately the goal was hard to achieve with a deepening depression and the group disbanded. Boyd was recruited by Donald Bear, the regional Federal Art Project Director, to help locate a New Mexico artist for the state director and she recommended Vernon Hunter who did get the job.

Hunter then assigned her to work on a mutual dream of theirs which involved documenting in color literal renderings of santos, altar screens, missal stands, etc. This became the forerunner of the *Portfolio of Spanish-Colonial Design in New Mexico* which became New Mexico's contribution to a federal project called the National Index of American Design. This nationwide project was established to record information on and the appearance of objects produced by Americans of European descent. Two hundred copies of the *Portfolio* were created in 1938 and Boyd wrote the text relying heavily on historic sources for her descriptions. From this she went on to write other books and became the internationally recognized authority on Spanish-Colonial Art of New Mexico. She continued to live and do her artwork in Santa Fe and was actively involved in the creation of the International Folk Art Museum. She was married four times and died on September 30, 1974 in Santa Fe.

POSSIBLE LOCATIONS OF NEW DEAL ARTWORK: Santa Fe (various sites), Roswell.

BURBANK, ELBRIDGE AYER (1858–1949)

Burbank was born in Harvard, Illinois 1858 and lived in Muskogee, Oklahoma and San Francisco, California where he died in 1949. Burbank was an expert in the use of crayons as well as oils and watercolors. He also did an autobiography called *Burbank Among the Indians*. His work is regarded as historically important because his portraits are, in some instances, the only visual records of some Indian subjects. Before Geronimo's death in 1909, he told Burbank that he liked him better than any white man he had ever known. Their friendship had begun in 1898 when Geronimo sat for his portrait, and thereafter Burbank often visited and painted the old warrior. Burbank made friends among the Indians not just because he paid them well for posing but because he liked them. Frequently they were his guests at meals, and on occasion they spent the night at his studio. They were painted whether they were famous or not, for Burbank chose them for their character. In all, he painted representations of more than 125 western tribes.

LOCATION OF NEW DEAL ARTWORK: Gallup

BURK, WILLIAM EMMETT

(Little known)

CASSIDY, GERALD aka IRA DIAMOND CASSIDY (1879–1934)

This Covington, Kentucky native was born Ira Diamond Cassidy on November 10, 1879 and was the son of a contractor and builder. He grew up in Cincinnati and went to the Mechanics Art Institute and took first prize for drawing at the early age of twelve. He was greatly influenced by Duveneck of Munich and became one of three best commercial lithographers in the country, living in New York and New Jersey. When he came to New Mexico in 1896 because of tuberculosis, he chose to change from commercial to fine art and also changed his name to Gerald at that time. He also included the Indian sign of the sun between the two names making it look like his name was Gerald O'Cassidy, the family's original name in Ireland. He worked in Albuquerque for ten years and also in Denver specializing in theatrical posters and portraits. In January 1912 he brought his new bride, Ina Sizer, to Santa Fe for their honeymoon. He was desirous of painting the Indians and she hoped to write about them.

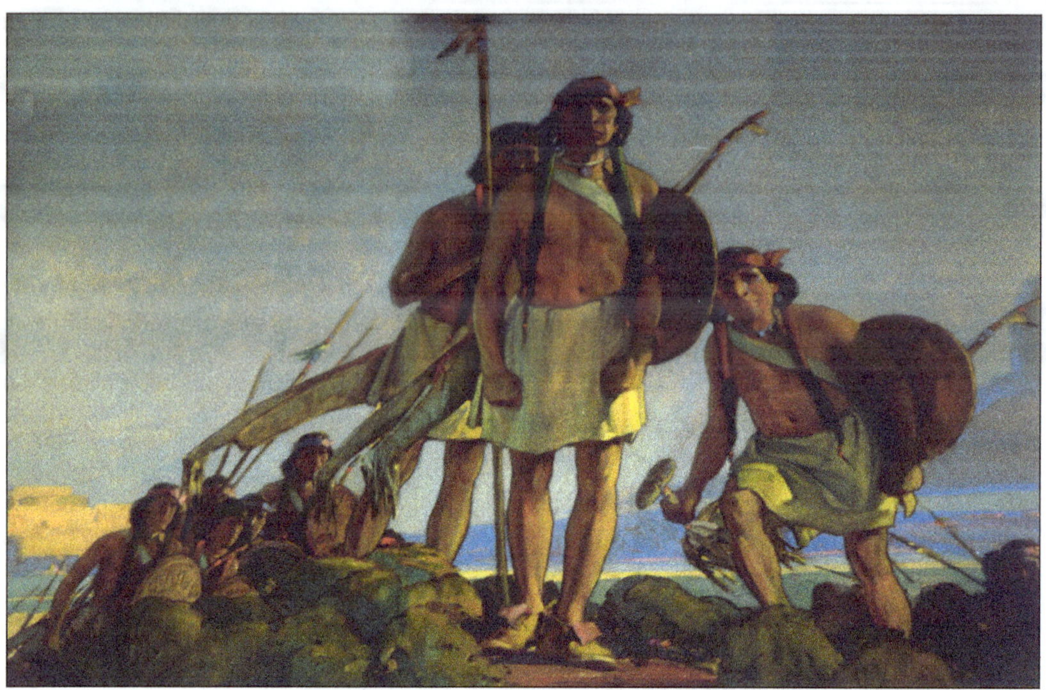

Gerald Cassidy, "Indians," oil, Santa Fe Main Post Office

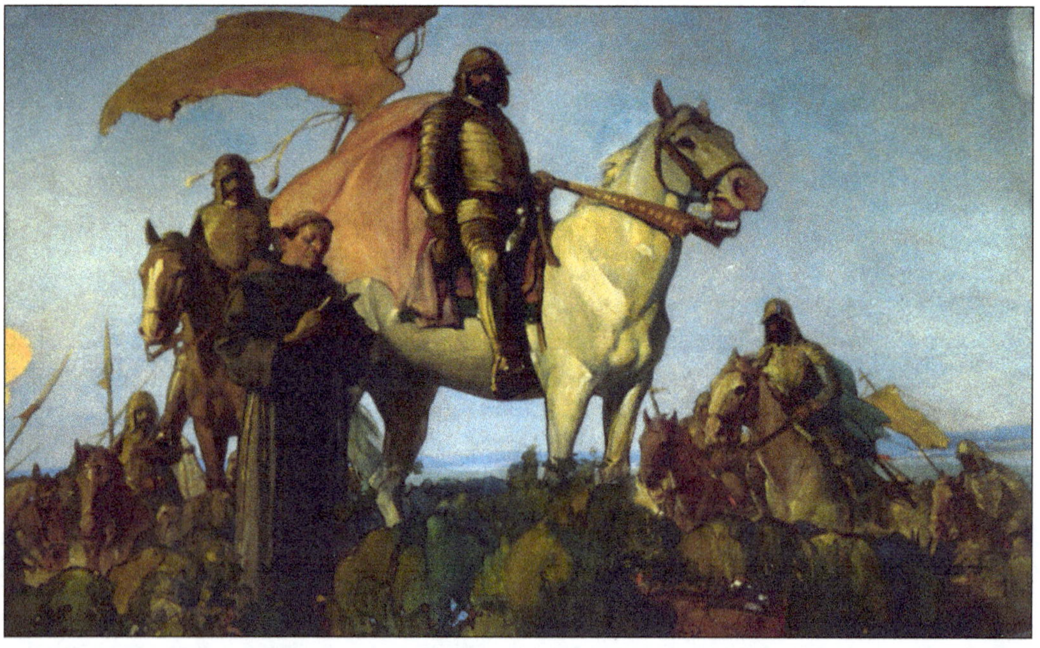

Gerald Cassidy, "Spaniards," oil, Santa Fe Main Post Office

These two large murals were not done as a New Deal project but rather privately for a theater on the Santa Fe Plaza where the First National Bank is currently. They are included to honor his talent because according to his wife, Cassidy "gave his life for the WPA" unexpectedly.

Gerald and Ira both accomplished their goals. In fact, he became known as "the last painter who painted Indians while they were still wild Indians," according to his wife. They both participated in the federally funded projects. She became the director of the WPA Federal Writers Project in New Mexico and he was the first local artist here to be chosen by the PWAP to do a large mural in Santa Fe. It was to be for the St. Francis Auditorium in Santa Fe. He planned to paint on a very large canvas so he rented a warehouse to work in. Unfortunately, the warehouse was poorly ventilated and Cassidy, working high on scaffolding, became very ill from carbon monoxide poisoning and died in a matter of weeks in 1934, as mentioned above. According to his fellow artist, Gus Baumann, he was a most prolific worker and this was the only project he failed to complete. Other fine work of this painter can be found in various locations in Santa Fe, including the Main Post Office, La Fonda Hotel, and around the world. These were all done privately.

CERVANTEZ, PEDRO "PETE" LOPEZ (1914–1987)

Cervantez was born in Wilcox, Arizona to parents of Mexican-Indian and Spanish heritage. The father worked for the Santa Fe Railroad and was transferred to Texico, New Mexico where the five children received their schooling. During the depression era he worked as an apprentice with Vernon Hunter on the historical murals located in the De Baca County Courthouse in Fort Sumner. It would appear that he never received recognition for his contribution to these murals.

For two years beginning in 1938, he studied art at Eastern New Mexico University in Portales and then he joined the Army. After serving in the armed forces in Europe during World War II, he returned to his studies at the Hill and Canyon School of the Arts in Santa Fe from 1949 to 1952. Pedro married Merle Hernandez who had two sisters who married the other two Cervantez brothers. Pedro and his growing family lived in Texico and Clovis, New Mexico where he worked as a sign painter for the Coca-Cola Bottling plant and later in the 1960s for the Clovis Municipal Schools. His wife is still working for the school system and may still have some of his floral paintings from the WPA period. She indicated that he quit painting in 1984 when his eyesight and arthritis worsened. He died in Clovis in July of 1987 at the age of 72 and was buried in the Bovina Cemetery.

LOCATIONS OF NEW DEAL ARTWORK: Fort Sumner, Melrose; Washington, DC.

CHALEE, POP aka Merina Lujan Hopkins (1906–1993)

One of five children, Pop Chalee was born in the Taos Pueblo to a Taos Indian father and an East Indian mother whom he met in Salt Lake City. Her grandmother gave her the Pop Chalee name which means 'Blue Flower." She was also known as Merina Luhan and was related to Mabel Dodge Luhan. All this gave this young girl quite a beginning. Her love of horses started early and she remembered riding around Taos and visiting many of the "big artists" in town; sitting and watching them paint but not realizing it was going to have such an effect upon her life. She went to school at the Santa Fe Indian School which she indicated was "military" but she was able to adjust. There she studied under Dorothy Dunn whom she noted "never really had to teach the Indians since it came natural for them. They worked primarily in watercolors since it was more like the earth colors and writing on skins. They worked in the two dimensional traditional style." While there she met and married a young man and soon was a young mother of a boy and girl. In 1937 when Dunn opened The Studio, an art school at the Indian School, Pop returned to study with her again for three years. As her own style emerged, she developed the horses and ponies with long hoofs and flying tails that she became famous for, along with other animals. She was the creator of "Bambi" for Walt Disney who came to Santa Fe and tried to get her and other Indians to go to California. She didn't go at that time but later was involved with Metro Goldywn Mayer studios in the movie "Annie Get Your Gun" and traveled all over the country promoting it. Later while working with Warner Brothers, she also worked with the Santa Fe Railroad and was present at the ceremonies when the Santa Fe Railroad connected at San Francisco and Oakland. She decorated many of the trains and also did murals for Howard Hughes in the Albuquerque Municipal Airport. Those murals now hang in the new airport. In 1990 she was honored at the 17th annual Governor's Achievement and Excellence Award ceremony and a large creation of her ponies hangs outside the Office of the Secretary of State in the State Capitol in Santa Fe. It was her last large commissioned work.

She worked in the Indian Division of PWAP and created a number of works that were distributed around the country. During an interview she reported, "This period was a happy time despite the economic difficulties [that] all artists were having due to the depression. The happiness was directly related to the love we artists had for one another. We were all like one big happy family." Pop was a small framed woman who packed quite a lot of living into her life and would probably say "Jiminy Crickets, it was a good one!" She died in Santa Fe in 1993 and a memorial service at the Laboratory of Anthropology included representatives from the Taos Pueblo, the Santa Fe artists, the East Indian Sikh religious group, family, and many friends.

LOCATION OF POSSIBLE NEW DEAL ARTWORK: Unknown

CHAPMAN, MANVILLE (1903–1978)

A Colfax County pioneer's son, Chapman grew up in Raton. Little was found about his youth. When designated to do the eight New Deal murals at the Shuler Theatre he spent weeks collecting photographs and stories of Raton's earliest day. This series shows trails blazed and towns created by the early settlers, stagecoach routes and railroad tracks. Chapman also lived in Taos and finally moved to California. He is well known for his woodcuts and paper batiks and during the New Deal activities an exhibit of his batiks traveled around the state and country. He created woodcuts for the Portfolio of Spanish-Colonial Design of New Mexico as part of the Index of American Design and did the woodcuts for the program of the opening of the Roswell Museum. He taught other WPA artists and other aspiring students in Raton.

POSSIBLE LOCATIONS OF NEW DEAL ARTWORK: Albuquerque, Clayton, Raton, Roswell, Santa Fe, Socorro.

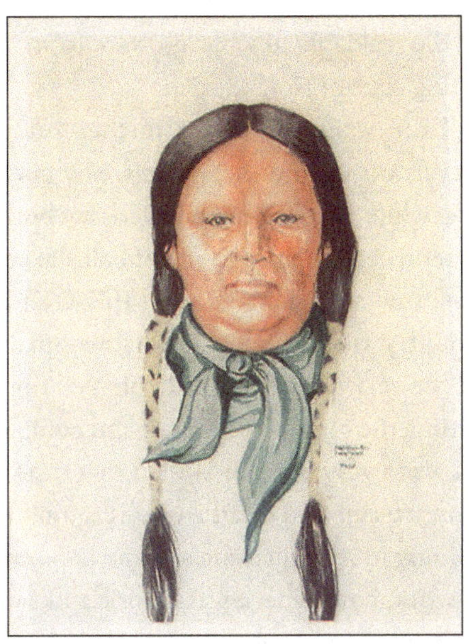

Manville Chapman, "Indian Man," Watercolor, Socorro, New Mexico Technical University

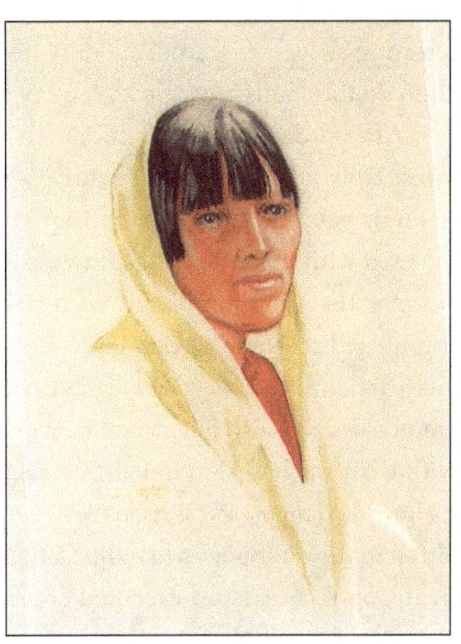

Manville Chapman, "Indian Woman," watercolor, Socorro, New Mexico Technical University

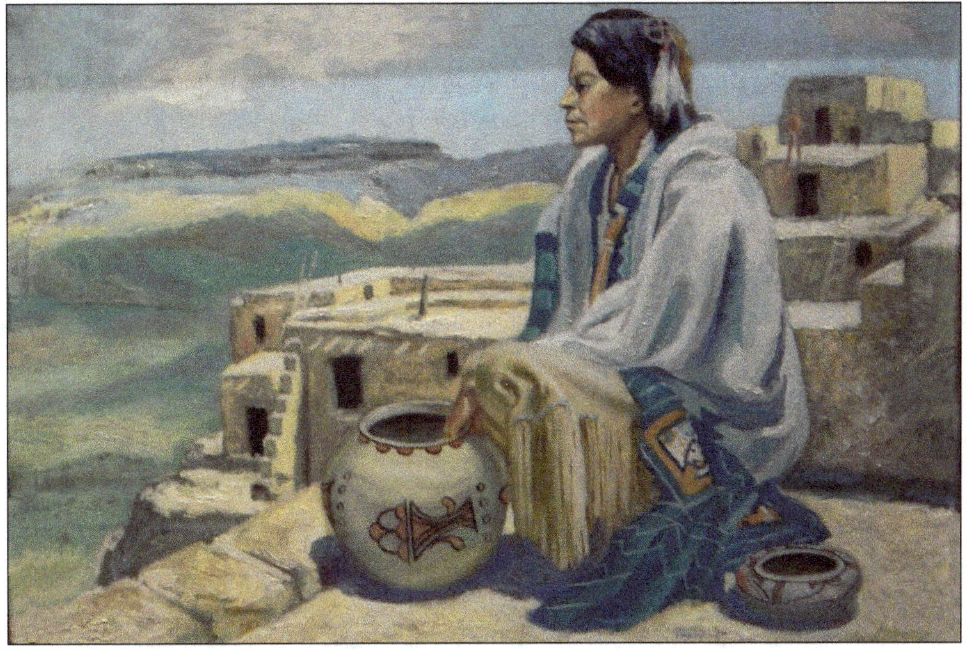

Manville Chapman, "Untitled," oil, Las Cruces, Farm and Ranch Museum

CLAFLIN, MAJEL (Dates Unknown)

This Michigan preacher's daughter from Eaton Rapids went to Chicago to study at the Art Institute, living at "Temperament Chambers," which used to be at the corner of Rush and Superior Streets. Her stories of the life and characters she knew there are said to be as interesting as were her amusing drawings. Some of the residents in Chicago were from Taos and no doubt that is how she learned of the enchanting state of New Mexico.

After completing her studies in Chicago, Claflin went abroad for further study in France, Holland, Spain, and Portugal—riding a bicycle on most of her travels. She became well known as a cartoonist and poster artist but once, while visiting New Mexico, she became fascinated with the indigenous tin work. When she returned to Chicago she did all she could to master the handling of this material, but she became so fascinated with this craft that she returned to New Mexico and went into the country visiting homes of native Spanish-American families who could teach her more about the very early patterns of pierced tin and painted glass. She also did a great deal of study regarding the origin of this craft and compared it with what she had seen in her European travels. It was a very popular craft at that time and the New Mexico Art Project of WPA employed many artisans and crafts persons to make tin lighting fixtures for places like the Little Theater building in Albuquerque and the Laboratory of Anthropology. Claflin executed copies of native work, embroideries, tin work and santos and bultos for the New Mexico Art Project and many of her copies were included in the *Portfolio of Spanish-Colonial Design* for the Index of American Design. She also did many of the original tin lighting fixtures for La Fonda Hotel.

Claflin often referred to herself laughingly as "Jill of all Trades." In addition to her art work, she was also active in the New Deal education programs. The Harwood Foundation of Taos is beholden to her for having been their cataloger of the Mabel Dodge Luhan collection.

LOCATION OF NEW DEAL ARTWORK: Melrose.

CONNELY, RUTH (Dates Unknown)

Little is known about this artist, but three portfolios of Native American rugs done by her have been found in the Laboratory of Anthropology in Santa Fe, the Center for Southwest Research at University of New Mexico's Zimmerman Library and at the Special Collections Library in Albuquerque at 423 Central. They are identified as a New Deal art project and we will watch for more to show up in the future despite their being virtually unknown. The author purchased a small woodcut by her at a garage sale some years ago. Watch for "Connely—with only one "l."

LOCATION OF NEW DEAL ARTWORK: Santa Fe—Laboratory of Anthropology; Albuquerque—Zimmerman Library and Special Collections Library

COOK, HOWARD (1901–1980)

Cook was born July 16, 1901 in Springfield, Massachusetts and began painting in high school. He later studied for three terms at the Art Students League of New York and at different intervals studied in France, Turkey, China, Mexico, and North and Central America. Some of this was funded by Guggenheim Foundation Fellowships. He arrived on the Taos scene in 1926 and later was involved with the New Deal projects but did none in New Mexico. His contributions to these projects included frescoes in the Law Library at Springfield, Massachusetts, the Federal Building in Pittsburgh, Pennsylvania and in post offices in Corpus Christi, Texas and San Antonio, Texas.

The San Antonio murals may be the largest pieces of art work in any post office in this part of the country and Cook did create life size frescoes on a wall of a structure in Taos in preparation for the many frescoes he was to do for that building. Later these "practice wall creations" were discovered and the wall was removed intact and made a part of a marvelous exhibit and book, *The Taos Artists and Their Patrons* by Dean Porter, former Director of the Snite Museum at Notre Dame University. This massive wall piece is now on view at the Witte Museum in San Antonio.

In 1967 he was the Roswell New Mexico's art center's first "Artist-in-Residence" and they have an extremely large collection of his work and information about him in their archives. A number of his paintings, created when he was a war correspondent, can be viewed in the McBride Museum of New Mexico Military Institute in Roswell and an obscure creation can also be seen in the lobby of the Sagebrush Inn in Taos. In addition to his fresco work, Cook did a number of etchings, woodcuts, and watercolors. He died in Santa Fe on June 24, 1980 and the Roswell Museum and Art Center was the recipient of his estate's art collection. His wife, Barbara Latham, a writer and artist, lived in Santa Fe until her death in 1988.

LOCATIONS OF NEW DEAL ARTWORK: Corpus Christi and San Antonio, Texas; Springfield, Massachusetts; Pittsburgh, Pennsylvania.

COOKE, REGINA TATUM (1902–1988)

Born in Corsicana, Texas on August 22, 1902, the daughter of a district judge, Mrs. Cooke was salutatorian of her high school graduating class, studied art at Ward-Belmont Junior College in Nashville, Tennessee, a girl's school and received her bachelor's degree in art from Colorado College. Her paintings were exhibited in the Denver Art Museum early on. She married in 1925 and had one son. She moved to Taos in 1933 and along with many Taos artists, found a livelihood with the Works Projects Administration painting a series of dioramas, now the property of the Museum of Fine Arts in Santa Fe. Cooke also worked on the *Portfolio of Spanish-Colonial Design*. Her body of artwork that is best remembered is her Southwestern mission church series. She is likewise and maybe better known for her writing career and impact upon the art movement in New Mexico. She was the arts editor of *The Taos News* for twenty three years and had a total of nearly fifty years in journalism with columns in *Southwest Art, New Mexico Magazine, Mademoiselle, Golden Magazine, Christmas Annual, El Crepusculo e la Libertad* and numerous brochures. Cooke also helped found the Taos Arts Association, the Taos Little Theater and started the Taos municipal school's art collection. Before her death at 86 in Taos, she had numerous art exhibitions and her artwork is in numerous private and public collections.

LOCATIONS OF NEW DEAL ARTWORK: Clayton, Melrose, Raton, Roswell.

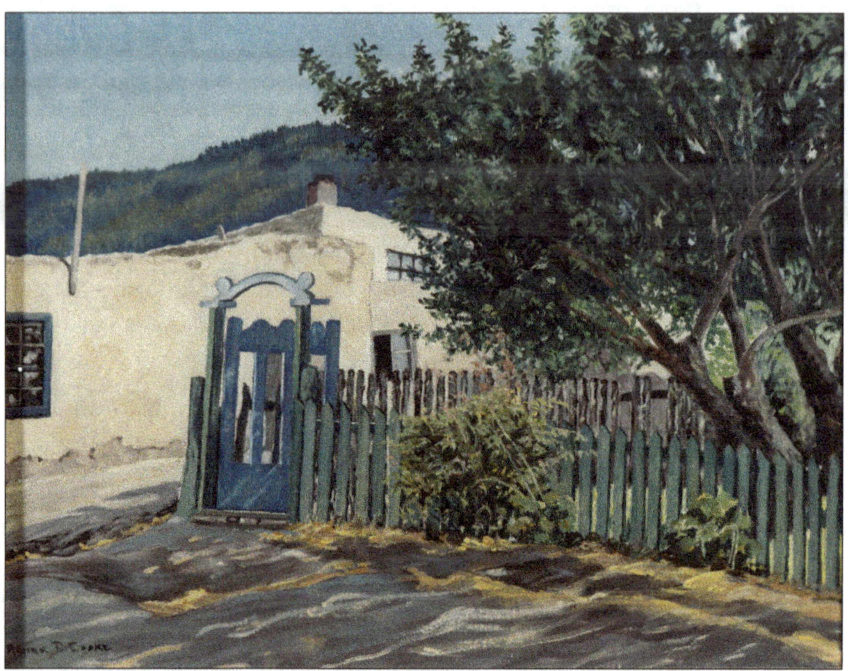

Regina Tatum Cooke, "Blue Gate," oil, Clayton High School

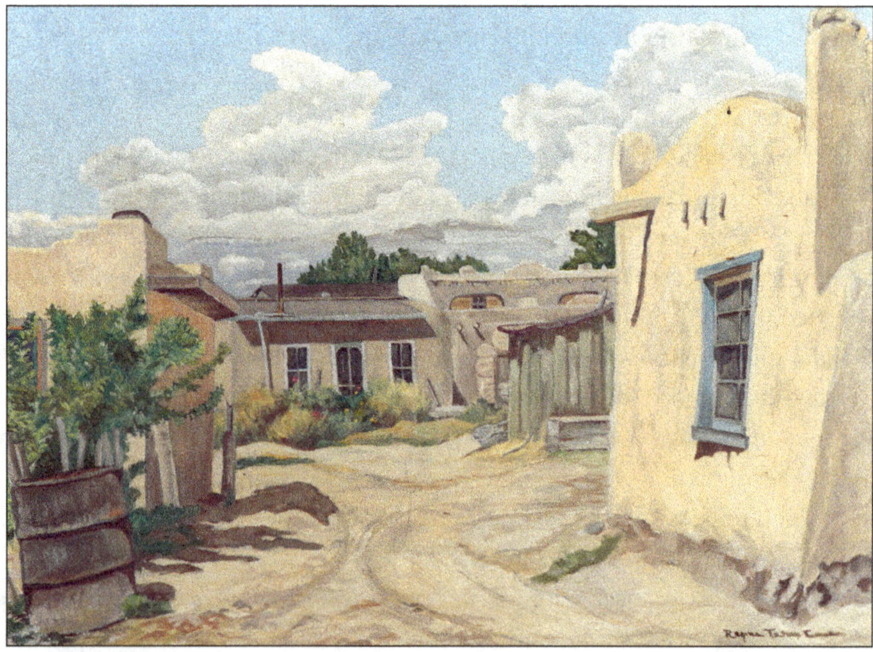

Regina Tatum Cooke, "Street in Taos," oil, Clayton High School

CRUMBO, WOODROW WILSON (1912–1989)

Born in Lexington, Oklahoma, of a Pottawatamie Indian mother and French father, Crumbo attended Chilocco Indian School through two years of high school and was offered a scholarship at the American Indian Institute at Wichita, Kansas. He studied art at the University of Wichita and then transferred to Oklahoma University. In 1938 he became the Art Director at Bacone College at Muskogee, Oklahoma. That was the first college in the US with curricula for Indian artists and taught by Indian artists. The following year he was selected to participate in the painting of six murals in the US Department of Interior Building in Washington, DC. During the war years, he worked as an aircraft designer for Douglas Aircraft in Tulsa, Oklahoma and was commissioned by the New Deal Treasury Section project to do a mural in the US Post Office of Nowata, Oklahoma. In addition to the painting, he received New Deal funds in1933 to take fourteen Indian boys to all Indian reservations. He reported, "We wanted to show the old time Indians on the reservations that by sending their children off to school they did not have to forget their tribal backgrounds. The youth did Indian dances and ceremonials to show them what school Indians could do, that we could have a modern education but retain our Indian background." This group also entertained at Indian Civilian Conservation Corps (CCC) camps to stimulate interest in the CCC projects among Indians.

Crumbo spent some summers in New Mexico during the depression years and made friends with many of the artists. He and Nat Kaplan shared living quarters and occasionally others joined them. He was credited as being the first to mass market Indian paintings to the public with the help of the Taos Pueblo Indians. His own outstanding work brought him the Rosenwald Fellowship and while serving as the "Artist-in-Residence" for the new Gilcrease Museum, he brought Mr. Gilcrease to Taos to select paintings and artwork for the museum. He was once again impressed by this area and moved his family to Taos in 1948 and again in 1973. During those years he was at other locations in professional capacities including El Paso in 1960 where he was the curator of their art museum. Upon retirement in 1988, Crumbo and his wife, Lillian, moved to Cimarron and opened an art gallery. After his death one year later, she returned to Oklahoma.

His son, Woody Crumbo II continues to promote his father's work to the public sometimes with the help of his son, Woody Crumbo III.

LOCATIONS OF NEW DEAL ARTWORK: Washington, DC; Nowata, Oklahoma.

DAVEY, RANDALL (1887–1964)

Davey was born May 24, 1887 in East Orange, New Jersey. He entered Cornell University in 1905 to study architecture and drawing and in 1908 studied painting with Robert Henri in New York City and with others in Holland, France, and Spain. His teaching career included positions at the Chicago Art Institute, Kansas City Art Institute, Broadmoor Art Academy (Colorado Springs) and the University of New Mexico. He came to Santa Fe with John Sloan in 1919 and became a resident in 1920 until his death in 1964, His Santa Fe home now houses the Audobon Society at the top of Upper Canyon Road and is open to the public. He was elected to the National Academy of Design in 1938 and named an Honorary Fellow in Fine Arts by the School of American Research, Museum of New Mexico, of Santa Fe in 1957. He is well remembered for his paintings of polo ponies and as part of the Works Project Administration, he created a polo mural that currently hangs in the Santa Fe State Capitol passageway between the Capitol and its Annex. It is on a long term loan from the New Mexico National Guard. This mural may have been planned to be placed at the New Mexico Military Institute in Roswell but actually started out at the state's Horse Calvary Unit in Albuquerque before being moved to the Military Museum (the New Deal built Armory) in Santa Fe. Over the years, it has been in three military related locations in Santa Fe. He had numerous works in both public and private collections. Davey was married twice; his second wife was Bell Holt.

LOCATION OF NEW DEAL ARTWORK: Santa Fe; Claremore and Vinita, Oklahoma.

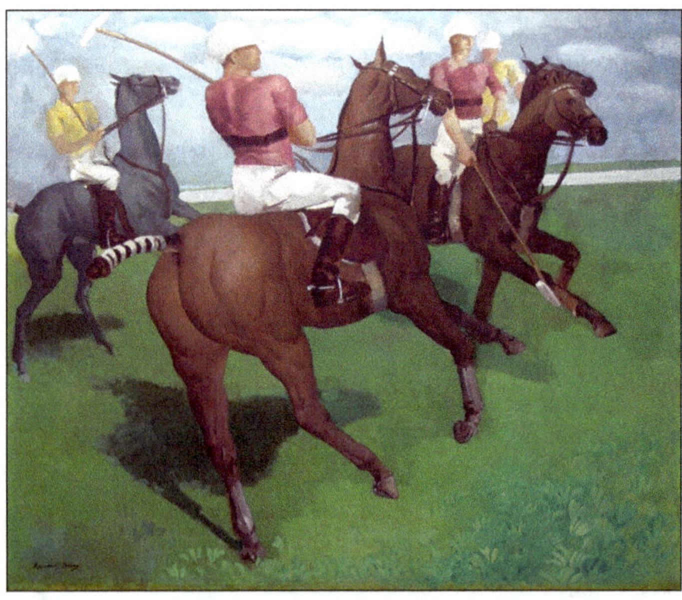

Playing polo was a hobby of the artist, Randall Davey and also his buddy, Peter Hurd, thus the subject of this mural and its original placement was at the state's Horse Calvary Unit site in Albuquerque. From there it has graced the walls of other New Mexico military facilities but is now on loan to the State Capitol and can be seen in the passageway between the Capitol and its Annex. It was restored in 2007 by Steve Prins, art conservator, thanks to NNDPA and the state legislature. Photograph by Steve Prins.

DELGADO, FRANCISCO (1858–1936)

The New Deal programs got underway in 1933, and one of the earliest art programs was the Public Works of Art Project (PWAP), which lasted from December 1933 to June 1934. This outstanding tin smith has been identified as being in that program. It appears from the records that he created eleven chandeliers and five lanterns for the "old museum" and the "state museum", but no one is sure whether this work is now in the Museum of Art in Santa Fe, the Palace of Governors or possibly even the Laboratory of Anthropology, where the PWAP offices were located. All of those institutions are in Santa Fe.

DELGADO, ILDEBERTO "EDDIE" (1883–1966)

Eddie Delgado, son of Francisco, was one of many generations of his family to do tin smithing. He did outstanding decorative light fixtures and other craft items in the original Albuquerque Little Theater (a New Deal structure), the National Park Service Building in Santa Fe, the Roswell Art Center, and the Cannon Airbase Officer's Club in Clovis, to name just four sites. The first three sites still have and use these masterpieces; however, the six or eight large chandeliers at the Officer's Club are gone. Considering their beauty, one wonders if they are hanging in some other military building. The collection at the Albuquerque site probably had the most in variety and volume, and his great-grandson, Jason Younis, was hired in 2006 by that organization to replace some of their missing Delgado pieces and to restore other existing items. As with many of the other artists, Delgado's achievements in the Federal Art Project (FAP) established and furthered his career. More details about Eddie's accomplishments can be found in *Sin Nombre* by Tey Mariana Nunn. His daughter, Angelina "Angie" Delgado Martinez of Santa Fe, worked alongside her father on some of the WPA projects, including the Albuquerque Little Theater.

LOCATIONS OF NEW DEAL PUBLIC ART: Albuquerque—Albuquerque Little Theater, Santa Fe, National Park Service building, Roswell—Art Museum.

DETWILLER, FREDERICK KNECHT (1882–1953)

Born in Easton, Pennsylvania on December 31, 1882. He studied in Lafayette College and New York Law School where he was admitted to the New York State Bar in 1906. He studied art, architecture and painting at Columbia University, Ecole des Beaux Arts in Paris, Art Student's League in New York City; Royal Inst. Di Belle Art in Florence, Italy and Ecole Americaine des Beaux Arts in Fontainebleau, France. He was the originator of Frederick K. Detwiller System of Graphic Art Education and had a traveling exhibition, used by schools and colleges in 1929. Until his death on September 20, 1953, he made his home in Easton with a summer studio in New Harbor, Maine.

LOCATION OF NEW DEAL ARTWORK: Gallup.

DEUTSCH, BORIS (1892–1978)

Deutsch was born in Krasnagorka, Lithuania, considered part of Russia. He received his art training in Russia and Germany and came to this country in 1919 where he settled in Los Angeles, California and became an American citizen. His work can be found in the Palace of the Legion of Honor; Portland Museum of Art; Denver Art Museum; San Diego Fine Arts Museum; Carnegie Institute; Mills College; and the Los Angeles Terminal Annex Post Office.

While local landscapes, history and industry were muralists' most common subjects, Boris Deutsch's winning design for the Hot Springs Post Office also embodied a sense of humor. His sketch for the national competition for post office mural designs, which is now in the National Archives, cleverly showed an Indian chief dancing out of the path of an Atchinson, Topeka & Santa Fe Super Chief. Deutsch's mural, apparently redesigned, does not show the train, but instead features background mountains. He did another post office mural called "Grape Pickers" located in Reedley, Calfornia and another one in the Los Angeles Terminal Annex Post Office.

LOCATIONS OF NEW DEAL ARTWORK: Truth or Consequences; Los Angeles and Reedley, California; Washington, DC.

DIXON, MAYNARD (1875–1946)

Dixon did not do any New Deal artwork in New Mexico having left in 1932 but did participate in one of the programs involving the post offices. Two of his creations can be found in the post offices of Canoga Park and Martinez, California. Information about his WPA work is included in a recent book about him, *Desert Dreams, The Art and Life of Maynard Dixon*. He was the first husband of New Deal photographer Dorothea Lange.

DORMAN, JOHN (1912–1982)

Dorman was born in 1912 in Berlin, Germany, to Teresa and Archibald B. Dorman, since his father was possibly doing advanced studies at the University of Heidelberg after having been in Berlin in the Consular Corps. Some years later his parents were divorced and Teresa returned to the United States with John and his brother, Ralph. She visited Santa Fe on occasion and once she came here in 1921 with the hope of meeting Jozef Bakos after admiring one of his paintings in an exhibit in Chicago. They met and two months later she moved to Santa Fe with her two sons and married Bakos in 1923. According to his stepfather, Jozef Bakos, John was a natural abstract painter. He designed cars at the age of ten—many of the modern treads they came to use later. He also assisted with the New Mexico's New Deal *Portfolio of Spanish American Colonial Design* most likely in 1937–38 and there is one of his other works in the University of New Mexico Fine Arts Museum collection. Photographic examples of his work can be found in the Kay Dorman (his third wife) photo files at the New Mexico. Records and Archives collection.

John Dorman had a daughter, Teresa, and a son, William Dorman. William is a professor emeritus of Government and Journalism at California State University, Sacramento. From William's records, his father lived in the San Francisco area in the early 1920s but then moved back to Santa Fe. Somewhat repeating his mother's romantic experience in Santa Fe, John and Carolyn Overbury Jones, a San Francisco young woman from a prominent Bay Area family, met in Santa Fe when she was visiting in the late 1930s. They were married in 1937 at San Ildefonso Pueblo. They had a small gallery in Santa Fe specializing in Indian art and others' work also. In February 1941, William was born and shortly after WWII began, the family moved back to California and his father worked at the Hunters Point shipyard. The management of the gallery was left in the hands of his mother, Teresa Bakos. After the war they moved to Carmel and Dorman tried to get established there as a significant artist but was unsuccessful. The couple divorced in 1947 and John went back to New Mexico. He married again for a brief time then later married his third wife, Kay, with whom he lived for a number of years until his death. He continued to produce art and work at various jobs. Towards the end of his life, he moved more from the abstract art to the Santos form and an exhibit of his Santos was scheduled in 1970 at a local gallery. Just prior to the opening, the gallery burned and his collection with it. He died in Santa Fe twelve years later. Kay died in 1988 and had been an archivist at the New Mexico State Archives for a number of years.

LOCATION OF NEW DEAL ARTWORK: Albuquerque—University of New Mexico Museum of Art, and *Portfolio of Spanish-Colonial Design*

DUNTON, W. HERBERT "Buck" (1878–1936)

Born in Augusta, Maine, on August 28, 1878, Dunton became enamored of the outdoors at an early age by accompanying his grandfather on forays into the New England countryside. These early excursions were the foundation of Dunton's life as a big-game hunter and chronicler of North American wild-life. The young Dunton began early to carry a sketch pad along with his rod or rifle during his outings. He quit school at sixteen to work in a clothing store to earn money to take a trip to the West and finally in 1896 achieved his goal. He ended up in Montana where he worked with a bear hunter for nearly two years. He cowboyed or hunted all over the southwest and Mexico in the summers but returned east to study during the rest of the year. He developed a career in illustrations with emphasis on the western subjects which was most timely since the country was fixed on the cowboy craze in literature. His accomplishments in that area were later ignored or forgotten following his permanent move to Taos in 1914 where he became the third resident artist of Taos—after Phillips and Sharp. He was one of the six founders of the Taos Society of Artists. In this setting he was well known for his portraiture and lithographs. As he matured, animals took on prominence in his work with the bear assuming the most prominent roles in his canvases. One he did in 1934 in the Public Works of Art Project in New Mexico was selected by President Franklin Roosevelt to hang in the White House. That painting is now in the National Museum of American Art in Washington. Another piece can be viewed in the offices of U. S. Federal Judge James Parker in Albuquerque. Dunton died in Taos at the age of 57 just when one of his works that focused on bears, "Crest of the Rockies, Grizzly" was being printed in New York.

POSSIBLE LOCATIONS OF NEW DEAL ARTWORK: Albuquerque; Mesa Verde, Colorado; Washington, DC.

EGRI, TED (1913–2011)

Taos sculptor, Ted Egri was a New Deal artist in New York City during the New Deal era but did no New Deal art in New Mexico. He moved to Taos in 1950 and once here became well known for his large sculptures, some done for public sites as funded by the 1% for Public Art, a contemporary version of the New Deal public art programs. He always enjoyed telling a funny story about living and working in New York with his brother and sister. All three of them were on the Federal Art Project. Legally only one was allowed per family so when the supervisor came to view and/or pick up their work, two of the three had to hide under the bed or go out the back door. Egri died early in 2011 and was still painting up to that time.

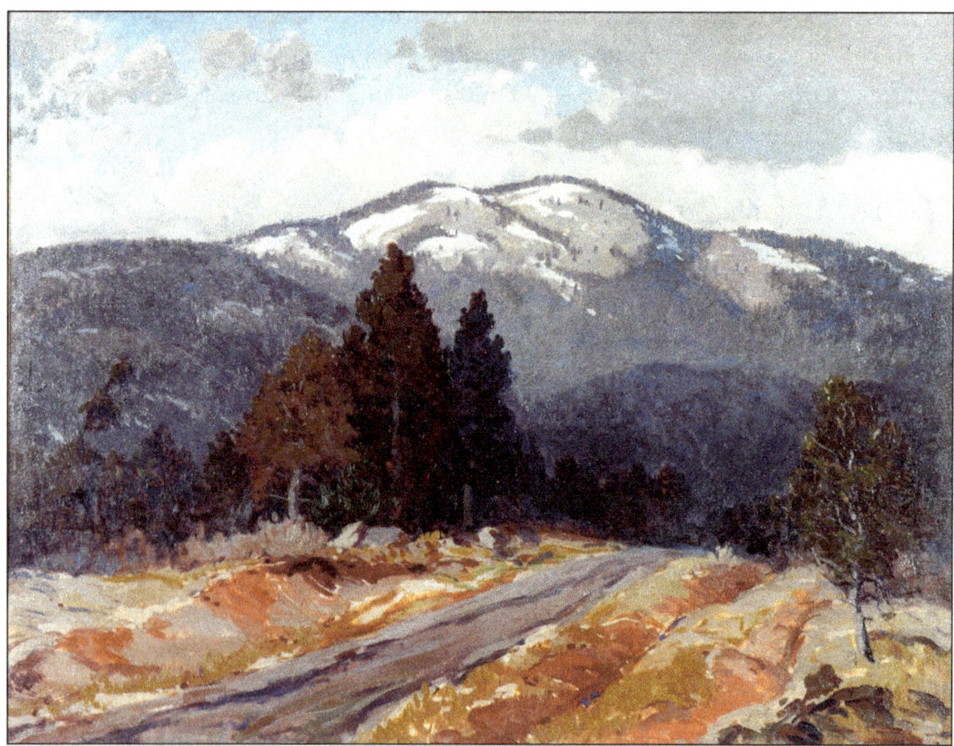

Fremont F. Ellis, "Winter Scene," oil, Albuquerque, Carrie Tingley Hospital for Crippled Children. Photograph by Pat Berrett.

ELLIS, FREMONT F. (1897–1985)

Born in Virginia City, Montana in 1897, Ellis trained briefly at the Art Students' League in New York and was strongly influenced by the American Impressionists. On a family trip to New York City at the age of 12, Ellis' mother took him to the Metropolitan Museum and he was fascinated by the lighting and the three dimensionality of Albert Bierstadt's western scenes. He returned as often as possible and at home tried to recreate this style. He trained to be an optometrist and moved to El Paso, Texas where he painted southwestern scenes and taught art in his spare time. Once discovering Santa Fe, he fell in love with northern New Mexico landscapes and a young woman named Lorencita who was from an old and aristocratic New Mexican family. Both were enough to motivate him to move north never to leave. The couple had two children, Fred and Bambi. He was the youngest of Los Cinco Pintores, a group that created an awareness of contemporary art which was essential to the foundation of an artist colony in Santa Fe in the early 1920s. Along with Jozef Bakos, Walter Mruk, Willard Nash and Will Shuster, the 24 year old Ellis held the principle to create art from the people and not surrender to commercialism. Each man's style varied greatly and each was a strong influence in the art movement over the years in New Mexico. Nearly all were a part of the Works Project Administration (WPA) contributions to the public's exposure to original fine art. Ellis died in his beloved hometown in 1985 at the age of 87.

POSSIBLE LOCATIONS OF NEW DEAL ARTWORK: Albuquerque, Las Vegas, Santa Fe, Springer; Washington, DC.

EMERY, IRENE (Date Unknown–1981)

Another arrival in Santa Fe due to health problems brings us Irene Emery. She came in 1931 and lived there until her death in 1981, with the exception of 1954, when she went to Washington, DC to continue her research for a book on textiles. She worked initially as a sculptor, and a bas relief by her is in the courtyard of the Palace of Governors in Santa Fe, but we don't know if that was done as a New Deal activity or not. In the National Archives we found reference to a wall sculpture featuring birds in flight done at Carrie Tingley Hospital for Crippled Children in Hot Springs (now Truth or Consequences), New Mexico. This has never been found. That facility was originally a New Deal program, so the bas relief referenced was most likely New Deal. That facility is now the state's Veterans' Center. Another New Deal project that has never been found is her creation of two coats of arms carved in wood for the State Museum, most likely the Museum of Art. She worked as an artist for Edward Hall at the Aztec Studio with Paul Ruthling.

By the 1940s she had become well known for her knowledge of the study of fabric structure. She wrote a book, *The Primary Structures of Fabric*, which was published in 1966 and has been known as the standard reference on this subject. There are records indicating that between 1947 and 1954 she worked at the Laboratory of Anthropology, but it is not known in what capacity.

LOCATION OF NEW DEAL ARTWORK: Unknown

EVERINGHAM, MILLARD (1912–Date Unknown)

Born in Eagle Village, New York September 8, 1912, Everingham studied at Syracuse University, Tiffany Foundation, and the University of Mexico. His work was exhibited at National College FA, Smithsonian, GGE, 1939; PAFA, 1940–1941, Coronado Quatro Centennial 1940; Museum of New Mexico, 1939–1940. A mural of mining camp scenes in southern New Mexico is reported as being done in Deming but has yet to be found there. He was a resident of Ranchos de Taos between 1939–1950 and during that time he was the recipient of a foreign studies fellowship from the Augusta Hazzard School.

POSSIBLE LOCATION OF NEW DEAL ART: Albuquerque—University of New Mexico, Santa Fe Museum of Art

EWING, LOUIE (1908–1983)

Ewing was born in 1908 in Pocatello, Idaho and later moved to Richfield, Idaho where the family lived on a farm. Here he learned to love people and nature and painted, sketched, and carved throughout his youth. He attended colleges that unfortunately had no art departments but took an art correspondence course. Finally in 1933 he moved to California to attend a junior college and live with the head of the art department. When this professor, Stanley Brenesier, moved to Santa Fe in 1935 to teach at the Endolon School of Art, Ewing followed and worked there also for the one more year that it survived. He got a teaching job elsewhere, did some weaving and married fellow teacher, Marie Brenesier. They had two sons. Fortunately, the WPA's Federal Art Project came to New Mexico a year after he arrived, helped him survive and provide for his young family. Once involved in this program, he was exposed to serigraph possibilities and soon found his medium of choice. His work in this medium brought him the opportunity of creating two thousand copies of the winning poster entry for the Intertribal Indian Ceremonials in Gallup every year from 1938 to the early 1970s. During the 1940s, he was most productive and may have been the first to illustrate a book using the silk screening process. The book was James MacMillan's *Fifteen New Mexico Santos.* He illustrated many more books during his life but was reportedly proudest of his illustrations in *Kiva Mural Decorations at Awatovi and Kawaika-a* by Watson Smith, published in 1952 by Peabody Museum, Harvard University.

The Laboratory of Anthropology in Santa Fe funded a WPA/FAP project for which Ewing made 200 silkscreen prints from his own paintings of fifteen Navajo blankets in the Laboratory's collection. His assistant was Eliseo Rodriguez, and they were pleased and proud of the squeegees they created from automobile tires, which speeded up the process of moving paint across their screens. He did another series for them called the "Masterpiece Series," which was a set of silk screened images selected from a collection of the Laboratory's and given as gifts to its members.

He continued to create but was not desirous of submitting his work for juried shows and therefore built no record of exhibitions and awards. Nevertheless his career and reputation flourished and his love, awe, and respect for nature was always featured. His love of gardening was also very special to him. For a period of time, he worked for Nambe Mills in Santa Fe. He died December 19, 1983, with his second wife Virginia Hunter Ewing at his side. Her first husband was Russell Vernon Hunter, who brought Ewing into the WPA program.

POSSIBLE LOCATIONS OF NEW DEAL ARTWORK: *Navajo Portfolio*—Santa Fe, Roswell.

FLECK, JOSEPH (1893–1977)

Born in Siegless, Austria in 1893, Joseph Amadeus Fleck studied at the Royal Academy of Fine Arts and also at the Royal Graphic Institute, both in Vienna, Austria. Fleck made his way from Vienna to America in 1922 and on to New Mexico in 1924, by way of Kansas City, where he saw his first Taos paintings. He went to Taos soon afterward, and once there became close friends with Ernest Blumenschein and others. In 1925 he married Mable Davidson Mantz and they moved to Taos to live. Fleck became an American citizen in 1927. He left Taos for two European painting tours and between 1942–1946 when he was Dean of Fine Arts and Artist in Residence at the University of Missouri in Kansas City. He died in Pleasanton, California.

Fleck worked in a variety of mediums—oil, tempera, watercolor as well as lithography. As with many representational painters, Fleck's paint application and use of color became freer as he parted from the discipline of his academic school years. Despite the expressive freedom of his later landscapes, Fleck's earlier portraits seem to be more individual and successful; they represent a firmer grasp on form-definition, where the paint was used to convincingly construct a volumetric mass. Whether the subject was an attractive Indian girl clothed in a geometrically-designed costume, or a pair of Spanish musicians in blue denim, all were painted in a simple, straight-forward manner without flourish of technique or decorative color. His work can be found in various collections in New Mexico and nationwide. One piece is in the New Mexico State Capitol.

LOCATIONS OF NEW DEAL ARTWORK: Albuquerque—State Fair, Gallup, Lordsburg, Santa Fe, Raton; Hugo, Oklahoma.

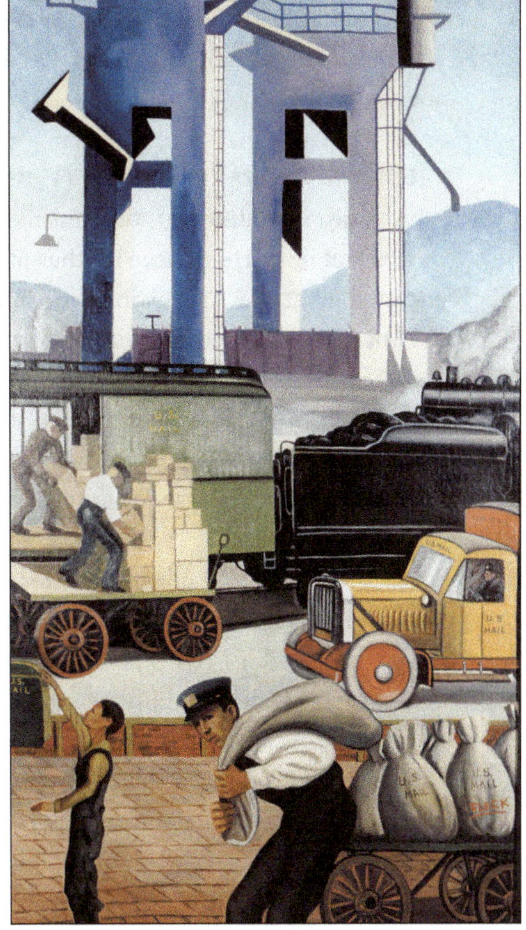

"Unloading mail at Raton." The Raton post office has two murals in it, both done by Fleck. They depict some of the steps in getting the mail from the writer to the reader. One is on view in the lobby but the other is in the staff conference room. Both were moved from the earlier post office to this location. Photograph by Pat Berrett from *A More Abundant Life, New Deal Artists and Public Art in New Mexico*, courtesy of Sunstone Press.

GILBERTSON, BORIS (1907–1982)

Born in Evanston, Illinois in 1907 of Russian and Norwegian stock, Gilbertson lived in Minnesota, Wisconsin, and Indiana and first went to Santa Fe on the Chili Line railroad when he was almost fifteen. He was quite a wanderer. He rode the rails and got construction jobs on the railroads helping the powder men with the explosives used to blast tunnels through mountains. He began to study sculpture in 1927 at the Art Institute of Chicago, winning major prizes in 1933 and 1943. He preferred the subjects of his sculpture to be animals, because he was first a naturalist, and also because creating animal sculpture rarely provoked negative or political criticism from the viewers and judges of his work. During the New Deal era, he created "American Moose" and "American Bison," a bas relief done in Missouri marble in 1939 for the first floor of the Department of Interior building. This was done under the auspices of the Treasury Department's New Deal program to decorate federal buildings. He also executed sculptural reliefs on two post offices in Wisconsin. Once settled in Santa Fe, he continued his art work and restored an old adobe house with his life partner, Charlotte White. Their historic home built in 1782 on Alto Street was one they worked on together for years after buying it in 1959. White donated it to the Historic Santa Fe Foundation prior to her death.

POSSIBLE LOCATION OF NEW DEAL ART WORK: Department of Interior—Washington, DC; post office buildings in Fond du Lac and Janesville, Wisconsin; Chicago's Chess Pavilion and Brookfield Zoo, Illinois.

GILBERTSON, WARREN "Bud" (1910–1954)

Born in Watertown, Wisconsin on August 7, 1910, Warren "Bud" Gilbertson became a ceramist of note. He was the brother of Boris Gilbertson and spent most of his life in Illinois and studied at the Art Institute of Chicago. While there he taught sculpture and ceramics at Hull House and completed his formal American training with a master's degree at the New York State College of Ceramics. He traveled in Mexico to study work of the Talavera potters and in 1941 he went to Japan to study with one of their top ceramists. One year he spent in Santa Clara Pueblo studying the techniques of this pottery making. It is possible that during that year he worked with the New Deal programs in New Mexico but this is not firmly documented.

Because of his knowledge of Oriental culture and languages, the Navy sent him across the Pacific during World War II as an intelligence officer. He returned to the Santa Fe area after the war and established his pottery workshop on Alto Street. By this time he was a recognized authority in his field and his writings on oriental ceramic technique had been published by the American Ceramics Society and reprinted in England and Italy. In early 1954 he was written up in *Time* magazine in connection with his discovery of a method of duplicating the oil-spot ceramics of the Sung dynasty—a feat no potter had accomplished in over 750 years. This technique may have been lost since he was killed in a car wreck in February of 1954.

POSSIBLE LOCATION OF NEW DEAL ARTWORK: Unknown.

GOODBEAR, PAUL "Flying Eagle" (1913–1954)

Paul Goodbear was the grandson of Chief Turkey Legs, a Cheyenne Indian who was in the battle of the Little Big Horn. He was born in Fay, Oklahoma and lived with other tribal members on disconnected farms. As a young man he enjoyed sharing old stories of his tribe and his ancestors and became interested in expressing the movement and color of the living figures of the ceremonial participants. He married a Choctaw who was also interested in teaching about the antecedents of her people. He became an educator of Indians of all tribes and injected his personality into manuscripts written about them.

During World War II he had little time for his dancing, painting, and writing and was wounded twice on the Normandy Landing and in the Battle of the Bulge. After returning to the United States after his discharge, he decided to become a staff artist with three American daily newspapers in Japan. During this time a comic strip was born, "Chief Ugh," and deep rooted humor poured from his pen.

His Indian name "Flying Eagle" was officially bestowed upon him after he returned from World War II. He studied art at the University of New Mexico and in Chicago and did many illustrations that have been reproduced in school books. Possibly his most outstanding contribution to New Mexico history came with the restoration of the prehistoric murals at Coronado Museum near Bernalillo. According to an article in the October 1961 issue of *New Mexico Historical Review*, "the techniques he used were akin to those of the Greeks and Italian masters. He was forced to paint on fresh plaster and his patience and understanding of this task and his fidelity to his own style of painting is amazing." The Museum of Fine Arts has a large collection of his work. These works give insight into his concern that the Indian artist's right to retain his own expression and reflect his heritage. His untimely death in a hospital in Chicago cut short a potentially significant contributor to his people and to his country. He left two small children that were raised by their mother while she taught in Indian mission schools.

LOCATION OF NEW DEAL ARTWORK: Santa Fe—Museum of Fine Art.

GRANT, BLANCHE CHLOE (1874–1948)

Born in Leavenworth, Kansas in 1874, Grant was a Taos landscape and Indian painter, illustrator, and author. She was one of five children and was educated at Indianapolis High School and was in Vassar College's first graduating class in 1896. She was a leader of working girls' clubs, living at College Settlement in Philadelphia for two winters and also heading a Brooklyn club. She studied at the Boston Museum School of Fine Arts, the Pennsylvania Academy of Fine Art, and the Art Students League. By 1914 she was established as a magazine illustrator and landscape painter. In 1920 she went to Taos where she planned only to vacation but chose to settle permanently since it was better than any place she had ever dreamed of. In addition to her painting, which she did with many of the local figures, Grant was the author and editor of books on the history of Taos and on Western personalities such as Kit Carson. She was the editor of the *Taos Valley News* as of 1922. Her books, *When Old Trails Were New* (now in a new edition from Sunstone Press) and *Taos Yesterday*, are important references on Taos history. At her death in 1948, she was buried from the Taos Presbyterian Church where she had created murals in 1921. They are now gone.

POSSIBLE LOCATIONS OF NEW DEAL ARTWORK: Santa Fe, Socorro.

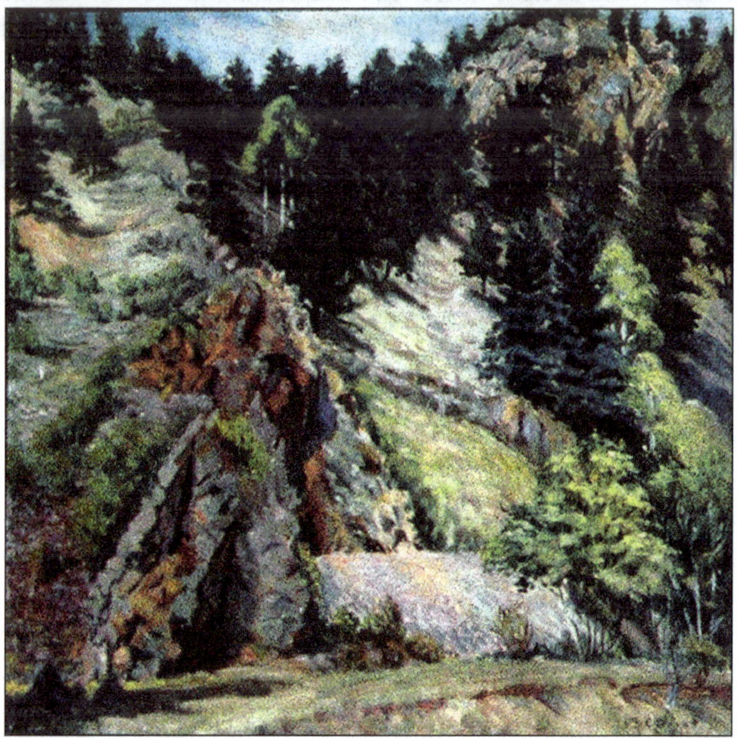

Blanche Chloe Grant, "Mine," oil, Socorro, New Mexico Technical University Library

GRANT, GORDON KENNETH (1908–1940)

Grant was born in Berkeley, California on January 21, 1908. His father was Walter Grant who ran art galleries in New York for a number of years. Between 1920–1925 Gordon studied drawing at the California School of Fine Arts in San Francisco and the Arts and Crafts School in Berkeley. He turned to studying architecture during his time at the University of California in Berkeley (1925–29). Records indicate that he was employed in 1926 by the Anderson Galleries Inc. as a salesperson and later the Assistant Exhibition Manager. The following year he was in charge of prints for the Century of Progress Exhibit at the Art Institute of Chicago. After the exhibition closed, he returned to New York and established his own gallery until the spring of 1935. While in New York, research noted, he assisted muralist Albert Herter, painting six murals at Wellesley College and some murals in the City Hall in Bronx, New York. These were most likely New Deal funded public art.

In 1935, he moved to New Mexico, and for the next ten years he worked at promoting an interest in American art through lectures and articles. He became interested in portraying Native American themes and during the New Deal he was commissioned by the Fine Arts Museum to do a series of murals featuring Native Americans and others who lived in New Mexico before it became a state, but there appears to be no one who is aware of their existence. A mural study featuring Indians performing the buffalo dance was once shown in Santa Barbara, California, and some feel that may have been the study for the mural in Santa Fe but the execution of that piece never took place. After three years in New Mexico he returned to Santa Barbara where he worked as a designer, silversmith, blacksmith, and post office muralist. While there he executed a mural decoration on board in oil emulsion tempera of Indians performing the buffalo dance. This may have been a study for his Santa Fe commission.

POSSIBLE LOCATION OF NEW DEAL ART WORK: Alhambra and Ventura post offices in California, and Brady, Texas post office. The piece in Brady, done in 1939, may be his only surviving post office mural and is titled, "Texas Immigrants."

GROLL, ALBERT LOREY (1866–1952)

Born in New York City, Groll was an etcher and also an Eastern landscape painter specializing in Western scenes. He was elected to the National Academy of Design in 1910. Groll studied with the few Americans who attended the Royal Academy in Antwerp. He became a landscape painter on his return in 1895, it is said, because he was then too poor to pay for models. In 1899 he studied at the Royal Academy in Munich under N. Gysis and Loefftz as well as in London. He painted landscapes in the vicinity of New York until about 1904. He then went West with Stuart Culin of the Brooklyn Museum, a famous ethnologist, who wrote a treatise on Indian games. Groll sketched desert and mountain scenes in Arizona and New Mexico. The resulting painting "Arizona" won a gold medal at the Penn Academy of Fine Art in 1906 and was reviewed by a critic familiar with the desert who said, "it glows like a gem with the indescribable color of the Colorado desert." Groll was the rare painter in northern New Mexico before WW I, choosing "bare mesas and towering cloud formations" rather than mountains. Laguna Pueblo was a favorite area, as it was for Thomas Moran. There are also many crayon paintings by Groll, particularly of the Taos area, as well as complete landscapes in crayon mixed with oil, the paper surface scuffed for texture. One of his paintings can be seen at the Octavia Fellin Public Library in Gallup. He died in New York City in 1952.

LOCATION OF NEW DEAL ARTWORK: Gallup

HEARN, OMAR W. (Dates Unknown)

Little is known about this man or his work. A reference by Supervisor Gustave Baumann states, "General Kearney probably never expected to have his portrait painted by a preacher—not until recently were we aware of having a reverend at work on the project. His painting is not so hot but the Las Vegas Historical Society is appreciative—altogether he gives the project an air of much needed sanctity." There was reference in another document to his doing a mural at the Old Veeder Museum in Las Vegas. That museum is no longer at that location and whereabouts of the mural or the portrait are unknown. We also wonder if these two art works may be one and the same.

POSSIBLE LOCATION OF NEW DEAL ARTWORK: Unknown

HENDERSON, WILLIAM PENHALLOW (1877–1943)
HENDERSON, ALICE CORBIN (1881–1949)

This couple had a partnership that worked well and was culturally productive.

He was born and raised in Medford, Massachusetts, and also lived for a time on a cattle ranch in Texas and in a small Kansas town. He studied at the Massachusetts Normal Art School and the Boston Museum of Fine Arts with Edmund Tarbell. Following further art training and travel in Europe, Henderson returned to the states to teach at the Chicago Academy of Fine Arts. In 1916, after more than a decade teaching and painting in Chicago, he moved to Santa Fe with his wife, the poet and editor, Alice Corbin Henderson, because of her tuberculosis. He painted in a flat, decorative style somewhat related to the manner of Whistler when he first came to Santa Fe. Gradually, under the influence of Nordfeldt and others, he embraced much of Cezanne. Henderson's emotive, high-keyed color and decorative special treatment suggest Post-Impressionism applied to distinctly Southwestern imagery. His interest in the Indian and Hispanic residents of the Southwest inspired work in several mediums. Although he is well known for his pastels and oils, Henderson's artwork also included outstanding murals, handcrafted furniture, stage designs and innovative architectural projects.

One of the more unique architectural structures he designed and built in Santa Fe is the Wheelwright Museum of the American Indian (originally known as the Museum of Navajo Ceremonial Art). It is built to resemble a Navajo hogan. Alice became the curator of the museum. He created illustrations for an edition of the well-known book, *Alice in Wonderland*, and during the Federal Arts Project, he completed easel paintings and six large murals for the Santa Fe Federal Court House which were later conserved by Steve Prins. They are various New Mexico landscapes which Henderson loved and wanted to "bring their beauty inside." With the exception of 1918, Henderson lived in the Santa Fe area from 1916 until his death from a sudden heart attack in 1943 at the age of 66.

Alice was born in St. Louis, Missouri and attended the University of Chicago. In 1904 she rented a studio in the Academy of Fine Arts and soon met and fell in love with one of the teachers, William P. Henderson. They were married on October 14, 1905. By 1912 Mrs. Henderson was the associate editor of *Poetry Magazine*, a Chicago publication where she got to know such writers as Carl Sandburg, Ezra Pound, and Robert Frost. Four years later, as mentioned above, she was diagnosed with tuberculosis and the couple moved to Santa Fe, the tuberculosis treatment mecca. She continued her position with the magazine long distance until 1922.

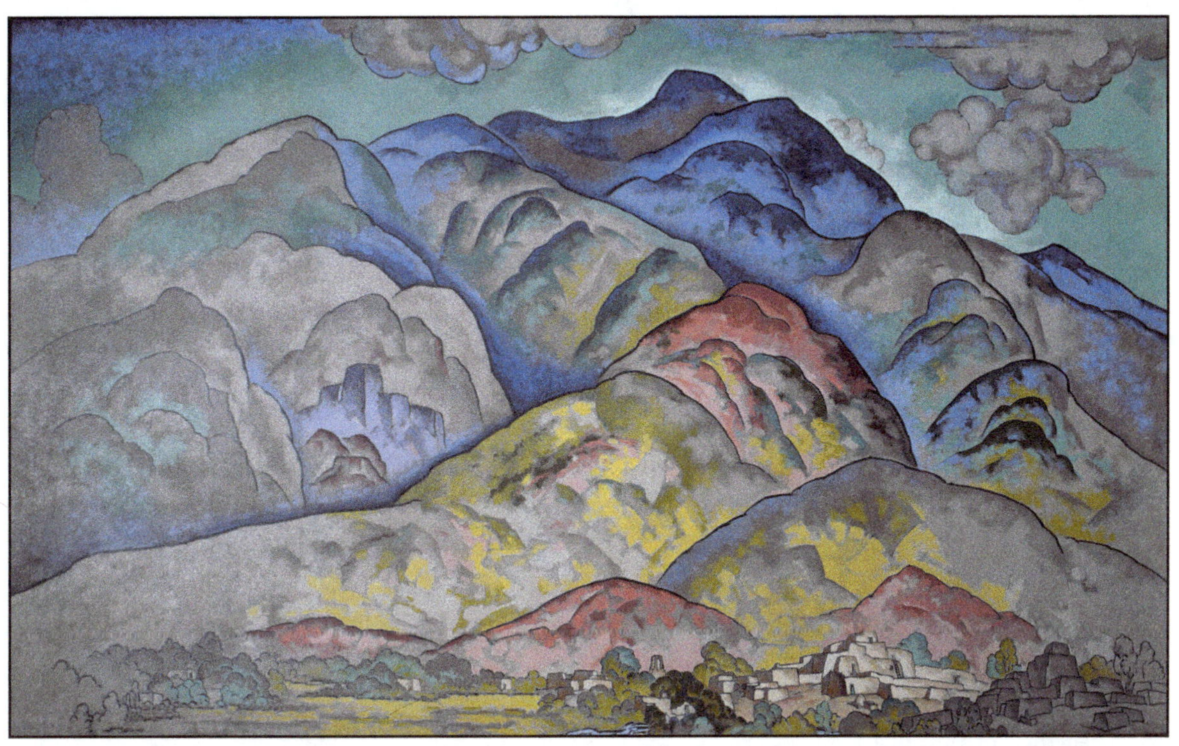

Six immense and rich murals ("Taos Mountains," above) can be seen in the U.S. Federal Courthouse in Santa Fe which was Henderson's attempt to bring New Mexico's wonderful landscapes inside to enjoy there as well. The power and beauty of these natural wonders is emphasized by the contrast in size between them and the buildings included in the artwork. They were preserved by Steve Prins. Photograph by Pat Berrett from *A More Abundant Life, New Deal Artists and Public Art in New Mexico*, courtesy of Sunstone Press.

Alice was successfully treated at Sunmount Sanitorium and then moved to a small adobe house on Telephone Hill, a dirt road that followed the telephone line into the center of town. This "road" had homes of the art group called *Los Cinco Pintores* and writer, Mary Austin, and one can assume that Alice's husband helped most of them build their homes since being primarily artists, they probably needed help with the physical construction of adobe houses. Alice was later instrumental in persuading the local officials to change the name of the road to Camino de Monte Sol. This area with its struggling artists and writers was "saved" by Roosevelt's New Deal programs since many were employed by the WPA Federal Art and Writers Projects. She was one of the writers and later the Director of New Mexico's Federal Writers Project after Ina Sizer Cassidy (wife of artist, Gerald Cassidy) left the program.

One of the projects that the couple did together in 1937 was the book, *Brothers of Light, The Penitentes of the Southwest*, which she wrote and he illustrated. An earlier and substantial work edited by Mrs. Henderson in 1928 was *The Turquoise Trail: An Anthology of New Mexico Poetry*. It contained poems by thirty-seven of New Mexico's most well known writers. The

Hendersons, enamored with northern New Mexico and its cultures, encouraged many of their Eastern and Midwest friends to come West and as such were considered among the founders of the original Santa Fe art colony.

The couple had one daughter, also named Alice, who married John Ganson Evans, the only son of Mabel Dodge Luhan, and one of their daughters, Letitia "Tish" Frank, was a prominent supporter of the arts for many years in Santa Fe prior to her death in 2009. Tish was frequently referred to as part of "New Mexico Royalty" considering the accomplishments and prominence of at least three of her grandparents.

LOCATION OF NEW DEAL ARTWORK: Santa Fe—Federal Courthouse.

HENNINGS, E. MARTIN (1886–1956)

Born in Pennsgrove, New Jersey 1886, Hennings studied at the Art Institute of Chicago, Munich Academy with Walter Thor, and the Royal Academy, Munich with Angelo Junk. He was elected to membership in the Taos Society of Artists in 1921 and lived at the Harwood Foundation apartments with his wife, Helen, during their residence in the village. He won many awards in this country and received honorable mention in the 1927 Paris Salon. He created various murals, one of which is "The Chosen Site" in the U. S. Post Office of Van Buren, Arkansas. His wife and daughter served as his models for the pioneers in the mural. He died in Taos in 1956.

POSSIBLE LOCATIONS OF NEW DEAL ARTWORK: Albuquerque, Dexter, Santa Fe; Van Buren, Arkansas; Washington, DC.

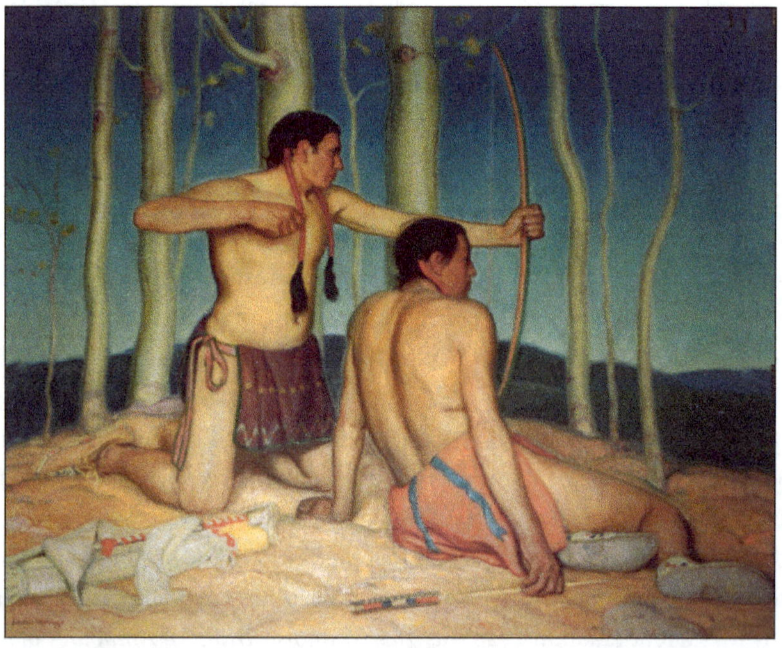

E. Martin Hennings, "Indian Hunters," oil, Santa Fe, Supreme Court

HERRERA, VELINO SHIJE (Ma-Pe-Wi, Oriole or Red Bird) (1902–1973)

Born at Zia Pueblo, New Mexico, Herrera was a self-taught artist whose painting career began in 1917 at the School of American Research in Santa Fe. He credited Dr. Edgar L. Hewett for getting him started in the field of art. His subjects included native dances, genre scenes from the pueblos, portraits, and hunting scenes. As his work grew in breadth and confidence, his style changed from flat, pattern like compositions to more naturalistic representations often with a delicate rendering of texture and detail. He taught at the Albuquerque Indian School and some of the murals created for that school can now be found in the library of the Santa Fe Indian School. In 1938 he reproduced ancient kiva murals found at Kuau (at Coronado State Monument near Bernalillo, New Mexico). He also painted murals for the Department of the Interior building in Washington, DC and illustrated several books on Pueblo life and art. With his skillful blend of tradition and innovation he became one of the most highly regarded figures in the Indian watercolor movement. "However when the State of New Mexico adopted the sun symbol of the Pueblo Indians as its official insignia, he was accused by his own people of betraying them by giving the design to the whites," according to references found in *American Indian Painters* by Jeanne O. Snodgrass.

He married Picuris native, Mary Simbola, and they had at least three children. Son Harold is also an artist and as of 2011 lives in Santa Fe with brother, Cliff. Daughter Olla lives near the Picuris Pueblo in Chamisal. Velino was also the cousin of José Rey Toledo, another New Deal artist. In the 1950s, he was in a tragic auto accident killing Mary and injuring his eyesight for life. Never totally recovering from the consequences of this accident, Herrera rarely ever painted again. He died in 1973.

LOCATIONS OF NEW DEAL ARTWORK: Santa Fe—Museum of Fine Art, Santa Fe Indian School, Kuana Kiva (near Bernalillo); Washington, DC.

HIGGINS, VICTOR (1884–1949)

Born in Shelbyville, Indiana, Victor Higgins left at the age of fifteen to study at the Art Institute of Chicago and the Academy of Fine Arts. Sponsored by ex-mayor and art collector, Carter Harrison, Higgins spent two and a half years in Europe studying with Rene Menard and Lucien Simon in Paris and Hans von Hyeck in Munich, The year after his return (1914), Harrison sent Higgins on a painting trip to New Mexico. He chose to live in Taos from then on but divided his time between Chicago and Taos. He taught for several years at the Chicago Academy of Fine Arts all the while exhibiting in New York and having an occasional showing in Europe.

Higgins found the strong light, brilliant color, and the lure of the New Mexico land a powerful antidote to the confines of academic training. He joined the Taos Society of Artists in 1917, and in 1923 was one of the co-founders of the Harwood Foundation with Bert Phillips and Louise Harwood. His Moses figure and landscape was part of the ten large frescos done in the Taos County Courtroom during the New Deal artwork projects. Those works were restored in the mid 1990s.

Another mural done thanks to the federal government is in a post office in Rocky Ford, Colorado and was completed between 1936–1940.

His perceptions and renderings of the land in paint, according to some observers, may be unsurpassed by any other artist of the Taos colony. Higgins' own intuitively derived visual harmonies resulted in a rich and varied body of work in still life, figure painting, and most significantly, landscape. Higgins' work is increasingly recognized as being among the most significant produced in New Mexico. He was married to Sara Parsons, daughter of Sheldon Parsons, and they had one daughter, Joan H. Reed, who is deceased.

LOCATIONS OF NEW DEAL ARTWORK: Albuquerque—University of New Mexico, Santa Fe & National Park Service, Taos; Rocky Ford, Colorado.

HOGNER, NILS (1893–1970) or (1887–1970)

In the 1956 *Who's Who in American Art*, Nils Hogner was reportedly born in Whiteville, Massachusetts on July 22, 1893. A recent Hogner researcher reports that indeed he was born in Sweden and came with his family to this country based on a ship's manifest that has them arriving in 1893 and he was listed as six years of age and had two sisters. The 1893 date was supported by his widow in 1981 and University of New Mexico catalogues (1930–34). He is known to have studied at the Boston School of Painting, the BMFA School, Rhodes Academy in Copenhagen (Denmark).

During the 1920s he went to the Southwest and was a pupil of Leon Gaspard and Ivar Nyberg. According to New Mexico author Frank Waters in his book about Leon Gaspard, Hogner told Gaspard that "he had been injured during the war, and came out West to recuperate. He married Teckla, a Navajo woman who belonged to a wealthy Navajo clan which was fortunate for Hogner because this clan that ran many sheep, goats and horses, were able to help him build up his trading post business. This business helped the clan sell their goods. What a happy couple they were!" The couple had four children according to some families in that area who remembered him and his family. This relationship did not survive and he moved into Albuquerque. Teckla was known to have told others in the area that Hogner was dead. Gaspard noted after Hogner came to see him enroute to the East that Hogner and Teckla were divorced and he had given up the trading post. Gaspard felt that the country had been too vast and overpowering for Hogner's creative instinct.

If he did go back east we are not sure but we do know that he was in Albuquerque in the early 1930s where he became a professor in the University of New Mexico art department for four years. While there he met and married Dorothy Childs, an author from Litchfield, Connecticut. In 1934 they moved to her home town and later to New York City where he painted murals for the Officers Club at Halloran Hospital, Staten Island, the dining room at Floyd Bennet Field, Long Island and the history of the Navy for Brooklyn's Navy YMCA. One can consider that these were most likely New Deal funded projects but this has not been verified as of 2011. Other mural work from that period is reportedly in the Oklahoma City public schools, Oklahoma Art Center, St. Louis Public Library, History Museum in North Carolina, and Whistler's House in Lowell, Masasschusetts.

According to *Who's Who in American Art* (1956), Hogner won various professional prizes and was a member of different professional organizations including the National Society of Mural Painters, and the American Artists Professional League and the Architectural League of New York City. His best known mural is the "Memorial to the Four Chaplains" commissioned by Daniel Poling commemorating the lives of the four chaplains who gave their life jackets to soldiers on the troopship Dorchester when it was sunk during World War II. This mural was dedicated by President Truman in 1951 at Temple University.

Nils and his wife, Dorothy Childs Hogner, collaborated on thirty-seven of her books; he provided the illustrations. Some of these books included *Navajo Winter Nights* (1935), *South to Padre* (1936), *Santa Fe Caravans* (1937), *Westward, High, Low, and Dry* (1938) and *The Bible Story* (1943). In 1938 he worked with Guy Scott to create *The Cartoon Guide of New York City*.

Three large and colorful paintings hang at Eastern New Mexico University's Music Department and were done during his time with the New Deal programs probably while living in Albuquerque. A fourth one, "Sanitation Isleta Pueblo," has disappeared. They were most likely painted based on his memories of his time spent on the Navajo reservation since they are various Navajo scenes.

Before his death in Litchfield on July 30, 1970, he had won many awards for his art.

LOCATIONS OF NEW DEAL ARTWORK: Portales—Eastern New Mexico University; Washington, DC and possible New Deal work in sites identified above.

HOKEAH, JACK (1902–1969)

This Kiowa Indian named White Horse, the warrior, was reared by his grandmother in western Oklahoma after being orphaned as a young boy. He attended the Santa Fe Indian School and was commissioned to do a mural at that school. During the 1930s he lived with Maria Martinez and her family in San Ildefonso Pueblo as her adopted son. He was on the New York stage for a short period and was later employed by the Bureau of Indian Affairs. He was known to be part of the Kiowa Five Artists who did work in Oklahoma. One of his pieces was transferred to Mesa Verde National Park by Edgar L. Hewett, an early director of the New Mexico Museum of Fine Art.

LOCATION OF POSSIBLE NEW DEAL ARTWORK: Santa Fe—Museum of Fine Art, Santa Fe Indian School; Mesa Verde National Park, Colorado.

HOUSER, ALLAN (1914–1994)

Born in Apache, Oklahoma, Allan Houser was proud of his Chiricahua Apache heritage and felt it inspired him to the greatness he achieved. His real name was Allan C. Haozous but since many people had difficulty with this Apache name, which means "Pulling Roots," he became well known as Allan Houser.

The need to help with the crops and other work on the family farm sometimes made education a luxury but he finally graduated from Chilocco Indian High School. In the early 1930s young Houser and his dad used their horses and wagon to haul rock for the WPA road building activities in that state. His aging father was sad when in 1936 the young man decided to go with others to the Santa Fe Indian School to pursue his budding talent in art. There he met Dorothy Dunn, the art instructor at that school. This woman, who became the devoted discoverer of many an Indian artist, tried to discourage this Oklahoma boy from trying to do three dimensional creations to which he felt drawn. Having been too busy working on the Oklahoma farm, Houser did not have the wealth of Indian stories that some of the New Mexico artists had so when he returned home for visits, he had his father share the family and tribal stories of his ancestor, Geronimo, and others. In 1937 he was the only Native American to be represented at the National Exhibition of American Art in New York and also had his first one-man show at the Museum of New Mexico. After graduating from the Santa Fe Indian School, he stayed on to study with Dunn in her extended art program called The Studio.

Paintings of the traditional two dimensional nature done by Houser during this time and as part of the New Deal programs can be seen today in the Gallup and Raton libraries. His mural painting won him national recognition. In 1939 he joined other Native Americans to create two murals in the Department of the Interior Building in Washington, DC. World War II brought another turning point in his career when he moved to California to work in a defense plant and while there continued his studies looking both at the old masters and investigating new art movements. As a result he broke out of the two dimensional creations and moved into the three dimensional medium of sculpture. He experimented with all kinds of materials but found he always stayed loyal to his favorite subject matter, the Indian.

In addition to his own painting and sculpting, Houser began to teach art and worked at the Inter-mountain Indian School in Brigham City, Utah from 1951 to 1962. Then he returned to Santa Fe to become an instructor at the new Institute of American Indian Arts. He later was named the head of the sculpture division until his retirement in 1975. Today the IAIA Museum includes an area that is named for him and features large three dimensional creations of Houser and others inspired by him.

Up until his death on August 23, 1994, he lived in Santa Fe creating and receiving numerous accolades for his special creative talents. In July 1992 he received the nation's highest art award, the National Medal of Arts, and it is on display along with numerous other awards and prizes at his studio south of Santa Fe. Although he never finished college, Houser received three honorary doctorates from the University of Oklahoma, University of Maine and Colorado State University. He was considered by many to be the most outstanding and highly respected Native American artist in the world.

He and his Navajo wife, Anna Marie Gallegos, had five sons. Houser had his studio south of Santa Fe along with artist son, Bob Haozous, and the land is dotted with their sculpture and teepees. An amphitheater was finished shortly before his death with the plan that he would be able to entertain his friends and family with his other talent, playing his Native American flute. This was the site of his memorial service with over five hundred attending and son, Bob Haozous, played the Native American flute in his memory. The three other sons were also involved in working with him prior to his death, and now all continue to promote his work as well as their own.

LOCATIONS OF KNOWN NEW DEAL ARTWORK: Gallup, Raton, New Mexico; Washington, DC.

HULLENKREMER, ODON (1888–1978)

Odon Hullenkremer was born in Hungary in 1888. He studied art in Budapest, Berlin, Paris and Munich and painted extensively in Europe before coming to America in 1912. Settling first in the east, he later moved to Santa Fe in 1933. He is a recognized artist in both Europe and the United States and is listed in *Who's Who in American Art*. In his early years he painted portraits, landscapes and murals extensively. He often depicted the people and times of the depression and the simplicity of life through a person's expressions. One of his most poignant works is the "Depression" which pictures a man and woman coping with their despair, the wife's arm around her husband offering comfort. Hullenkremer could also depict the simple joy of children as seen in the Carrie Tingley Hospital for Crippled Children painting of "Children on a Teeter Totter" and "Boy in Helmet" paintings of his neighbor's children. Also at that hospital is a painting of workers during the Depression constructing an adobe structure. Two large pieces depicting the construction of Conchas Dam and the adjacent village can be viewed at the Visitor Center at the dam and at the National Park Service building in Santa Fe is another large portrait of the first director of the National Park Service. Smaller and more finite work was done by him as one of the artists/copyists who worked on the state's *Portfolio of Spanish-Colonial Design*.

He set aside his painting later in life for an active role as a community leader in the American Red Cross and the Santa Fe Civil Defense Organization. He was awarded the American Red Cross Medal of Honor in 1946 and was honoree of a City of Santa Fe Resolution in 1960. He never married and died in 1978 leaving behind a long record of humanitarian efforts.

LOCATIONS OF NEW DEAL ARTWORK: Albuquerque, Conchas Dam, Raton, Santa Fe.

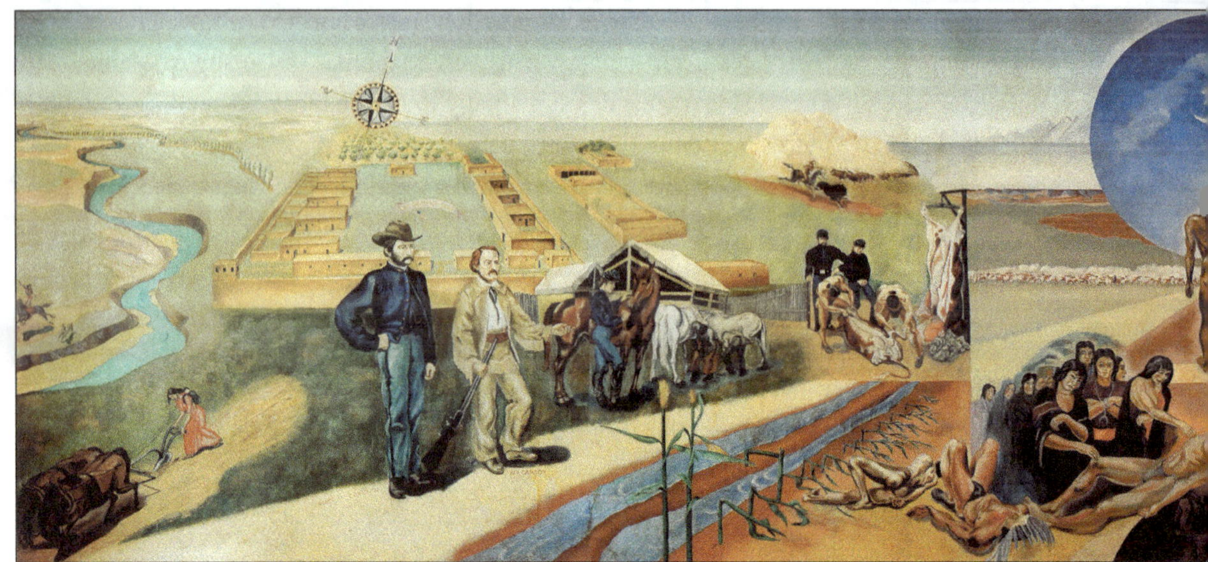

Hunter, Russell Vernon, "The Last Frontier" mural, De Baca County Courthouse, Fort Sumner, continued on next page. Hunter was the director of the state's WPA Federal Art Project and he saved himself a location to paint the history of eastern New Mexico where he grew up. It covers the four walls of the second floor in Fort Sumner's courthouse for De Baca County and is a powerful piece full of history—both good and bad. Photograph by Pat Berrett from *A More Abundant Life, New Deal Artists and Public Art in New Mexico*, courtesy of Sunstone Press.

HUNTER, RUSSELL VERNON (1900–1955)

Hunter was born in Hallsville, Illinois and raised in eastern New Mexico. He studied at the Art Institute of Chicago and was always interested in teaching and encouraging all types of art activity. A long-time resident of New Mexico, his career began as an art instructor in the Los Cerrillos schools near Santa Fe. During the twenties, he continued his teaching at the State Teacher's College (now New Mexico Western University) in Silver City and the Otis Art Institute of Los Angeles (1923–27). Then he taught at the Master Institute of Roerich Museum in New York (1929–31). In the early thirties, he returned to his roots in eastern New Mexico. He painted the Fort Sumner Courthouse murals as a PWAP project. In November of 1934 he married and went to live in Puerto de Luna, New Mexico where he organized a State Vocational Education school. In the late fall of 1935, he was asked to take the job of New Mexico State Director for the WPA Art Project and the Hunters moved to Santa Fe to give him the opportunity to carry out these duties. This involved working with local, state, and federal groups and discovering all the artists who might participate in the various projects.

Early in 1942 Washington closed the New Mexico Art Project and one might note that Hunter was one of two state directors who survived in his position throughout the entire program. Others came and went in other states. Unfortunately, the New Mexico office was instructed to destroy all records, since copies had been sent to Washington. Some key material has yet to be found. Hunter went on to plan and supervise the interior decoration of the

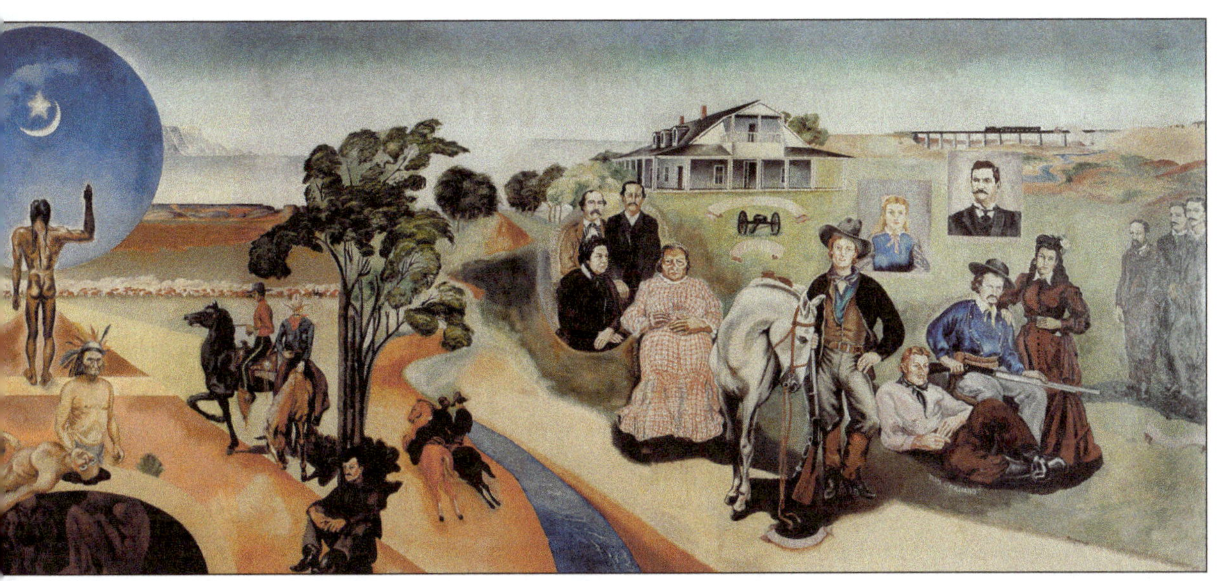

Officer's Club at the airbase in Clovis, then to Regional Buildings supervisor for USO in the east, then Administrative Director, Dallas Museum of Fine Arts, and back to New Mexico as the Director of the Roswell Art Museum which had been started as one of the state's four art centers under WPA. He died in Roswell in 1955.

LOCATION OF NEW DEAL ARTWORK: Fort Sumner.

HUNTINGTON, ANNA VAUGHN HYATT (1876–1955)

Anna was born in Cambridge, Massachusetts on March 10, 1876, to Alpheus and Audellas (Beebe) Hyatt. Her father, Alpheus Hyatt, was an eminent palaeontologist. Hyatt studied in private schools and at the Art Students' League in New York. As a sculptor, she loved to create both domestic and wild animal pieces. Her small bronzes were exhibited in over 200 museums and art galleries and featured the animals and historic figures Don Quixote in New York City, Abraham Lincoln in Austria, works in Springfield and Portland, and Andrew Jackson in Georgia. She also created an equestrian statue of Joan of Arc in Riverside Drive, New York (1915) and a wall statue of the same martyr in the Cathedral of St. John the Divine in the same city in 1922. She created Torchbearers statues for Madrid, Spain, Havana, Cuba, and Norfolk, Virginia. In 1923 she married Archer M. Huntington, a railroad heir, and they purchased Brookgreen Plantation in South Carolina. This home place became a public sanctuary after her death. She received many awards, prizes, and Medals of Honor from this country, France, and Spain. She was a member of the National Sculptor Society of Federation Arts and the first woman to ever be named a member of the Spanish Academia de Bellas Artes de San Fernando as well as a member of the American Academy of Arts and Letters. One of her pieces is in the Gallup library and a small bronze can also be seen at the Roswell Art Museum.

LOCATION OF NEW DEAL ARTWORK: Gallup, Roswell.

HURD, PETER (1904–1984)

Peter Hurd was born in Roswell, New Mexico February 22, 1904, and lived there during his youth. As a painter and illustrator, he studied at the Pennsylvania Academy of Fine Arts where he was a pupil of N. C. Wyeth and married his daughter, Henriette Wyeth. He was a member of the Fellowship Pennsylvania Academy of Fine Arts and the Wilmington Society of Fine Arts. He exhibited widely throughout the United States and received several awards of national distinction. Hurd received a bit of notoriety over a portrait he did of President Lyndon Johnson in 1966 for the White House Historical Association. He was represented in a number of leading galleries and collections including the Art Institute of Chicago; Nelson Gallery of Art, Kansas City; Rochester Memorial Art Gallery; and the Metropolitan Museum of Art, New York City. Not only was he a fine painter of oils, tempera and watercolor paintings, but Hurd was also an excellent lithographer. He was an illustrator of numerous books such as *The Last of the Mohicans* by James Fenimore Cooper and *American History* by T. S. Lawler. Peter Hurd was also a *Life* magazine correspondent in European, African and Oriental theaters during World War II. His work is included in the *Encyclopedia Britannica* Collection of Contemporary American Painting. He created a mural for New Mexico Military Institute, one of his alma maters, but it was lost in a fire in 1938 that was allegedly started by a disgruntled individual. Other murals were done as part of the New Deal project and can be seen on the exterior of the Otero County Office Building in Alamogordo and the post offices of Big Spring, Dallas and El Paso, Texas.

This cowboy artist was also well known for his great love of horses and polo. In the early 1970s he had a serious fall during a polo game and it seemed to have a lingering effect upon his general health. Later that year he virtually retired and was a patient in an Albuquerque nursing home at the time of his death in 1984.

Both his daughter, Carol H. Rogers, and son, Michael are also artists as is Carol's son, Peter De La Fuente. A gallery near the family home in San Patricio houses works of all members of this talented family while Peter has the Wyeth-Hurd gallery in Santa Fe.

LOCATIONS OF NEW DEAL ARTWORK: Post Offices in Alamogordo New Mexico; Big Spring, Dallas Terminal Annex Building; Lubbock, Texas Institute of Technology's Holden Hall, and El Paso, Texas; Washington, DC.

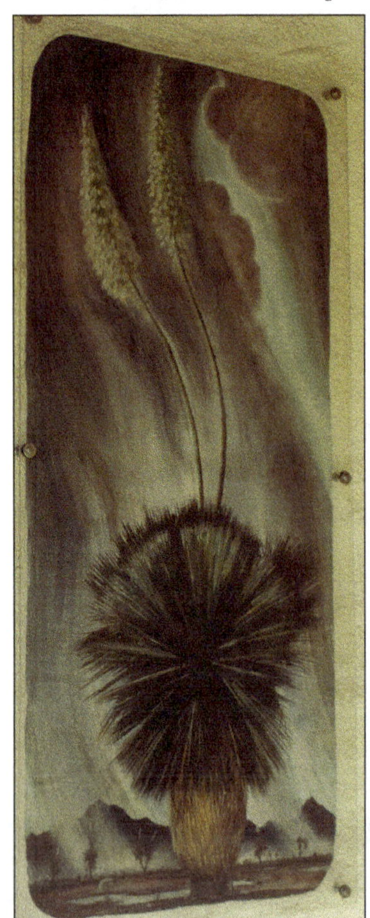

Peter Hurd, "Yucca," fresco, Alamogordo, Otero County Building. This is one of the two side pieces to two large frescos Hurd painted around the exterior of the front doors leading into the New Deal former post office.

IMHOF, JOSEPH ADAM ANDREW JOHN (1871–1955)

Born in Brooklyn, New York in 1871, Imhof lived in New York, Europe, Albuquerque and Taos, New Mexico. Imhof's paintings of Indians are so anthropological that some critics have deprecated their importance as art. From his observations of Pueblo culture, he had become aware of the importance of corn in their lives and had used the art medium to explain its secular and ceremonial use. His lithographs received better treatment from the critics. Although largely self-taught, he was an excellent draftsman and print maker. He had the first lithographic press in Taos which he set up sometime after his arrival in 1929. Imhof was not a newcomer to New Mexico, however, since he lived in Albuquerque from 1906 to 1912. The University of New Mexico Department of Anthropology has six of his oil paintings.

LOCATIONS OF NEW DEAL ARTWORK: Albuquerque—University of New Mexico Art Museum, Anthropology Department.

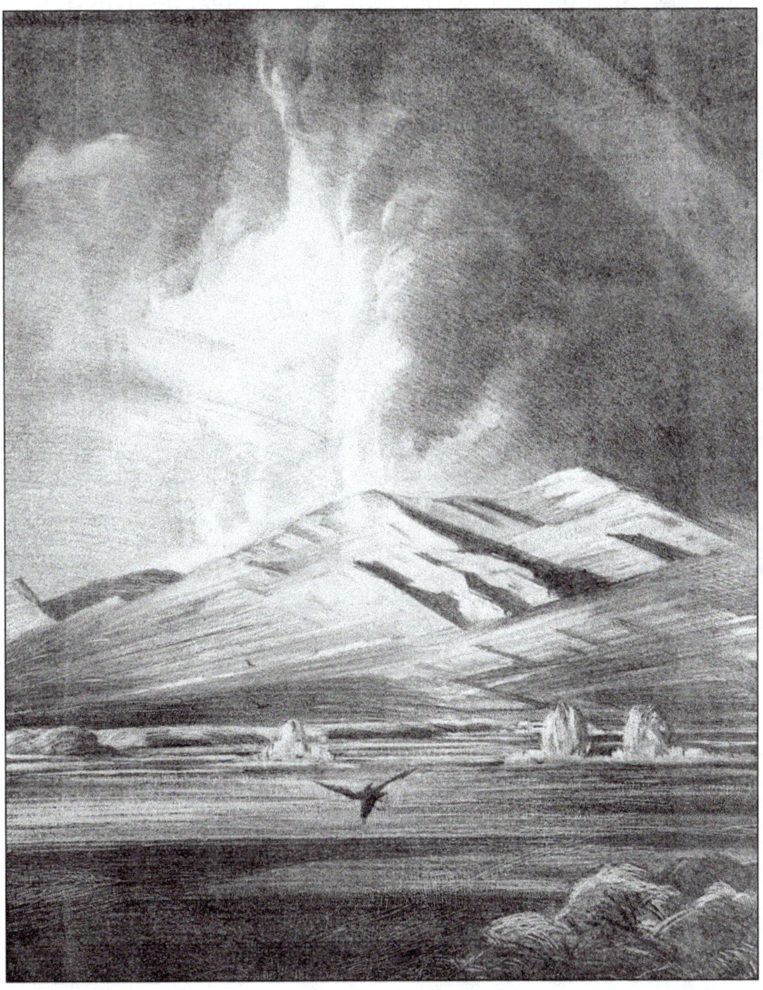

Joseph Adam Andrew John Imhof, "The Storm," lithograph, Albuquerque, University of New Mexico Art Museum

JELLICO, JOHN (1914–2005)

Born in Koehler, New Mexico in 1914, Jellico was a graduate of the Art Institute of Pittsburgh and studied at Phoenix School of Design and Grand Central School of Art, both in New York, and at evening sessions at the University of Pittsburgh. From 1946 to 1950 Jellico was an instructor of commercial art and design, advancing to assistant director at the Art Institute of Pittsburgh, 1950–1956. In the fall of 1956 he went to Denver to become director of the Colorado Institute of Art, becoming the president in 1962. As an artist Jellico has painted numerous murals for the Third Air Force chapels and seven larger murals for a church in Raton, New Mexico. He joined with Juanita Lantz to create twenty-seven ceiling decorations in the Old Library (Carnegie) in Raton but they were later demolished when the building was destroyed to reroute the highway. Today there are still two of his WPA works in the existing Raton Library and Public Schools. In 1993 he was one of the few remaining WPA artists of New Mexico and lived in Littleton, Colorado with his daughter until his death.

LOCATION OF NEW DEAL ARTWORK: Raton.

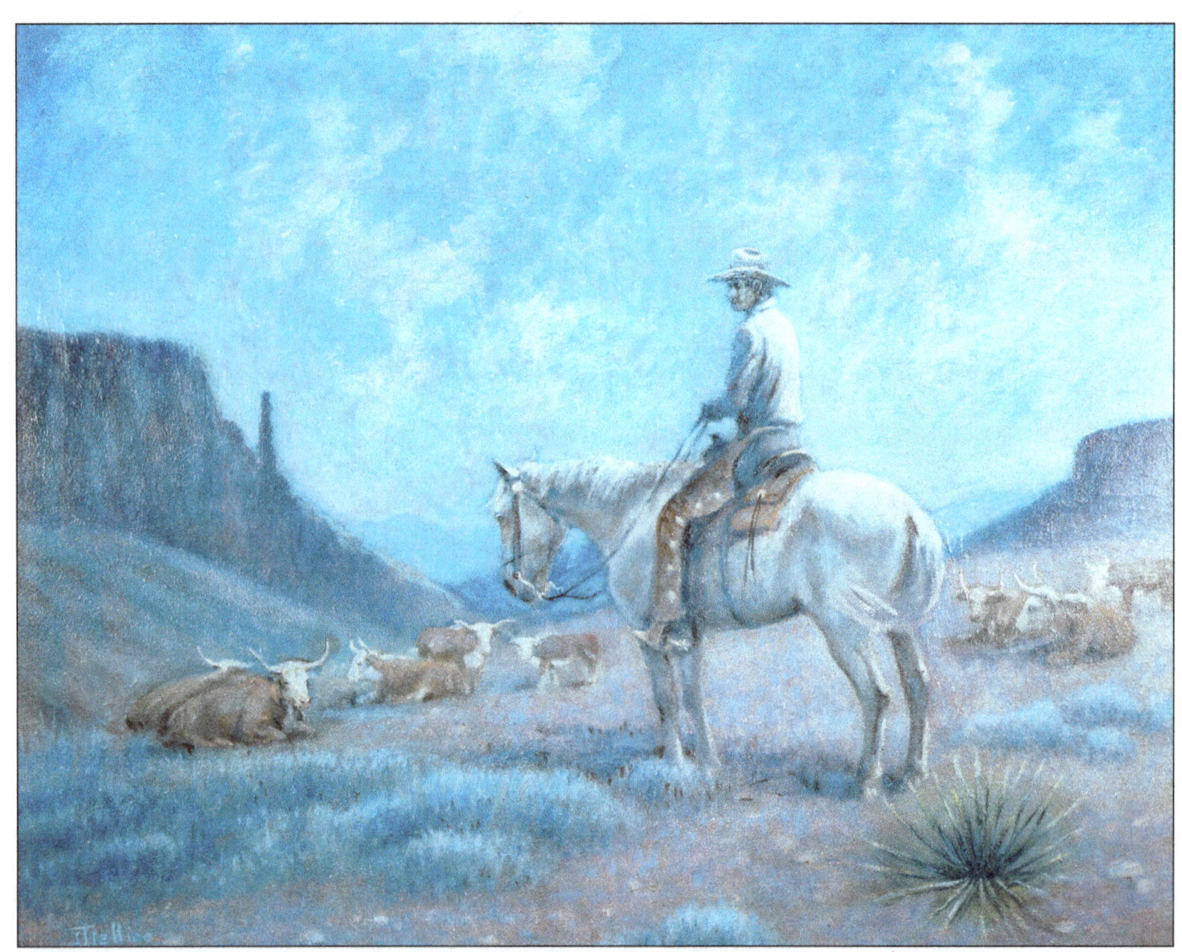

John Jellico, "Untitled," oil

JONES, D. PAUL (dates unknown)

Born in Maryland, Jones grew to manhood and first studied art there. As a young man he found himself in France during World War I, and kept his sanity by subconsciously studying form and movement and the play of color over the tortured landscapes while dreaming of peace in a land of solitude. After the war he went to Phoenix, Arizona and worked in a bank but needed more solitude, nature and art so he bought some art supplies and food and went into the wilds of the Hopi and Navajo country. He learned all about these people, their country, and customs and was given the Navajo name of Kla-chi-yezzy or Little Dog, because of his gift of imitating animal sounds. After several years of the nomad life, he went to Colorado Springs for further study under Robert Reid and John Carlsen at the Broadmoor Art Academy and later became one of the teachers there himself.

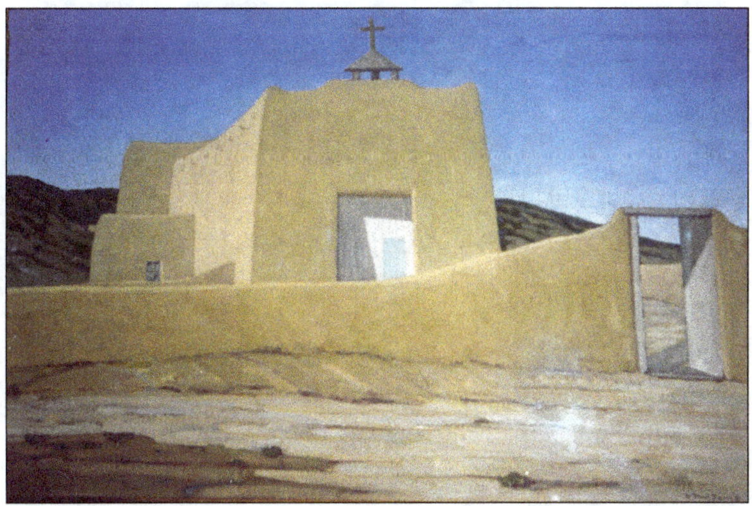

D. Paul Jones, "Hernandez Church," oil, Santa Fe, Supreme Court. There is a second painting of the same subject located at Carrie Tingley Hospital for Crippled Children in Albuquerque.

In 1933 or thereabouts he moved to Alcalde, New Mexico and maintained a studio with his friend, Lloyd Moylan. During this time both men were involved in creating beautiful artworks thanks to the financial resources of the New Deal Programs. Being an artist on the Portfolio project was one of the activities. He did murals for the Northern New Mexico Community College (then called, Spanish American Normal School) at El Rito and they are hanging in the Bronson Cutting Hall. Two paintings of the mission church of Hernandez, north of Española, can be seen today in Albuquerque at Carrie Tingley Hospital for Crippled Children and the Supreme Court in Santa Fe. Ina Sizer Cassidy noted about the mission church paintings that one can "trace in his brush strokes, the bleak setting, and meager life to which it is the spiritual sustenance, the earthy symbol of a living faith, the central pivot about which revolves the social structure of this primitive village."

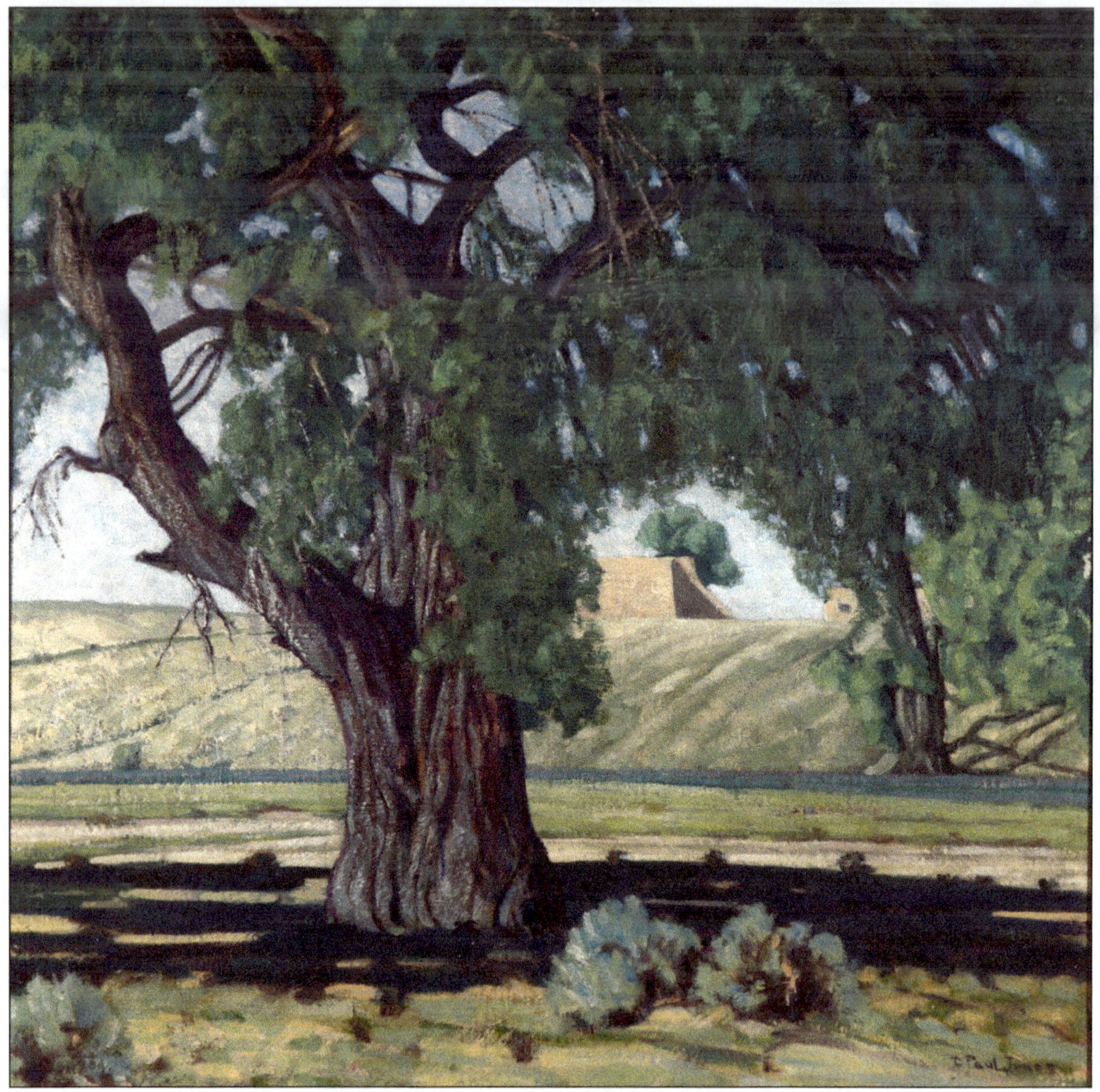

D. Paul Jones, "Cottonwood Tree," oil, Socorro, New Mexico Technical University Library

LOCATIONS OF NEW DEAL ARTWORK: Albuquerque—Carrie Tingley Hospital for Crippled Children, Clayton, El Rito, Gallup, Las Cruces, Melrose, Santa Fe, Socorro.

JONSON, RAYMOND (1891–1982)

Born near Chariton, Iowa in 1891, Raymond Jonson moved often during his childhood. At age twenty Jonson had a spiritual experience in which he felt challenged to dedicate his life to art. His art training began at the Portland Art Museum School and continued when he moved to Chicago and attended the Chicago Academy of Fine Arts, later enrolling at the Art Institute. Encouraged by his teacher, BJO. Nordfeldt, Jonson became art director at the Chicago Little Theater (first American experimental theater). His experimental stage-design work and Bauhaus concepts influenced his painting, which took on distinctly abstract qualities. A summer visit to Santa Fe in 1922 prompted a permanent move for Jonson and his wife, Vera White, two years later. For the following twenty-five years. Jonson taught and painted in Santa Fe and then moved to Albuquerque to become a University of New Mexico professor. He lived there until his death in 1982. A strong and dedicated artist and a man of great industry and curiosity, Jonson was a one-man task force for modern art isolated in New Mexico for more than forty years and as such was an active member of the Transcendental Movement. After his death, his home housed his art work as the Jonson Gallery for a number of years but that collection has been transferred to the University of New Mexico Art Museum to make up a portion of that museum referred to as The Raymond Jonson Gallery.

Two interesting, personal anecdotes about Jonson include the fact that he insisted that his name be pronounced "Joanson" and toward the end of his life, he chose to eat only ice cream.

LOCATIONS OF NEW DEAL ARTWORK: Albuquerque—Jonson Gallery, University of New Mexico Art Museum, Portales—Eastern New Mexico University and Washington, DC.

KABOTIE, FRED (1900–1986)

Kabotie was born on the Second Mesa of Hopi Land in Arizona on February 20, 1900. His Native American name was Nakayoma meaning Day After Day. When he was six years old the family joined others who left old Oraibi and established Hotevilla as an attempt to escape the efforts of the government to force them to abandon their customs. They were forced to return and in 1913 the children were placed in schools for the first time. Kabotie was sent to Santa Fe Indian School at the age of ten as a further disciplinary action but there his artistic talents blossomed with the encouragement of Mr. and Mrs. DeHuff of the school's administration. After 1920 his work and his name usually appeared wherever Indian art was mentioned. His career included teaching, painting, writing, lecturing, and good will ambassadorship to India in 1960. A Guggenheim Fellowship awarded to him in 1945 to study ancient paintings on Mimbres pottery may have been the beginnings of his abstract pictorial metaphor work. He married a Hopi woman in 1931.and they had two children.

LOCATION OF POSSIBLE NEW DEAL ARTWORK: Unknown in New Mexico, but much in Arizona at the Petrified Forest Monument and Grand Canyon.

KAPLAN, NAT (1912–1996)

Kaplan was born in New York City and received his bachelor's degree in Zoology and Civil Engineering from the University of Connecticut. During the Depression days, he got a job at the university in Texas Station thanks to an old friend. From there he moved on to Red River and later Taos around 1936 where he did picture framing at a shop that assisted most of the known artists of the time. While in northern New Mexico he roomed with Woody Crumbo, lived next door to Herbert Dunton, and was friends with Gisella Loeffler and many of the others in the area. By the age of twenty eight, he was involved with the WPA project in Gallup. Teaching art classes at the art center paid him $90 a month since he was the assistant director. The classes included both fine art and furniture making. He later became the art center director. Kaplan also loved woodcarving. He also did mapping in 1939 of the Navajo reservation and noted "they were not easy days but they were GREAT days."

Kaplan went on to become a highly respected and successful engineer, architect, and builder in the Albuquerque area where he lived until his death. His daughter, Susan K. Lentz, lives in his Albuquerque home.

LOCATION OF NEW DEAL ART: Unknown.

KAVIN, ZENA (1912–2003)

Born in Berkeley, California on October 25, 1912, this painter and engraver studied at the California School of Fine Arts in San Francisco and privately with A. Kravchenko in Moscow. She was a lifelong resident of Berkeley and Oakland except for four years in New Mexico during the 1930s. During that time she participated in the New Deal programs and five of her paintings are in the New Mexico Museum of Art collection. She also created two frescoes as part of the kiva murals done in Bernalillo, New Mexico. She married artist Jon Cornin in 1940 and returned with him to a studio-home in Oakland. Using the pseudonym Corka, the Cornins produced cartoons for the *Saturday Evening Post* and *The New Yorker*. During her active life as an artist, she specialized in figure studies in casein tempera, however, she also sculpted and contributed wood engravings for a number of books and magazines. She was a member of various California organizations and exhibited in numerous California venues.

POSSIBLE LOCATION OF NEW DEAL ART: Bernalillo, Santa Fe.

KITTS, CORA EASTON(Dates Unknown)

Cora Easton Kitts was born in Greenfield, Iowa. She lived in Taos between 1938–1960. She used oil and watercolors primarily. In Mabel Dodge Luhan's 1947 book, *Taos and Its Artists* she was described thusly: "Cora Kitts, stripped of even the minor ease and comfort of her youth, alone, without encouragement from anyone, began to paint when all else failed her. In her small, meticulous pictures there are an appealing naivete that somewhat recalls the primitive Rousseau. No lions in the jungle, but the sunflowers and horses and blue skies of her environment. Her little paintings are becoming collectors' items among the cultivated, blasé sophisticates who are familiar with all the techniques of the art world, and who find, in the simple untutored observations of a child, a comfort and consolation too often lacking in more accomplished work."

LOCATION OF NEW DEAL ARTWORK: Unknown

KLOSS, GENE (ALICE GENEVA GLASIER KLOSS) (1903–1996)

Born Alice Geneva Glasier in Oakland, California in 1903, Gene chose to change her name since she felt it was too much "name" for a young girl. She graduated from the University of California, Berkeley with honors in art in 1924. An academician of the National Academy of Design, she was given numerous awards and critical acclaim and her work has been extensively exhibited. Since 1925 she painted and etched both the country and the people of the Southwest after visiting "out West" and moving to Taos in 1928. She is best known for her etchings and as of 1930 began receiving acclaim and prizes for her work in this medium. Sunstone Press in Santa Fe published a book under her authorization and direction, *Gene Kloss Etchings*, which provides a list of six hundred of her prints, but her oil painting "Rain Priest" at the Albuquerque Museum is a favorite of many. Her etching "Christmas Processional at Taos," which was not a New Deal creation, received First Place in 1952 from the Chicago Society of Etchers. It is similar to the New Deal etching, "Christmas Eve, Taos Pueblo," which is part of the group of nine etchings of New Mexico scenes. Two hundred reproductions were distributed to New Mexico schools and institutions as part of the Federal Art Project. Today, a majority of them are missing from those sites or may have simply not been located.

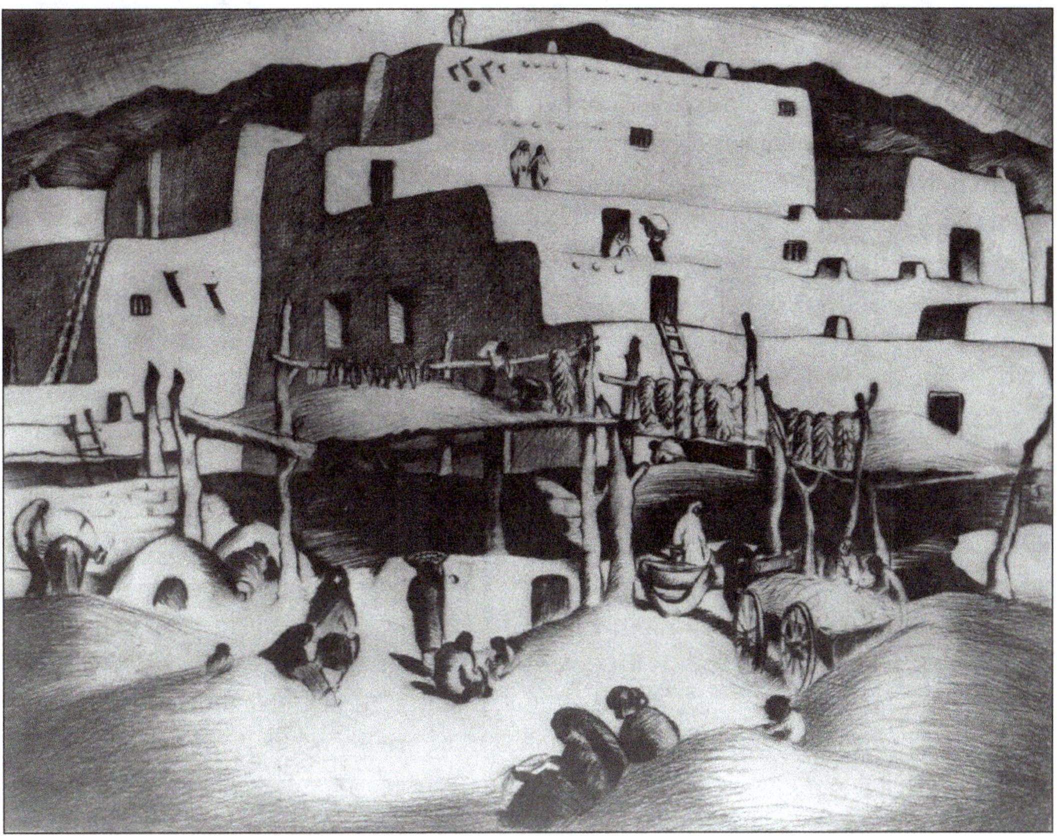

Gene Kloss, "Indian Harvest," etching, various New Mexico schools

Kloss lived in Taos, New Mexico with her husband Philip Kloss, who was a poet, until her death in 1996. They did a book together in 1980, *The Great Kiva: A Poetic Critique of Religion*, published by Sunstone Press, which included her etchings and his poetry. Her book, *Gene Kloss Etchings*, was also published by Sunstone Press under the guidance of the artist and includes the works Kloss felt best represented her.

POSSIBLE LOCATIONS OF NEW DEAL ARTWORK: (Not all have been located.) Albuquerque—University of New Mexico, Anthony, Artesia, Aztec, Bernalillo, Carlsbad, Clayton, Carrizozo, Clovis, Cuba, Deming, Elida, Farmington, Hot Springs, Hurley, Las Vegas, Lordsburg, Magdalena, Melrose, Milne, Mountainair, Mora, Portales, Raton, Roswell, Santa Fe, Silver City, Tierra Amarilla, Tucumcari, Tularosa; Washington, DC.

KNEE BROOK SCHNAUFER, GINA (1898–1982)

Born in Marietta, Ohio in 1898, Gina Knee lived in Sag Harbor, New York and began painting early as a child but never really thought "art" until she arrived in New Mexico. She came to Santa Fe in 1931, after seeing a 1930 New York City exhibition of Marin's Taos watercolors. She studied one summer with Ward Lockwood and taught at a girl's school. Her watercolors at first showed the influence of Marin, and later incorporated Klee symbolism to produce abstracted Indian and landscape motifs. She remained in Santa Fe for 15 years, with one artist exhibitions beginning in 1942. "Up to 1945" she said, "I painted everything I could see: Indian dances, the Spanish Americans—the desert and mountains—but after a few years I started trying to paint more abstractly, expressing forms in their spirit, or sound, or smell—a more complete picture—a sensual statement—as important as the forms." Later she lived in Georgia, Spain, New York and the West Coast, but the shapes, feelings and memories of New Mexico were always with her. Gina Knee was married to the photographer Ernie Knee and the artist, Alexander Brook.

LOCATION OF POSSIBLE NEW DEAL ARTWORK: Unknown

LA GRONE, OLIVER (1906–1999)

Born in 1906 in McAlester, Oklahoma, LaGrone was a creative man. Besides being fond of expressing himself in poetry, he spent time making images out of the red clay of Oklahoma. He spent his formative years in Albuquerque and received his formal education at several universities including the University of New Mexico where he earned a Bachelor and Master of Arts degrees and was the first African-American graduate of the school's art department. During his stay in New Mexico, LaGrone, through the WPA, created the "Mercy" sculpture in 1935 as a reminder of the comfort given to him by his mother when he had malaria as a boy. It stood first in the clinic lobby in its original white plaster form at Carrie Tingley Hospital for Crippled Children in Truth or Consequences and later also in the clinic lobby at the Carrie Tingley Hospital for Crippled Children in Albuquerque. In 2008, it was moved to the children's wing (Barbara and Bill Richardson Wing) of the University of New

Mexico Hospital. Carrie Tingley Hospital for Crippled Children was a New Deal facility built to care for the state's young victims of polio.

Oliver LaGrone remained a friend to the hospital and its children returning to be honored during the 50th anniversary in 1987. The sculpture was finally bronzed nearly 60 years after its creation and was financed by funds from 1% for Public Art and funds from the University of New Mexico. At that time, a duplicate of the sculpture was made and placed in the sculpture garden of the Albuquerque Museum.

His love of poetry and sculpture led him through a life of teaching in Detroit, Marygrove, and Pennsylvania State University. His last appointment in 1974 was as special assistant artist-in-residence to the vice-president of undergraduate education. LaGrone and his wife, Lillian Graham LaGrone, lived in Hamlet, North Carolina at the time of his death.

LOCATION OF NEW DEAL ARTWORK: Albuquerque—University of New Mexico Hospital, Richardson Pediatric Wing, and Albuquerque Museum Sculpture Garden.

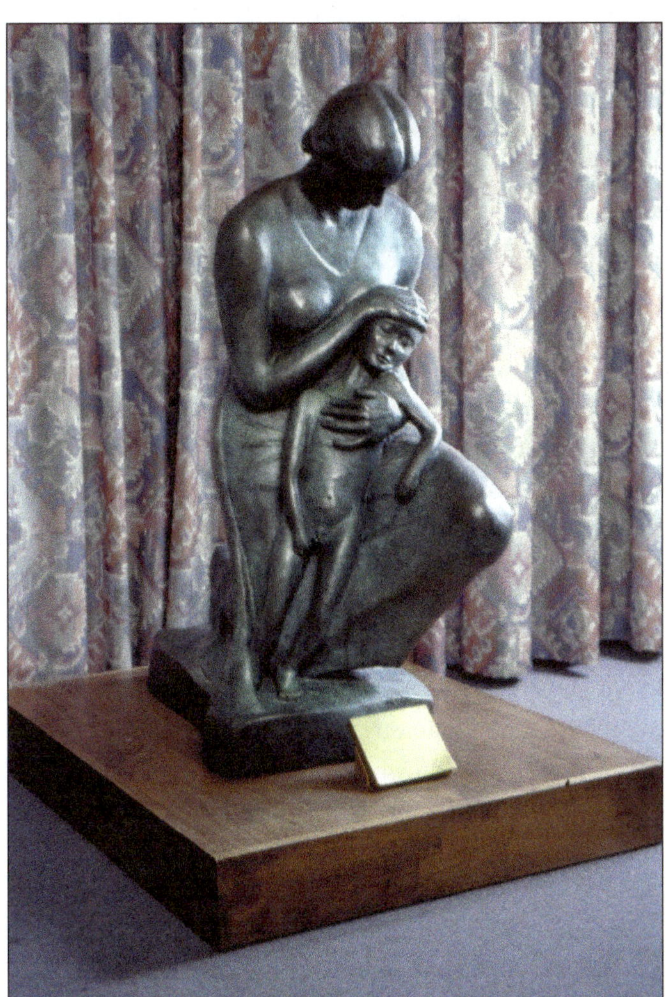

Oliver La Grone, "Mercy." This young African-American artist elected to portray his memories of the time in his childhood when his mother nursed him through his suffering with malaria. The sculpture stood in the lobby of Carrie Tingley Hospital for Crippled Children both in its original site in Truth or Consequences and later when the program moved to Albuquerque. The one on the left is now in the Richardson Pediatric Wing of the University of New Mexico Hospital. Photograph by Pat Berrett.

LANTZ LEIGHTON GOODWIN, JUANITA (1920–1969)

Juanita Donnell Lantz Leighton Goodwin grew up in Texas and eastern New Mexico. At one time she was married to Paul Lantz and assisted him with the paintings he created in La Fonda Hotel in Santa Fe. She later married Fred Leighton, an importer, and Walter Goodwin of Santa Fe and continued to paint all her life. She worked on twenty-seven ceiling decorations with John Jellico for the Raton Carnegie Library during the New Deal era but they were later demolished when the building was destroyed to reroute the highway. Conducting art classes for the Hispanic children of Roswell was another activity she engaged in as the result of New Deal funding. She died in Tucumcari, Arizona, below Tubac, in 1969. According to her son, Chris Lantz of Santa Fe, she had a one woman show in the National Gallery in Washington in the 1980s.

LOCATION OF NEW DEAL ARTWORK: Albuquerque—University of New Mexico Art Museum

LANTZ, PAUL (1908–1998)

Born in Stromburg, Nebraska February 14, 1908, Lantz lived and painted in New Mexico from 1930 to 1939. His murals decorated La Fonda Hotel and other places in Santa Fe and could also be seen at the old mine headquarters in Madrid. During the mining days of that area he was hired by the mining company to make drawings of men killed in mine accidents for records and identification purposes since many people could not read or write. He was married to Juanita Donnell (see above) by whom he had one son, Christopher. His wife and he were divorced when the son was six, but Lantz later remarried and had two other children. After leaving New Mexico, he lived, traveled and painted in New York, Kansas, San Francisco, Oregon, and the east coast. He maintained homes in Santa Fe and New York City.

Lantz led a productive life as an artist even illustrating some 30 books and some magazines. He was an individual who "had to paint or would become very fidgety" according to an old friend. He has five works displayed at the Museum of Fine Art in Santa Fe and the Metropolitan Museum of Art in New York City. The portraits of Clyde and Carrie Tingley at Carrie Tingley Hospital for Crippled Children in Albuquerque are just two of many that Lantz painted in his long career. His talents were extended to landscapes and murals which reflect the different areas of the country in which he lived and worked. There is one still in Clovis, New Mexico in a former post office called "Clovis Main Street" now an architect's office. He lived for some time in the Springer area but his last known place of residence was Phoenix, Arizona, where he died. His brother, Walter, was known for his creation of the Disney cartoon character, Woody Woodpecker.

LOCATIONS OF NEW DEAL ARTWORK: Albuquerque—University of New Mexico Art Museum, Clovis, Gallup, Raton; Washington, DC. A painting named "Jungle Warfare" by Private Lantz and a second titled "March Field" by Captain Lantz are part of the national CCC office collection now stored in the Smithsonian Museum in Washington, DC.

LEA, TOM (1907–2001)

Born on July 11, 1907, Lea studied at the Art Institute of Chicago from 1924 to 1926 and under John Norton in Chicago from 1926 through 1933. He worked on his first murals in Italy in 1930. He moved to Santa Fe in 1933 where he continued to paint while carrying on studies in Southwestern history and working as a part-time staff member of the Laboratory of Anthropology. In addition to his mural work in Las Cruces, which he did in the early 1930s while living in Santa Fe, he completed murals at South Park Community Building (Chicago), Court House (El Paso), State of Texas Building (Dallas), Post Office Department Buildings in Odessa and Seymour, Texas and Washington, DC, to name just a few. His work as an artist-correspondent for *Life* magazine during World War II brought him considerable recognition and throughout his career he had illustrated over fifty books about the American West and the war, seven of which he also wrote. His works are in the collections of the University of Texas and the Dallas Museum of Fine Art. He has had numerous exhibits including one at the Whitney Museum of American Art, New York in 1938. At least three books have been done about his life and creations. Lea lost his sight before his death in El Paso.

LOCATIONS OF NEW DEAL ARTWORK: Las Cruces—New Mexico State University Art Museum; Branigan Cultural Center, Chicago, Illinois; Dallas, El Paso, Odessa, Seymour, Texas; and Washington, DC.

LEIGH, WILLIAM ROBINSON (1866–1955)

Born in Robinson, West Virginia in 1866, Leigh, son of impoverished Southern aristocrats, was educated privately. He studied art under Hugh Newell at Maryland Institute in Baltimore from 1880 to 1883. He then went to the Raupp Royal Academy in Munich 1883–1884, the pupil of Gysis 1885–1886, of Lofftz 1887, and of Lindenschmid 1891–1892. He became adept at drawing animals as a boy, winning a $100 award for a sketch of a dog from W. W. Corcoran of Washington, DC. In 1897, *Scribner's* magazine sent him on an assignment to North Dakota. In 1906 Leigh persuaded the Santa Fe Railroad to give him free transportation for his first trip to the West in exchange for a painting. Five more paintings were commissioned, permitting Leigh to make an elaborate sketching trip through Arizona and New Mexico, living with the Indian tribes and cowboys. His realistic paintings are represented in major museums throughout the United States. His critics who had not seen the West said that the resulting paintings were of "purple horses with yellow bellies," a "ridiculously false color," and only illustrations. It was not until the 1940s that Leigh's Western work was completely accepted. An author of several short stories and books on the Southwest, his studio and many of his works are on exhibit at the Gilcrease Institute in Tulsa. He died in New York in 1955, the year he was elected to the National Academy of Design.

LOCATION OF NEW DEAL ARTWORK: Gallup.

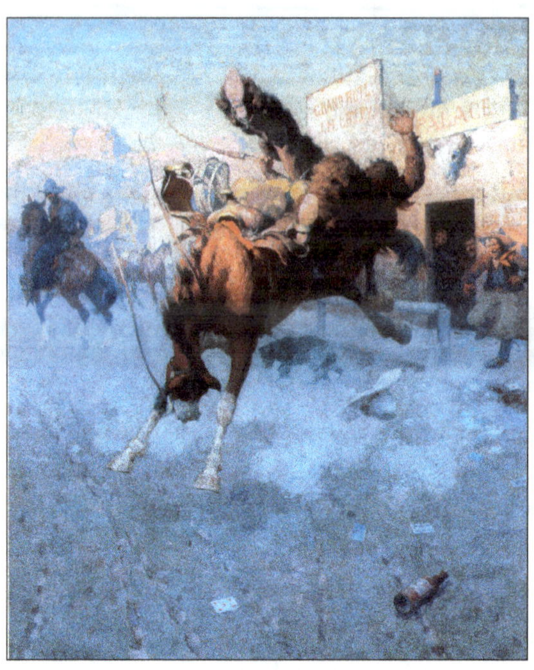

William Robinson Leigh, "Horses & Whiskey Don't Mix," oil, Gallup, Octavia Fellin Library

LOCKWOOD, JOHN WARD (1894–1963)

Born in Atchinson, Kansas in 1894, Ward Lockwood received his artistic training at the University of Kansas, Pennsylvania Academy of Fine Arts and at the Academie Ransom in Paris. Further studies with Andrew Dasburg at Woodstock, New York, preceded his move to New Mexico in 1926. In addition to his contact with Dasburg, Lockwood also spent a good deal of the time fishing and sketching with John Marin, and painting with fellow Kansan, Kenneth Adams. He ended up in Taos because of these friends and because living was cheaper there. He was a member of the Taos Heptagon. In his landscapes, form rather than storytelling was the major concern; the painted landscapes had a raw vigor which was conveyed through a variety of simple shapes and sharp contours, with an influence from Dasburg's tamed and modified cubism. During the 1930s, when Lockwood participated in WPA mural projects, he responded to the taste for American Scene realism in various post offices, i.e. "Daniel Boone Leading His Men Into Kentucky," a post office rendering in Lexington, Kentucky and two in Washington called "Building the West" and "Opening the West." He was also one of the Taos Fresco Quartette that did the large frescoes in the old Taos courthouse on the Plaza.

A versatile artist in many media, Lockwood was also a sought-after teacher. He taught at the University of New Mexico 1936–37 and University of Texas where he served as Chairman of the Department of Art (1938–39). Later he taught at the University of California at Berkeley (1939, 1949–61). Although he spent many years away from Taos, teaching art in California, he always retained contact with the Taos artist colony, visiting there from time to time throughout his life and died there in 1963.

LOCATIONS OF NEW DEAL ARTWORK: Taos; Edinburgh and Hamilton, Texas; Lexington, Kentucky; Washington, DC.

LOEFFLER LACHER, GISELLA (1900–1969)

Born in Vienna, Austria (Wertherburg, Austria-Hungary) in 1900, Mrs. Gisella Loeffler Lacher lived in New Mexico as of 1932 residing in Taos and Albuquerque. This painter of egg tempera, enamel and lacquer maintained her own individual decorative and illustrative folk style and was said to have painted everything in her sight. She studied at the Washington University School of Fine Arts in St. Louis and while in that city painted the ceilings in the Children's Hospital. She also studied in Gloucester, Massachusetts and was the pupil of Mary McCall and Hugh Breckenridge. Her work has been exhibited at the Museum of New Mexico and in Los Angeles and two large murals can be seen at the Carrie Tingley Hospital for Crippled Children in Albuquerque. In addition to her painting and mural work, she illustrated a number of children's books and one, *Franzi and Gizzi*, which she both wrote and illustrated, was critically acclaimed. Another was *Spanish Games of New Mexico*. She also did a poster for the *New York Herald Tribune* called "The Little Boy Dance of Taos." Her work was the basis of the décor of The Shed Restaurant in Santa Fe. The facility that may own the largest collection of her art is the Panhandle-Plains Museum in Canyon, Texas.

LOCATIONS OF NEW DEAL ARTWORK: Albuquerque—Carrie Tingley Hospital for Crippled Children, Las Cruces, Santa Fe—Museum of Fine Art.

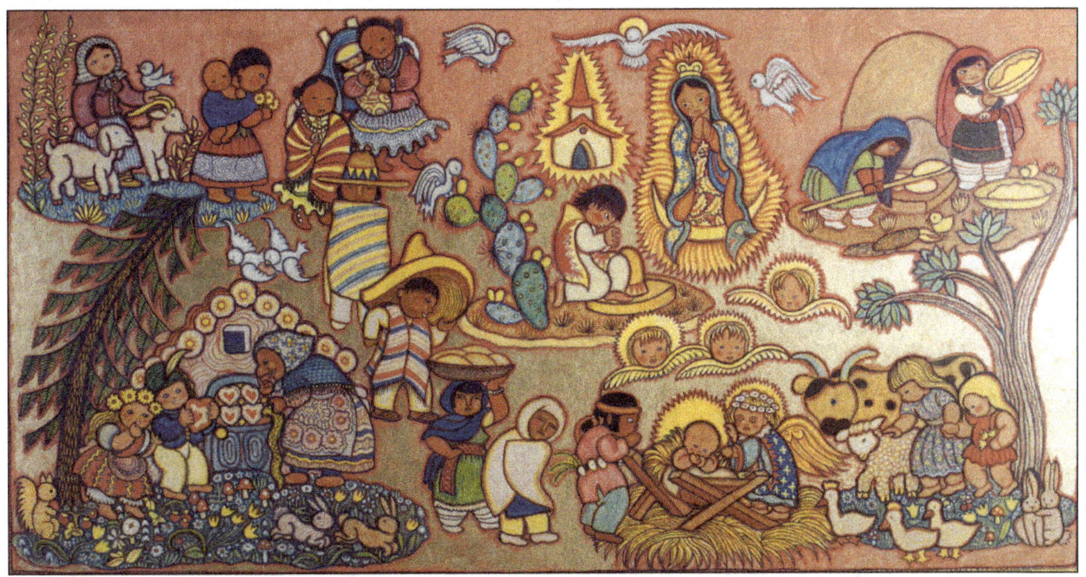

Gisella Loeffler Lacher, "Nativity Scene and Ethnic Children," oil/gold leaf on fiber board, Albuquerque, Carrie Tingley Hospital for Crippled Children

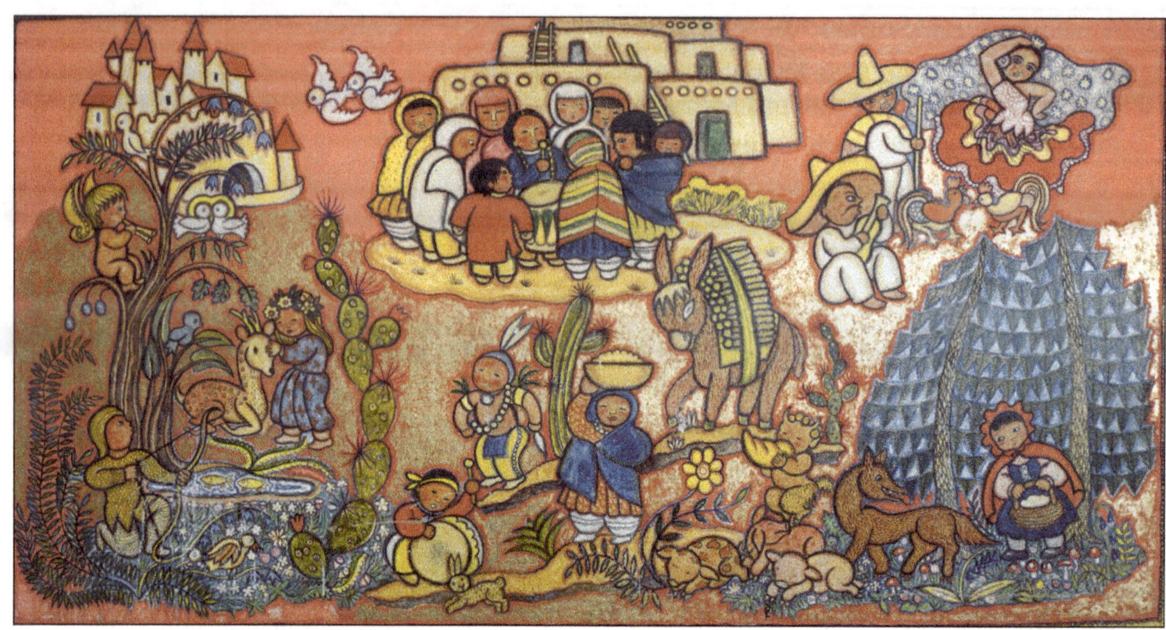

Gisella Loeffler Lacher, "Fairy Tale Young Children and Ethnic Children" oil/gold leaf on fiber board, Albuquerque, Carrie Tingley Hospital for Crippled Children

LUCERO, ABAD ELOY (1909–2009)

Lucero was born in Cerrillos, New Mexico in 1909 and spent a lifetime carving everything from signs to furniture to santos. Between the state's vocational schools and the WPA's Federal Art Project and the National Youth Administration (NYA), a great deal of Spanish furniture was created, either by the crafts persons or those they taught. Abad was one the lead teachers, and his furniture is found all over the state, or at least all over Northern New Mexico in public buildings and some private hotels like La Posada. He started in 1933 and while in his early 90s, he was still teaching in Senior Citizen Centers—this time it was how to create paintings. Through the New Deal programs, he worked with the National Youth Administration to teach young people woodworking. He also worked for the Vocational Division of New Mexico Department of Education and the United States Forest Service.

Moving to Dayton, Ohio, in 1943 he worked at Wright Patterson Field to try his skills at pattern-making, which was followed by working as an aircraft woodworker while in the service at Biac, New Guinea, during World War II. After the war, he came to Santa Fe with his wife to work and raise their family, including three children. They later moved to Albuquerque, and he worked for the Forest Service, making beautifully carved signs for them. Teaching all ages and in various settings, including detention facilities for youth was not a problem for Abad. Like some of the other talented artists, he also did tinwork, retablos, and got serious about painting in 1991.

During his retirement years and while teaching his fellow seniors, he took one of his classes to Cerrillos, his home town, to show off the WPA gymnasium he remembered playing basketball and dancing in. They didn't try their basketball skills but all had a wonderful time dancing. After the death of his beloved wife, Emma, who had been with him through all his teaching ventures, he finally began to slow down and the family determined that he needed more care. Initially, he went to a retirement home, but he came home on the week-ends and continued to create, according to his daughter, Jackie Gutierrez, and son, Leonard Lucero, who live in Santa Fe and Albuquerque.

LUJAN, MERINA, see Pop Chalee (Dates Unknown)

LUMPKINS, WILLIAM (1909–2000)

Born on a ranch near Clayton in the territory of New Mexico in 1909, Lumpkins made a name for himself in the field of architecture and art. He grew up on his family's ranches in Lincoln County and in Arizona. As a young man, Lumpkins and his friend, Peter Hurd, frequently went on camping trips where they did a great deal of sketching and studying art books provided to them by the librarian at New Mexico Military Institute, Paul Horgan.

Since the family's resources were not adequate for supporting a young aspiring artist, Lumpkins focused his educational activities on architecture at the University of New Mexico where he started in 1929 and while there he took courses in art, anthropology and journalism. Then he left to study architecture at the University of Southern California in Los Angeles but hitchhiked back to New Mexico where he finally graduated from the University of New Mexico in 1934. He began looking for work during the depression era when jobs were tough to come by. He was involved with the New Mexico Vocational School craft programs and then secured employment with the Public Works of Art Project (PWAP) by presenting some samples of his art work to the supervisor Gustave Baumann who seemed to like his work and commented, "Yes, you are an artist, now go home and paint for us." He did just that for six months and three of those works are now in the Museum of Fine Arts in Santa Fe and one in Portales. Another watercolor has been located in Carville Maine Hospital in Los Angeles.

Six months later he was transferred to the WPA Architectural Division as a junior grade architect and was assigned along with an old friend from Roswell, Frank Standhart, to design a state hospital for children who had been stricken with polio. Since neither of them knew what was needed for such treatments they consulted with Mrs. Eleanor Roosevelt, wife of the President, himself a polio victim. She made arrangements for them to obtain the architectural plans of the Warm Springs facility where her husband had received his treatments. The WPA funded institution was built in Hot Springs, New Mexico and served its original purpose for over 50 years and then became the home of the New Mexico Veterans' Center. Lumpkins went on to become "the grand old man of solar adobe architecture" and is world renowned in this capacity.

Architecture did not keep him from continuing with his artwork. During the college days at the University of New Mexico he was strongly supported by Raymond Jonson and others in the beginnings of his abstract style. This was not the most popular or acceptable form of art and they met with some opposition when they formed their Transcendental Painting Group in 1938 in Taos. The purpose of the group was to carry painting beyond the appearance of the physical world, through new concepts of space, color, light and design to imaginative realms that are idealistic and spiritual. Unfortunately World War II shortened the duration of this group and pilot Lumpkins found himself somewhat limited to creating portraits during his many hours of "waiting and ready" status.

Lumpkins felt that he was early influenced by a man who had traveled throughout the Orient and later came to the family ranch when he was pre-adolescent. Others along the way who made some impact on his style included Peter Hurd, Nils Hogner, John Marin, Loren Mozley and Cady Wells—many involved with the New Deal programs in New Mexico. It is also interesting to note that he had two brothers-in-law also working as artists in the programs: Howard Barton and Brooks Willis.

His talents in architecture and art seemed to come together in 1935 and over the years he noted that painting freed up his architecture. His artwork is in both private and public collections. At his death, a memorial service was held at the St. Francis Auditorium of the New Mexico Museum of Art in Santa Fe, and it was filled to capacity.

LOCATIONS OF NEW DEAL ARTWORK: Portales—Eastern New Mexico University, Santa Fe—Museum of Fine Arts; Los Angeles—Carville Maine Hospital.

LUNA, MAXIMO L. (1896–1964)

Furniture maker and carver "par excellence" from Taos according to many and particularly in the book, *The Taos Artists, A Historical Narrative and Biographical Dictionary* by David Witt and *Sin Nombre* by Tey Mariana Nunn. He was involved in the vocational programs in northern New Mexico training the young men in building the traditional Hispanic furniture.

MALDONADO, MANTHER (Circa 1920–Date unknown)

This man was one of four junior high students who were chosen to do two murals for the public library in Raton. It is unknown whether he did other artwork. William Warder was one of those four to go on with his art.

LOCATION OF NEW DEAL ARTWORK: Raton.

MARFYAK, JAN (1907–1990)

Born in Gnazda, Slovakia, Marfyak immigrated with his family to the United States in 1912, settling in New Britain, Connecticut. On graduating from high school, he attended the Hartford Art School for two years before enrolling at the Art Student's League in New

York City (1926–1931). Taking classes from Walt Kuhn, Kenneth Hayes-Miller, Boardman Robinson, John Carroll, and George Groez, he was a monitor for Thomas Hart Benton, as well as Walt Kuhn. In January 1934, Marfyak was hired as a project artist with the CWA in New York City, working with Benjamin Knotts. It was during this period that he began work on a mural panel, "Agamemnon", a 4' by 9' oil on gesso panel, which was to be placed in a New York City high school. In 1938, as part of the Works Project Administration/Federal Arts Project, he relocated to Roswell, New Mexico, to work with Roland Dickey, Director of the Roswell Federal Art Center, and Vernon Hunter, the Regional Supervisor in Santa Fe. He was responsible for collecting and cataloging Native American works of art, as well as teaching drawing to students and adults. In 1939, he returned to New York City, resigned from the WPA, and was hired as a cartographer with the Coast and Geodetic Society, transferring to the Office of Coordinator of Inter-American Affairs. During World War II and subsequent years, he continued to paint and exhibit works in Madison, Wisconsin and Washington, DC while holding full time jobs as a cartographer and draftsman. He created no known artwork in New Mexico while working in Roswell.

He was a friend of Peter Hurd, Ben Shahn, Sandy Calder, and Jackson Pollock, as well as other artists who had attended the League in the late 1920s. He roomed with Edward Laning and they spent summers together on Nantucket. They also worked together on a New Deal mural at Ellis Island.

Marfyak considered himself an Abstract Expressionist, working in oils, pastels, and acrylics. As of 2011, his son, Jan, lives in Rio Rancho, New Mexico, and has the body of his father's work. He is also a board member on both the National and New Mexico chapters of the National New Deal Preservation Association.

LOCATION OF NEW DEAL ARTWORK: Roswell; Ellis Island murals; Julia Richmand High School—Bronx, New York.

MARTINEZ, JULIAN (1879–1943)

This San Ildefonso Indian was known in his pueblo as Po-Ea-No, which means "herd of animals." As a young man he began working with Dr. Edgar L. Hewett of the School of American Research. He was also chosen in 1903 to go to the 1904 World's Fair in St. Louis. He was eager to go and he wanted to take Maria Montoya, a young San Ildefonso girl, with him as his wife. After this was worked out between the families, the marriage was planned and held on the same day that they left for St. Louis. While there they both worked as singers and dancers and helped to educate the world about the Native American life in the Southwest. Upon their return, Julian again worked with Hewett between 1907–1910 on the excavation of Puye Cliff dwellings. Initially his wife and son stayed at their pueblo home but later they went up to the excavation site also. In 1908 he began to be recognized for his drawings which he began doing as the result of seeing the petroglyph drawings and the designs on the ancient pottery. By 1909 he and Maria began working together to make and design pottery. During the winter months of 1909 Julian worked at the Palace of the Governors as a janitor and maintenance person and in 1910–1912 Maria and the children joined him. While living there, a market for their regular pottery and their new black pottery became a major activity in their lives. They were involved in the Indian New Deal project but we have not found any detailed records of what they did and where it ended up. Making the black pottery, which came about as a firing error, changed their lives financially and they became most successful. Over the years the Martinez's attended the World Fairs in Chicago, San Francisco, and Washington. They met with the President and Mrs. Roosevelt and were honored by them. En route home Julian collected clay from each state for the purpose of their trying to create pottery from clay from every state. He was elected governor of his pueblo in 1940 and saw some major changes in the pueblo at that time.

LOCATION OF POSSIBLE NEW DEAL ARTWORK: Santa Fe—Laboratory of Anthropology; Washington, DC.

MARTINEZ, MARIA (1886–1980)

Martinez is probably the best known American potter in the world. Born in the San Ildefonso Pueblo to Reyes and Tomas Montoya she was named Povika, which means "flower leaf" and christened Maria. She had three sisters. Maria began making pots at the age of 14 and her keen intelligence was noticed by her school teacher and the tribal council. Both she and her sister, Desideria, were chosen by the council to go to St. Catherine's Indian School for two years in Santa Fe and then back to the pueblo for further study with one of the government teachers, Miss Grimes. At 17 she married Julian Martinez (Po-Ea-No). He was chosen to go to the World's Fair in St. Louis that year and they left for the fair directly after their wedding feast. This was the first of four world expositions in which they participated together as potters and dancers and just the beginning of their numerous experiences.

Their special pottery came together as a result of their early work with Dr. Edgar L. Hewett, Director of the School of American Research in 1907. First Julian worked with him on the excavations of prehistoric pueblo sites. Maria remained at the pueblo to care for their firstborn son and later a baby girl who did not survive her first winter. After this Maria joined Julian at the Puye Canyon site so the family could be together. Together they studied the prehistoric potsherds when asked by Hewett to reproduce the old pottery again if possible. They achieved making the "new old pots" and in the process also had a batch that were fired poorly and turned out all black. Maria put these "bad" pots away but years later they were brought forth when they were trying to keep up with the orders they were getting once they moved into Santa Fe and worked at the Palace of the Governors. The "blackened pots" immediately became very popular. In addition to making fine pots, Maria was a good business woman and was always planning for having their own place to sell their pots and ways to improve their life style like having a new stove in her kitchen. They worked together for thirty-nine years recreating and creating designs on a matte band on a polished black body which made them both famous.

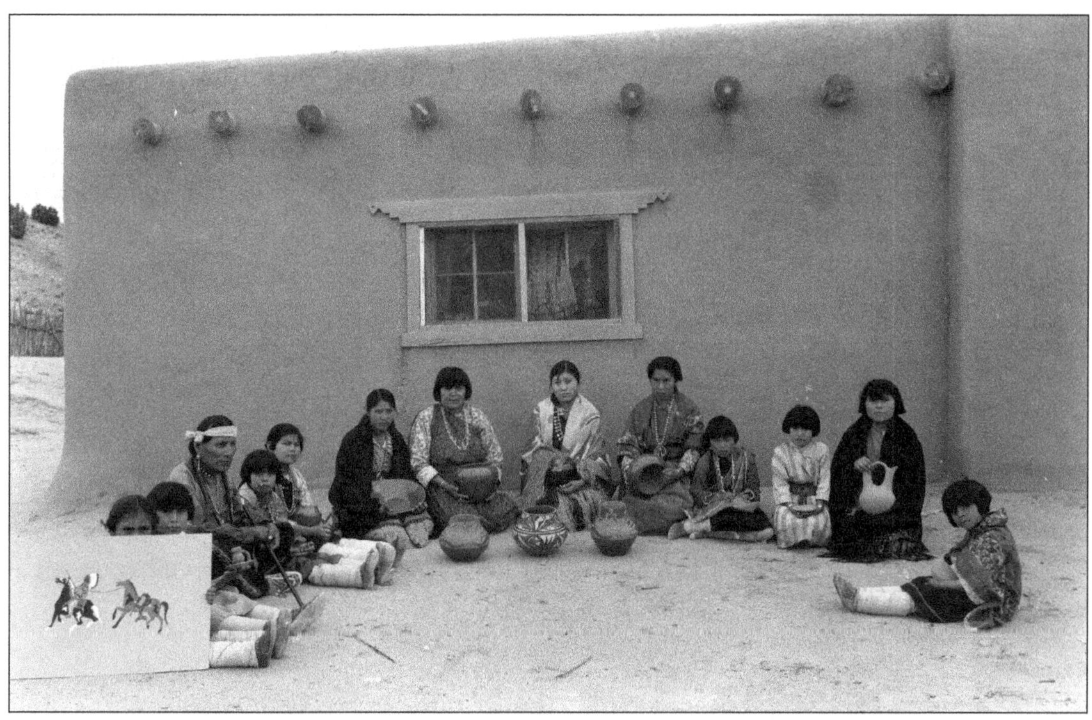

Maria (7th from left) and Julian (3rd from left) Martinez with pottery class, San Ildefonso Pueblo, San Ildefonso Pueblo

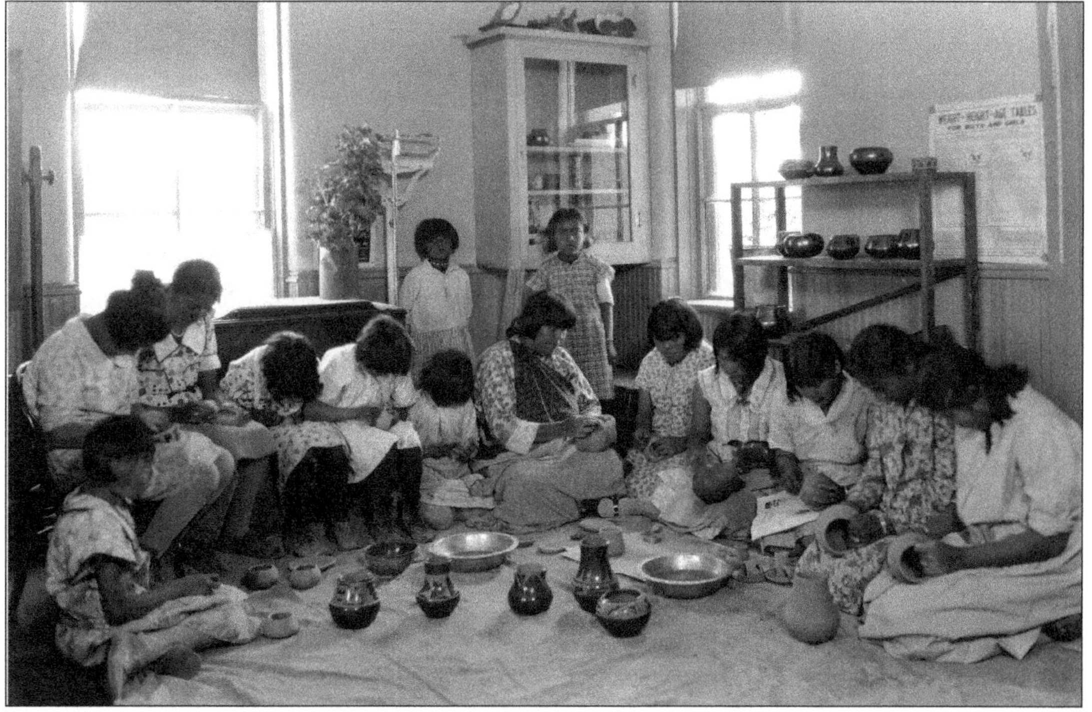

Maria Martinez pottery class in progress, San Ildefonso Pueblo, c. 1935

Maria's mastery of the old pueblo pottery making gave her family a way out of their economic struggles but then it also did the same for the whole pueblo village. Other women and then other husbands and wives began making the pottery in order to survive financially. However, no one's work became as revered as the Martinez's and in particular, Maria's. Finally the signing of the pots became important to keep track of who made what. It is interesting to note that Maria varied her own signature from time to time with different spellings.

Maria raised four sons and her baby sister, Clara, who was deaf. One son, Popovi Da, helped her make her pottery after the death of her husband, Julian. Other family members also assisted. For over seventy years this working mother with five children created for her people and this nation, pottery works that are extremely valuable. It also brought her honorary doctorates, the last when she was 94 and just prior to her death. The other awards and decorations from various countries are too numerous to mention.

LOCATIONS OF NEW DEAL ARTWORK: Santa Fe—National Park Service, Museum of Art, Laboratory of Anthropology; Washington, DC.

McAFEE TURNER, ILA (1897–1995)

Ila McAfee Turner was born in 1897 and raised near Gunnison, Colorado. As a young girl she assisted her father, who had the use of only one hand, in his work with the farm animals. She became a lover of horses very early on. Later she went to California on $100 where she became a student of James E. McBurney in Los Angeles and later studied art in Chicago and New York City. She settled in Taos in 1928 with her husband, Elmer Page Turner. She is well known for her pictures of animals, particularly horses. Ila McAfee illustrated the children's book, *All the Year 'Round with the Furry Fold,* and furnished her home with many of her own hand carved pieces. The Turner's studio was named "White Horse Studio" after a plaster sculpture of a white horse which served as a model for her life-size sculpture of Joan of Arc on her horse. McAfee designed fabrics, wrapping paper, dishes, calendars, and wood carvings, and she provided the illustrated cover for Walter Foster's book, *How to Draw Horses.* She was delighted to get to do a mural in the post office of her hometown during the New Deal and has other murals in Gunnison, Colorado, Clifton, Texas, and Cordell and Edmond, Oklahoma. In her later years she enjoyed hot air ballooning. She moved to Pueblo, Colorado to live with her sister, after living in Taos for nearly 65 years. She died there after the death of her sister.

LOCATIONS OF NEW DEAL ARTWORK: Albuquerque—City Council chambers and Albuquerque Museum, Taos schools; Clifton, Texas; the post offices in Cordell, Edmund, and Florence, the library in Greeley, and the Civic Center in Gunnison, Colorado; Washington, DC.

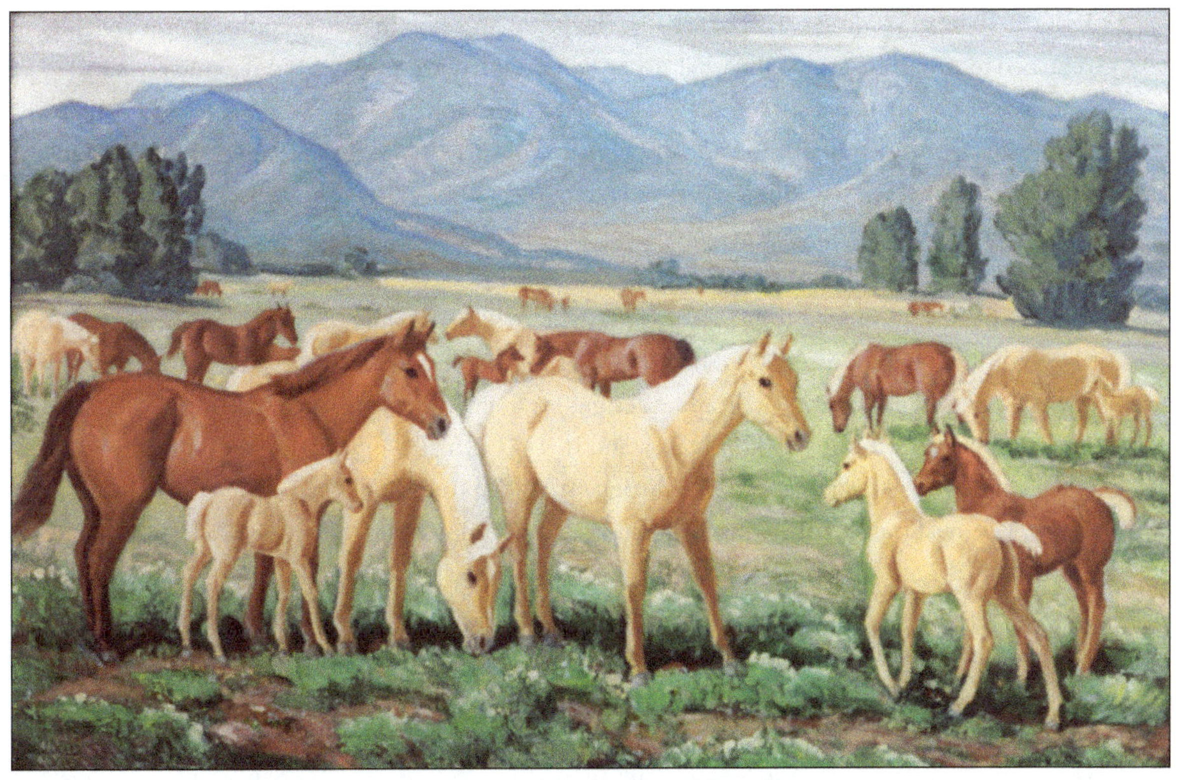

Ila McAfee Turner, "Palominos and Chestnuts," oil, Taos High School Library

McMURDO, J. T. (Dates Unknown)

Supervisor Bauman indicated that McMurdo lived in Albuquerque and "continued to wear cowboy boots long after the advent of the automobile." He was a self-taught or a "natural born artist." One of his paintings, "A Salty Bobcat" is said to have hung in Mayor Clyde Tingley's office in Albuquerque. That work has not been located nor two other paintings that appeared to have been sent to Washington.

LOCATION OF NEW DEAL ARTWORK: Unknown

MEAD, BEN CARLTON (1902–1986)

Born in Bay City, Texas, Mead lived in Texas and Oklahoma before settling in Amarillo. During high school he painted theater posters and stage sets, and worked as sports editor for the *Amarillo Daily News*. After graduating from Amarillo High School in 1923, Mead studied at the Art Institute of Chicago for three years, and later with painter, Hugo D. Pohl in San Antonio. While working as a commercial artist in San Antonio in 1929, Mead met the noted folklorist J. Frank Dobie and eventually illustrated several Dobie books including *Coronado's Children* (1930), *On The Open Range* (1931), *I'll Tell You a Tale* (1960), and *Cow People* (1964).

From 1930 to 1932 Mead was staff artist at the Witte Museum in San Antonio, after which he returned to Amarillo. He taught art at Amarillo Junior College and in his downtown Amarillo studio, and maintained a studio near Palo Duro Canyon. In 1934 he began the first of three murals for the west wall of the Panhandle Plains Historical Museum's Pioneer Hall. Painted under the auspices of the Public Works of Art Project (PWAP) that preceded WPA, the first mural depicts Coronado and his party in Palo Duro Canyon. Another Coronado mural is located in the Quay County courthouse in Tucumcari. After moving to Chicago and back to Amarillo, Mead moved to Dallas in 1941 where he again worked as a commercial artist. One of his war bond posters was shown in over 17,000 theaters in the United States. Braniff Airlines hired him to create new graphic designs for their airline which proved most successful. He continued to live and work in Dallas and in 1973 actually appeared in an episode of the television series "Gunsmoke." After enduring virtual blindness for some three years in the late 1970s, a corneal transplant enabled Mead to begin painting again. He moved to California in the early 1980s, and died there in 1986.

A student of Western history, Mead took great pride in the historical accuracy and attention to detail found in his work. Careful sketches and drawings of historical artifacts supplied Mead with a large pictorial vocabulary upon which he would depend for his compositions. He was a member of the Western History Association, the Texas State Historical Association, and the Panhandle-Plains Historical Society. Mead's inclusion in Jeff Dykes' *Fifty Great Western Illustrators* indicates the high regard in which his work is held. Eleven pieces of his art work can be found in the Panhandle-Plains Museum collection in Canyon, Texas. A biography of him was written by Robert Duncan in his book, *The Bounty of the Woods.*

LOCATIONS OF NEW DEAL ARTWORK: Tucumcari; Canyon, Texas.

MEEM. JOHN GAW (1894–1983)

Meem is included in this book since he was the designer of so much New Deal architecture in New Mexico and served on the committee that determined what mural art would be placed in which buildings. Other architects also participated but Meem had to be at the top of the list in terms of quantity, quality, and recognition.

According to Jan Dodson Barnhart in her book, *The Pueblo Revival Architecture of John Gaw Meem*, this talented architect was born in Pelotas, Brazil. His parents were Episcopalian missionaries. He came to the United States in 1910 to attend the Virginia Military Institute which was a family tradition. While there he studied civil engineering and got his degree in 1914. After this he worked for his uncle in New York City helping build the city's subway system until being drafted into the Army during World War I. He was an army captain at a training camp in Iowa for most of his service time. After the war was over, he tried his hand at banking and since he was trilingual (German, Portuguese and English), he served as a credit manager of a branch of the National City Bank of New York in Rio de Janeiro. While there he contracted tuberculosis and ended up in Santa Fe, New Mexico. Supposedly he noticed a poster that was advertising the Santa Fe Railroad so he bought a ticket and arrived at the Sunmount Sanatorium in Santa Fe in 1920. Once he was cured, he moved to Denver and worked with an architectural firm there plus taking night courses in design. It proved too much for him when the tuberculosis returned and he came back to the sanatorium in 1924.

Shortly after arriving, he formed an architectural firm with a fellow patient, Cassius McCormick. This partnership continued until 1929 and it was during that time that Meem got involved in preservation with the initial emphasis on preserving and restoring New Mexico's old churches. He was also one of the founders of the Old Santa Fe Association.

One of his first major commissions was an addition and restoration of La Fonda Hotel followed by the design of the planned Laboratory of Anthropology funded by John D. Rockefeller, Jr. His innovative Pueblo Revival style was born and that was what he became famous for in future buildings. As a New Deal project, he redesigned the Santa Fe Indian School from its old red brick structures to its Pueblo Revival appearance. Another one of these building projects (the Colorado Springs Art Center) took him to Colorado. While there he met and worked with the uncle of Faith Bemis, a young unemployed architect, whom he married in 1933.

About this same time, President Franklin D. Roosevelt's New Deal projects got underway and Meem became the architect of choice by University of New Mexico's President and Board of Regents. He designed Scholes Hall, the Student Union Building (now Anthropology), the Heating Plant and Zimmerman Library—one of his Spanish Pueblo Revival style jewels. (Refer to Albuquerque University of New Mexico structures for more specifics on these structures.) He continued as the school's major architect for a number of years and his papers can be researched in the John Gaw Meem Archive of Southwestern Architecture at the Zimmerman Library's Center for Southwest Research. This archive also houses holdings of all the New Mexico surveys done by the New Deal's Historic American Buildings Survey (HABS). This was started in 1933 employing many architects all over the nation and continues on today.

Meem's career was full of personal and professional honors due to his accomplishments in a number of areas including architecture, historic preservation, civic concerns, education and his Episcopal faith and family. Later his wife was active in the community and now his daughter, Nancy Wirth, continues to sell his Southwestern furniture and doors when not creating her own pottery. As of 2011, she is an active cultural preservationist.

MIRABEL, VICENTE (1918–1946)

Chiu Tah (Dancing Boy) was born at the Taos Pueblo and graduated from the Santa Fe Indian School. He was an assistant painting instructor there when he entered the Army during World War II and his budding art career was cut short when he was killed in the Battle of the Bulge. He was married to a Navajo woman and they had three sons.

LOCATION OF POSSIBLE NEW DEAL ARTWORK: Unknown.

MORANG, DOROTHY (1906–1995)

Born in Bridgton, Maine in 1906, Dorothy's first artistic talent was focused on music. She was trained as a pianist and later taught in West Bridgton, Maine in 1922–1923. In 1928 she went to Boston to study at the New England Conservatory of Music. After marrying artist Alfred Morang in 1930 she taught piano and performed as a soloist in Maine from 1928 to 1936. The couple moved to Santa Fe in 1939 where he became involved as an artist. She had begun developing her fine art talents as a result of being with him and many other artists. As a result, she also became active in the New Deal projects both with easel painting and as a music teacher. They both carried on the visionary work of artist/philosopher Wassily Kandinsky of Paris and they joined others who were active in his Transcendental Movement. The others included Bisttram, Morang, Lumpkins and Jonson and they referred to themselves as the Transcendental Painting Group. She was one of the unsung heroes of that movement in New Mexico.

She worked for the Museum of Fine Arts for over 20 years beginning in 1942 and served as curator during that time. She was a prominent and visible force in Santa Fe's art community and received numerous awards at juried shows throughout the region. Her vision and style always challenges the viewer and Kim Wiggins commented that "Morang's world is an ethereal, spiritual one. Trying to understand it, one has to be willing to enter his or her own fantasia." Dorothy Morang became interested also in working with enamels and that was as close to any form of commercialism in art that she touched. She lived in Santa Fe until her death.

LOCATION OF NEW DEAL ARTWORK: Albuquerque—University of New Mexico Art Museum.

MORRIS, JAMES S. "JAY" (1902–1973)

Born in Marshall, Missouri, Morris variously listed his birth date as 1898 or 1902. He studied at the Cincinnati Art Academy from 1925 to 1926 and at the Pennsylvania Academy of the Fine Arts. In the late 1920s he was encouraged to come to Santa Fe by Willard Nash and while visiting in the city he met John Sloan and became entranced by the southwestern landscape. Sloan subsequently arranged a scholarship for Morris at the Art Students League in New York. During the Depression, Morris returned to New Mexico with Charles Barrows and they were found sleeping in the park their first night in town by poet Witter Bynner. He befriended them and they both got settled in the community. Morris worked on the New Deal *Portfolio* at one point. As he continued to paint, Morris' boldly executed oils and more delicate watercolors grew increasingly abstract, then shifted to a more representational, social-commentary style. During World War II he was in the Seabees in Alaska and afterward his work took on elements of fantasy, perhaps reflecting his concern about the diminishing coherence of twentieth century society. Morris worked with Barrows on a mural for the vocational school at El Rito but it has not been found.

LOCATIONS OF NEW DEAL ARTWORK: Albuquerque—University of New Mexico Art Museum, El Rito.

MOSES, TRINIDAD (Dates Unknown)

Moses was one of four junior high students who were chosen to do two murals for the public library in Raton. It is unknown whether he did other artwork. William Warder was one of those four to go on with his art.

MOYLAN, LLOYD (1893–1963)

Moylan was born in St. Paul, Minneapolis and studied at the Minneapolis Art Institute. Further art training followed at the Art Students League of New York between 1917 and 1919. A teaching position at the Broadmoor Art Academy in Colorado Springs brought him West. Moylan was a resident of New Mexico as of 1939, living for a time in Gallup. One of his largest murals can be seen in the McKinley County Courthouse. His work both as a painter, primarily in watercolor, and his printmaking in the form of lithographs has been exhibited throughout several principal cities of the United States and Mexico. Trips to Mexico exposed Moylan to the burgeoning mural movement there and inspired him to execute several murals in the Colorado Springs area. Eventually, investigating Indian themes for his work, he gravitated to New Mexico where his mural work continued under WPA sponsorship. In addition to the mural in Gallup, two other outstanding murals can be found at Highlands University in Las Vegas and Eastern New Mexico University in Portales. He also did at least seven paintings of Indian dances for the Kirtland Air Base and six are still in the Officers Club Bar area. A traveling show of fourteen paintings depicting Navajo life was also created by Moylan. His style could be described as being abstract and expressionistic in nature. Before his death, he was the museum curator of the Museum of Navajo Ceremonial Art (now Wheelwright Museum) in Santa Fe.

LOCATIONS OF NEW DEAL ARTWORK: Albuquerque—Kirtland Officer's Club and University of New Mexico Art Museum, Gallup, Las Vegas—New Mexico Highlands University, Portales—Eastern New Mexico University; Washington, DC; San Francisco, California; Newark, New Jersey.

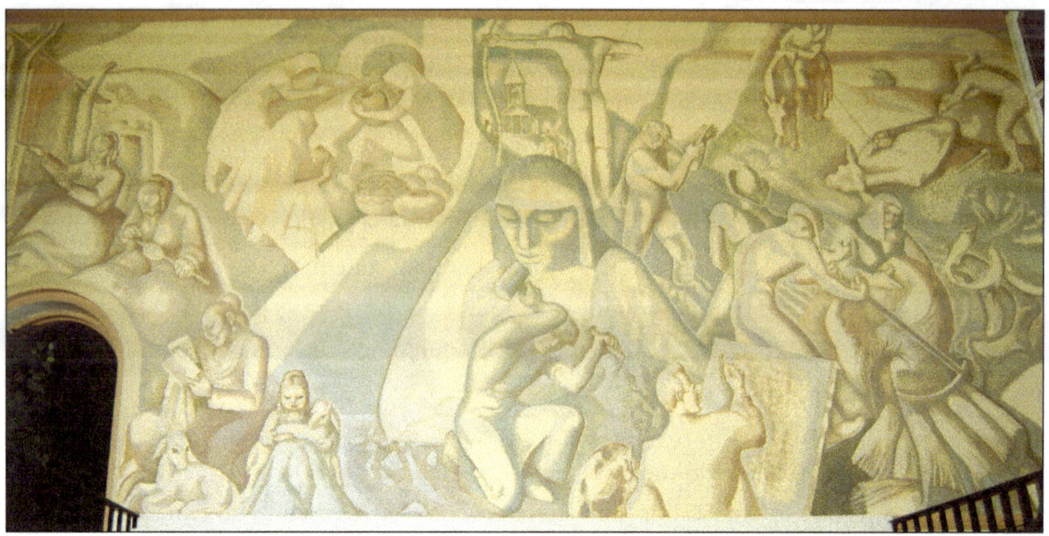

Lloyd Moylan, "The Dissemination of Education" is a mural covering all the walls of the second floor in the Administration Building at New Mexico Highlands University in Las Vegas. Photograph by Pat Berrett.

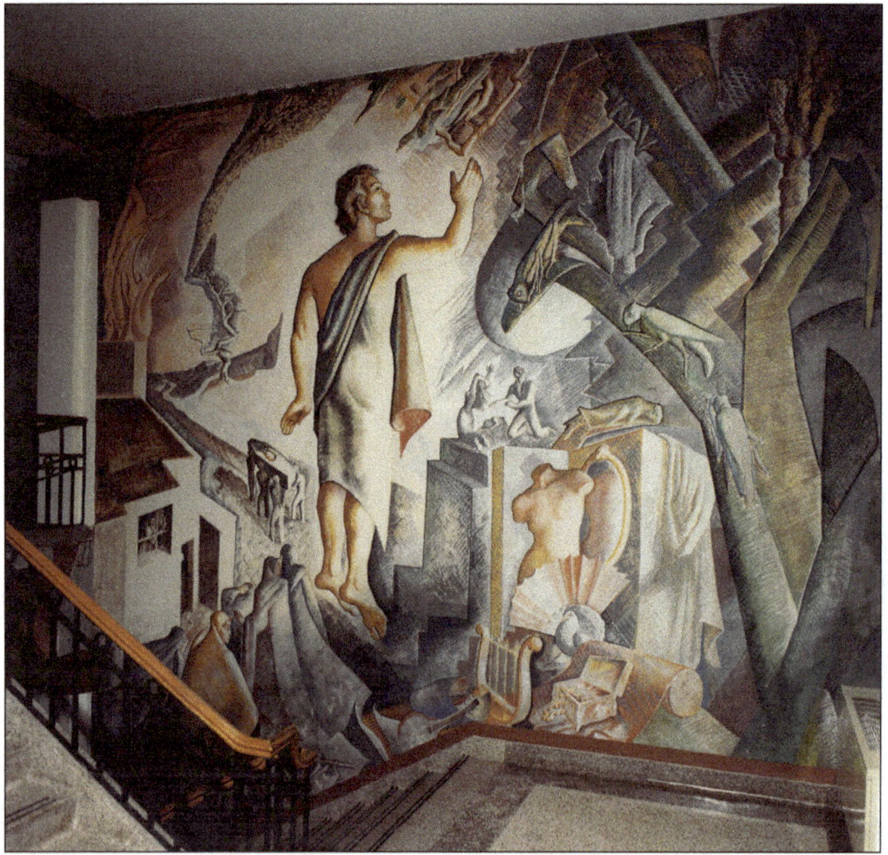

Lloyd Moylan, "The 12th Chapter of Ecclesiastes," oil, on one side of wall, Portales, Eastern New Mexico University Administration Building.

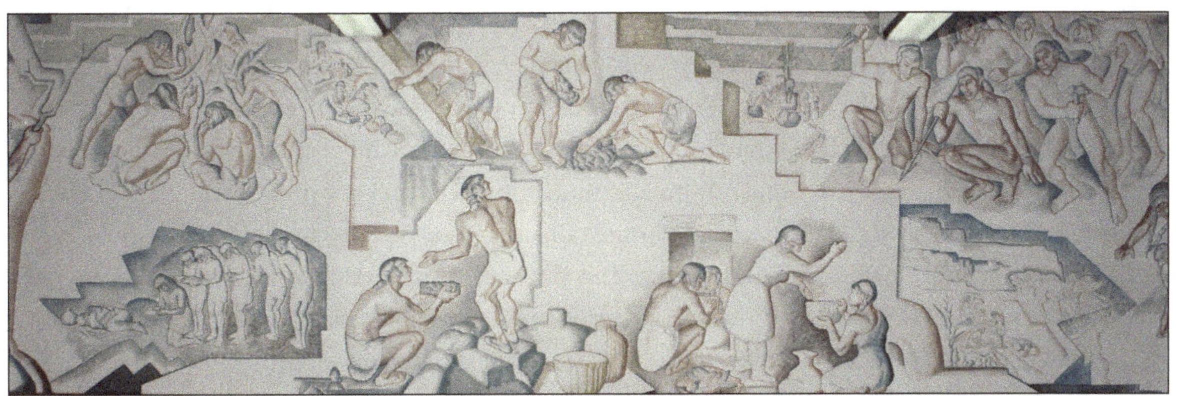

Lloyd Moylan, "History of McKinley County" oil, Gallup Courthouse

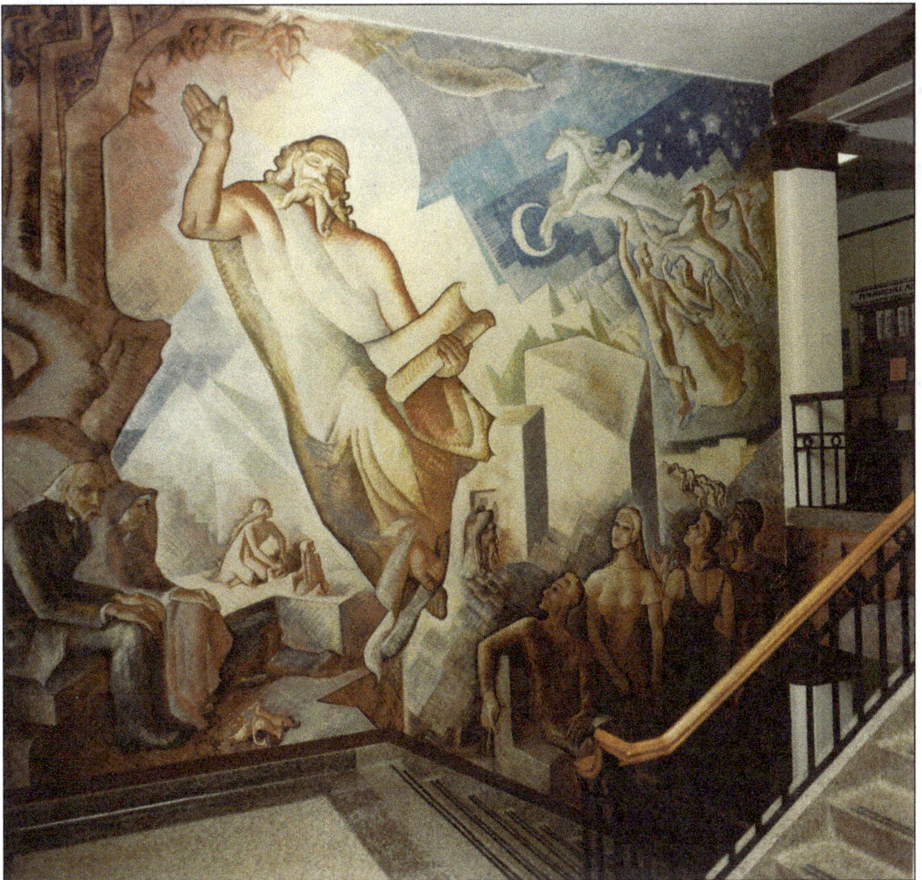

Lloyd Moylan, "The 12th Chapter of Ecclesiastes" oil, on the other side of wall, Portales, Eastern New Mexico University Administration Building.

A third large mural by Moylan can be found in the Administration Building at Highlands University in Las Vegas, New Mexico

MOZLEY, LOREN NORMAN (1905–1989)

Mozley's family moved to New Mexico shortly after he was born on October 2, 1905 in Brookport, Illinois. His father became a "cow country doctor" so Mozley was educated in country schools, Indian schools and finally studied at the University of New Mexico. He primarily studied art independently but did study three years in Paris in the early 1930s at the Academie Colarossi and the Academie Grande Chaumiere. Over the years he held many jobs in order to support himself and his painting. This included being an Indian trader, lumber camp merchant, museum curator, hotel clerk, bartender, lithographer, commercial photographer retoucher and airplane plant worker. In 1924 he moved to Taos and was a member of the Taos Art Association and the Taos Heptagon. Later, after moving to Austin, Texas, Loren Mozley executed murals in Alvin, Texas, the United States Post Office in Clinton, Oklahoma and the Federal Building and U. S. Courthouse in Albuquerque. He was the author of *Yankee Artist,* a monograph on John Marin and exhibited his work at the Museum of Modern Art, New York for the Marin Exhibition in 1936.

LOCATION OF NEW DEAL ARTWORK: Albuquerque, New Mexico; Alvin, Texas and Clinton, Oklahoma.

MRUK, WALTER (1883–1942)

Walter Mruk attended the Art Student League in New York City. Josef Bakos and he were childhood friends and first came to Santa Fe with their instructor, John E. Thompson, in 1920. Mruk and Bakos chose to settle in Santa Fe and considered themselves, by dint of their work along with that of others, as Modernists. In 1921, Mruk and Bakos joined up with Will Shuster, Willard Nash and Fremont Ellis to form *Los Cincos Pintores* (the Five Painters) in order to get more publicity and marketing for their art. They also helped one another build their homes along Canyon Road. There are references to his New Deal work, but nothing has been found to date. Mruk died in 1942.

LOCATION OF NEW DEAL ARTWORK: Unknown

MYERS, DATUS ENSIGN (1879–1960)

Myers was born in Jefferson, Oregon and studied at the Art Institute in Chicago between 1905–1910. While there he met Alice Clark who became his wife. She became one of the first women architects in the country. He painted as much as was possible while trying to make a living and raising a family. In 1926 the family moved to Santa Fe and Mrs. Myers designed a large home for them on the Camino de Monte Sol and many parties were held there including all of the Santa Fe artists and their families.

While in the Southwest, he was named the Field Coordinator for the Indian Division of the PWAP. In 1939 he was chosen to do a mural for the post office in Winnsboro, Louisiana entitled "Logging in Louisiana Swamps." For this he was paid $530 by the Section portion of the New Deal projects. He also did a watercolor called "Clowning Koshares" that may have ended up in Washington. Another work can be seen in the museum at West Texas State University in Canyon, Texas. Over the years he combined his Egyptian and Oriental art research with his love of American Indian painting. According to his daughter, his work is not as well known as some of the others of his time primarily because he did not sell through the local established galleries.

He was active in the I AM movement, a religious group, while living in Santa Fe and continued this association in his work when he moved in 1953 to Shasta Springs, California, where he died. A daughter, Eve Myers Foley, lived in Santa Fe and was known for her modern dance work.

LOCATION OF NEW DEAL ARTWORK: Canyon, Texas; Winnsboro, Louisiana; Washington, DC.

NAILOR, GERALD (1917–1952)

Pinedale, New Mexico was the birthplace of this Navajo whose name was Toh Yah meaning Walking By the River. He later married a Picuris Pueblo woman, Santana Simbola, and moved to her pueblo.

Gerald Nailor graduated from the Albuquerque Indian School and later studied with Dorothy Dunn, Kenneth Chapman, and the Swedish muralist, Olaf Nordmark. He created murals for the U. S. Department of the Interior in 1939–1940 with Allan Houser, Velino Herrera and other Native American artists. Houser and Nailor shared studio space in Santa Fe over the years and were close friends. Nailor also did murals for the Mesa Verde Post Office in Colorado and the Navajo Tribal Council House in Window Rock, Arizona.

LOCATION OF NEW DEAL ARTWORK: Washington, DC—Department of Interior; Mesa Verde, Colorado; Window Rock, Arizona.

NARANJO, EULOGIA

Pottery vessel created by Naranjo is on exhibit at the National Park Service in Santa Fe.

NASH, WILLARD (1898–1943)

Born in Philadelphia, Pennsylvania, Nash studied in Detroit with John P. Wicker. He then moved to New Mexico in 1920 in search for a more stimulating artistic environment. Known as the Santa Fe "modernist," Willard Nash's early work was still academic in conception, as he used rather subdued tones and conventional compositions. However, after studying with Dasburg, he experimented with the techniques of the Fauves and Post-Impressionists, especially Cezanne. By the end of his first year in Santa Fe a greater brilliance and feeling for luminous color began to characterize his canvases.

He became a founding member of *Los Cinco Pintores* and built a home alongside his colleagues on Camino del Monte Sol. All the artists in this group were struggling financially except Nash who had a wealthy patron. His growing devotion to the architectonic structure of Cezanne in the thirties and to abstraction in the forties marks him as one of the more daring New Mexico modernists. Nash was frequently able to reduce the forms of nature to visually exciting notations of color and shape which had ingenious harmonies and geometric rhythms. In 1936 Nash left Santa Fe for California, where he taught at the San Francisco Art School and the Art Center School in Los Angeles but returned to Albuquerque in 1942 where he died. Some of the panels at UNM were restored by Luis Neri-Zagal.

LOCATION OF NEW DEAL ARTWORK: Albuquerque—University of New Mexico Art Museum.

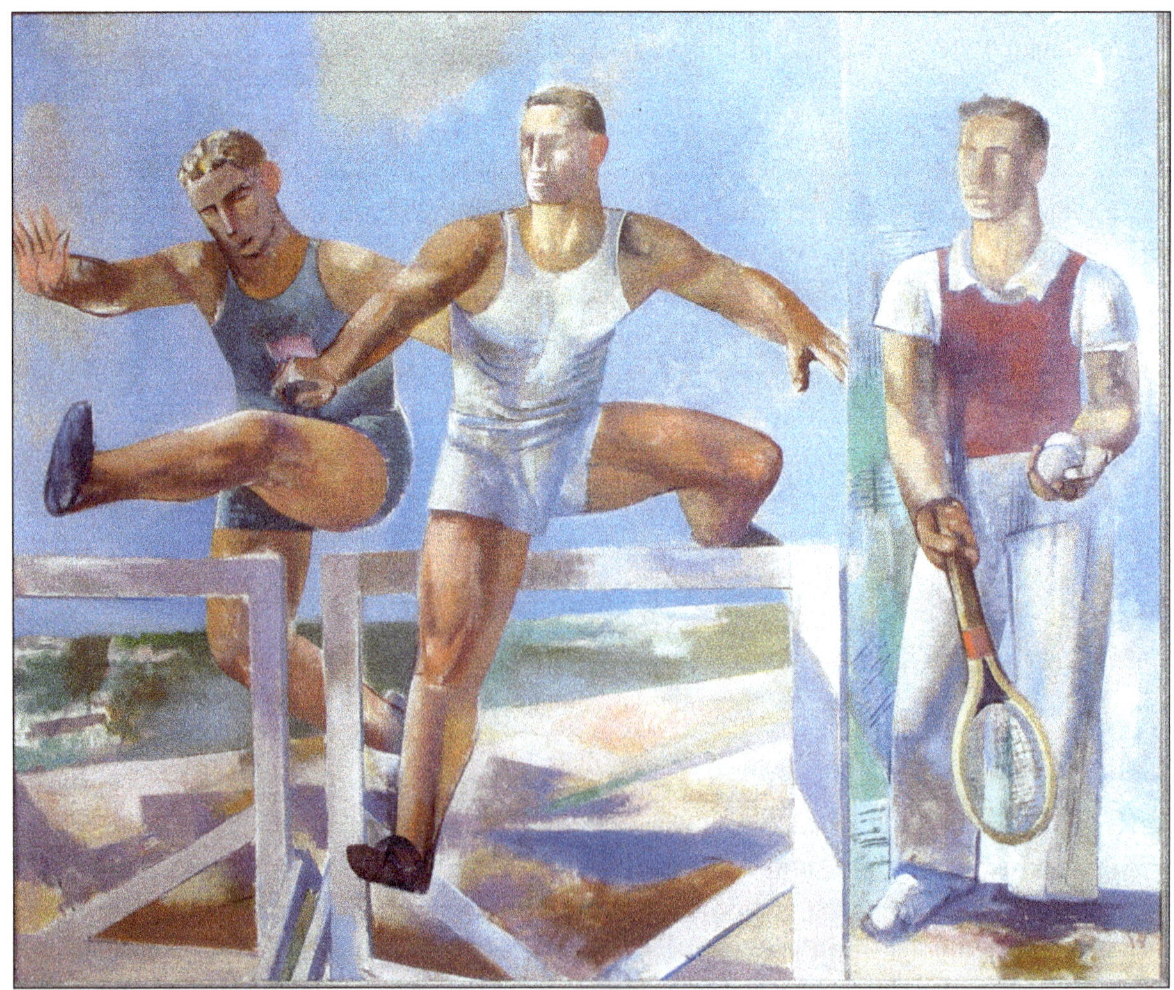

Willard Nash, "Men's Track and Tennis," oil, Albuquerque, University of New Mexico Fine Arts Museum. This is one of five panels depicting men and women's athletic scenes. They were originally in Carlisle Gymnasium but are now part of the school's museum collection. Photograph by Luis Neri-Zagal.

NAUMER, HELMUTH (1907–1989)

Reutilingen, Germany, near Stuttgart, was the birthplace of Naumer who fell in love with the romantic West through the books of Karl May. At age 17 he left Germany for the life of a sailor and traveled around the world twice. By 1927 he was living with the Santo Domingo Indians learning about New Mexico. A year or so later he moved to Santa Fe to further develop his talents as an artist among other artists. As part of that he was one of the artists involved with the *Portfolio*. One of his mentors, Carlos Vierra, provided regular opportunities for growth with other European trained artists at his home in the southern part of Santa Fe. Naumer built his initial slab cabin outside Santa Fe with the help of other artists such as Tom Lea and Harper Henry. Naumer was also a fine accordion player and musician and enjoyed playing at local dances where he met his future wife, Tomee Reuter, a resident of Pecos.

Naumer continued his close relationship with the Native Americans throughout his life, yet he himself loved and lived the cowboy image. He was an avid horseman and marksman who was a member of the Santa Fe County Sheriff's Posse for 30 years. However, his life's focus was to capture the spirit of New Mexico through his favorite medium, pastels, which he felt was ideal for catching the fleeting effects of sky and earth in New Mexico's changing landscape. He believed that when properly handled, pastels were a more permanent medium than oils and portrayed New Mexico's vast pallet of colors better than any other medium. In many of his paintings he would use the full array of the 1,000 colors available in his especially produced European pastel boxes.

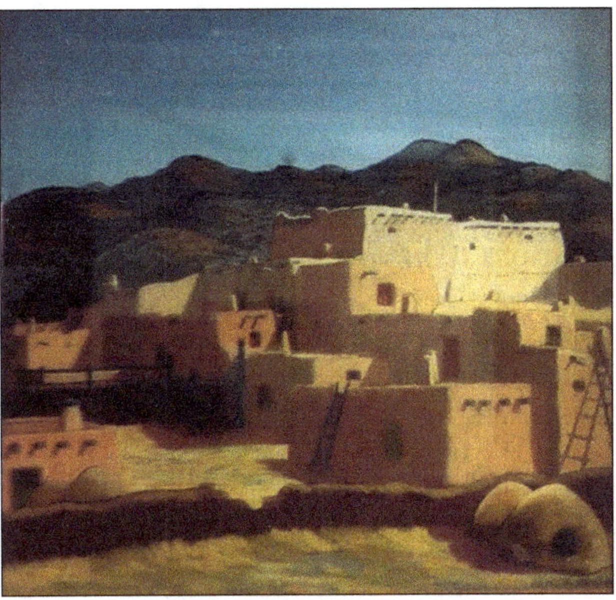

Helmuth Naumer, "Taos Pueblo," pastel, Santa Fe, New Mexico Taxation and Revenue Department. This is one of seven pastels located in the Taxation and Revenue offices.

Naumer studied art in Germany and later at the Frank Wiggins School of Art in Los Angeles. New Mexico was always his favorite subject, but he painted throughout the United States and around the world. His paintings are in private and museum collections throughout the world. He is well known for a series of pastels of Pueblo communities created in the 1930s under the New Deal program and these works can be found at the Bandelier National Monument. Other creations can be enjoyed around the state and in the state's Museum of Fine Arts which is part of the state's museum system that his son, Helmuth J. Naumer, administered prior to his death in 1994.

LOCATIONS OF NEW DEAL ARTWORK: Albuquerque, Bandelier, Clayton, Gallup, Melrose, Roswell, Santa Fe.

NORDFELDT, BROR JULIUS OLSSON (B.J.O.) (1878–1955)

Nordfeldt immigrated to Chicago in 1891 from his native Sweden. After a year of training at the Art Institute of Chicago, he began a decade of further art studies, painting, and printmaking in this country and Europe. In 1919 he established residence in Santa Fe, where he lived for the next twenty years and was referred to primarily as "Nordy." His wife was a local psychoanalyst. In his paintings, etchings, and lithographs he analyzed the rugged southwestern landscape or expressed fascination with his Hispanic neighbors. Elements of Cezanne and the Fauves are present in his work, along with a personal strain of expressionism. Six lithographs were done by Nordfeldt as part of the PWAP and then reproduced and distributed to many public schools and universities around the state. Some are still on view while most have disappeared. The New Mexico Chapter of the National New Deal Preservation Association continues to look for the missing ones and in 2010 rematted the existing ones with acid free mats and backings in order to protect them.

From 1934 to 1937 Nordfeldt divided his time among Wichita, Minneapolis, and Santa Fe, where he taught, painted portraits, and made lithographs for the PWAP. In 1937 he moved to Lambertville, New Jersey, which became his home for the rest of his life. He died in Henderson, Texas in 1955.

POSSIBLE LOCATIONS OF NEW DEAL ARTWORK (Not all have been located in the public schools/institutions): Alamogordo, Albuquerque, Artesia, Belen, Capitan, Carlsbad, Carrizozo, Clayton, Clovis, East Vaughn, El Rito, Grants, Hurley, Las Cruces, Las Vegas, Lordsburg, Mosquero, Portales, Raton, Roswell, Santa Fe, Santa Rosa, Silver City, Socorro, Springer, Taos, Wagon Mound; Washington, DC.

NYE, TINKLE VIRGINIA "GINNY" (1911–1997)

Virginia Nye was born in New York but grew up in Kansas City, Missouri. In early adulthood she worked as a copywriter in radio in New York but contracted tuberculosis and like others, moved to Albuquerque in 1928. After recuperating, she worked on the WPA/FAP program and was one of the copyists on the *Portfolio of Spanish-Colonial Design*. A small drawing done by her during this time can be found in the McKinley County Courthouse and is called "The Little Engineer." She later got a job working as an interviewer and copywriter for the local radio station that broadcasted out of the Kimo Theater in Albuquerque. This is the place where she also met a young actor named C.E."Tip" Dinkle since both were involved with the Albuquerque Little Theater. They performed out of the Kimo prior to the organization having its own theater which was built by the New Deal. It is an active theater still in 2011. They married and Ginny was able to take art classes at the University of New Mexico while Tip was involved in the Albuquerque banking world for 42 years. They had one daughter, Susan D. Lindley, who followed her mother's interest in art and after graduating from the University of New Mexico became a Master Printer in Albuquerque for some years before moving to California.

LOCATION OF NEW DEAL ARTWORK: Gallup.

ORTIZ, MAX (Dates Unknown)

Very little is known about this weaver from Pena Blanca. According to Tey Mariana Nunn's book, *Sin Nombre*, he taught weaving at the Melrose Art Center as part of the Federal Art Project. Nunn found a newspaper clipping that referenced the opening of the gallery at the Melrose Art Center on June 22, 1938, and Ortiz was listed as being on staff there. It further noted that he had been in the weaving business for four years.

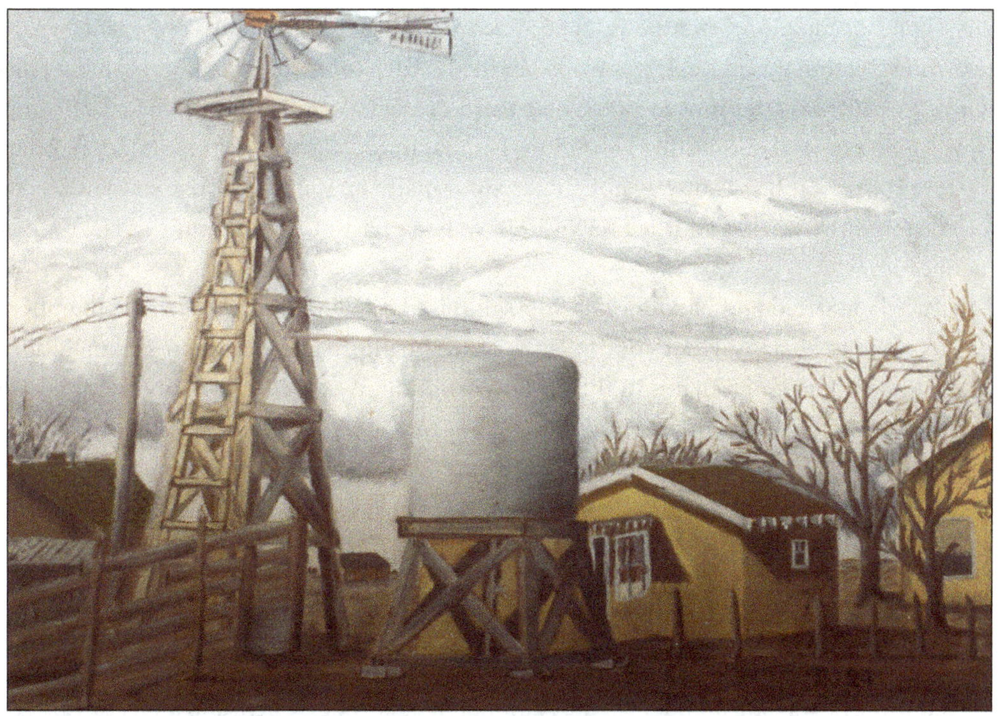

Max Ortiz, "Windmill and Water Tank," oil, Melrose School Library

There is also information that indicates that before his work at Melrose he worked with the Native Market and El Parian Analco programs in Santa Fe. Nunn also references him as being a teacher in the state's vocational education classes and various WPA supported programs, including the Melrose Federal Art Center. Considering that the Ortiz family of Chimayo is very well known for their weaving, one can wonder if he might not have been related to that family of weavers.

PADILLA, EMILIO (1913–1970)

Born in Springer, New Mexico, Padilla came to Santa Fe with his family as a young child. He began carving early in his life. According to Tey Mariana Nunn, in her book, *Sin Nombre*, he took art classes from Howard Kretz Coluzzi in the Santa Fe Art School as a teenager. Another budding young artist, Eliseo Rodriguez, was also a student at this school. The teacher introduced Padilla to Mary Austin, who was working with the state's Public Works of Art project, in the hope that Padilla would be able to get accepted into that program. This did not work out, but later he and Rodriguez were accepted into the WPA's Federal Art Project.

Sources are confident that Padilla created some wooden carvings while in this program, and there are references by E. Boyd to his three dimensional religious sculptures. Their whereabouts are unknown but may be at the Museum of International Folk Art. The one piece that is known to have been done by Padilla at age twenty-three is a large wooden relief panel featuring the Entrada of Diego de Vargas and his party coming into Santa Fe during their second occupation Santa Fe in 1695. Records indicate that Padilla was paid $16.00 a week while creating this piece. It was placed in the D.A.R. Room near the library in the Palace of Governors. It was later moved to the courtyard of the Palace and then may have been put in storage due to its deteriorating condition. Padilla, upon learning of this situation, offered to restore it or get it back but was not successful. Finally in 1983, his artist and jeweler son, Nino, restored the work, and it is known to have been part of the Museum of New Mexico Art collection.

Padilla married and had four children, all raised in Santa Fe. He became a plumber in order to support his family but continued to carve furniture and other objects, including a bust of Vincent Van Gogh that is in the family collection. A carved chest done privately is in the collection of the Museum of International Folk Art.

LOCATION OF NEW DEAL ARTWORK: Unknown—Santa Fe or Coronado Monument?

PARSONS, SHELDON (1866–1943)

Sheldon Parsons was born in Rochester, New York in 1866 and became known for his portraiture in the early 1900s. President McKinley and Susan B. Anthony were two of the famous Americans whose portraits Sheldon Parsons painted. His talent for portraiture had emerged while he was still a student at the National Academy of Design, and a successful career in New York seemed assured. But his wife's death in 1913 abruptly changed his plans. The artist was granted a commission to paint murals for the Panama-Pacific Exposition to be held in San Francisco so he and his young 12 year old daughter, Sara, sold all their possessions and took the train west. He was also able to make an arrangement with Santa Fe Railroad to let him paint for them in exchange for free passage. Upon arrival in Denver, Parsons suffered a relapse from a previous attack of tuberculosis and was advised by doctors to try New Mexico's climate. Two months later and well enough to travel, Parsons and his daughter boarded a southbound train. In Santa Fe they were welcomed into the community by helpful citizens willing to exchange the necessities of life for Parsons' paintings. As the artist recovered his health, he began painting landscapes which became a longstanding interest of his. Absorbed with the color and light of his new environment, he recorded the town, nearby Indian pueblos, and the imposing New Mexico desert and mountains. In time Parsons became a well-known artist, accommodating his early Barbizon and Impressionist training to the light-drenched scenes of the Southwest. He worked on the *Portfolio* and did numerous paintings for the New Deal art projects. He also served in 1918 as the first director of the Museum of New Mexico. However, he was later fired from this position because it was felt he was including too many modernist painters in the exhibits.

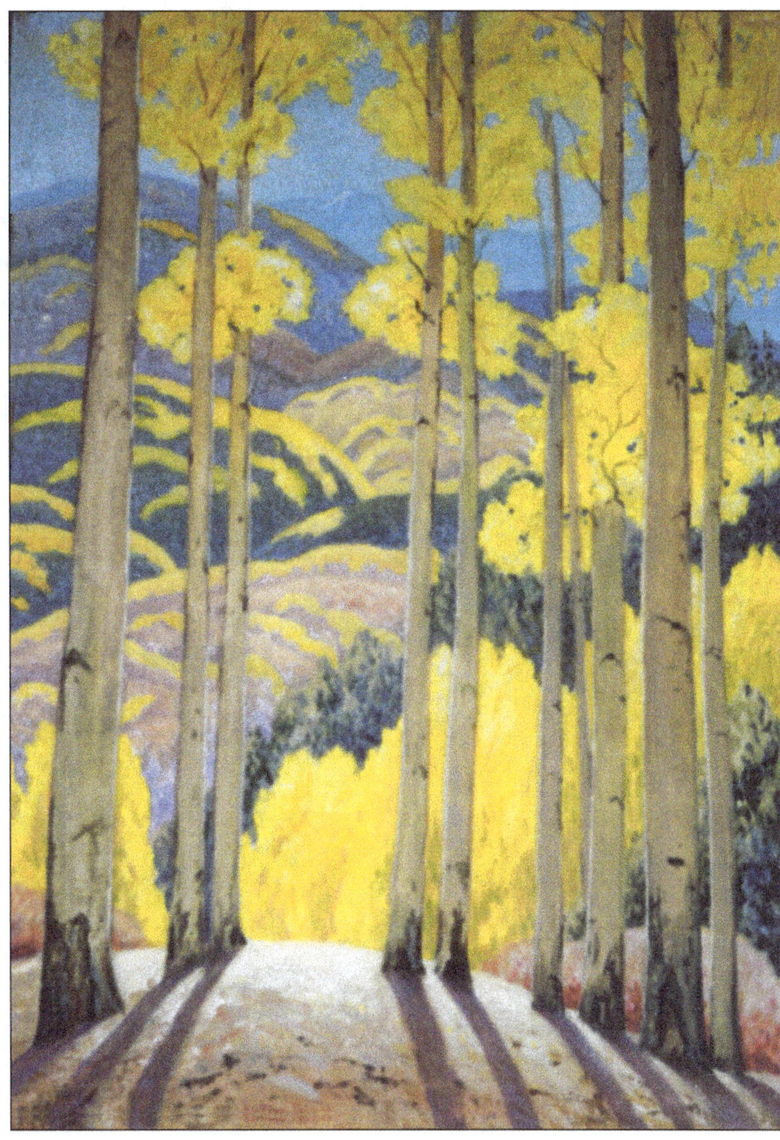

Sheldon Parsons, "Untitled" (Aspens), oil, Santa Fe, Supreme Court

Parsons' daughter Sara grew up to be a distinguished painter herself and later married artist, Victor Higgins and then later Robert Mack. She became a fine photographer and worked on contract for *Vogue* magazine. Parsons died in 1943 in Albuquerque.

LOCATIONS OF NEW DEAL ARTWORK: Albuquerque—Carrie Tingley Hospital for Crippled Children, Melrose, Roswell, Santa Fe; Washington, DC.

PAYNE, EDGAR ALWIN (1882–1947)

Born in Washburn, Missouri in 1882, Payne left home at fourteen to paint in the Ozarks, followed by a trip to Mexico. He had begun as a house and sign painter and also as a decorator. He became known, however, as a western landscape painter and muralist and, while living in Chicago, became a member of the Chicago Society of Artists. In 1911 a sketching trip West took him to Laguna Beach, California where he settled in 1917, and where he did many coastal scenes in the Monterey and Laguna Beach areas. His paintings are in many collections and his murals are in commercial and public buildings in several western states as well as Indiana and Illinois. Payne, a largely self-taught artist, is well known throughout the Southwest for his mountain and desert landscapes, the latter frequently depicting Indian life as he saw it in northern Arizona. He also painted in New Mexico, the Grand Canyon, Canyon de Chelly, and the mesas. His work is displayed at the National Academy of Design, New York; Southwest Museum, Los Angeles; University of Nebraska, Lincoln; Hubbell Trading Post Museum, Ganado, Arizona. Edgar Payne was a member of the Alumni Association of the Art Institute of Chicago. He died in Los Angeles, California on April 8, 1947.

LOCATION OF NEW DEAL ARTWORK: Gallup; Long Beach Library, California.

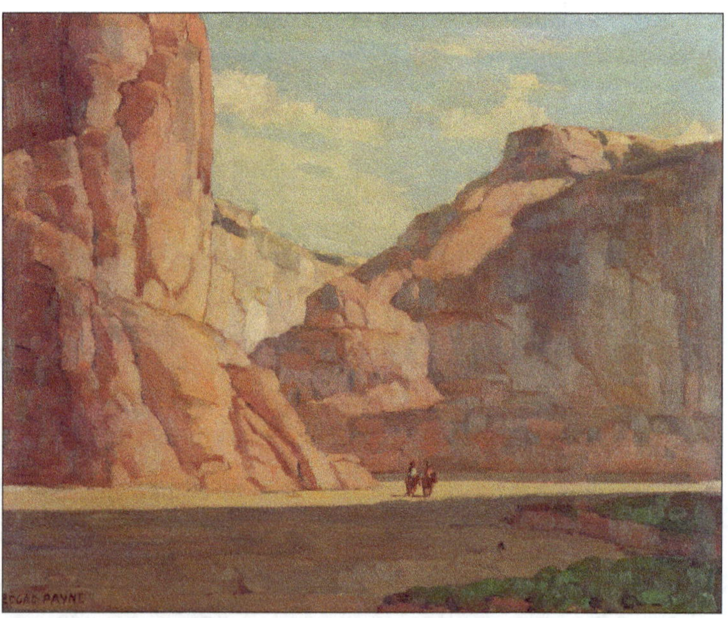

Edgar Payne, "Canyon del Muerto," oil, Gallup

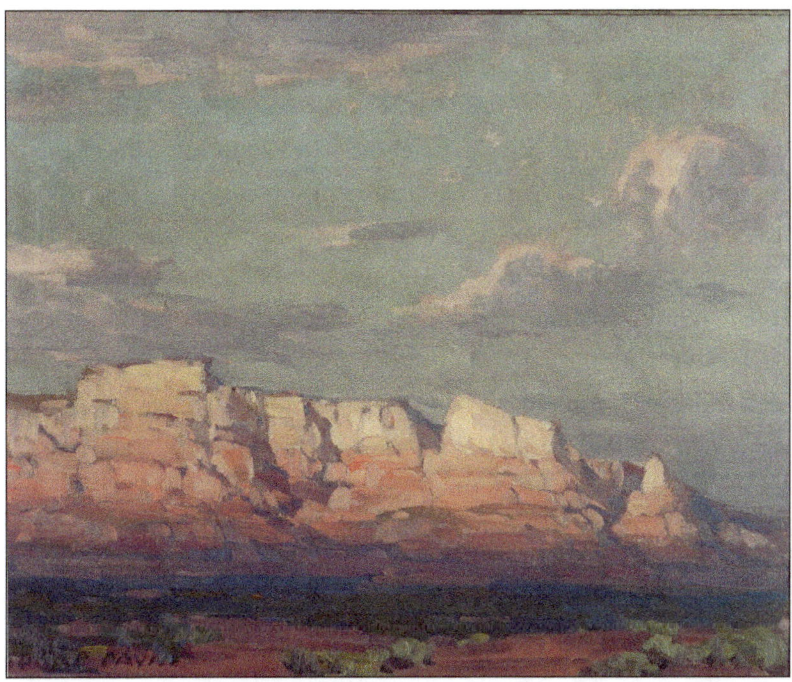

Edgar Payne, "Mountain Redonia," oil, Gallup

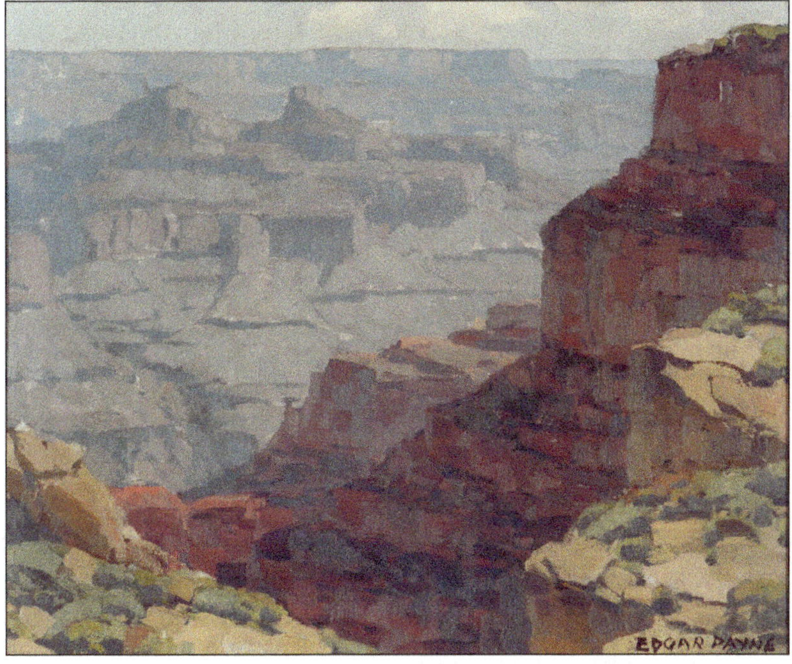

Edgar Payne, "Grand Canyon," oil, Gallup

The three oil paintings above are part of the large collection owned by the Gallup Public Schools.

PENA, TONITA (1895–1949)

Tonita's San Ildefonso tribal name was Quah Ah meaning White Coral Beads. She was born at the pueblo on June 13,1895 and was raised by an aunt, Martina Vigil. As a child of seven, she was already painting. She attended the Santa Fe Indian School and was one of the eight painters who completed 13 panel mural paintings at the school and numerous watercolor paintings. Her first husband, Juan Chaves, was from Cochiti Pueblo and after he died she married Felipe Herrera and their son, Joe Herrera, also became an outstanding painter. Pena was one of the first Indian painters to reject the tradition that Indian women painted only on pottery. She came to use painting as a form of personal artistic expression and as such was the first pueblo woman to win independent recognition as a painter. Granddaughter Yvonne Herrera Lewis continues the artistic traditions of her grandmother and father, in a variety of media.

LOCATION OF NEW DEAL ARTWORK: Santa Fe Indian School.

PHILLIPS, BERT GEER (1868–1956)

Born in Hudson, New York, Phillips grew up with a passion for art. He studied at the National Academy of Design and the Art Student League in New York. After five years in a New York studio, he went to Paris where he enrolled at the Academie Julian and studied with Constant and Laurens. There he met Joseph Sharp, who convinced him and fellow student, Ernest Blumenschein, to visit Taos, New Mexico where Sharp had been two years earlier. In 1898, Phillips and Blumenschein acquired a wagon, team and outfit in Denver and started out on a painting expedition southward but due to major misfortune with their wagon ended up in Taos. It may have been fate for Phillips established his home there and was a resident of New Mexico from that time on. He became a founding member of the Taos Society of Artists and committed himself to New Mexico for the next sixty years. At one point he almost lost his eyesight and decided to stop painting for four years. During that time he worked for the Carson National Forest Service and he later expressed that this experience "opened his eyes and heart" allowing him to create his best works. His vivid, realistic oil paintings fostered a romantic view of Native American life. Phillips wrote, "I believe it is the romance of this great pure-aired land that makes the most lasting impression on my mind and heart." In his contact with the Indians, Phillips attempted to break through their native reserve by patience and understanding, which gave his paintings an aura of idealized ethnology, and instilled in his subjects a visionary and unreal conceptual quality. His work is exhibited widely throughout the United States and is represented in several State Capitols and a number of museums including the Museum of New Mexico. He died in San Diego, California in 1956.

LOCATIONS OF NEW DEAL ARTWORK: Raton, Taos.

PIERCE, EDMA (Dates Unknown)

Pierce is thought to have gone to Albuquerque from Melrose or Carrizozo (unable to verify) and studied art at the University of New Mexico circa 1937. She worked on the *Portfolio of Spanish Design*, and her supervisor, Roland Dickey, recalled "she was in tears when he came to pick up her work that involved painting numerous drops of blood in the renderings of Jesus on the cross." She was a devout Protestant and may have done a mural at the First Baptist Church in Albuquerque at the corner of Broadway and East Central Avenue. Two murals by her have been located in the dining room in the New Mexico School for the Deaf in Santa Fe. In 1947, a *New Mexico Magazine* article referenced her as being at New Mexico State University in Las Cruces. One person who remembered her described her as "very shy, talented and sweet" and Gustave Baumann described her work as "rather melancholy in tone due to the subdued color and deep shadows, her work is marked by broad simplicity of treatment." One reference to a Mamie Edma Pierce has been found but there is no assurance it is the same person, otherwise little else has been found about her.

LOCATION OF NEW DEAL ARTWORK: Santa Fe—School for the Deaf.

PILLIN, POLIA SUNOCKIN (1905–1992)

This artist was born in Poland where her father was an instructor in the Czenstokowa Teck in crafts, specializing in metal and leather—beginning her life in a creative atmosphere. She came to the United States when she was fifteen and settled in Chicago. In 1932 she visited Santa Fe for the first time and vowed to return as soon as possible. She accomplished this in 1936 and worked consistently to grasp the essential quality of the countryside. She noted that an artist "must experience New Mexico before he/she can hope to paint it." Records indicate she was part of the New Mexico New Deal program in October 1938.

Prior to locating in New Mexico, Pillin had studied art at the Art Students League in New York, the Art Institute in Chicago and worked with private teachers with emphasis on the School of Expressionism. Once in New Mexico she found these styles not suited to the aesthetic presentation of Southwestern landscapes and evolved a style of her own. Her watercolors were her strongest works because it was through this medium she felt the ability to express the ever changing moods of light and shadow that passed so rapidly. She was always sure of herself and knew what she wanted. This carried over in her painting. If something did not come out in her first attempt, she would destroy it and immediately start over. She did not paint for the acclaim of the world but for the satisfaction of her own creative ego and its expression. Later in her career, while living in California, she became a renowned ceramicist. She died in Los Angeles, California in 1992.

LOCATION OF NEW DEAL ARTWORK: Albuquerque, Clayton.

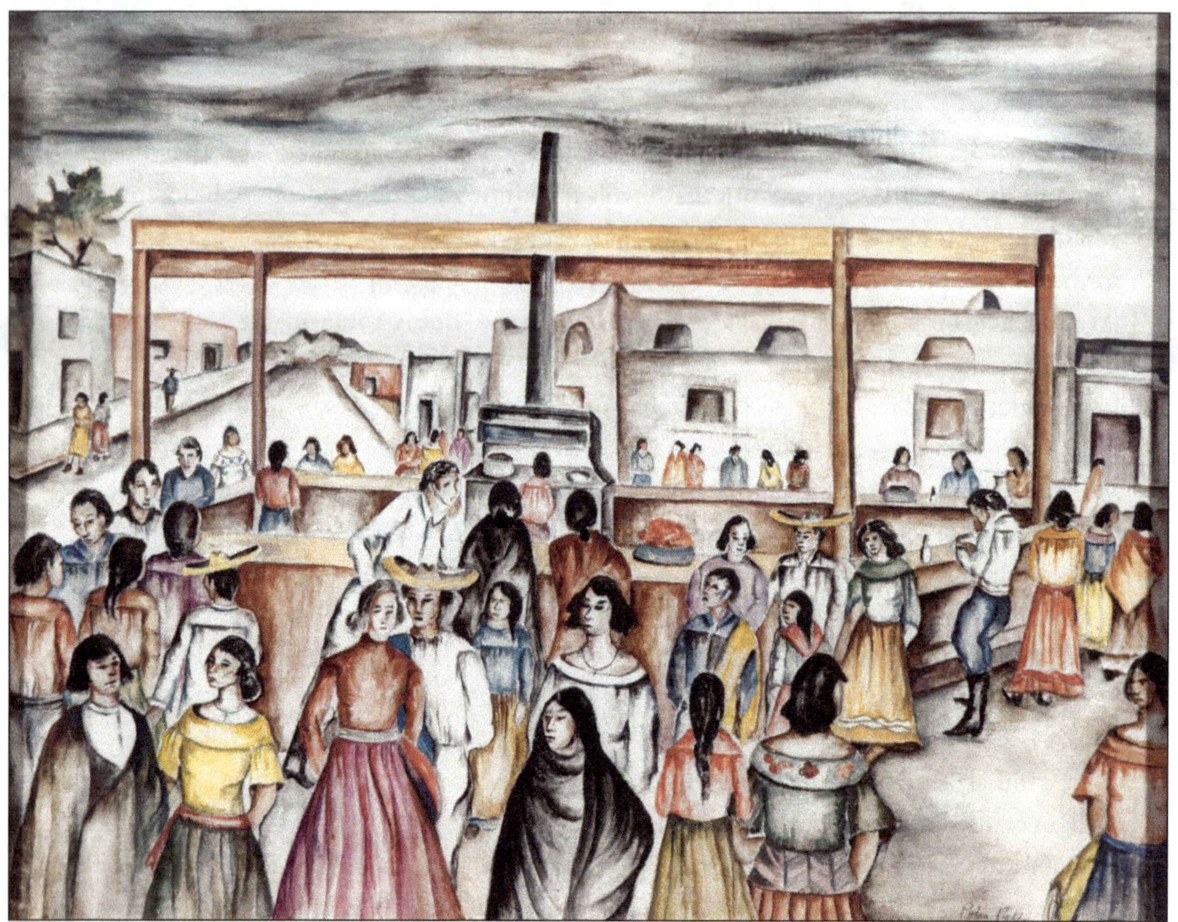

Polia Sunockin Pillin, "Santa Fe Fiesta Booth," watercolor, Clayton High School. This is one of the paintings in the largest school art collection in the state. They are featured in the school's WPA Museum which is not limited to paintings. Photograph by Pat Berrett.

QUINTANA, AGRAPINA (Dates Unknown)

From Cochiti Pueblo. Pottery on exhibit at National Park Service in Santa Fe.

QUINTANA, PEDRO (Dates Unknown)

Little known tin smith. Refer to the book, *Sin Nombre*, for more information.

REDIN, CARL (1892–1944)

Carl Adolf Hjalmer Persson Redin was born in southern Sweden and while still a youngster began covering household objects with his creations. He was frequently caught not doing his chores but rather drawing and sketching his family and surrounding scenery. The young boy also had a great desire to come to America and dreamed of it during many periods of illness and poverty. When Redin was 14, the village doctor's wife made arrangements for him to study art in Stockholm at night while he worked during the day to help support his family. Finally, in 1913 he was able to immigrate to the United States and lived in Chicago for three years until he went west to New Mexico in 1916 to improve his health which was failing due to tuberculosis. During his recovery he became close friends with an Albuquerque dentist and amateur painter who spoke fluent Swedish and they went on sketching trips once a week.

During and after his recovery Redin had various benefactors who provided him with opportunities to continue his painting. He taught in 1929–1930 in the University of New Mexico art department but some have suggested that his heavy accent kept him from a lengthier teaching career. Other New Mexico painters chose to live and paint further north, but Redin remained in Albuquerque and through his painting mythologized "his" town. His style was perfectly congruent with the popular tastes of the day and his images and vision became part of what most people think of today when they imagine New Mexico. Dying at age 52, not associating with any particular group or school of art, and choosing to work in a town with less artistic reputation may be the key reasons why his outstanding work is not as well known as others during that time. However, his artwork hangs in many public and private collections.

POSSIBLE LOCATIONS OF NEW DEAL ART WORK: Albuquerque, Hatch, Las Vegas, Los Lunas, Silver City, Springer; and Washington, DC.

RODRIGUEZ, ELISEO (1915–2009)

Rodriguez was born in Rowe, New Mexico and lived all his life in Santa Fe near the area where *Los Cinco Pintores* lived so he knew all of them. He began his art studies at fourteen, when his talent was noted and he was given a scholarship to the Santa Fe Art School. While there he painted for three years. In 1936, he was one of a group of New Mexico artists assigned to paint murals for the Texas Centennial, which featured Coronado's entry into New Mexico. As part of the New Deal projects in New Mexico, he worked on building the rock retaining walls of the Santa Fe River along Water Street. When that job was finished, he was encouraged to join the WPA's Federal Art Project and did some paintings, one known in the Dexter schools and another one recently located in the rafters at the Gallup City Hall.

He assisted his artist neighbor, Louie Ewing, in creating a mosaic tile base around a sculptured water fountain of turtles at Carrie Tingley Hospital for Crippled Children in Truth or Consequences. The fountain was the creation of Eugenie Shonnard, another Santa Fe New Deal artist. That facility is now a Veterans' Center and the turtle water fountain is still there in the courtyard but their mosaic creation in the base is no longer visable. We assume they have been painted or tiled over. He also worked on the *Portfolio of Spanish-Colonial Design* in New Mexico and Ewing and Rodriguez also created another portfolio collection of Indian rugs and were particularly proud of an implement they created to help spread the paint on the paper evenly. Sets of these Indian rug portfolios are known to be in the possession of the Laboratory of Anthropology, two libraries in Albuquerque and at the Branigan Library in Las Cruces.

The art work that Eliseo ultimately became famous for as a result of his time with the Federal Art Project was the straw inlay art form, an early Egyptian craft that died out in the latter part of the nineteenth century. Eliseo decided to try it when the WPA staff person presented the art work to him and others. He was the only artist interested and while he was learning how to do it, so was his wife Paula as they both sat at their kitchen table with straw, tweezers, glue, patience and their strong faith. This couple became famous for their achievements with this intricate medium and their crosses of all sizes and various portrayals of religious stories and/or designs can be found across the nation.

After World War II, Rodriguez taught cabinet making and design for the New Mexico Department of Vocational Education and worked for several years for a company specializing in church architecture in California, Colorado and New Mexico. One of his creations—a fifteen panel Stations of the Cross—took him eight years, completed in 1964. It was located in Our Lady of Grace Catholic Church in Castro Valley, California but currently appears lost. A smaller Stations mural can be seen at the Penitente Morada in Cordova, New Mexico.

LOCATION OF NEW DEAL ARTWORK: Dexter Schools, Gallup City Hall, Santa Fe and the tile work on the interior of the turtle fountain in the court yard at the Veterans Center in Truth or Consequences, formerly Carrie Tingley Hospital for Crippled Children.

ROGERS, R. HUBERT (Dates Unknown)

Little is known about his life. During the New Deal era, he created a mural painting called "Federal Road Work" for the Federal Building (early Post Office) in Santa Fe. This building is located across from the St. Francis Cathedral/Basilica and now houses the Institute of Indian Arts Museum. This art work was later transferred to Denver by the U.S. General Services Administration. Rogers also did two murals called "San Felipe Man" and "San Felipe Woman" that are believed to have been sent to Washington.

POSSIBLE LOCATIONS OF NEW DEAL ARTWORK: Denver, Colorado; Washington, DC.

ROLLINS, WARREN ELIPHALET (1861–1962)

Born in Carson City, Nevada on August 8, 1861, Rollins was raised in California. He was the pupil of Virgil Williams at the San Francisco School of Design, becoming assistant director of the school. In 1887 after further study in the East he moved to San Diego. He began to specialize in Indian subjects, traveling through the Western states. He was one of the first artists allowed to live among the Indians and admitted to their ceremonies. In 1900 he was in Arizona painting Hopi Indians. He also worked at the Chaco Canyon ruins in northern New Mexico and had a studio near El Tovar at the Grand Canyon. Rollins was an early member of the Santa Fe artists colony, painting and teaching along with Carlos Vierra, Gerald Cassidy, Kenneth Chapman, and Sheldon Parsons, arriving in 1915 through his friendship with E. I. Couse. He had previously spent years at Pueblo Bonita. Rollins had the first formal exhibition in Santa Fe, showing Indian paintings before 1910 so that he was properly regarded as the "dean of the Santa Fe art colony." Some of his work can still be seen at Bishop's Lodge in Santa Fe. Three paintings created for the former Gallup Post Office have been restored and are displayed in the United States Federal Courthouse, Santa Fe, in the second floor lobby, along with interesting interpretive information about their history and Rollins' talent.

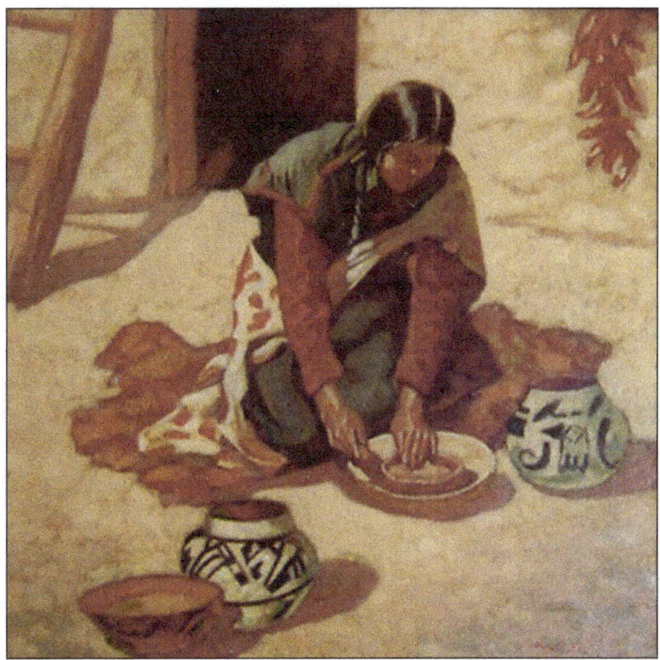

Warren Eliphalet Rollins, "Potter," oil, Santa Fe, Federal Courthouse

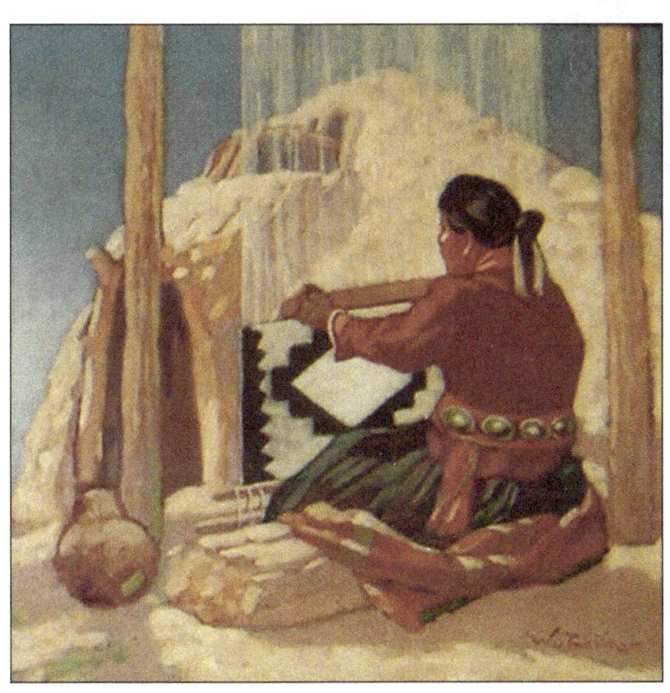

Warren Eliphalet Rollins, "Weaver," oil, Santa Fe, Federal Courthouse

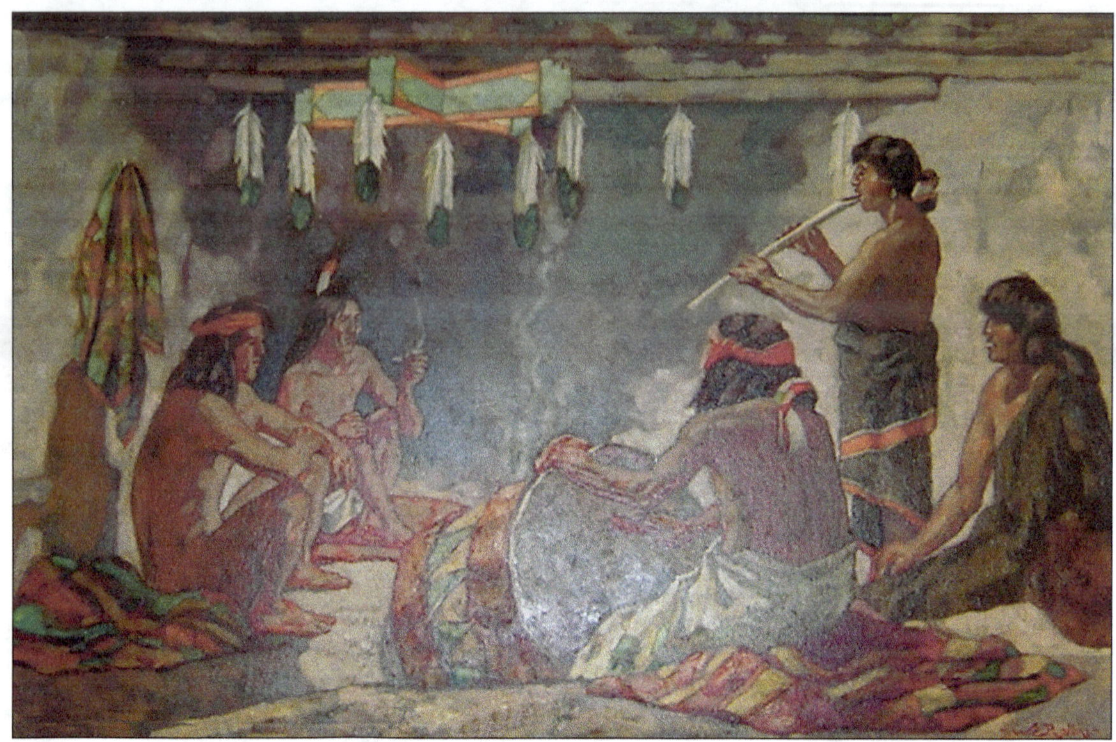

Warren Eliphalet Rollins, "A Ceremony in the Kiva," oil, Santa Fe, Federal Courthouse

The three New Deal pieces above are the only works by Rollins in the state and were originally in Gallup.

Although Rollins worked primarily with oils, he began in 1925 some experiments with wax crayons which became a life time interest. "Crayon gives stability," said Rollins. "It never fades or cracks, and may be viewed from almost any angle." Many of his Arizona desert and Santa Fe area scenes were done in that medium. Rollins and his wife, Birdella, had two daughters, Ramona and Ruth. Late in his life he was stricken with a palsy condition which impeded his ability to do his painting. He died January 15, 1962 with his family in Winslow, Arizona. An unpublished biography of his life was written by his grandson, Warren Griffin, and a copy is on file in the New Mexico State Records and Archives.

LOCATION OF NEW DEAL ARTWORK: Santa Fe Federal Courthouse; Fort Worth, Texas.

ROMERO DE ROMERO, ESQUIPULA (1889–1975)

Born in Cabezon, New Mexico in 1889, Romero de Romero was an early New Mexico artist who settled in Albuquerque in 1904. He established a successful outdoor advertising company and turned to serious painting in 1926. By the 1930s he was well known locally for his portrait, landscape, and Penitente paintings. In 1936 Romero sold his combined home, studio, and art gallery, built in 1924, and left Albuquerque to live and paint in Latin American countries. He exhibited widely and was still preparing for solo exhibitions at age 73. That year, 1962, he returned to Albuquerque, assisted in the building of a new home, and on occasion was seen riding a motorcycle. Records indicate he did a New Deal PWAP mural along with Brooks Willis and Stuart Walker for the Bernalillo County Courthouse; that work is now privately owned and its whereabouts are unknown. Also, a mural and possibly other paintings were done privately by him in the old Villa de Romero Inn, later Sunset Inn, which he managed. That structure, or parts of it, are the Manzano Day School now, but the art work is gone, possibly painted over or burned in an early fire. From the stories included about Esquipula in *Sin Nombre*, we deduce that he was a colorful personality, a traveling man and a character with a broad spectrum of artistic endeavors, as well as a builder of homes in Albuquerque, San Francisco and El Paso.

LOCATION OF POSSIBLE NEW DEAL ARTWORK: Unknown

ROYBAL, ALFONSO "AWA TSIREH" (1895–1955)

This San Ildefonso native was commissioned in 1917 by Alice Corbin Henderson to execute paintings for her. Later without formal education beyond the primary grades, he painted with others at the School of American Research. In 1933 the *St. Louis Post Dispatch* quoted the artist, John Sloan, as saying that "when Awa Tsireh sits down to paint a leaping deer he remembers not only the way a deer looks when leaping over a log but he feels himself leaping in the dance, with antlers swaying on his forehead and two sticks braced in hands for forelegs." Fred Kabotie, Velino Hererra and Roybal were the first Pueblo Indians to win individual recognition as artists. By 1950, according to *El Palacio*, he had abandoned his painting, silver smithing and other unrelated jobs due to poor eyesight, shaky hands and other personal reasons. His great nephew, Gary Roybal, is the curator of Bandelier National Monument as of 2011 and an artist himself, with special interest in elaborate beading of moccasins.

LOCATION OF NEW DEAL ART WORK: Unknown

ROYBAL, SEVERINO (1900–1986)

San Ildefonso Pueblo

RUSH, OLIVE (1873–1966)

Olive Rush was born in Fairmount, Indiana in 1873 and studied at the Art Students League in New York and with Howard Pyle in Paris. She was an independent spirit, experimenting with many styles during her lengthy career as an artist. Best known as a proficient painter in oils, watercolor, and fresco, she was able to combine "old world" sophistication with a daring sense of adventure. There is a refreshing spontaneity in her work, and a subtle feeling for the design of basic shapes which Rush intensified by daring color application to suggest the piercing light of New Mexico.

She was a long time resident of New Mexico, making her home in Santa Fe and that home she gave to the Quakers for their Meeting House and it is in use as such as of 2011. Her work has been widely exhibited in the United States and she won numerous awards including an Honorary Doctor of Fine Arts from Earlbain College. Rush's work is represented in various museums and public buildings around the country. Here in New Mexico, as part of the New Deal, she created a fresco in the old Santa Fe Public Library which is now the state's Chavez History Library and a large mural was also done in Las Cruces on the exterior of the Biology Building at New Mexico State University. Unfortunately, that work was "repainted" with enamel paint by some individuals who did not necessarily know better. Early in 2000, the New Mexico of National New Deal Preservation Association was able to hire art conservator, Luis Neri-Zagal, to remove the enamel paint and restore it to its original fresco beauty.

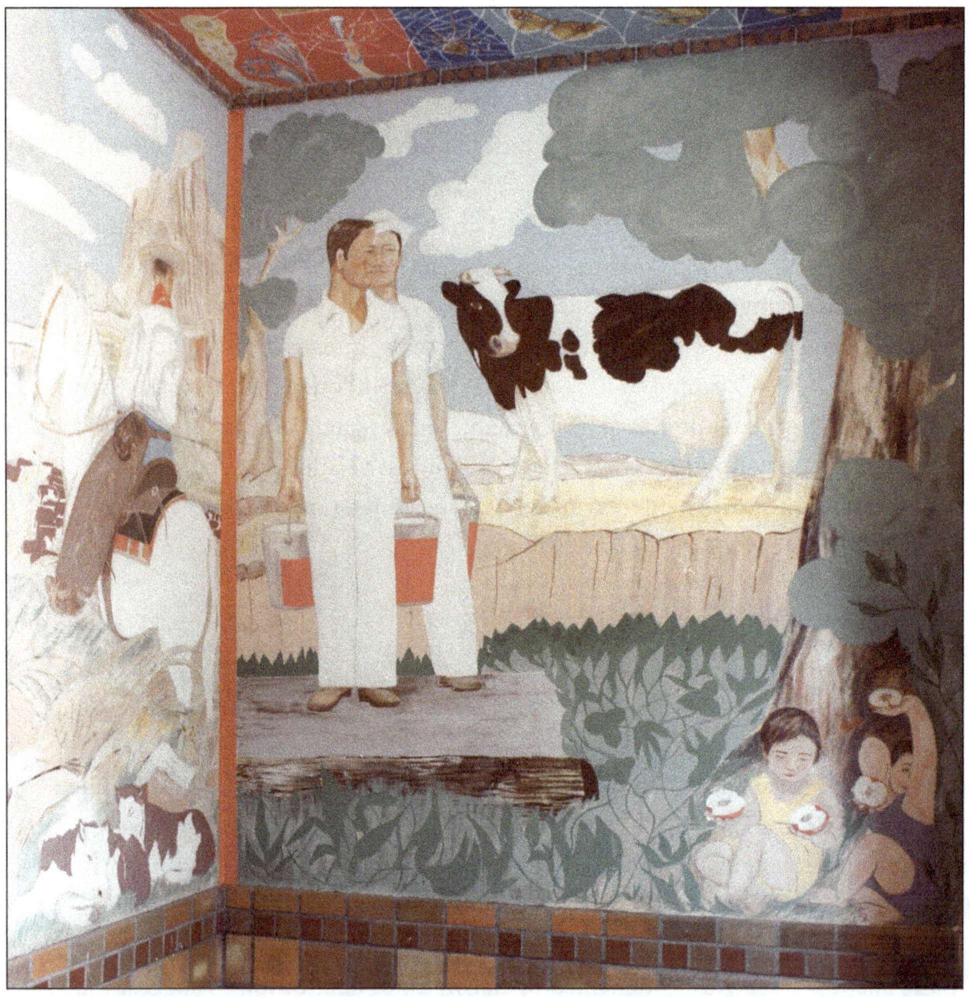

Olive Rush, "Agricultural Industries of Dona Ana County," fresco, Las Cruces, New Mexico State University

Rush did other work at the Indian School in Santa Fe, but the funding source is unknown. Privately known works included the exterior entrance walls of La Fonda Hotel in Santa Fe and Maisel's Trading Post in downtown Albuquerque where she was commissioned and included young Indian students from the Santa Fe Indian School to assist her. Most of her students went on to achieve some recognition on their own. Two other New Deal murals were created for post offices in Pawhuska, Oklahoma and Florence, Colorado.

LOCATIONS OF NEW DEAL ARTWORK: Las Cruces, Roswell, Santa Fe; Florence, Colorado, and Pawhuska, Oklahoma.

SANCHEZ, JUAN AMADEO (1901–1969)

Sanchez was born in Rio Pueblo, near Taos but grew up in Colmer, New Mexico. At the age of twelve a most unfortunate "prank" was played on him by other boys in the village. He was placed in a wooden box which was nailed shut and hours later when he was let out, he had difficulty walking. As a result of this, rheumatism developed early on leaving him with severe paralysis in his legs for the rest of his life. In 1936 he was hired by the WPA-Federal Art Project not only because of his developing painting skills as a santero but as a possible form of rehabilitation of his physical limitations. His religious creations adhered strictly to the traditional form and he was also included as one of the artists on the *Portfolio*. Over one hundred religious creations done by Sanchez, can be found in New Mexico and Colorado Museums.

Tom Riedel did a master's thesis in 1994 on Sanchez and his artistic work but Tey Nunn's material on this artisan in *Sin Nombre* is informative. She indicates that his physical disability (partial paralysis of his spine and legs) "also affected how his sculpture and painting skills were perceived." This may have been because at that time the public was not as open to looking past a person's physical limitations to see and appreciate their fine talents. Holger Cahill, the National Director of the FAP, was reported to have seen his work and highly approved of it and his ability to make a sculptural record of the old New Mexican santos. He lived out his life in Raton making both retablos and bultos with a goal of making future generations aware of the beauty and significance of colonial New Mexico santos.

In *Sin Nombre,* Nunn shares that Sanchez did not consider himself a santero despite being a very religious man. He is quoted as saying: "Even though I have to deal with some physical disability, God granted me the ability to reproduce this old Colonial art, and I live in hopes that my work may be kept for many centuries, so that the future generations may see what colonial-New Mexican santos were."

LOCATIONS OF NEW DEAL ARTWORK: Carlsbad Art Museum, Raton Museum, Roswell Art Center, Santa Fe International Folk Art Museum, Palace of the Governors and Museum of Art; Colorado Springs, Colorado—Taylor Museum, and Boulder, Colorado—University of Colorado and the Denver Art Museum.

SANCHEZ, RAMOS (1926–Unknown)

Oqwa Owin or Kachina Town or Rain God Town was born in San Ildefonso Pueblo March 17, 1926. He married Marie Gertrude Montoya in 1949, and they had three children.

SAVILLE, BRUCE WILDER (1893–1938)

Little has been found about this sculptor but we believe he was born in Massachusetts. He designed and executed many symbolic figure groups including war memorials in Maine, Ohio, New York, Michigan, Mississippi, and Missouri. A photograph and reference presented a sculpture piece of soldiers of various wars and it was planned for the National Cemetery in Santa Fe. However, such a statue has never been known to have been placed in this cemetery nor does the cemetery have any records about it. An early letter between Vernon Hunter, the New Mexico State Director, and Holger Cahill, the National Director of Public Art, references a horizontal panel of dance figures in clay that was to be cast soon and sent to the Laboratory of Anthropology in Santa Fe. One might wonder if the six bronze Indian Dancers piece at the Museum of Fine Arts could be that work.

Saville also did portrait busts that are in Santa Fe. One of E. Dana Johns is part of the New Mexico Museum collection. In 1938 friends and comrades of Bronson Cutting commissioned Saville to do a bronze bust to honor Cutting, a former U. S. Senator who supported the New Mexico New Deal projects. He was also one of the founders of the American Legion and owner of *The Santa Fe New Mexican*. Upon completion, the bust was placed on an island on the street across from the west side of the Capitol. In 2006 the NNDPA hired Dale Kronkright, local art conservator, to restore the lost patina on the bust and when completed, the bust was placed in a more viewable location on the east side promenade up to the New Mexico State Capitol. Saville died in Santa Fe.

LOCATION OF POSSIBLE NEW DEAL ARTWORK: Santa Fe.

SCHLEETER, HOWARD (1903–1976)

Born in Buffalo, New York, Schleeter studied early in his years at the Albright Art School in his hometown. He later made his living as an airplane mechanic and got to know Lindbergh, Earhart and Doolittle. He came to New Mexico in 1929 and became a permanent resident as of 1930, the year he also married his wife, Ruth. Howard Schleeter studied under Brooks Willis and became known as an experimenter both with media and image. The various media he worked in included oil, watercolor, gouache, scratch board as well as wood engraving. His style can best be described as abstract fantasy but the five large New Deal murals in Melrose Public School library are highly realistic portrayals of the West. Local ranchers and Schleeter's mother-in-law provided critical guidance on these murals.

In the 1930s, Schleeter evolved a style of pigment application which gave his surfaces a raised mosaic appearance. This technique was coupled with conventionally organized and selected subject matter ranging from landscapes to still-life motifs. In 1936, while studying with Brooks Willis, he became involved with the New Deal art programs. This was a great help to the family income since he had been digging ditches. He worked on the *Portfolio* and the five murals mentioned earlier. His wife also became a part of the program working as a timekeeper and as part of a sewing project.

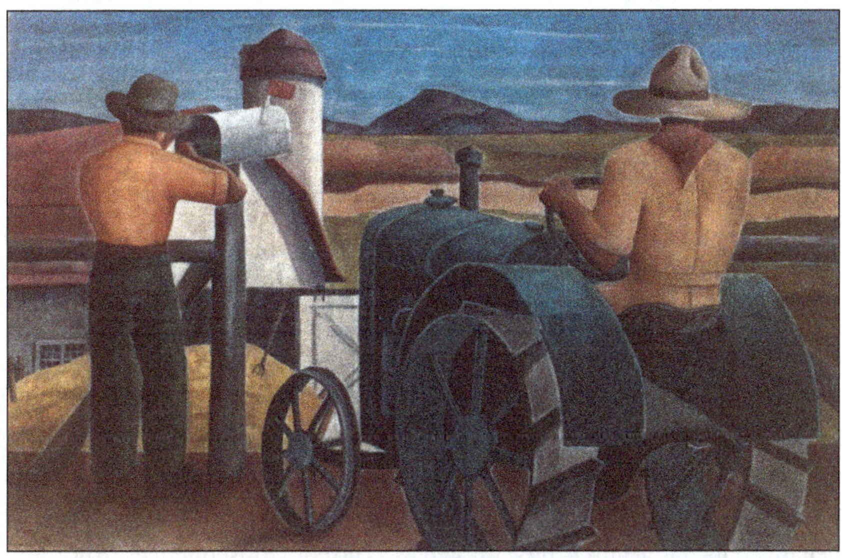

Howard Schleeter, "Farmer on Tractor," oil, Melrose School Library. This is one of five panels depicting early scenes on the eastern frontier of New Mexico.

He was one of the first New Mexico artists chosen by Jane Mabry and Peter Hurd as contributing significantly to New Mexico's art and was referred to in the 1945 *Encyclopedia Britannica* as "an artist's artist." Later in his career, Schleeter left this articulated surface treatment and concentrated upon a more abstract and visionary type of imagery. In addition to his murals in several New Mexico public buildings, his work is represented in the Institute of Religion, Cedar City, Utah, and he is well known in Europe. He died in Placitas, New Mexico May 27, 1976.

LOCATIONS OF NEW DEAL ARTWORK: Clayton, Melrose, Santa Fe; Washington, DC.

SHONNARD, EUGENIE F. (1886–1978)

Born in Yonkers, New York on April 29, 1886, Shonnard was a descendent of Francis Lewis, one of the signers of the Declaration of Independence. She was a fragile and lonely child who spent many hours with the animals she loved. As a young woman she studied first at the New York School of Applied Design, but when she first held a piece of clay in her hands she knew that she had found the reason for her life. Over the protests of her doctor and family who thought a frail, semi-invalid person would not be able to handle being a sculptor, she decided to go to Paris to study sculpture. She has said that from the moment she set out for

Europe in 1911 she became strong and healthy—a testament to her faith and need to create. In France she studied with the sculptor Emile Bourdelle and with Auguste Rodin. Back in New York she worked on many important sculpture commissions before discovering Santa Fe and making it her home in 1927.

In New Mexico Miss Shonnard, also known as Mrs. George Ludlum, formed close friendships with many Indian people, and an especially strong bond with Maria Martinez, famed potter of San Ildefonso who taught her much about working in clay. She also worked in stone, bronze, wood, and in a material she developed herself which she called "Keenstone." Through the years Eugenie Shonnard received many honors including a fellowship from the School of American Research, and inclusion in museum collections such as the Luxembourg Museum in Paris. She exhibited work at the Museum of Modern Art in New York, The Pennsylvania Academy, The Art Institute of Chicago, The Whitney Museum, and the Brooklyn Museum.

In New Mexico she carved the reredos at Rosario Chapel in Santa Fe, did architectural sculpture for the Episcopal Church in Las Cruces, and a PWAP funded outdoor sculpture and a fountain at the Carrie Tingley Hospital for Crippled Children in Hot Springs, New Mexico in 1936. That institution has relocated to Albuquerque, New Mexico but the fountain remained with the buildings that became the home of the New Mexico Veterans' Center. The town also changed its name and is now known as Truth or Consequences. Another New Deal work includes two wooden carvings in the post office at Waco, Texas.

A private piece, "The Desert Maiden," done during the New Deal era, has had a history of traveling between its original site, Sandia Preparatory School in Albuquerque and New Mexico Technical University in Socorro. It was originally commissioned for the early girl's school, Sandia Girls School, but when that school closed, the work moved with the art teacher to New Mexico Tech in Socorro. Years later, the new Sandia Prep requested it be returned to their campus, which was by then co-educational, and it was placed on a long term loan there. While there, this sandstone piece was restored after having been painted green as a prank by students at New Mexico Tech. Just a few years later, New Mexico Tech discontinued the loan and returned it to that campus. After a few years in storage, it was put in a prominent place in a newer part of the campus.

Shonnard also did bronze busts and bas reliefs of many leading New Mexicans. In 1976 she was honored by an exhibition of her work at the Governor's Gallery in Santa Fe sponsored by Governor and Mrs. Jerry Apodaca. In the following statement by Eugenie Shonnard we feel she identifies the honest and shining purpose of her life. "God created form and color in this world. Also He gave some of us talents for the use of these. Therefore, we human beings must need them in our daily lives. There is perhaps no other answer; and so, we artists must fulfill life's commission as artists and craftsmen." She died in Santa Fe in 1978.

LOCATION OF NEW DEAL ARTWORK: Truth or Consequences—Veterans' Center, and New Mexico Institute of Technology—Socorro; Waco, Texas Post office.

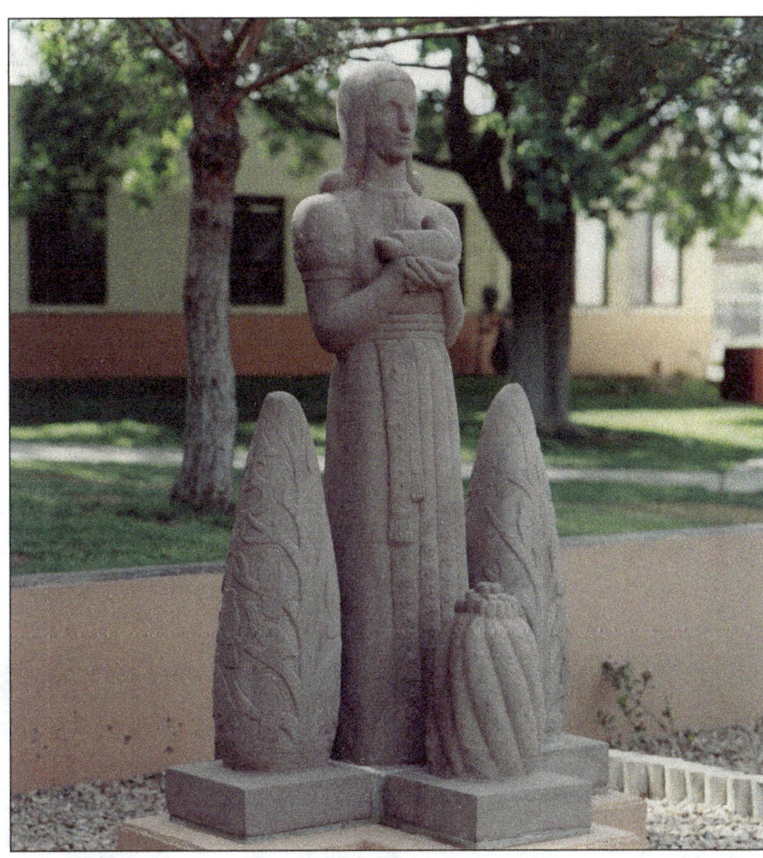

Eugenie Shonnard, "Desert Maiden," limestone, Socorro, New Mexico Institute of Mining and Technology.

SHUSTER, WILL (1893–1969)

Born in Philadelphia, Pennsylvania, Shuster trained early with J. William Server and John Sloan. He was gassed in World War I and developed tuberculosis so he was another one of the artists who came to the West for health reasons. He moved to New Mexico in 1920 and lived in Santa Fe for the rest of his career. Like many of his fellow artists, he was an painter as well as a print maker, working with etchings. The style of Shuster's work is generally considered to be expressionistic. His artwork is represented in Newark Museum, New Jersey, Brooklyn Museum; and the Museum of New Mexico.

Shuster was one of the noted *Los Cinco Pintores* of Santa Fe and was the creator in 1925 of the Zozobra figure of the annual Santa Fe Fiesta. As a New Deal artist, he created four paintings of the Carlsbad Caverns, now in the National Park Service storage area in Arizona. One has been returned to the new Visitor Center at the caverns. A series of fresco murals with Indian subjects are in the inner courtyard at the New Mexico Fine Arts Museum in Santa Fe. More about him can be found in chapter 5 by Louise Turner and in the biography she wrote, *Will Shuster, A Santa Fe Legend*, with Joseph Dispenza.

LOCATIONS OF NEW DEAL ARTWORK: Santa Fe—Museum of Art, Carlsbad Caverns; National Park Service in Arizona.

SMALL LUDINS, HANNAH MECKLEM (1903–1992)

Born in New York City January 9, 1903, Hannah Small was the daughter of Eugene and Grace Workum Small. While in her teens she enrolled at the Art Students League in New York and studied under Boardman Robinson and sculptor A. Sterling Calder, among others. Married in 1937, she and her husband, Eugene Ludins, were early residents of Woodstock, New York.

In 1933, en route to California, the Ludins discovered Santa Fe and decided to stay temporarily. She became involved in the PWAP and was commissioned to do two stone sculptures in conjunction with the Olive Rush fresco mural for the lobby of the old Public Library. The stones were quarried in Las Vegas and she worked on the pieces at their rented adobe. The placement of those statues today is in the newer Santa Fe Public Library, a building which was also created as the result of the New Deal projects. Mr. Ludins, her husband, was not involved with the New Deal projects of New Mexico but after they left and returned to Woodstock, he became the WPA supervisor there in 1937–38 and the New York State supervisor in 1938–39. His papers and some of Hannah's are archived in the art center.

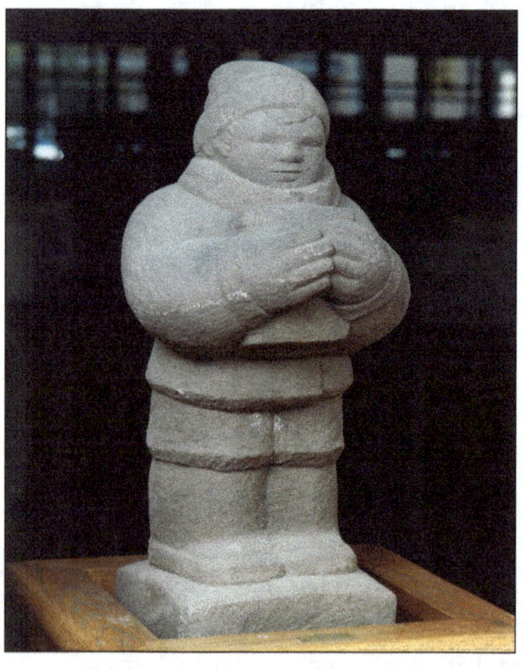

Hannah Mecklem Small Ludins, "Boy," granite, Santa Fe Main Public Library

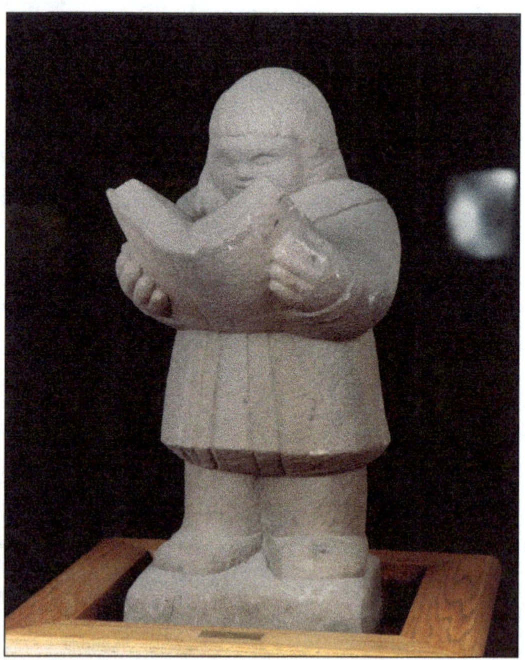

Hannah Mecklem Small Ludins, "Girl," granite, Santa Fe Main Public Library

The two granite sculptures shown above were first placed in the children's section of the original public library, but now welcome visitors in the entry area of the current Main Library which was once the New Deal built City Hall and Fire Station.

Hannah Small won many prizes including the Logan Award at the Chicago Art Institute in 1940. She was honored by her home artists association by receiving the 1984 Sally Jacobs Award in Woodstock and had her work shown at the Metropolitan and Whitney Museums and the National Academy in New York. Her work is represented in many private and public collections. She died April 25, 1992 at the Kingston (NY) Hospital at the age of 89.

LOCATION OF NEW DEAL ARTWORK: Santa Fe—Main Library.

STEWART, DOROTHY NEWKIRK (1891–1955)

Born in Philadelphia, Pennsylvania, Dorothy Stewart began drawing portraits in her early teens. As a young child she stopped talking as the result of an illness but got what she wanted by drawing pictures of objects. She was never an outstanding student in school; however, she later took courses in chemistry, Spanish, Greek and French and studied at the Academy of Fine Arts in Philadelphia. She came to be considered one of the most talented students of her period. She moved to New Mexico in 1925. Her work was mainly in oil and fresco painting and linoleum cut; her style varied from realistic to expressionistic to abstract. She exhibited in several venues including the Artists for Victory show at the Metropolitan Museum, New York City. Stewart's work is represented in the Museum of New Mexico.

The WPA fresco she did on the front of the Albuquerque Little Theater titled "Los Moros" was done in 1936 but was later destroyed during remodeling activities. In the fresco Stewart depicted the annual re-enactment of the Christians doing battle with the Moors held in Santa Cruz.

Stewart lived on Canyon Road and reportedly loved Shakespeare and painted murals of Shakespearean creations on the walls of her home. She died on Christmas Day in 1955.

LOCATION OF NEW DEAL ARTWORK: Destroyed.

TAFOYA, LEGORIA (Dates Unknown)

Sister of Pablita Velarde. Pottery at Bandelier National Monument.

TAMOTZU, CHUZO (1888–1975)

Tamotzu was born on a Japanese island below Kyushu on February 19,1888 and came to the United States in the 1920s to continue his painting. He did no New Deal art in New Mexico but an interesting story is included here to share his experience with the New Deal project in New York in the 1930s. He applied and was accepted to do easel paintings and graphic art for the Public Works of Art Project. He was paid $40.00 a week and expected to paint one painting a month. When that program (PWAP) was over in 1934, many of the artists transferred to the WPA programs but one only got paid $28.00 a week and were required to file and go on relief. At that time he was denied participation in the program because he was not an American citizen. There were other artists like him who were denied and they organized a march to Washington and appeared before Harry Hopkins, close associate of President Franklin Roosevelt, who stated, "He felt sorry for them but it's up to the Congress. I can't do it myself." Interestingly, he volunteered and was accepted as a member of the United States Army's Office of Strategic Service during World War II where he served our country but bore no arms.

Tamotzu moved to Las Vegas, New Mexico in 1948 with his American bride, Louise, who had been a WAC during WWII. She had friends there who had invited them to come to New Mexico. After two months in Las Vegas they moved on and settled in Santa Fe where they lived on Canyon Road, in the former home of John Sloan. Tamotzu was a most active painter in Santa Fe for many years until his death in 1975. His lithographs are in many museums all over the country and Japan. Prior to her death, his widow put a plaque on their home noting the studio location where both her husband and John Sloan had created their works.

TERKEN, JOHN RAYMOND (Dates Unknown)

Four busts of historical figures in Chaves County were done by this sculptor and can be found in their historical museum in Roswell. This appears to be the only work done in New Mexico prior to his moving to New York.

LOCATION OF NEW DEAL ARTWORK: Roswell.

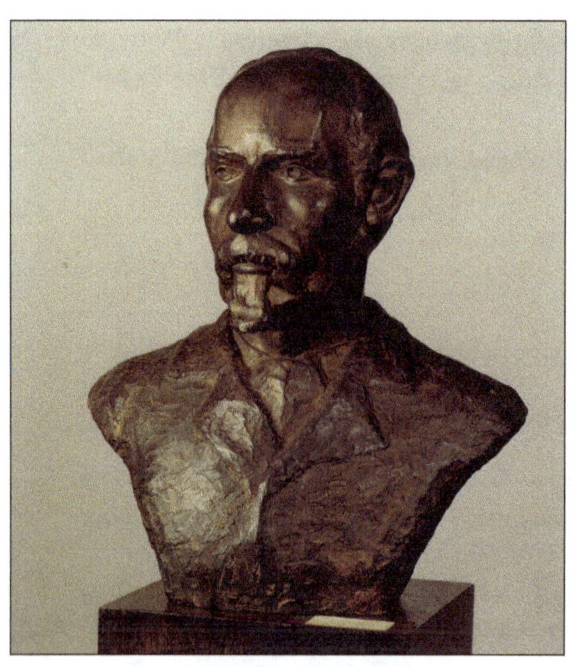

John Raymond Terken, "Joseph C. Lea," bronze sculpture, Roswell, Historical Center for Southeast New Mexico

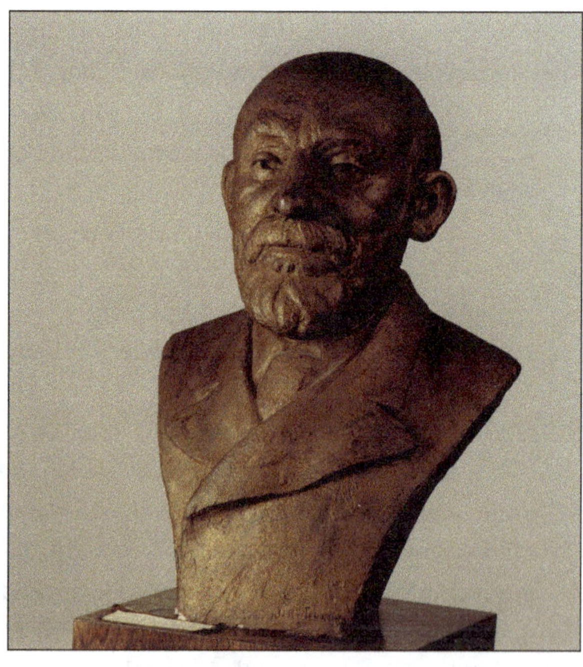

John Raymond Terken, "John J. Hagerman" bronze sculpture, Roswell, Historical Center for Southeast New Mexico

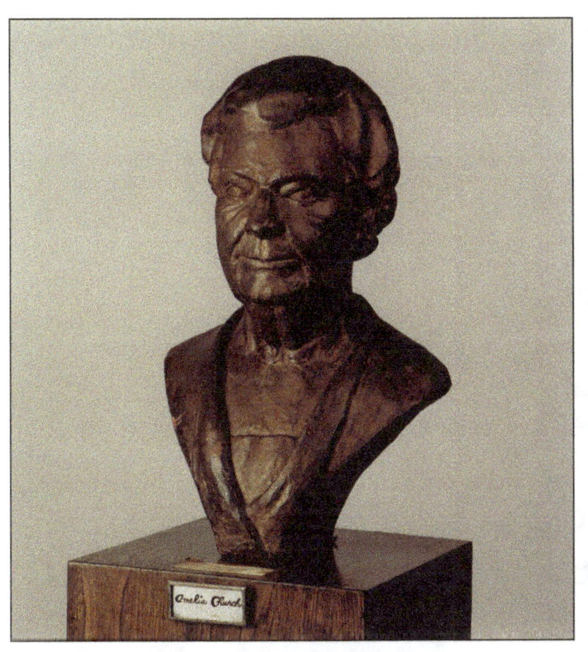

John Raymond Terken, "Amelia B. Church,"
bronze sculpture, Roswell,
Historical Center for Southeast New Mexico

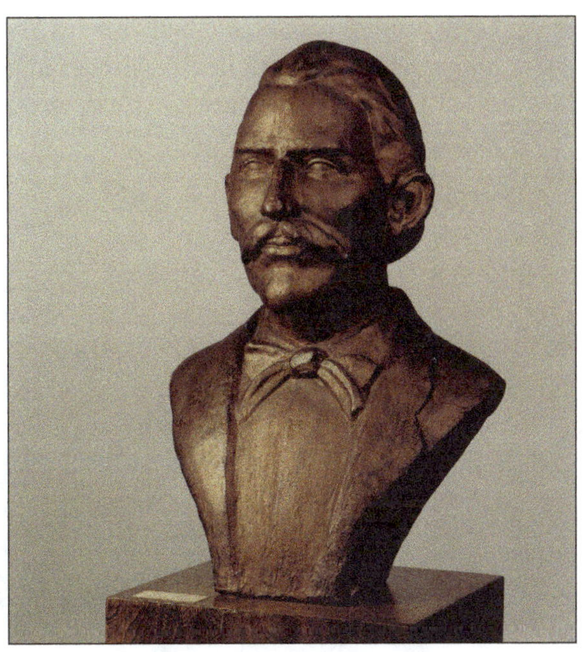

John Raymond Terken, "John E. Chisum,"
bronze sculpture, Roswell,
Historical Center for Southeast New Mexico

TOLEDO, JOSÈ REY (1915–1994)

Born in Jemez Pueblo, New Mexico in 1915, Toledo was a painter of the San Ildefonso movement, a muralist and teacher. He also signed as Morning Star (Shobah Woonhon). His father was chief of the Jemez Arrow Society, a warrior lodge, and the first Indian owner of a modern general store in the pueblo. Toledo was influenced toward art by his cousin, Velino Shije Herrera. He attended Albuquerque Indian School and earned his MA in art education from the University of New Mexico in 1955. He had more formal training than was usual for Native American artists but his style and subject matter remained pueblo-oriented. He painted with the WPA in 1940–1941, primarily in his home, which he felt was a great opportunity and reward because it allowed him to do what he loved—recording his tribal activities in his painting. At the same time he was able to be at home and assist in the raising of his eight children.

During World War II Toldedo went to work in the shipyards in California but later returned to be an instructor from 1949–1957 at the Santa Fe and Albuquerque Indian schools. He was an active member of the pueblo watercolor movement until the early 1960s when he had less time to paint due to his full time employment as a Health Education specialist for the U.S. Public Health Service and later with the New Mexico Health Department. In 1980 he suffered a heart attack and retired to return to his painting in his home. A year prior to his death in 1994, his children built him his first studio and his wife no longer had to share their dining room table with him as she created her pottery.

LOCATION OF NEW DEAL ARTWORK: Washington, DC.

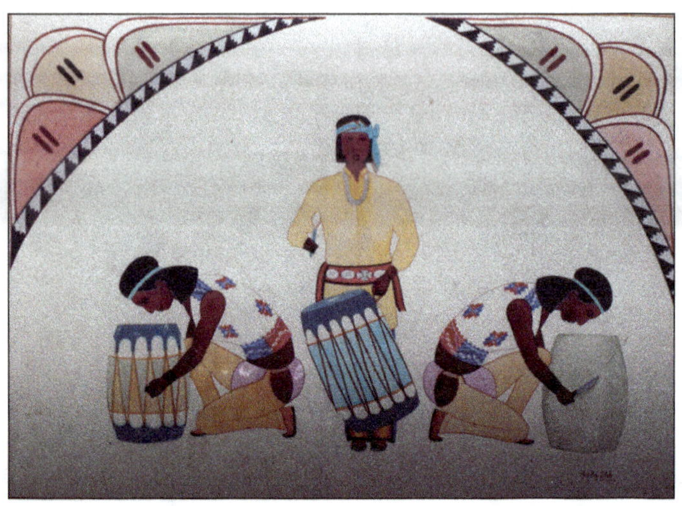

José Rey Toledo, "The Drum Makers," watercolor, Melrose School Library

TREVORS, FRANZ (Dates Unknown)

One oil painting is on exhibit at Carrie Tingley Hospital for Crippled Children in Albuquerque along with their other New Deal artwork. He was also one of the *Portfolio* artists.

LOCATION OF NEW DEAL ARTWORK: Albuquerque—Carrie Tingley Hospital for Crippled Children.

TSCHUDY, HERBERT BOLIVAR (1874–1946)

Born in Plattsburg, Ohio in 1874, Tschudy's work is displayed in Brooklyn Museum, Museum of New Mexico, Yellow Springs Public Library, National Museum, Warsaw, National Museum, Sofia, Bulgaria, and Gallup Public Library. About 1914 Tschudy was on a Western sketching expedition which included Arizona, California, and Glacier National Park and his sketches were to be used in making installations at the Brooklyn Museum. A regular visitor to the West thereafter, Tschudy in time achieved recognition as an artist, and by 1930 was receiving favorable reviews in New York City. About half of his paintings for a 1934 exhibition at "Fifteen Gallery" were of New Mexico, painted during the previous summer. By 1935 Tschudy was identified in New York reviews as a painter of the Southwest. During the early years of Tschudy's career he sometimes simplified the spelling of his name. An oil called "Hubbell Hill," at Hubbell Trading Post Museum in Ganado, Arizona, is signed "Judy." The first volume of *Brooklyn Museum Quarterly* also used that spelling.

LOCATION OF NEW DEAL ARTWORK: Gallup.

TSIHNAHJINNIE, ANDY REY (1918–2000)

A Navajo, Andy was born in Rough Rock, Arizona in 1918. His Native American name is Yazzie Bahe, Little Grey, and his long last name has been spelled five different ways. As early as five he was drawing on stone and later on wrapping paper and the back sides of can labels. He was at the Santa Fe Indian School as of 1932 and graduated in 1936. He is thought to have created murals around the country during his stint in the Army during World War II. His artwork created during the New Deal period was sent to the U.S. Indian Service for distribution. One work was done for the Indian school in Phoenix, which was later demolished. He is believed to have done some art at the Santa Fe Indian School. He lived in Scottsdale, Arizona and later died there.

LOCATION OF NEW DEAL ARTWORK: Unknown.

TYNDALL, CALVIN T. (Dates Unknown)

Little is known about this Omaha native whose Indian name was Umpah, meaning Elk. He attended the Santa Fe Indian School and participated in the creation of the 13 panel murals done as part of the PWAP. These have since been destroyed, when the building was demolished in 2009.

UFER, WALTER (1876–1936)

Born in Louisville, Kentucky in 1876 (late July or early August), Ufer was the son of an immigrant German gunsmith. He received early art training from his father who engraved gun stocks. Around 1890 he left high school to work in the Lithography Department of the *Louisville Courier Journal* and in 1893 he went to Hamburg, Germany to study with German lithographer Johan Jergens and on to the Royal Applied Arts School and the Dresden Royal Academy under Thor, and the Art Institute of Chicago. By 1898 he had returned to work in Louisville, Kentucky before going to Chicago to study at their Art Institute. Ufer continued to study, alternating between Europe and America until 1914 when he was offered a trip along with Victor Higgins to the Southwest by Carter H. Harrison, former Mayor of Chicago and local art patron. In 1915 he and his artist wife, Mary Frederickson, settled in Taos and he was elected a member of the Taos Society of Artists. In this new environment his style became more academic. He received many awards and did well financially until 1927 when he was near bankruptcy. David Witt's book, *The Taos Artists* noted that "his studio had a sign on it marked, 'Danger . . . Explosives,' which seemed to say something about his personality at that time."

He survived by giving private art lessons and did some painting for the New Deal project. He died unexpectedly of appendicitis on August 2, 1936, just a few days after his 60th birthday. Today he is remembered as one of the most colorful of the Taos artists of his time, painting in a bold aggressive style until his death.

LOCATION OF NEW DEAL ARTWORK: Albuquerque—University of New Mexico.

VAN SOELEN, THEODORE (1890–1964)

Born in St. Paul, Minnesota in 1890, Van Soelen first studied at the Institute of Arts and Sciences in his hometown, and then at the Pennsylvania Academy of Fine Arts, where he earned a travel-study scholarship to Europe. By 1916, when he moved to New Mexico for his health, he was a thoroughly trained painter. He spent his early years in Albuquerque as a painter-illustrator, but by 1920, seeking a closer view of Indian subjects, moved to an Indian trading post in San Ysidro. In 1922 he moved to Santa Fe, living there for four years before making his permanent home in nearby Tesuque. Prior to this move, he also spent some time on a Texas ranch to observe cowboy life. He recorded the Southwest and its people with keen accuracy and harmonious composition. His work is represented in a number of recognized galleries and in public buildings including the Pennsylvania Academy of Fine Arts; National Academy of Design, New York; and the Museum of New Mexico. As a muralist, he spent much painstaking time on research of his subjects, along with extensive preparation in creating truly accurate depictions of the land, the animals, the vegetation, the people and spirit of the Southwest. His New Mexico New Deal artwork can be seen in the Portales Post Office and the Court House in Silver City. The two murals in Silver City were restored by Steve Prins in 2009. Van Soelen died on May 15, 1964.

LOCATIONS OF NEW DEAL ARTWORK: Portales and Silver City; Wawrika, Oklahoma, ("Wild Geese"); two in Livingston, Texas ("Buffalo Hunting" & "Landscape"); Washington, DC.

VELARDE, PABLITA (1918–2007)

Born in Santa Clara Pueblo in 1918, she was also known as Tse Tsan—Golden Dawn. She is perhaps the best-known Indian woman artist today. A childhood eye disease caused temporary loss of sight. "Temporary darkness made me want to see everything," she said. "I have trained myself to remember, to the smallest detail, everything I see." Tse Twan was sent in to Santa Fe to attend grades one through six at St. Catherine's Indian School and later studied with Dorothy Dunn during her educational days at the U.S. Indian School in Santa Fe. She worked with other Indian students on a mural on the exterior of Maisel's store in Albuquerque, which is still there. As a member of the Santa Clara Pueblo, she sold her work under the portal of the Palace of the Governors in the early days. As a young woman she traveled all over the county with the Ernest Thompson Seton family caring for their child but finally became homesick and asked to return to her pueblo.

About this time, the WPA came to her rescue and she always credited it as giving her the opportunity to become an artist. Her work was primarily done at Bandelier National Monument, creating a vast collection of WPA paintings featuring daily life in her pueblo. While working she would live at the park with the ranger's family. She always enjoyed sharing that she made $5.00 a day, which was more than the men in the Civilian Conservation Corps were making at Bandelier. With that "vast amount" of pay, she was able to save and build her own home on the pueblo, which was unusual for a pueblo woman to accomplish financially at that time. The art work is still there, as is some work done by her sister, Legoria Tafoya.

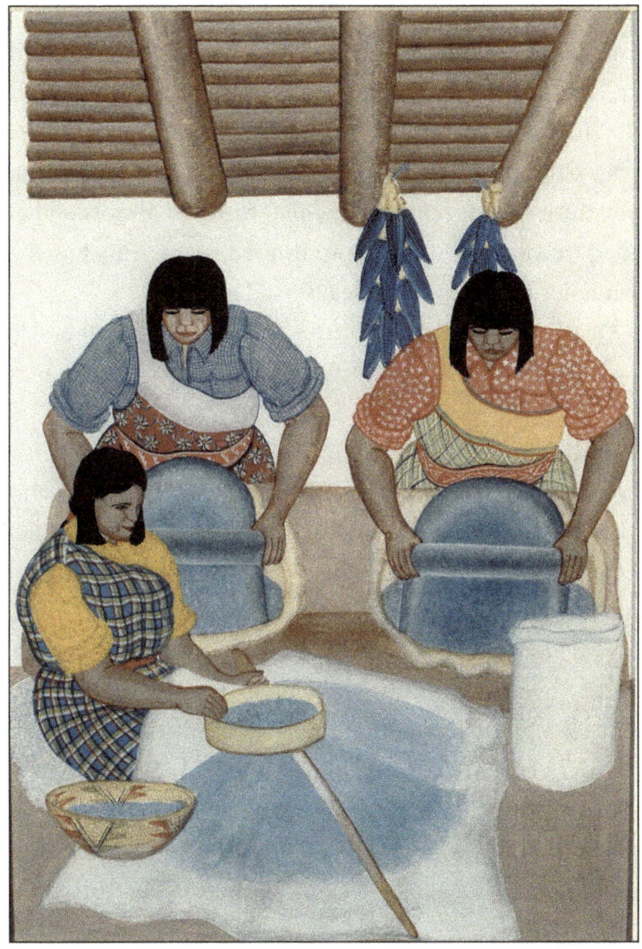

Pablita Velarde, "Grinding Blue Corn," watercolor, Bandelier National Monument

Once married in 1942, Velarde moved to Albuquerque, although always keeping her pueblo home. She raised a son and daughter, by and large as a single mom. Her daughter, Helen Hardin, now deceased, followed in her mother's creative footsteps, although with a different style. Now, as of 2011, her granddaughter, Marguerite Bagshaw, is carrying on the family's art tradition with her own contemporary style and gallery in Santa Fe. Pablita's son, Herbert Hardin, became a pipe fitter by trade and moved into iron sculpture for his creative outlet.

Prior to her death and due to impaired vision, Velarde did less painting and turned her creative energies to making and dressing dolls with traditional clothing typical of each pueblo and tribe. Those dolls quickly became collector's items. Pablita was honored in a number of ways and had numerous one woman shows, including one in the Governor's Gallery in Santa Fe. Even though she did not live in Santa Fe, she was included in the collection of Living Treasures, based on the outstanding person she was. The New Mexico Chapter of the National New Deal Preservation Association also included a reproduction of one of her large paintings from Bandelier as part of its five New Deal Legacy front license plates. When presented to Pablita, she was thrilled, exclaiming, "Now, they will have to see my art work coming and going!" This was typical of the sense of humor Pablita shared with family and friends. Following her death, the Museum of Indian Arts and Culture in Santa Fe created a major exhibit in cooperation with Bandelier, which featured almost all her stored work done at that facility and had been rarely seen due to limited space. This has changed now that the Visitor Center at Bandelier has been remodeled.

LOCATIONS OF NEW DEAL ARTWORK: Bandelier, and other United States Indian Service facilities.

WALKER, W. STUART (1888–1940)

Very little has been found on this artist. He lived in Albuquerque and painted at least six and maybe nine watercolor sketches of forest scenes as part of the Public Works Art Project for the District Office of the U. S. Forest Service which was located in the post office building. The six identified titles were "Fencing," "The Red Gate," "Sawmill," "Five O'Clock," "Bridge Gang," and "Logging." The whereabouts of these watercolors is unknown. He also created a mural in the Old Post Office across from one done by Brooks Willis. Both may have gone to private collections. In 1938 he became a member of Emil Bisttram's Transcendental Artist group and in 1939 he had artwork exhibited in the World's Fair in New York and a Golden Gate Exhibition in San Francisco. One painting is on display in the Golden Library at Eastern New Mexico University in Portales.

LOCATIONS OF NEW DEAL ARTWORK: Albuquerque, Portales; Washington, DC.

WARDER, WILLIAM "WILLIE" (1920–1999)

Born in Mora, New Mexico with a variety of ethnic ancestors, Warder considered himself an American since he was Comanche, Pueblo Indian, Spanish, and English. His grandfather was a wagon master in the very early territorial days. Warder attended school in Raton, graduating in 1940. At age nine he won the opportunity to paint, along with three classmates, two paintings for the children's section in the Raton Library. This was part of a New Deal project, possibly NYA, and many years later he restored two of these youthful paintings about children's books for the library. As an adult, he said that his first painting job was to improve upon the tail of a horse painted by his teacher, Manville Chapman. The first payment he received for a painting job was art supplies (oil paints, brushes, etc.) provided by a local bank and he noted he immediately went up on the east slope of Raton Peak and painted a mural on the largest flat rock face he could find.

He went to the University of New Mexico and later joined the armed forces during World War II and ended up in the South Pacific. He painted all over those islands in USO buildings before returning to the New York Art Institute, University of California at Los Angeles, and other schools. He also studied with some of the New Mexico masters—Berninghaus, Bisttram, Dasburg and Chapman.

He had six daughters, two sons and thirteen grandchildren and lived in Albuquerque most of his adult life.

Warder was primarily a mural painter, feeling that murals are "humanizing our environment." He did murals in numerous locations around New Mexico, including the El Portal Hotel and Yucca Hotels (formerly Swaztika Hotel) in Raton, the Legends Hotel in Angel Fire and other sites. Warder was responsible for starting New Mexico's Artist-in-Residence Program. His daughter Alice Seely became well known for her jewelry, which features the state's petroglyphs.

LOCATIONS OF NEW DEAL ARTWORK: Raton, New Mexico; Washington, DC.

WELLS, CADY (1904–1954)

It is not clear whether Wells was ever a New Deal artist, since he came from a family of financial means, but two of his pieces of art are included in public collections and identified as New Deal. It is possible they could have been done under the auspices of the Public Works of Art Project (PWAP) or the Treasury Section Project, since being on relief was not a prerequisite, or the art may have been donated by some family or friends. Beyond that Wells was a strong supporter of the local artists, particularly the Hispanic artists during his time.

Born in Southbridge, Massachusetts in 1904 to a wealthy family, Wells initially studied music and theater design. He attended Harvard and trained as a concert pianist and early on tried to develop a business career for himself. However at the age of 28 he came to Taos to study painting with Andrew Dasburg and decided on art as a career along with Ward Lockwood and Kenneth Adams. To find his own way in expression, he went to Fogg, Massachusetts in 1933 to learn art history before returning to Taos and Dasburg. He also studied in France and was greatly influenced by the French cathedrals and their stained glass windows. Not happy with Taos, Wells moved to Santa Fe and by 1934 found a secluded spot in Jacona outside of Santa Fe. He worked with architect John Gaw Meem to create a cluster of small buildings where he lived with his six dogs who loved to sing whenever he would play the piano. He was passionate about music and frequently traveled to Chicago to attend the opera. He was a loyal friend to many and reportedly had a wicked but beautiful sense of humor. He was a member of the committee that supported the creation of the *Portfolio of Spanish-Colonial Design in New Mexico.*

Prior to Pearl Harbor, he enlisted in the United States Army Engineers and served in the European Theater Operation (ETO) from D-Day until the end of the war. Upon his return in 1945 the proximity of Los Alamos and atomic bomb research reminded him of the war and seemed to inhibit his painting. In 1949 he moved to St. Croix in the Virgin Islands and in 1950 he donated his large and rare santo collection to the Museum of New Mexico and established E. Boyd as the curator of the Spanish-Colonial Arts Department. He also helped establish the Jonson Gallery at the University of New Mexico. By 1952 he had returned to Jacona but did some traveling and studying in France. A bad heart condition began to limit his abilities to paint and early in 1954 he had two heart attacks, later dying in Santa Fe on November 15, 1954. A significant retrospective exhibition was organized by the Museum of New Mexico and School of American Research in 1956 and toured throughout the country. In 2011 exhibits of his work have been done in Santa Fe and Albuquerque.

LOCATION OF NEW DEAL ARTWORK: Portales—Eastern New Mexico University, Taos Public Schools.

WEST, HAROLD "HAL" (1902–1968)

West was born in Honey Grove, Texas on October 16, 1902 but grew up in Tishamingoe, Oklahoma. During his early years he won first prizes at the county fairs with the best acre of cotton, the best pig and the best painting. At 17 he had a small studio of his own and worked as a commercial artist apprentice between his first and second tries at high school graduation. With the the educational hurdle out of the way, he set out to see the world and had numerous experiences traveling about this country during the severe depression era. He settled in New Mexico in 1920 and lived some twenty years on a ranch south of Santa Fe on Highway 14.

He studied under Vernon Hunter but otherwise was self-taught. He painted realistic scenes of the Southwest depicting ranch life. He also was a print maker and serigrapher, making linoleum cuts and wood cuts of scenes he knew well—many having stories to go with them. In 1938 he got involved again with his painting as part of the New Deal projects in order to feed his growing family and worked on them for two years.

According to his artist son, Jerry West, "Hal loved his art, people and children so in 1950, about the time his five children were in high school, he opened a shop and studio on Canyon Road and became a full-time artist. Before that he had limited his painting to time when he was freer—generally in winter." For this reason, West noted that he generally painted from memory and imagination rather than "on location," because as a part-time naturalistic artist, he did not have time or opportunity to paint what he saw when he saw it. His shop became a popular site for all the local painters to gather, socialize and compare notes on their work.

LOCATIONS OF NEW DEAL ARTWORK: Clayton, Melrose.

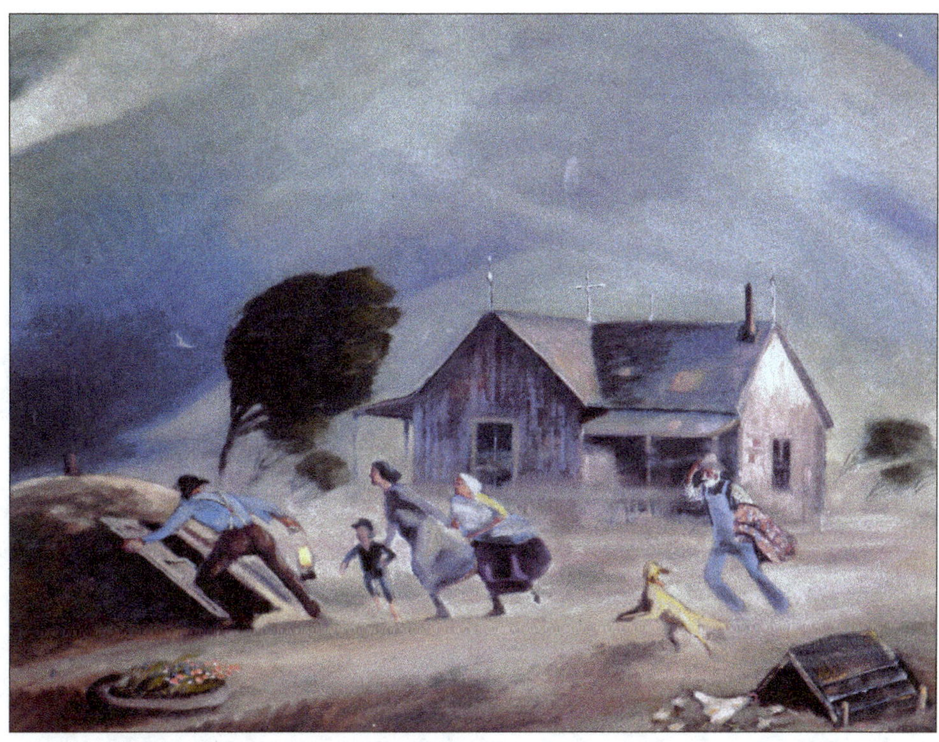

Hal West, "Oklahoma Storm," oil, Clayton School collection. A typical dust storm like those during the Great Depression can be seen here as the family runs to the root cellar to keep from being blown away. Photograph by Pat Berrett.

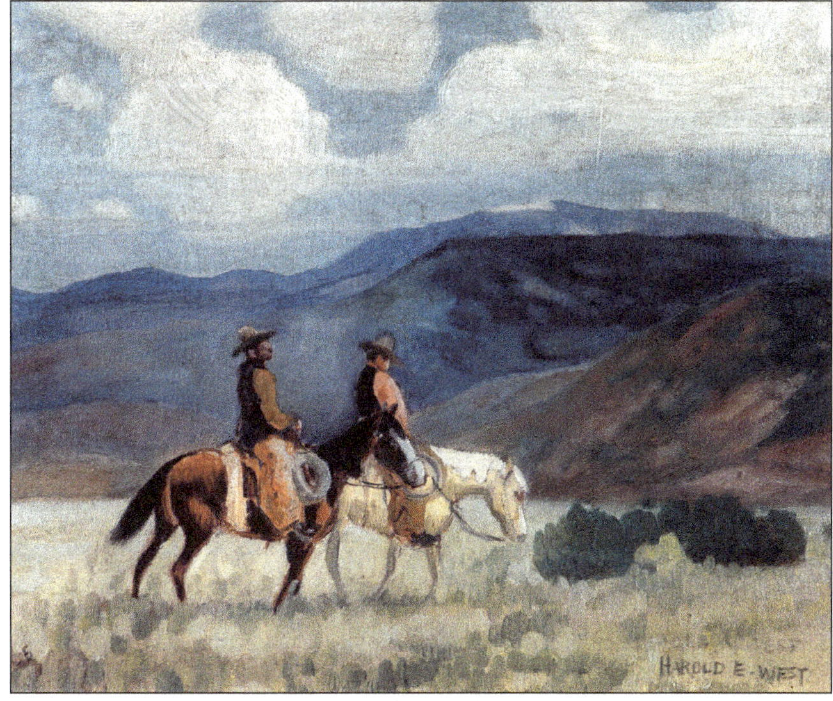

Hal West, "Bored Cowboys," oil, Melrose School Library

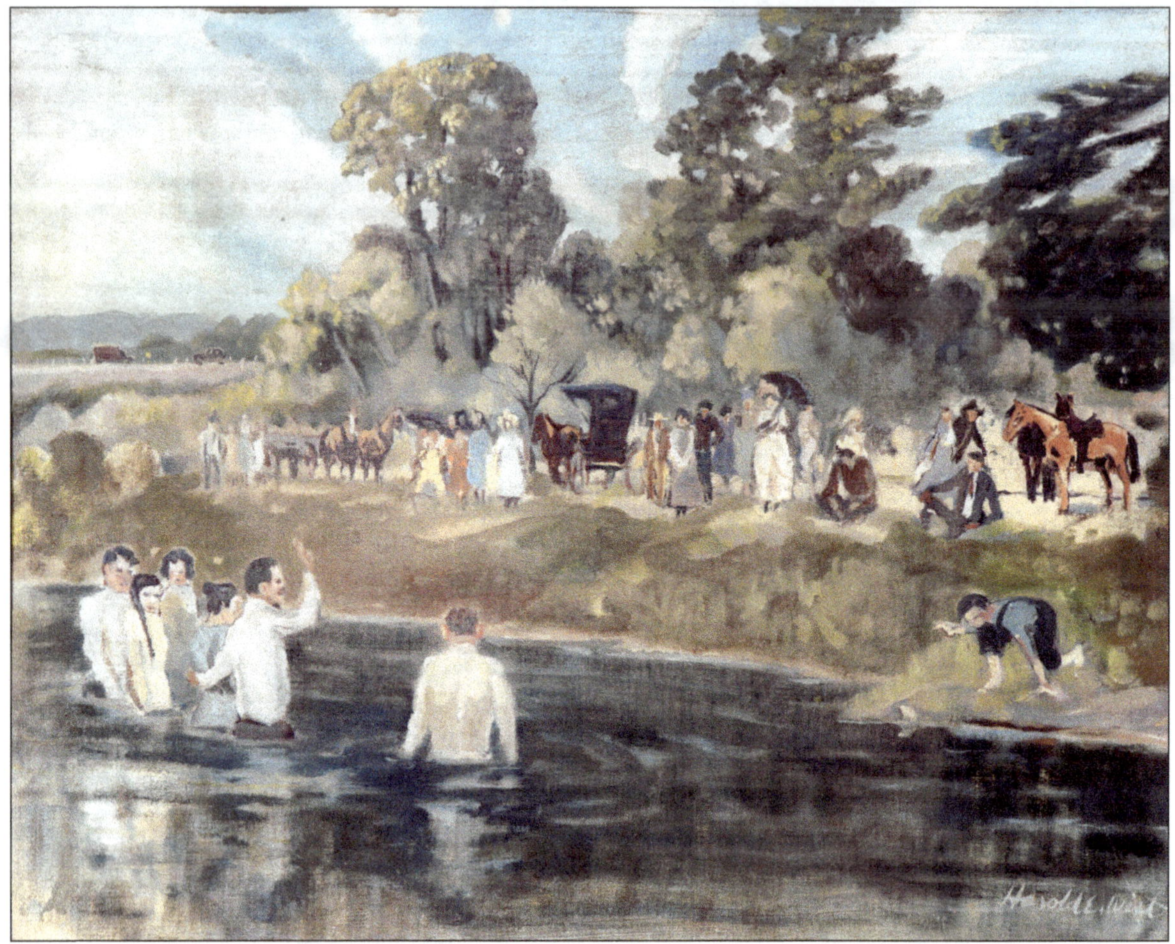

Hal West, "Baptism," oil, Melrose School Library

WHITEMAN, JAMES RIDGELY (1910–2004)

Whiteman was born in Portales, New Mexico January 15, 1910 when the state was still a territory and lived the last years of his life with his daughter Katherine and son-in-law Don McAlavay a few miles outside of Clovis. He considered himself a full blooded American since he had many nationalities represented in his genes. His early ancestors were German. During the New Deal era he was involved with the WPA project for four years and during that time he helped hand paint many of the color plates and assisted his father in the printing of the *Portfolio of Spanish-Colonial Design.* Whiteman also designed an embroidery pattern for the theater curtain in the Melrose school auditorium. Unfortunately, after it was completed by local Melrose and Clovis WPA colcha embroiderers, the auditorium caught fire, destroying the curtain. In Gallup and Albuquerque, Whiteman taught metal craft, including jewelry making, and did research for a book about Hopi kachinas. He was never able to publish the book, due to the controversy over his presenting information not allowed to be shared with the outside world, according to the Native American people.

LOCATION OF NEW DEAL ARTWORK: curtain design for Melrose stage curtain.

WILL, BLANCA (1881–Date Unknown)

Born in Rochester, New York July 1881, Will studied at Rochester Mechanics Institute, the Grande Chaumiere in Paris, and privately with many others. Her work appeared in numerous exhibits and she was listed in *Who's Who in American Art* in 1985.

Will worked in Santa Fe long enough to be included in *Representative Art and Artists of New Mexico*, published by the School of American Research in 1940 and was in another show in 1947 as part of the Santa Fe Fiesta. She painted in oil and watercolor and did sculpture. One source indicated she did a mosaic tile creation in the porch floor of a Hot Springs, New Mexico bath house as part of a New Deal project. This may have been in the State Bathhouse which no longer exists. We have not been able to confirm this but it was the only public owned bathhouse in Hot Springs at that time. Records indicate that she spent a large part of her life in Rochester, New York but she spent her summers in Blue Hill, Maine from 1919 on.

LOCATIONS OF POSSIBLE NEW DEAL ARTWORKS: Albuquerque—University of New Mexico Art Museum, Clayton, Melrose, Truth or Consequences.

WILLIS, BROOKS (1903–1981)

Willis was born in Farmington, New Mexico but lived his early years in Durango and Colorado Springs, Colorado. As a young man he went to Paris to study art but this was interrupted when World War I broke out. He joined some friends when they all decided to enlist in the American Volunteers Ambulance Corps which was attached to the French Army. Upon his return to the United States he enjoyed being the Executive Director of the Harwood Foundation particularly since there were so many fine artists in Taos at that time. This was around 1939 and then he moved to Albuquerque to be an instructor at the University of New Mexico Art Department. In the early 1940s he moved his family to California where they lived for thirty years. The family eventually returned to New Mexico and he continued to paint until his death in 1981.

He created numerous paintings during the WPA activities and another exterior mural at Los Ojos. He joined his good friend, Stuart Walker, in creating a mural for the Bernalillo Courthouse but when that building was destroyed the mural went to a private collection. Another one of his creations was a series of oil on canvas murals over the exits of New Mexico Highlands University's Ilfeld Auditorium. Unfortunately, they were later painted over with five or six coats of white paint. They depicted art, music, drama, health, literature, education, history, and science and were symbolic creations being primarily decorative and quite different from the New Deal work in New Mexico or elsewhere. The National New Deal Preservation Association's New Mexico chapter was finally able to obtain funds to hire Steve Prins, Santa Fe conservator, to remove the white paint. During the restoration, the one depicting the Department of English was determined missing after there was nothing found in the eighth location.

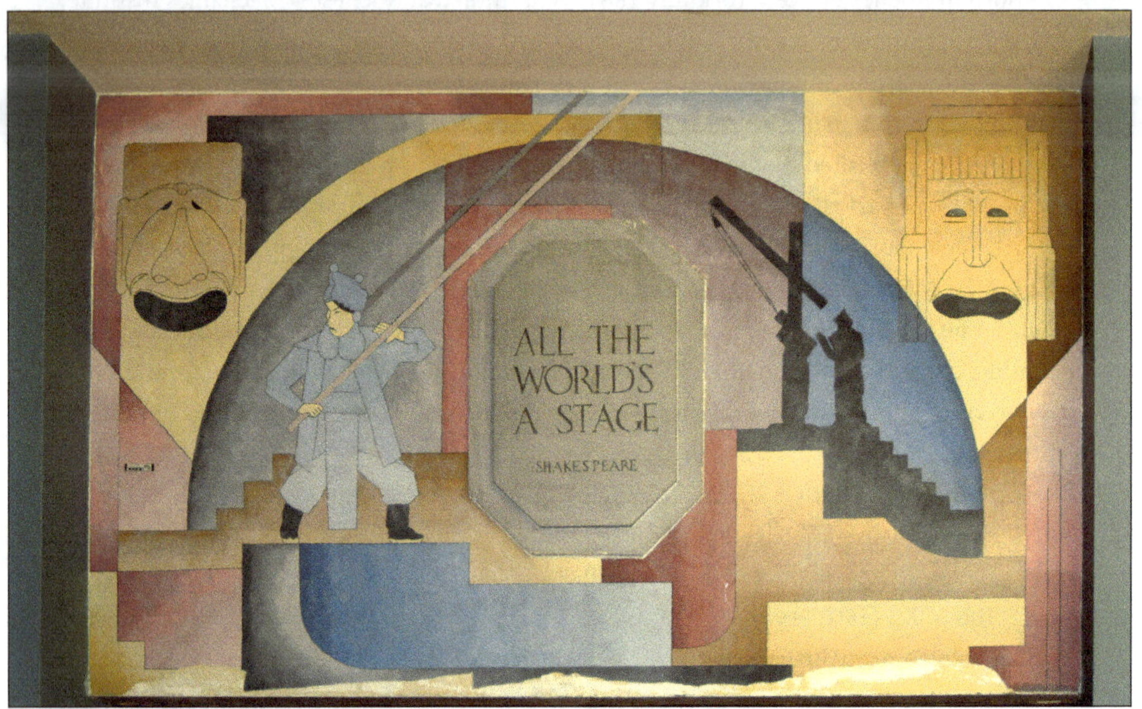

Brooks Willis, "All the World's A Stage," oil, Las Vegas, New Mexico Highlands University. One of the seven murals over the eight doors in the lobby of Ilfeld Auditorium at New Mexico Highlands University after restoration. The Drama Department mural exposed a total of seven murals after the six coats of white paint were removed. Photograph by Charley Akers.

Willis was a representational painter using oils, watercolors, acrylics, and unique collages to portray the world in which he lived. His realism sometimes blended with impressionism as he responded to color and light. An example of this was created in a mural for the old Bernalillo County Courthouse but is missing.

He also taught painting and two of his students and good friends were New Deal artists, Carl Redin and Howard Schleeter. Two of his brothers-in-law were also in the New Deal art projects, Howard Barton and Bill Lumpkins. As of 2011, a collection of his private works can be found at the Gerald Peters Gallery in Santa Fe.

LOCATIONS OF NEW DEAL ARTWORK: Albuquerque—University of New Mexico Art Museum, Carlsbad, Clayton, Gallup, Las Cruces, Las Vegas—Highlands Ilfeld Auditorium, Los Ojos, Portales, Santa Fe; and Washington, DC.

WILLIS, JOSEPH ROY (1876–1960)

Born in Sylvania, Georgia on Thanksgiving Day, November 24, 1876, Willis was once described by Ina Sizer Cassidy in her *New Mexico Magazine* column as "a soldier of fortune for the arts, for he has been a reporter, actor, cartoonist, illustrator, painter of murals and portable art work." After trying newspaper reporting in Atlanta, he decided to try art and moved to New York in 1902–03, studying at the New York School of Art. He studied with Robert Henri, gave chalk talks in vaudeville and then drew cartoons for the *Chicago Inter-Ocean* and in California. While in California he painted backdrops for Universal Studios.

In 1917 he started out for New York again but decided to stay in the Southwest and located himself in Gallup where he was a photographer. While giving tours of the Native American reservations he began sketching many of their inhabitants. Later he used his photographs as a basis of some of his paintings and as postcards, which he sold in his curio shop/studio to tourists.

In 1932 he moved to Albuquerque and was active there for years with various projects, which included painting murals at the Court Cafe on Fourth Street. That building later burned down. He designed homes in the Country Club area and did a home there for his family while also creating and selling post cards depicting Southwest and Native American scenes. In 1936 he was commissioned by the WPA to create seven murals depicting the Spanish settlement of New Mexico. Those works can still be seen in the Gallup High School library.

Another set of three WPA paintings by Willis can be viewed at the Alamogordo Women's Club (a WPA building), and this work has been restored as a project of the New Mexico chapter of the National New Deal Preservation Association. For years he and his wife held parties in the family home for friends and associates. He died in Albuquerque in 1960. He had two daughters, Louise and Emily, and one son, D. F. Willis.

LOCATION OF NEW DEAL ART WORK: Gallup, Alamogordo.

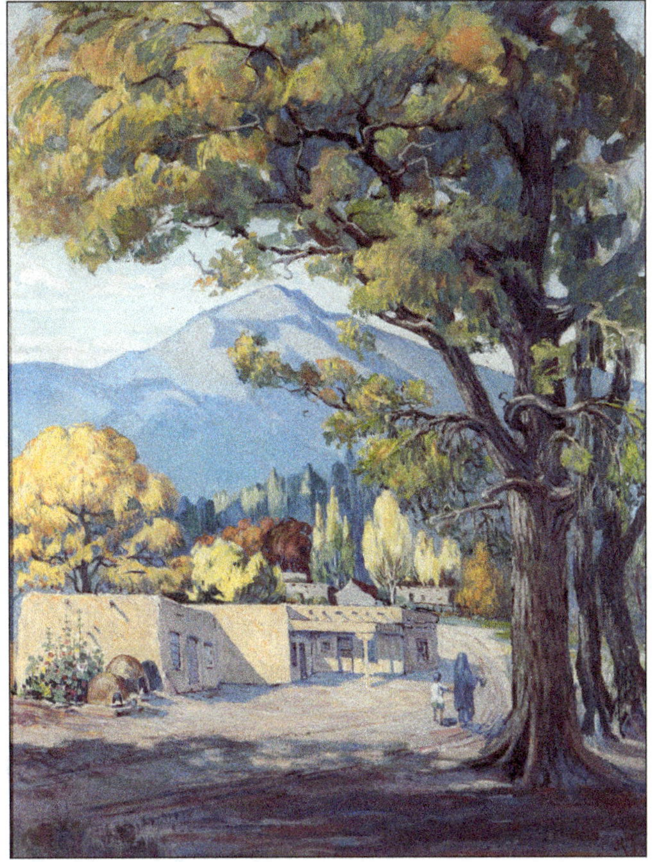

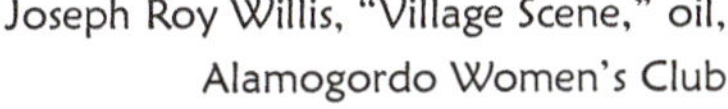

Joseph Roy Willis, "Village Scene," oil, Alamogordo Women's Club

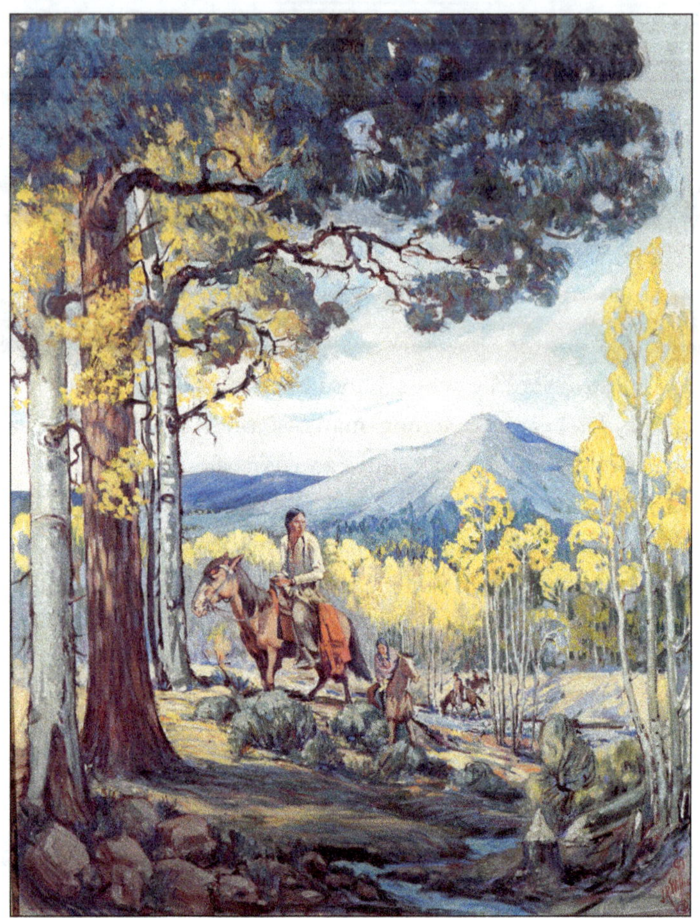

Joseph Roy Willis, "Indian on Horseback" oil, Alamogordo Women's Club

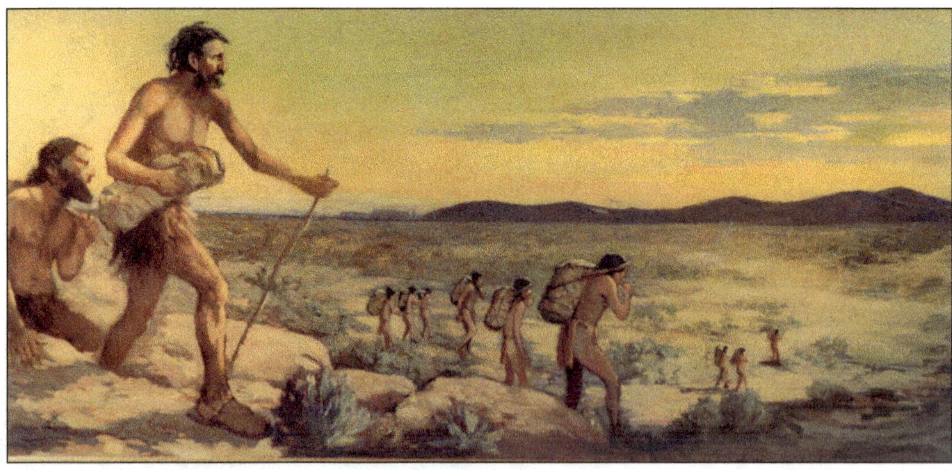

Joseph Roy Willis, "Unclad Explorers," oil, Gallup High Library

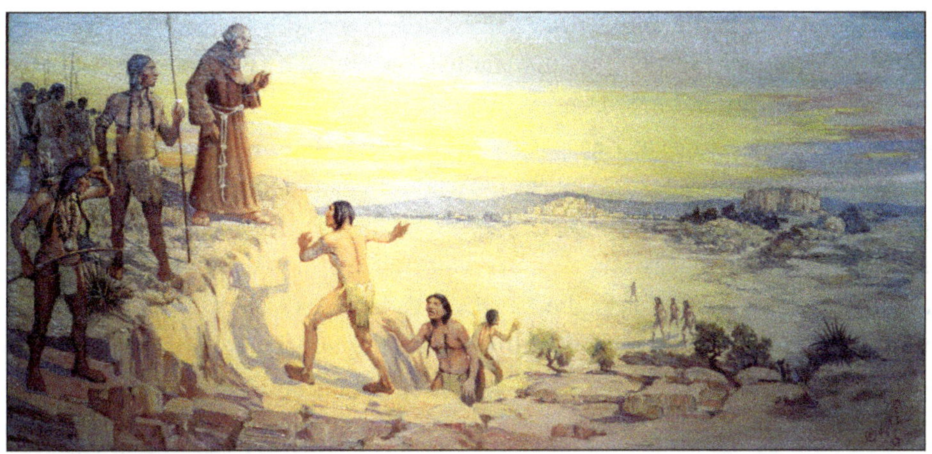

Joseph Roy Willis, "Franciscan Missionaries," oil, Gallup High Library

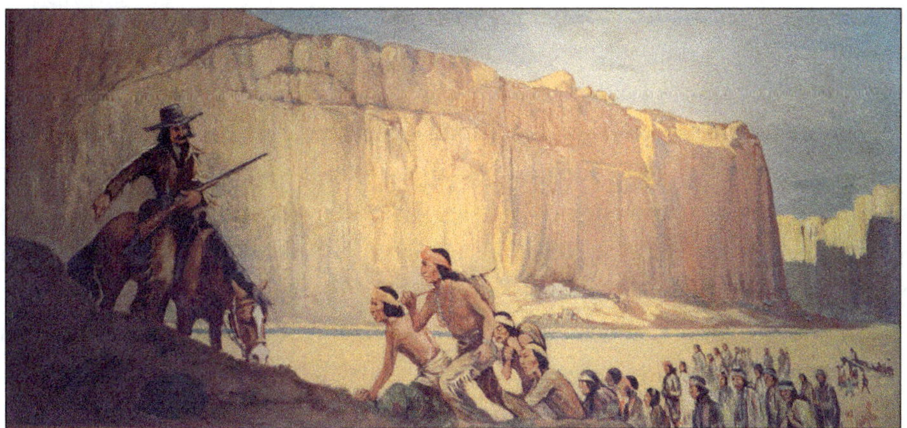

Joseph Roy Willis, "Kit Carson Leading Indians Out of Canyon de Chelly," oil, Gallup High Library

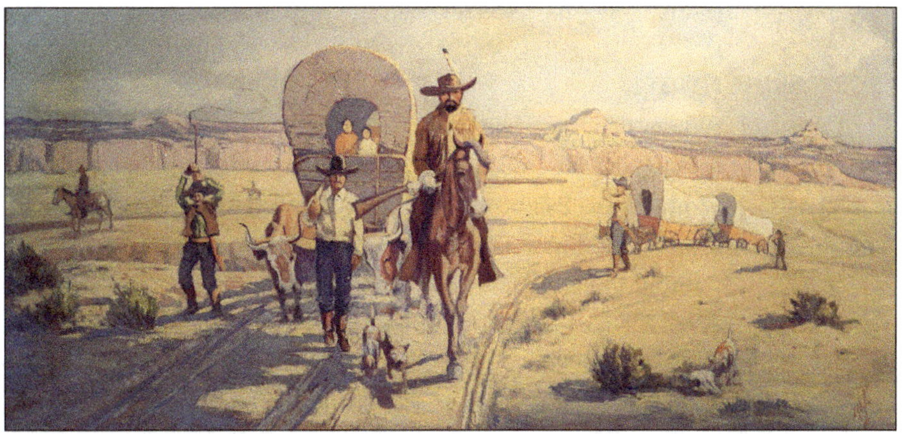

Joseph Roy Willis, "Wagon Train with the Red Rocks," oil, Gallup High Library

WILTON, ANNA KEENER, aka ANNA E. KEENER (1895–1982)

Born in Colorado in 1895, Wilton studied, assisted and taught under Birger Sandzen while receiving her BA and BFA Degrees at Bethany College in Lindsborg, Kansas. She also studied at Chicago Art Institute, Kansas City Art Institute, Detroit School of Design, Colorado State Teacher's College, California College of Arts and Crafts and in Mexico with well known masters in painting, block printing etching, mural painting, lithography, calligraphy and sculpture. She was a member of the U. S. Navy during World War I. In her early career days, she lived in the Gallup area and ran the New Deal Federal Art Center, one of four in the state. From the early twenties she did much to promote the understanding and appreciation of Indian and Spanish art. She became fascinated by the crafts of the Spanish-American people she came to know and while attending a vocational school, she learned how to make her own furniture and santos. Later she completed a survey of colcha embroidery. Her interest in, and respect for, the Navajo land and its people became the inspiration for many of her paintings that won various awards. The research for and creation of, her mural "Zuni Indian Pottery Women" still located in the McKinley County Courthouse became the basis of her Master's degree from the University of New Mexico.

As an art teacher she worked in various states, and in New Mexico this included a stint in a one room school house in Red River all the way to the Head of the Art Department at Eastern New Mexico University in Portales. The latter responsibility she held for many years prior to her retirement. As a New Mexico artist, she was a member of the early Taos art colony, well known in Gallup and Portales and active in Santa Fe upon her move there in 1952. Santa Fe provided the opportunity for her to be surrounded by her grown twin daughters and young granddaughter, to be continually stimulated artistically and to continue her professional activities in the field. Wilton was instrumental in establishing the New Mexico Arts Commission and other art related organizations in the state and southwest region. She died in Santa Fe.

LOCATION OF NEW DEAL ARTWORK: Gallup.

WOOLSEY, CARL E. (1903–1965)

Born April 24, 1903 in Chicago Heights, Illinois, Carl Woolsey moved to Indianapolis with his family as a teenager and later accompanied them to Long Beach, California where he was associated with some of the Pacific Coast artists. While there he and his two brothers, Wood and Jean, established a commercial art studio. For the most part the brothers were self-taught artists and captured many art awards. Carl was curious about the Southwest after seeing the art work of Walter Ufer in a gallery in Indianapolis in 1927 so by summer of that year he was a resident of Taos. By spring he had a southwestern scene painting accepted in the National Academy of Design show in New York. His southwestern landscapes and still life scenes became a trademark and his brother, Wood, soon joined him in Taos creating paintings which included human life scenes. Their varied styles and subjects made for interesting "family" exhibitions and both became popular. Brother Jean also came to Taos and made a name for himself framing art. Carl joined the Army in 1940 and after his discharge lived in New Hampshire. A sister, Mary Jane "Major" Woolsey, was an editor of a parenting magazine for some years. At the time of his death, Carl was residing with Wood in East Strasburg, Pennsylvania.

POSSIBLE LOCATIONS OF NEW DEAL ARTWORK: Carlsbad, Santa Fe; Washington, DC.

ZDNUICH, MIKE (dates unknown)

Zdnuich was one of four junior high students who were chosen to do two murals for the public library in Raton. It is unknown whether he did other artwork. William Warder was the one known of those four to go on with his art.

LOCATION OF NEW DEAL PUBLIC ART: Raton—Arthur Johnson Public Library.

10

YOUNG BOYS BECOME MEN IN THE CIVILIAN CONSERVATION CORPS (CCC) AND CONSERVE OUR NATION'S LANDS AND PARKS

Vincent T. Wathen, Vincente Ximenes and Kathryn A. Flynn

Criteria for getting into the Civilian Conservation Corps (CCC) was specific:

The family had to be destitute.

The young man had to be at least eighteen, although the age was lowered to seventeen. Even then since most families were destitute, the parents often lied about his age to get a young boy into the CCC since most of his monthly pay would be sent home to the family to help cover their needs in caring for the rest of the family.

He had to weigh at least one hundred and seven pounds. Some did not weigh that much and, according to reports, ate a lot of bananas prior to weighing in.

He had to have at least three good masticating teeth, at least one up and one down.

The young man could not have communicable diseases.

On March 31, 1933, just days after being inaugurated, President Franklin D. Roosevelt signed into law the funding for a New Deal program that was arguably the most successful program to come out of the troubled 1930s. There were more than five million young men and World War I veterans out of work at that time, so the CCC program was created to save our young boys by providing employment for this group of able bodied men. It was also a way that Roosevelt and others saw to save our valuable land, which was fast blowing away into the ocean and atmosphere. At the program's closing on June 30, 1942, more than three million young men had passed through the ranks of the CCC in its nine and a third years of existence. From that total, there were fifty-six thousand young men who served in New Mexico and over thirty thousand of them were from New Mexico, while the others were sent to New Mexico from other states.

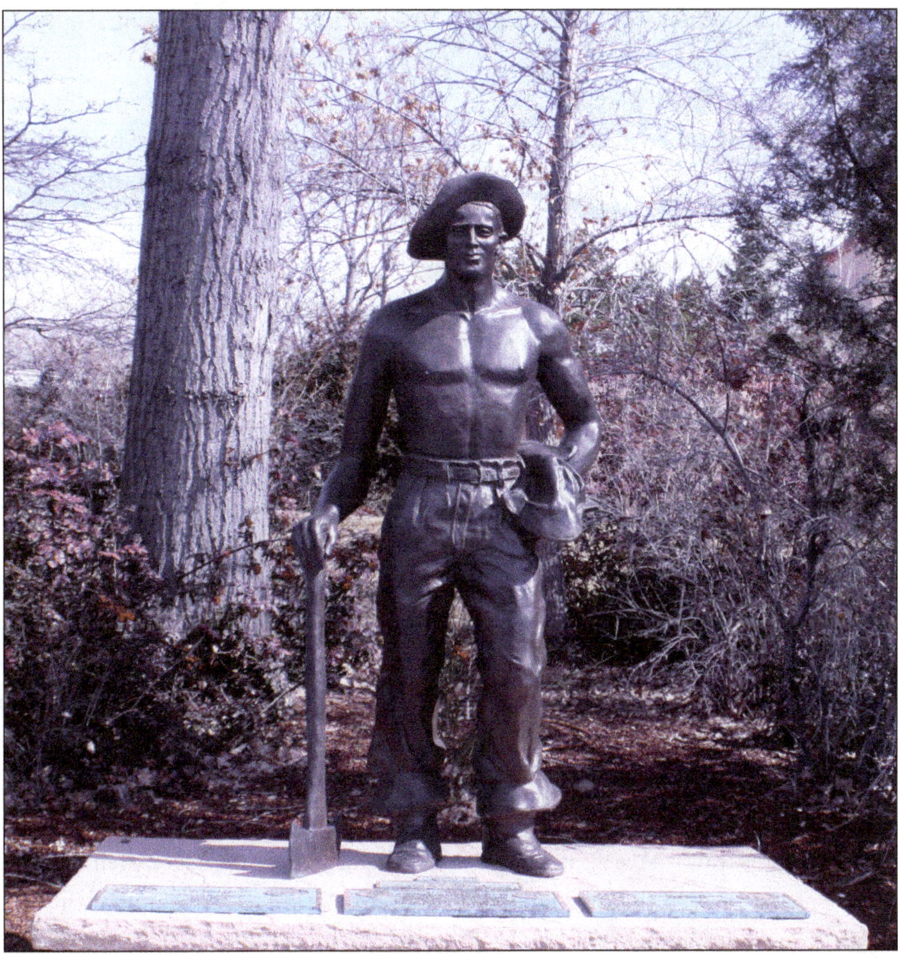

One of these statues honoring the successful work of the Civilian Conservation Corps (CCC) participants stands on the west side of the State Capitol directly across from the Bataan Memorial Eternal Flame monument. Another one is located at the Elephant Butte Damsite near Truth or Consequences. The statue was designed by Sergey Kazaryan in New York and created in a New York foundry. In 2011 there were fifty-eight statues located around the country. This statue at the Capitol was paid for with funds obtained by the New Mexico Chapter of NNDPA from the legislature and personal memorial donations. The one in the Truth or Consequences area was funded by the New Mexico State Parks Division and the Youth Conservation Corps (YCC) a current CCC type program. Photograph by Jan Marfyak.

Once accepted, young men could serve for six months, renewing up to two years. They were frequently sent to areas some distance from their homes. They were paid $1.00 a day, or $30.00 per month. In reality, they received $5.00 a month for their personal expenses and the remaining $25.00 was sent home to their families, in order to help them survive. This was a most appreciated factor, since $25.00 was a large amount each month to help feed the parents and siblings of the CCC boys.

In addition to their work activities, the boys were provided educational opportunities, many receiving their GEDs, as well as being taught a vocational skill. All their clothing, lodging (their own beds), and food were supplied by the federal government, primarily the United States Army, which ran the CCC camps where the boys lived, so that the boys could spend their money on luxuries like sodas, candy, cigarettes and dates if and when they ever got to go into town. Most of the alumni have reported that this program taught them valuable lessons such as discipline, a work ethic, how to get along with other people who might be different from oneself, particularly those from different parts of the country or different cultures with different values. For many, it was the most valuable thing that happened in their young lives.

After finishing their time in the CCC, and particularly after the beginning of the Second World War, these young men were drafted or volunteered to serve in the military and provided the backbone of the armed services—20% of tour military forces—because their experience on the CCC prepared them for military life. Other recruits did not have that advantage. Various generals have said that we could not have won the war without those CCC men.

At this writing, many of those 'boys' are now in their twilight years, while others have passed on. The ones remaining are extremely proud of having been in the CCC, and in 1977 many joined the new CCC Alumni, a non-profit organization named the National Association of CCC Alumni. Their main objective is to "preserve American pride, principles, purpose and progress." Today, the organization has changed its name to the CCC Legacy and desires to recruit, in addition to the dwindling number of alumni, the wives, sons, daughters, grandchildren and friends, to help keep their legacy flag flying. There is an alumni chapter in Albuquerque.

Some states today have similar work and education programs for their young people, but none are at the level of the original CCC program. New Mexico is one of the states that is fortunate to have a similar program, called the Youth Conservation Corps (YCC). It is administered by the New Mexico Department of Energy, Minerals and Natural Resources.

Various Agencies Were Involved

The United States Army 8th Corps was responsible for running camps all over the state. The work activities of the camps were based on the needs in the geographical area and were guided and funded by various federal agencies. Those included the United States Forest Service (FS), United States Soil Conservation Service (SCS), United States Department of Grazing Bureau of Reclamation (BR), and National Park Service (PS). Labeling of the camps included the agency's acronyms, which helped identify the kind of work going on, the numerical order in which the camp began, and the letter N for New Mexico. During the more than nine years that the camps operated in New Mexico, some $1.065 million per month came into this state, which included paying the boys, money going back home and monies going into local towns that provided personnel and supplies—a large win-win arrangement for many in New Mexico.

About the camps

The following data from 1936 was selected to represent the usual locations and activities of the camps.

I. Albuquerque District Camps:

Besides being the District Headquarters, Albuquerque oversaw these camps and offices:

Army Personnel Office, Rio Arriba Sub-District

Co. 1818 (F43N) La Madera
Co. 2843 (SCS3N) Espanola
Co. 2832 (SCS4N) Espanola
Co. 2834 (SCSSN) Espanola
Co. 2831 (F31N) Jemez
Co. 815 (New Mexico-I-N) Espanola
Co. 837 (SCS7N) San Ysidro
Co. 2836 (SCS8N) San Ysidro
Co. 3834 (DG42N) Magdalena
Co. 3837 (SCS9n) Albuquerque
Co. 2837 (SCS-19N) Grants
Co. 833 (SP1N) Santa Fe
Co. 835 (SCS6N) Fort Stanton
Co. 3808 (DG40N) Carrizozo
Co. 814 (F8N) Sandia Park
Co. 3835 (F41N) Corona

Some of the projects that were carried out at these camps are still viable sites around the state today. For example, the New Mexico Co. 815 (originally the F7N group) worked mostly in Bandelier using the existing rope cable way that lowered the supplies and trucks that the boys had to disassemble to send down to the work areas below and then reassemble to carry supplies and build a road back out of Frijoles Canyon. According to records, 2,500,000 pounds of equipment went down the cable way to build all the needed facilities, which are in use today. A steep access road was built in and out of the canyon and a quarry was established, from which stones were taken to use in the buildings that comprise Bandelier National Monument. Note: In 2009 this National Monument started a long overdue renovation of the work done by the CCC and other work done by the Park Service or contractors. The Visitor Center has also been expanded to include a theater area and the exhibit areas visibly enhanced and upgraded. Overall the quality work of the CCC was quite visible during the renovation.

The Soil Conservation and Department of Grazing camps worked on numerous projects to prevent erosion, replant range land, control pests, and stabilize stream watersheds. A significant project was the Rio Puerco watershed, which accounted for holding back 80% of the silt being washed into Elephant Butte Lake.

Co. 833 in Santa Fe constructed the large adobe Southwest Regional Headquarters Building for the National Park Service on Old Santa Fe Trail. It is the largest known adobe office building (24,000 square feet) in the nation—thousands of bricks were made from dirt dug on site. The CCC also did grading and rock work along the Santa Fe River through downtown. Today, people still enjoy this area as a park, as well as a water way.

Those camps, during their stays at the locations indicated, also operated several "side," temporary or seasonal camps at or near project sites. The crews built roads, hiking trails, camp grounds, picnic areas, and other recreational facilities. Notable among them are the facilities in the Sandia and Manzano Mountains built by Co. 1818 and side camps, under the direction of the Forest Service. Other camps near other cities like Santa Fe and Espanola created similar recreational areas in the mountains (Hyde Park camp grounds and ski basin). The Headquarters camp in Albuquerque did major repair on trucks and equipment for the District and operated a cooks and bakers school for the Southwest.

II. Fort Bliss District Camps

The camps in the southern part of New Mexico and Texas were designated primarily out of Las Cruces. Those included:

Co. 3833 (SCS15N) Las Cruces
Co. 3829 (BR39N) Las Cruces
Co. 3832 (DG38N) Radium Springs
Co. 855 (BR54N) Elephant Butte
Co. 3831 (DG37N) Cochillo
Co. 2873 (A4T) Berlino

Company 2873 was located on the Army Target Range in Dona Ana County. The fellows in that camp constructed access roads, and did flood control and erosion work for the area. The most notable work of the other camps and their side camps include the buildings of the Bosque del Apache National Wildlife Refuge, Elephant Butte Lake State Park facilities, landscaping and erosion control, and Pancho Villa State Park.

III. Carlsbad Sub-District Camps

Co. 1830 (BR3N) Carlsbad
Co. 2868 (F37N) Carlsbad
Co. 2842 (DG41N) Lake Arthur
Co. 2845 (DG39N) Tularosa
Co. 1850 (F32N) Mayhill

These camps did work similar to that outlined for the Albuquerque District. They were responsible for Bottomless Lakes State Park, Bitter Lakes National Wildlife Refuge, Sumner Lake State Park, and President's Park in Carlsbad. They built the access trails in Carlsbad Caverns National Park, did the wiring for electric lights in the caverns, and developed a water supply for Rattlesnake Springs. They engaged in flood control and watershed stabilization work along the length of the Pecos River and its tributaries, reforestation of the surrounding mountains and reseeding of much of the grazing land in the area.

IV. Colorado District Camps

These camps served northern New Mexico and moved established companies from Colorado to New Mexico, after completion of their tasks there. Camps were located at or near Raton, Clayton, Farmington, and Bloomfield. They reforested and replanted forest and grazing land and stabilized and built facilities near the ruins of Chaco Canyon. We do not have a complete list of these camps and the works they performed, but it would appear that there were eight or nine major camps and a number of side camps. Archival CCC documents about these activities can be found at the Salmon Ruins Museum in Bloomfield, New Mexico.

Conclusion

All in all, there were fifty-two main camps in New Mexico with about half that many side camps, for a total of about eighty-five general locations around the state. Many camps have been completely destroyed or subsequently covered over by new construction, such as the Carlsbad camps that were obliterated and the grounds now occupied by the Guadalupe Medical Centers. Some of the buildings were torn down or moved elsewhere, leaving only the foundations, generally unmarked and forgotten.

What else did they leave behind in New Mexico? Some of their accomplishments include eight hundred bridges, six hundred sixty dams, numerous state and national parks and monument facilities. They planted six million trees and reseeded thousands acres of grazing land.

In addition to the heavy manual laborers in these camps, it is known that there were artists employed to visually record the efforts put forth by these young men but it has been difficult to identify those artists within the CCC program. However, some of Oden Hullenkremer's New Deal art features activities of the CCC projects like two large images on view at the Conchas Dam Visitor Center featuring the construction activities and another one of the first Director of the National Park Service that hangs in that agency's regional office in Santa Fe which was built by the CCC and WPA. Another painting of young men building with adobes may well be a scene from the construction of that building, and can be viewed at Carrie Tingley Hospital for Crippled Children in Albuquerque. It is titled "Convicts at Work" but closely resembles a photograph from the Park Service building archives. The architecture and enhanced interiors (tinwork, furniture, corbels) of the CCC structures are wonderful examples of the New Mexico folk art so one has to credit them as contributing significantly to New Mexico's art and architecture as well as to its environment.

The impact of the CCC on its generation and subsequent American history is incalculable. The legacy far exceeds a list of good and durable works and convincingly demonstrates the powerful and guiding influence that an ethic can have on a generation and a nation's future.

CCC Worker Statues

Two life-size bronze CCC Worker statues can be found in New Mexico in commemoration of the work that was done by the CCC "boys." One is on the west side of the State Capitol grounds and was made possible with funds from the legislature and private donations to the New Mexico chapter of the National New Deal Preservation Association. Another one is located at Elephant Butte Damsite near Truth or Consequences provided by the New Mexico State Parks and installed by the state's Youth Conservation Corps, the current CCC similar program. These two are part of collection of at least 58 such statues located around the nation as of January 2012. Some states do not have one of these statues while other states have more than one. Most have been funded in memory of members of the various CCC alumni members. Contact the CCC Legacy at www.ccclegacy.org or www.newdeallegacy.org to find out where to order these statues and the cost of same if you would like to have one installed at a memorable site and/or for a memorable person/s.

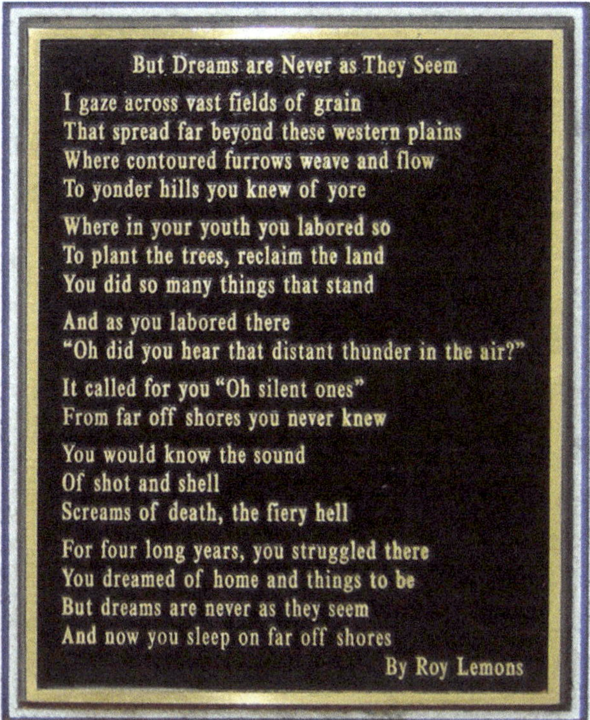

CCC "boy" Roy Lemons did his CCC work stringing telephone lines across the Grand Canyon. While there he met a young woman who was a Fred Harvey Girl hostess and they were later married. After his WWII stint, he had a successful career as an off shore oil driller. Upon retirement he was active in the National CCC Alumni Association and during that time wrote this poem. It is now on their headstone in Grand Canyon cemetery. Photograph by Kathryn A. Flynn.

LIST OF SOME EXISTING CCC STRUCTURES in NEW MEXICO

Northern Portion of State

- Bandelier National Monument
- Chaco Canyon National Historic Park
- Coronado State Monument
- El Vado State Park
- Hyde Park State Park
- Jemez State Monument
- National Park Service Building
- Santa Fe River Park

Central Portion of State

- Bosque del Apache Refuge
- Conchas Dam and Lake State Park
- Oasis State Park
- Juan Tabo Recreation Area
- Kiwanis Hut-Sandia Crest

Southern Portion of State

- Bottomless Lake State Park
- Carlsbad Caverns National Park
- Elephant Butte Damsite
- Sitting Bull Falls
- White Sands National Monument

Author Note: To the best of my knowledge, there were never any female CCC camps in New Mexico. In one reference source* on Eleanor Roosevelt, information indicates that she fought hard to get female CCC camps established. Her success was limited since there were only eighty-six female CCC camps created across the country serving sixty-four hundred women, while at the same time hundreds of thousands of men were working in CCC camps. The women received fifty cents each week, whereas men earned generally one dollar a day or thirty dollars a month.

**Eleanor Roosevelt: First Lady of American Liberalism* by Lois Scharf. Boston: Twayne Publishers, 1987.

APPENDICES

ALL KNOWN NEW DEAL ARTISTS IN NEW MEXICO

Note: Those with an asterisk have brief biographies in Chapter 9.

Abeyta, Emiliano*
Abeyta, Narcisco
Adams, Kenneth Miller*
Appleton, Carolyn TenEyck
Archuleta, Tony
Austin, E. J.
Bahe, Stanley K.*
Bakos, Jozef Gabyrel*
Bakos, Teresa*
Barela, Patrocinio*
Barger, Erik
Barrows, Charles*
Barton, Howard A.*
Baumann, Gustave*
Begay, Harrison*
Berninghaus, Julius Charles*
Berninghaus, Oscar Edmund*
Bisttram, Emil James*
Black, LaVerne Nelson*
Blumenschein, Ernest L.*
Boyd, E. (Van Cleave)*
Burbank, Eldridge Ayer*
Burk, William Emmett
Cassidy, Gerald*
Cervantez, Pedro Lopez*
Chalee, Pop*
Chapman, Manville*
Chosa, Alma
Claflin, Majel*
Connely, Ruth
Cook, Howard*
Cooke, Regina Tatum*
Corson, Stanley B.
Cowboy, Nellie
Crumbo, Woodrow Wilson*
Davey, Randall*
Delgado, Ildebert "Eddie"
Delgado, Francisco*
Detwiller, Frederick Knecht*
Deutsch, Boris*
Dixon, Maynard*
Dorman, John*
Dunton, Nellie G.
Dunton, W. Herbert*
Easton Kitts, Cora*
Egri, Ted
Ellis, Fremont F.*
Emery, Irene*
Everingham, Millard*
Ewing, Louie*
Fleck, Joseph*
Gilbertson, Boris
Gilbertson, Warren*
Goodbear, Paul "Flying Eagle"*
Grant, Blanche Chloe*
Grant, Gordon Kenneth*
Groll, Albert Lorey*
Gutierrez, Evangelio
Gutierrez, Lela
Hearn, Omar W.*
Henderson, William Penhallow*
Hennings, E. Martin*
Herrera, Velino Shije*
Higgins, Victor*
Hogner, Nils*
Hokeah, Jack*
Houser, Allan*
Hullenkremer, Odon*
Hunter, Russell Vernon*
Huntington, Anna Vaughn Hyatt*
Hurd, Peter*
Imhof, Joseph*
Jellico, John*
Jim, Mrs. John
Jones, D. Paul*
Jones, Wendell
Jonson, Raymond*
Kabotie, Fred
Kaplan, Nat*
Kavin, Zena*
Kinlichini, Sally

Kitts, Cora Easton*
Kloss, Gene*
Knee Brook Schnaufer, Gina*
La Grone, Oliver*
Lantz Leighton Goodwin, Juanita*
Lantz, Paul*
Lea, Tom*
Leigh, William Robinson*
Lockwood, John Ward*
Loeffler Lacher, Gisella*
Lopez, José Dolores
Lucero, Abad Eloy*
Lujan, Merina*
Lumpkins, William*
Luna, Maximo L.
Maldonado, Manther
Marfyak, Jan*
Marmon, Miriam
Martinez, Julian*
Martinez, Maria*
Matta, Santiago
McAfee Turner, Ila*
McMurdo, J. T.*
Mead, Ben Carlton*
Meem, John Gaw*
Mirabel, Vincente*
Morang, Dorothy*
Moreno, Samuel J.
Morris, James S.*
Moses, Trinidad*
Moylan, Lloyd*
Mozley, Loren Norman*
Mruk, Walter*
Myers, Datus Ensign*
Nailor, Gerald*
Naranjo, Eulogio
Nash, Willard*
Naumer, Helmuth*
Nordfeldt, Bror Julius Olsson*
Nye, Tinkle Virginia
Ortiz, Max
Pablo, Mrs. Elizabeth
Padilla, Emilio
Parsons, Sheldon*
Payne, Edgar Alwin*
Pena, Tonita*
Phillips, Bert Geer*
Phillips, Mary
Pierce, Edma*
Pillin, Polia Sunockin*
Quintana, Agrapina
Redin, Carl*
Rodriquez, Eliseo*
Rogers, R. Hubert*
Rollins, Warren Eliphalet*
Romero de Romero, Esquipula*
Roybal, Alfonso (Awa Tsireh)
Roybal, Severino
Rush, Olive*
Sanchez, Juan Amadeo*
Sanchez, Ramos*
Saville, Bruce Wilder*
Schleeter, Howard Behling*
Shonnard, Eugenie F.*
Shuster, Will*
Sizes, John Allen
Small Ludins, Hannah Mecklem*
Stewart, Dorothy Newkirk*
Tafoya, Legoria
Terken, John Raymond.
Tamotzu, Chuzo*
Toledo, José Rey*
Trevors, Franz*
Tschudy, Herbert Bolivar*
Tsihnahjinnie, Andy Rey*
Trevors, Franz
Tyndall, Calvin T.*
Ufer, Walter*
Van Soelen, Theodore*
Velarde, Pablita*
Walker, W. Stuart*
Warder, William*
Wells, Cady*
West, Harold*
Whiteman, James Ridgely*
Will, Blanca*
Willis, Brooks*
Willis, Joseph Roy*
Wilton, Anna Keener*
Woolsey, Carl E.*
Zdnuich, Mike

ARTISTS FROM OTHER STATES WITH ART IN NEW MEXICO

For names of the numerous Hispanic artists identified by Tey Mariana Nunn, PhD for her book, *Sin Nombre*, refer to Chapter 7 and/or find the information directly in that publication.

The following names have also been identified by the University of New Mexico Fine Arts Museum as New Deal artists whose works are included in their collection. For the most part the list includes artists who were involved in the New Deal projects in other states. This was confirmed by the U. S. General Services Administration staff in Washington who also has works by these artists in various locations around the country. The best explanation of why these works ended up in New Mexico relates to the likelihood that they were part of a traveling art exhibit and were in Albuquerque at the time the Federal Art Project closed. Rather than going to the expense of having them returned to Washington, the FAP administration determined that the items would remain where they were at the time.

Abelman, Ida
Abramoritz, Albert
Anderson, Carlos
Arnold, A. Grant
Borne, Mortimer
Breslow, Louis
Botts, Hugh
Campbell, Blendon
Chaney, Ruth
Davis, Hubert
Dorman, John
Dwight, Mabel
Eldred, Thomas
Fruhauf, Aline
Good, Minetta
Grossman, Elias
Hicks, William
Kouner, Saul
Kruse, Alexander
Limbach, Russell
Lowell, Nat
Mongel, Max
Murphy, Minnie Lois
Nooney, Ann
Parish, Betty
Sanger, William
Skolfield, Raymond
Steffen, Bernard
Supfer, Blanche
Wahl, Theodore
Weissbuch, Oscar

ARTISTS AND CRAFT PERSONS WHOSE WORK WENT TO THE UNITED STATES INDIAN SERVICE

Note: Very little is known about the whereabouts of the artwork these artists created during their time on New Deal programs.
In some cases, little is known about some of the artists themselves.

ARTISTS:

Abeyta, Emiliano
Archuleta, Tony
Connely, M. Ruth (see Chapter 9)
Herrera, Velino (see Chapter 9)
Hokeah, Jack
Pena, Tonita (see Chapter 9)
Toledo, José Rey (see Chapter 9)
Tsihnahjinnie, Andy (see Chapter 9)
Tyndall, Calvin
Velarde, Pablita (see Chapter 9)

COPYISTS:
(worked on *Portfolios*)

Appleton, Carolyn TenEyck
Chosa, Alma
Corson, Stanley B.
Delgado, Jr., S.
Dunton, Nellie G.
Marmon, Miriam
Sizer, John Allen

POTTERS:

Gutierrez, Evangelio
Gutierrez, Lela Naranjo
Naranjo, Eulogia (see Chapter 9)
Quintana, Agrapina (see Chapter 9)

TIN SMITHS:

Delgado, Francisco and Eddie (see Chapter 9)

WEAVERS:

Bah
Cowboy, Nellie
Jim, Mrs. John
Kinlichini, Sallie
Pablo, Mrs. Elizabeth
Phillips, Mary

WOOD CARVERS:
Lopez, José Dolores (Refer to *Sin Nombre*)
Padilla, Emilio (see Chapter 9)

ARTWORKS AT THE NATIONAL MUSEUM OF AMERICAN ART, SMITHSONIAN INSTITUTION CREATED BY NEW MEXICO NEW DEAL ARTISTS

Note: An asterisk denotes New Deal Art

Adams, Kenneth
- "Harvest"
- "Juan Duran"*
- "Deer Track"

Barela, Patrocinio
- Nine carvings*

Barrows, Charles
- "Crosses"*

Baumann, Gustave
- Four prints

Berninghaus, Oscar
- Mural study for Phoenix Post Office*
- "Red Peppers"

Bisttram, Emil James
- "Justice Tempered with Mercy" (Mural in old US Federal Courthouse, Albuquerque)*
- "Justice Tempered with Mercy" (Mural Study in Roswell Museum and Art Center)*
- "Upward"

Black, La Verne Nelson
- "Jicarilla Apache Fiesta"

Cervantez, Pedro
- "Los Privados"*
- "View of Artist's Home'*

Deutsch, Boris
- "Indian Bear Dance" (Mural in Truth or Consequences post office)*
- "Mother and Child" Portrait - Man
- "Sleeping Woman" (private)
- "The Tailor"

Dunton, W, Herbert
- "Fall in the Foothills"*
- "The Enemies' Horses"

Goodbear, Paul
- "Flying Eagle"
- "Buffalo Dance Oklahoma"

Henderson, William Penhallow
- "Alice in Wonderland Series"

Hennings, Ernest Martin
- "Homeward Bound"*
- "Riders at Sunset"

Herrera, Velino Shije
    "Bronco Busting"
    "Calf Roping"
    "Comanche Dance"
    "Story Teller"
Hurd, Peter
    "Big Whit Whitaker"
    "Day's Work"
    "The Night Watchman"
    "Windmill Well at Night"
    "Untitled"
Jonson, Raymond
    "Monument to Sound"*
    (Four paintings not WPA)
Kloss, Gene
    (Five paintings not WPA)
    "Midwinter in the Sangre de Cristo"*
Lockwood, Ward
    (Four paintings believed to be WPA)*
Martinez, Maria and Julian
    Three pottery pieces*
McAfee, Ila
    "Mountain Lions"*
Moylan, Lloyd
    (Three works)*
Nordfeldt, B. J. O.
    (60 private pieces)
Redin, Carl
    "A Madrid Coal Mine, New Mexico"
Schleeter, Howard B.
    "Mexican Landscape"*
Toledo, José Rey
    "A Stick Race"*
Tsihnahjinnie, Andy
    "Navajo Women"
Ufer, Walter
    "Callers"
Van Soelen, Theodore
    "Buffalo Range-Study" for Portales Post Office*
Warder, William
    "Sandia Mountains, New Mexico"*
Willis, Brooks
    "Country Store"

Other artists from New Mexico are also included in this collection.

FEDERAL / STATE SUPPORTED VISUAL ARTS PROGRAMS IN NEW MEXICO

PUBLIC WORKS OF ART PROJECT (PWAP)

December 1933–June 1934

National Director: Edward Bruce
Region 13: Arizona and New Mexico Regional Director: Jesse Nusbaum
Arizona Art Coordinator: Howe Williams
New Mexico Area Coordinator: Gustave Baumann
Indian Division: Datus Myers

TREASURY SECTION OF PAINTING AND SCULPTURE (THE SECTION)

October 1934–October 1938

National Director: Edward Bruce
Region 13: Arizona and New Mexico

TREASURY RELIEF ART PROJECT (TRAP)

July 1935–June 1939

National Director: Olin Dows
Region 13: Arizona and New Mexico
Regional Director: Jesse Nusbaum
Southern New Mexico Supervisor: Jesse Nusbaum
Northern New Mexico Supervisor: Emil Bisttram

WORKS PROGRESS ADMINISTRATION FEDERAL ART PROJECT (WPA/FAP)

August 1935–September 1939

National Director: Holger Cahill
Regional Supervisor for Southwest States (7): Joe Danysh
Regional Advisor Region 5: (Arizona, New Mexico, Colorado, Utah, Wyoming) Donald Bear
Arizona Supervisor: Mark Voris
Phoenix Federal Art Center Director: Philip Curtis
New Mexico Director: Russell Vernon Hunter
Roswell Federal Art Center Director: Roland Dickey
Melrose Federal Art Center Director: Martha Kennedy

Las Vegas Federal Art Center Director: Mary E. (Toni) Thoburn
Gallup Federal Art Center Director: Mary E. (Toni) Thoburn and Anna Keener
Indian Project: John Collier, Sr.

WORK PROJECTS ADMINISTRATION – ART PROGRAM (WPA FEDERAL ART PROGRAM)

September 1939–March 1942

National Director: Holger Cahill
Regional Supervisor for Southwest States: Joe Danysh
Regional Advisor Region 5: Arizona, New Mexico, Colorado, Utah, Wyoming: Donald Bear
Arizona Superintendent: Philip Curtis, Thomas Wardell
New Mexico Director: Russell Vernon Hunter

GRAPHIC SECTION OF THE WAR SERVICES DIVISION

March 1942–April 1943

National Director: Holger Cahill

OTHER FEDERALLY FUNDED NEW DEAL PROGRAMS

(Not limited to Art and not a complete list)

Civilian Conservation Corps (CCC), 1933–1942
Public Works Administration (PWA), 1933–1939
Federal Emergency Relief Administration (FERA), 1933–1934
Civil Works Administration (CWA), 1933–1934
National Youth Administration (NYA), 1933–1940
Federal Deposit Insurance Corporation (FDIC), 1933 to the present
Historic Architectural Building Survey (HABS), 1933 to the present
WPA Federal Art Project (FAP), 1935–1942. State Director, R.Vernon Hunter
WPA Federal Writers Project (FWP), 1935–1939. State Director, Ina Sizer Cassidy, Alice C. Henderson
WPA Federal Theater Project (FTP), 1935 (none in New Mexico)
WPA Federal Music Project (FMP), 1935–1943. State Director, Helen Chandler Ryan
WPA Historical Records Survey (HRS), 1935–1939
Social Security Administration (SSA), 1935 to the present
Rural Electric Administration (REA), 1935 to the present
Soil Conservation Service (SCS), 1935 to the present
Farm Security Administration (FSA) Photography project, 1937–1942

NEW DEAL PROGRAM REFERENCES

BOOKS/CATALOGS:

Adams, Clinton. *Printmaking in New Mexico 1880–1990.* Albuquerque: University of New Mexico Press. 1991.

Artists of the 20th Century. New Mexico Museum of Fine Art Collection. Museum of Fine Arts. Santa Fe: Museum of New Mexico Press, 1992.

Barnhart, Jan Dodson. *The Pueblo Revival Architecture of John Gaw Meem.* Albuquerque: Albuquerque Museum Foundation.

Bermingham, Peter. *The New Deal in the Southwest: Arizona and New Mexico.* Tucson: The University of Arizona Museum of Art, 1980.

Bickerstaff, Laura M. *Pioneer Artists of Taos.* Denver: Sage Books, 1955, Also Reprint Ed. Denver: Old West Publishing Co., 1985.

Biebel, Charles. *Making the Most of It, Public Works in Albuquerque During the Great Depression, 1929–1942.* An Albuquerque Museum History Monograph. The Albuquerque Museum, 1986.

Braeman, John, Robert H. Bremmer, and David Brody, eds. *The New Deal,* Vol. 2: *The State and Local Levels.* 2 vols. Columbus: Ohio State University Press, 1975.

Broder, Patricia J. *Taos: A Painter's Dream.* Boston: New York Graphic Society, 1980.

Brown, Lorin W., with Charles L. Briggs and Marta Weigle. *Hispano Folklife of New Mexico: The Lorin W. Brown Federal Writers' Project Manuscripts.* Albuquerque: University of New Mexico Press, 1978.

Burchill, Mary D. *Lady of the Canyon: Evelyn Cecil Frey.* Otowi Crossing Press, 2001

Cahill, Holger. *New Horizons in American Art.* New York: Museum of Modern Art, 1936.

Coke, Van Deren. *Taos and Santa Fe: The Artist's Environment: 1882–1942.* Albuquerque: University of New Mexico Press for the Amon Carter Museum of Western Art, 1963.

Cordova, Gilberto Benito, compiler. *Bibliography of Unpublished Materials Pertaining to Hispanic Culture in the New Mexico WPA Writers Files.* Santa Fe: New Mexico State Department of Education, December, 1972.

Dickey, Roland. *New Mexico Village Arts.* Albuquerque: University of New Mexico Press, 1949.

Dunn, Dorothy. *American Indian Paintings of the Southwest and Plains Areas.* Albuquerque: University of New Mexico Press, 1968.

Eldredge, Charles C. Schimmel, Julie, & Truettner, Wm. H. *Artists in New Mexico 1900–1945: Paths to Taos and Santa Fe.* New York: Abbeville Press, for the National Museum of American Art, Smithsonian Institution, Washington, DC 1986.

Fisher, Reginald, compiler and editor. *An Art Directory of New Mexico. For the School of American Research and the University of New Mexico.* Albuquerque: University of New Mexico Press.

Foster, Barbara Spencer. *Fremont Ellis, Last of Los Cinco Pintores of Santa Fe.* Santa Fe: Sunstone Press, 2010.

Garmhausen, Winona. *History of Indian Arts Education in Santa Fe.* Santa Fe: Sunstone Press, 1988.

Griffin, Warren. *A Circle of Light.* Unpublished biographical manuscript on Warren Rollins. Santa Fe: New Mexico State Records and Archives. Miscellaneous Records / Miscellaneous Persons.

Gordon, Linda. *Dorothea Lange: A Life Beyond Limits.* London/New York: W. W. Norton & Company, 2009.

Hagerty, Donald. *Desert Dreams, The Art and Life of Maynard Dixon.* Layton, Utah: Gibbs Smith Publishers, Peregrine Smith Books. 1993.

Hastings, Peter. ed. *Who's Who in American Art.* Sound View Press, 1985.

Hefner, Loretta L. comp. *The WPA Historical Records Survey: A Guide to the Unpublished Inventories,* Indexes and Transcripts. Chicago: Society of American Archivists, 1980.

Hewett, Edgar L. *Paths to Taos and Santa Fe.* Washington. Smithsonian Institution.

——— *Representative Art and Artists of New Mexico.* Santa Fe: School of American Research, Museum of New Mexico, 1940.

Hoefer, Jacqueline. *A More Abundant Life, New Deal Artists and Public Art in New Mexico.* Santa Fe: Sunstone Press, 2003.

Hooker, Van Dorn. *Only in New Mexico: An Architectural History of the University of New Mexico. The First Century, 1889–1989.* Albuquerque: University of New Mexico Press, 2000.

Howard, Donald S. *The WPA and Federal Relief Policy.* New York: Russell Sage Foundation, 1943.

Hyde, Hazel. *Maria Making Pottery.* Santa Fe: Sunstone Press, 1973.

Hyer, Sally. *One House, One Voice, One Heart, Native American Education at the Santa Fe Indian School.* Albuquerque: Museum of New Mexico Press, 1990.

Kimbro, Harriet. *Tamotzu in Haiku.* Santa Fe: Sunstone Press, 1977.

Kloss, Gene, and Phillips Kloss (text). *Gene Kloss Etchings.* Santa Fe: Sunstone Press, 1981.

Kloss, Phillips, and Gene Kloss (illustrations). *The Great Kiva, A Poetic Critique of Religion.* Santa Fe: Sunstone Press, 1980.

Light & Color, Images from New Mexico. Masterpieces from the Collection of the Museum of Fine Arts, Museum of New Mexico. Introduction by Norman A. Geske, Director, Sheldon Memorial Art Gallery, University of Nebraska-Lincoln. Museum of New Mexico Press, 1981.

Luhan, Mabel Dodge. *Taos and its Artists.* New York: Duell, Sloan and Pearce, 1947.

Manno, Lois. *Visions Underground: Carlsbad Caverns Through the Artist's Eye.* Albuquerque: Rio Grande Books, 2009.

Marling, Karal Ann. *Wall to Wall America: A Cultural History of Post Office Murals in the Great Depression.* Minneapolis: University of Minnesota Press, 1982.

Marriott, Alice. *Maria the Potter of San Ildefonso.* Norman: University of Oklahoma Press, 1948.

May, Esther V. Cordova. *Antes: Stories from the Past, Rural Cuba, New Mexico, 1769–1949.* Santa Fe: Sunstone Press, 2011.

McDonald, William F. *Federal Relief Administration and the Arts: The Origins and Administrative History of the Arts Projects of the Works Progress Administration.* Columbus: Ohio State University Press, 1969.

McKinzie, Richard D. *The New Deal for Artists.* Princeton: Princeton University Press, 1973.

Mecklenburg, Virginia. *Art in Federal Buildings. Vol. 1. Mural Designs 1934–36.* Bruce & Watson Publishing Co.

——— *The Public as Patron.* College Park: University of Maryland Press, 1979.

Melzer, Richard. *Coming of Age In the Great Depression:The Civilian Conservation Corps Experience in New Mexico, 1933–1942.* Yucca Tree Press, 2000.

Minton, Charles Ethridge (State Supervisor). *Guide to 1930s New Mexico: A Guide to the Colorful State.* Compiled by the Workers of the Writers Program of the WPA in the State of New Mexico. American Guide Series. Foreword by Clinton P. Anderson. First Edition, New York: Hastings House Publishers.1940. Sponsored by the Coronado Centennial Commission and University of New Mexico. Current Edition, Phoenix: University of Arizona Press. 1989.

Morris, Margaret. *Masterworks of the Taos Founders.* Gerald Peters Gallery Catalog. September 10 through November 25, 1984.

Nabokov, Peter. *Architecture of Acoma Pueblo: The 1934 Historic American Buildings Survey Project.* Santa Fe: Ancient City Press, 1985.

Nelson, Mary C. *The Legendary Artists of Taos.* New York: Watson Guptill Publications, 1980.

Nunn, Tey Marianna. *Sin Nombre: Hispana & Hispano Artists of the New Deal Era.* Albuquerque. University of New Mexico Press, 2001.

O'Connor, Francis V. *Federal Support for the Visual Arts: The New Deal and Now.* Greenwich, Connecticut: New York Graphic Society, 1969.

——— *Art for the Millions: Essays from the 1930s by Artists and Administration of The WPA Federal Art Project.* Boston: New York Graphic Society, 1973.

——— *Federal Art Patronage 1933–1943.* College Park: University of Maryland, 1966.

Ostrander Dawdry, Doris. *Artists of the American West I-111*: Sage Books, Swallow Press, Inc., 1985.

Park, Marlene & Markowitz, Gerald E. *New Deal for Art.* Gallery Association of New York State, 1977.

——— *Democratic Vistas: Post Offices and Public Art in the New Deal.* Philadelphia: Temple University Press, 1984.

Porter, Dean A. *Victor Higgins: An American Master.* South Bend: Snite Museum. Museum of Art Notre Dame, Peregrine Smith Books, 1975.

Reid, J. T. *It Happened in Taos.* Albuquerque: University of New Mexico Press, 1946.

Reily, Nancy Hopkins, and Lucille Enix. *Joseph Imhof, Artist of the Pueblos.* Santa Fe: Sunstone Press, 1998.

Robertson, Edna & Nestor, Sarah. *Artists of Canyons and Caminos: Santa Fe, the Early Years.* Salt Lake City: Peregrine Smith Inc. 1976.

Samuels, Peggy & Harold. *The Illustrated Biographical Encyclopedia of Artists of the American West.* New York: Doubleday & Co., Inc., 1976.

Schimmel, Julie & White, Robert R. *The Taos Art Colony.* Albuquerque: University of New Mexico Press, 1994.

Sheppard, Carl D. *Creator of the Santa Fe Style: Isaac Hamilton Rapp, Architect.* Albuquerque: University of New Mexico Press. 1988.

——— *The Saint Francis Murals of Santa Fe, The Commission and the Artists.* Santa Fe: Sunstone Press, 1989.

Short, C.W. & Stanley-Brown, Rudolph. *Public Buildings: Architecture Under the Public Works* . Volume 1. Introduction by Richard G. Wilson, Da Capo Press, Inc., New York, 1986.

Snodgrass, Jeanne O. *American Indian Painters: A Biographical Directory.* Contributions from the Museum of the American Indian. Heye Foundation, Vol. 21, Part 1. New York: Museum of American Indian, Heye Foundation, 1969.

Taggert, Sherry Clayton & Schwartz, Ted. *Paintbrushes and Pistols, How the Taos Artists Sold the West*. Santa Fe: John Muir Publications, 1990.

Tanner, Clare Lee. *Southwest Indian Painting, A Changing Art*. Tucson: University of Arizona Press, 1957, 1973.

Taylor, Anne. *Southwestern Ornamentation & Design, The Architecture of John Gaw Meem*. Santa Fe: Sunstone Press, 1989.

The New Deal Art Projects. *An Anthology of Memoirs*. Washington, DC. Smithsonian Institution Press, 1972.

Udall, Sharyn Rohlfsen. *Modernist Painting in New Mexico 1913–1935*. Albuquerque: University of New Mexico Press, 1984.

——— *Santa Fe Art Colony 1900–1942*. Gerald Peters Gallery Catalog. July 1–August 8, 1987.

United States General Services Administration. *WPA Artwork in Non-Federal Repositories*. Washington, DC: GSA Public Building Service. Cultural Affairs Division, Fine Arts Program, May 1996, 1999.

Wachs, Mary, Project Editor-Numerous Contributors. *Recording A Vanishing Legacy: The Historic American Buildings Survey in New Mexico 1933–Today*. Santa Fe: Museum of New Mexico Press, 2001.

Weigle, Marta & Larcombe, Claudia and Sam. *Hispanic Arts and Ethno History in the Southwest*. Santa Fe: Ancient City Press, 1983.

———, and Fiore, Kyle. *Santa Fe and Taos, The Writer's Era 1916–1941*. Santa Fe: New Edition, Sunstone Press. 2008.

——— *New Mexico Artists and Writers: A Celebration*. Santa Fe: Ancient City Press, 1940.

Whisenhunt, Donald W. *New Mexico Courthouses*. El Paso: Texas Western Press, University of Texas at El Paso, 1979.

White, Charlotte. *Greatness in the Commonplace, The Art of Boris Gilbertson*. Santa Fe: Sunstone Press, 1988.

Witt, David. *The Taos Artists, Historical Narrative and Bibliographical Dictionary*. Ewell Fine Art Publications, 1984.

——— and Gonzales, Edward. *Spirit Ascendent: The Art and Life of Patrocinio Barela*. Santa Fe: Red Crane Books, 1996.

Wroth, William, ed. *Russell Lee's FSA Photographs of Chamisal and Penasco. New Mexico*. Santa Fe: Ancient City Press; Colorado Springs: Taylor Museum of the Colorado Springs Fine Arts Center, 1985.

ARTICLES/PAPERS:

Note: Where the author of an article is unknown, the paper is referenced by the town being discussed.

Numerous Papers in the WPA Reports/Records. *New Mexico State Records and Archives Center*, and Record Group 69, Civil Records Section. *National Archives*, Washington, DC. Numerous papers and correspondence.

Bates, Zelpha. "A Homemaking Department Built From Community's Own Resources," *Practical Home Economics*. December 1939.

Baumann, Gustave. "A Retrospect of Work and the Artists Employed in the Thirteenth Region Under the Public Works of Art Project." WPA Reports/Records. *New Mexico State Records and Archives.*

Bisttram, Emil. "Abstract Memories, Transcendental Groups." *Albuquerque Journal*, August 29, 1982.

Bisttram, Emil. "WPA Murals-Fine Art From Hard Times." *New Mexico Magazine*, November 1982.

Bruce, Edward. "Implications of the Public Works of Art Project, American Scene in All Its Phases." *American Magazine of Art*, March 1934.

Bulow, Ernie. "Depression Art Not Wallpaper." *Gallup Independent,* January 18, 1990.

Campbell, Suzan & D'Emilio, Sandra. "Modern Women in Taos," *Antiques & Fine Art*, July/August 1991.

Campbell, Suzan. "Aesthetic Energies, Early Women Traditionalists in Taos,"*Antiques and Fine Art*, September/October 1991.

Chapman, Manville. "Blazed Trails." A series of Colfax County historical narratives based on the mural paintings in the Shuler Auditorium of Raton, New Mexico, done under PWA project and written by the artist, Manville Chapman. Copyright, 1935.

Cassidy, Ina Sizer. "Memorial Library, Las Cruces." Art and Artists of New Mexico. *New Mexico Magazine*, April 1938.

——— "Blumenschein in Retrospect. Art and Artists of New Mexico." *New Mexico Magazine,* July 1948.

——— "Teresa Bakos. Art and Artists of New Mexico." *New Mexico Magazine,* March 1939.

——— "Adventures in Tin. Art and Artists of New Mexico." *New Mexico Magazine,* August 1937.

——— (Numerous other articles featuring New Deal artists were written by Cassidy in her monthly column, "Art and Artists of New Mexico," of *New Mexico Magazine.*)

Coke, Van Deren. "Why Artists Came to New Mexico, Nature Presents a New Face Each Moment."*Art News*, January 1974. Vol. 73, No. 1.

Crane, Cathy. "Courthouse Mural Holds Mysterious Tale." *Roswell Daily Record*, October 29, 1991.

D'Emilio, Sandra. "The New Deal Was a Great Deal: Federal Patronage and Mural Painting in New Mexico-1933–1943." Unpublished manuscript compiled as result of personal interviews done by author and Virginia Ewing with New Deal artists still alive and living in New Mexico. c. 1991.

Dumont, Andre. "Ina Sizer Cassidy and the Writers Project." *Albuquerque Journal-IMPACT Magazine,* January 19, 1982.

Ewing, Virginia. "Some Memories Concerning New Mexico's WPA Federal Art Project." Unpublished. Santa Fe, 1988.

——— "Russell Vernon Hunter's Mural, The Last Frontier in the DeBaca County Courthouse." Unpublished paper. March 23, 1984.

Ford, D'Lynn. "Depression Era Art Still Lifts Spirits." *New Mexico Magazine*, November 1990.

Fort Sumner. "Ft. Sumner-Vernon Hunter Historic Murals." *Curry County News,* June 21, 1934.

Gallup. "Art Project is Aid to Beauty of Courthouse." *Gallup Independent,* October 7, 1939.

Gibson, Daniel. "Art Around Town: Public Places Host Array of Art." *Santa Fean Magazine*, January/February 1990.

Gugliotta, Guy. "VIPS Get the Pick of the Paintings Store for Museum." *Washington Post,* March 29, 1994.

Hendrickson, P. & Streeter, Lynne. "White Sands National Monument." A Handout.

Hodges, Carrie. "The Spanish American Craftsmen." *WPA Archives Reports/Records*. New Mexico State Records and Archives. 1937.

Howe, Elvon L. "The Man Who Saved Union County." *Rocky Mountain Empire Magazine*, May 16, 1948.

Kirk, Ruth. "New Courthouse Murals Are Complete History." *Gallup Independent.* Date Unknown.

Laine, Don. "Taos County to Restore Frescoes." *Albuquerque Journal North,* June 8, 1993.

Las Vegas. "Brooks Willis Completes WPA Commission at Las Vegas." *Albuquerque Journal*, January 17, 1937.

Lofton, Ray J. "Art Projects in Melrose Under the WPA." Unpublished article by School Superintendent 1941–58.

Loh, Jules. "WPA Injected Life Into Paralyzed Areas." *Albuquerque Journal: Associated Press.* July 28, 1991.

Lordsburg. "Present Library Built in 1937." *Lordsburg Liberal,* February 10, 1958.

Murphy, Chris. "WPA Art Returns to Public Library." *Gallup Independent,* May 27, 1992.

Nathanson, Rick. "Anti-Depression Transfusion: WPA." *Albuquerque Journal*, July 28, 1991.

Ortega, Joaquin. (Introduction by.) "New Mexico Artists: New Mexico Artists Series #3." *New Mexico Quarterly* Spring 1949–Winter 1950–51. Albuquerque: University of New Mexico Press, 1952.

Portales. "Large Mural Placed at Post Office." *Portales News*, July 28, 1938.

Raton. "Call for Historical Pictures and Library Paintings."*Raton Range*, 1934.

Sandlin, Scott. "Roswell's Missing Mural Finds a Home." *Albuquerque Journal,* October 30, 1991.

Santa Fe. "Henderson Murals Installed at Federal Building by Art Project Chief Are Landscapes." *Santa Fe New Mexican*, 1938.

Smith, Janet. "The Arts in Albuquerque." WPA Archives Reports/Records. New Mexico Records and Archives. *1937.*

Wroth, Will. "New Hope in Hard Times-Hispanic Crafts Are Revived During Troubled Years." *El Palacio. Vol. 89* (Summer 1983).

NEW MEXICO CENTER FOR SOUTHWEST RESEARCH NEW DEAL ARCHIVES INFORMATION

University of New Mexico Zimmerman Library
Albuquerque

The following subjects as compiled by Nancy Brown Martinez, Archivist at the library as of 2012, can be researched when looking for information on New Mexico New Deal subjects. They include collections of documents from key individual's papers, books, oral histories, photos, catalogs, theater programs, county records, Spanish translations, music collections, forms, scrapbooks, and much more. This list may not be complete.

WPA at University of New Mexico
WPA Architecture in New Mexico
WPA Agriculture-Farm Programs
WPA Photo Project
WPA Federal Writers Project
New Mexico Historical Records Survey
WPA Art Programs
WPA in the Schools
NYA and WPA Community Neighborhood Youth Work
WPA Community Education-Adults
WPA Relief Work
WPA Social Work and some Health Work
WPA Bug Control and Forest Work
Other Material to Portray What Was Happening in 1938 or Near to That Date

OTHER NEW MEXICO ARCHIVAL SOURCES FOR NEW DEAL INFORMATION

SANTA FE

New Mexico State Archives
New Mexico State Library
New Mexico Musuem of Art Library
Fray Angelico Chavez Library
New Mexico History Museum
Laboratory of Anthropology
Museum of Indian Arts and Culture

ALBUQUERQUE

National Hispanic Cultural Center
Albuquerque Special Collection Library
Albuquerque Museum

OTHER LOCATIONS

New Mexico State History Museum, Las Cruces
Roswell Museum and Art Center, Roswell
New Mexico Tech University, Skeen Library, Socorro

INTERVIEWS

1963 interviews done by Sylvia Loomis for the Santa Fe Office of the Archives of American Art are available on microfilm or possibly more current media at the Archives of American Art in Washington, DC. A large collection of these interviews can be obtained by local libraries through the Inter-Library Loan program. There are copies of these microfilm interviews in the files of the National New Deal Preservation Office in Santa Fe.

Kenneth Adams
Jozef and Teresa Bakos
Patrocinio Barela
Charles Barrows
Emil Bisttram
E. Boyd
Ina Sizer Cassidy
Roland Dickey
Olin Dows
Louie Ewing
Virginia Hunter Ewing
Joy Yeck Fincke, secretary to R.V. Hunter
Gene Kloss
Jesse L. Nusbaum
Olive Rush
Eugenie Shonnard
Will Shuster
Harold E. West

1992–1994 interviews were done by Kathryn A. Flynn for material for her earlier book, *Treasures on New Mexico Trails*. Family members are identified. These interviews are either on CDs made from a video interview, the video copy and others are on audio tapes. Hard copies of some are also in files. They are located and available to review in the National New Deal Preservation Office. Call (505) 473-3985 for appointment.

Josephine Baca
Emily Otis Barnes
Harrison Begay
Jane Cahill Blumenfeld (Holger Cahill's daughter)
Dorothy Berninghaus Brandenbury (Oscar Berninghaus's daughter)
Suzan Campbell
Kitty Carlisle re: the Federal Theater Project
Pop Chalee
Andrew Connors
Roland Dickey
Teresa Ebie
Bambi Ellis (Fremont Ellis's daughter)
Virginia Ewing (widow of Vernon Hunter and Louis Ewing)
Octavia Fellin, Gallup librarian emeritus
Joseph Fleck, Jr. (son of Joseph Fleck)
Tish Frank (granddaughter of William P. Henderson and wife, Alice)
Joy Y. Fincke McWilliams
Edward "Ned" Hall (former husband of E. Boyd)
Susan Herter
Glee Homan, New Mexico Military Institute historian/librarian
Van Dorn Hooker
Allan Houser
John Jellicoe
Lee Roy Jones
David Kammer
Nat Kaplan
Gene and Phillip Moss
Ellen Landis
Oliver LaGrone
Chris Lantz (Paul and Juanita Lantz's son)
Sam Larcombe
Tom Lea
Betty Lloyd
Ray Lofton
Abad Lucero
Edgar Ludins (Hannah S. M. Ludins' husband)

William Lumpkins
Ila McAfee
Elizabeth McGorty
John Meigs
Dorothy Morang
Helmuth Naumer, Jr.
Rod Peterson
Sarah Woolsey Pirkl (daughter of Jean Woolsey)
Dean Porter
Eliseo Rodriguez
Helen Schleeter (Howard Schleeter's widow)
William Spurlock
Myrtle Stedman (Wilfred Stedman's widow)
Louise Tamotzu (Chuzo Tamotzu's widow)
Andrew Tsininhjinnie
José Rey Toledo
Pat Smith (Step-granddaughter of Mabel Dodge Luhan)
Don Van Soelen (Theodore Van Soelen's son)
Bill Thomas
Pablita Velarde
William Warder
Alicia Weber
Marta Weigle
Jerry West (Hal West's son)
Mary Wheeler
James Ridgely Whiteman
Helen Willis (Brooks Willis' widow)
Woodrow Wilson
David Witt
Will Wroth
Vicente Ximenes

Since the above were interviewed, there have been additional interviews with New Deal artists and writers located in other states—Ted Egri, Stetson Kennedy, and Studs Terkel. Other interviews have also been conducted with those who were children of the artists or who have been closely involved with the New Deal in their own professional work: Jan Marfyak, son of Jan Marfyak, New Deal artist; New Mexico architects Van Dorn Hooker and Joe McKinney; and professional art conservators in New Mexico, Dale Kronkright, Patricia Morris, Luis Neri Zagal and Steve Prins.

DISSERTATIONS AND THESES

Contreras, Belisario R. "Treasury Art Programs: The New Deal and the American Artist, 1933 to 1943." Unpublished PhD. dissertation, American University 1967.

LeBovit, Linda, "Government Art Patronage of the 1930s." Master's Thesis, Santa Fe, 1993–95.

Randall, Mallory B. "Murals and Sculpture of the Public Works of Art Project and the Treasury Section in the Southwest." Master's Thesis in American Civilization, University of Texas, 1967.

Riedel, Thomas L. "Copied for the W.P.A.": Juan A. Sanchez, American tradition and the New Deal politics of saint-making. 1992 Master's Thesis.

Spurlock, William Henry, II. "Federal Support for the Visual Arts in the State of New Mexico 1933–1943," Master's Thesis, University of Texas, 1974.

CONTRIBUTORS

ANDREW CONNORS has been Assistant Curator at the National Museum of American Art, Smithsonian Institution, Washington, DC and as of 2012 is Curator at the Albuquerque Museum. His fields of research include Hispanic art, Native American art, and folk art and crafts.While at the Smithsonian, he did an exhibition project that included "Pueblo Indian Watercolors" and "Paintings of the American Southwest." He coordinated the Washington, DC venue of the national touring exhibition "Chicano Art: Resistance and Affirmation, 1965–1985."

For Smithsonian Folkways Recordings, he compiled an album of folk songs and stories for children, "A Fish That's a Song," which received a Notable Children's Recording Award from the American Library Association and a Parents' Choice Foundation 1991 Recording Award.

Connors received his B. A. in Architecture and Art History from Yale University in 1984. He grew up in Colorado.

SANDRA D'EMILIO was the curator at the New Mexico Museum of Fine Arts for the Depression era. She wrote articles and books related to this time period. With Suzan Campbell, she did *Vision and Visionaries: The Art and Artists of the Santa Fe Railroad.* D'Emilio and Campbell joined with John L. Kessell to write, *Spirit and Vision: Images of Ranchos de Taos Church.*

SALLY HYER, PhD, worked for tribal organizations and museums in the American Southwest since 1975. She was the author of the oral history, *One House, One Voice, One Heart: Native American Education at the Santa Fe Indian School*, co-edited a volume on the Historic American Buildings Survey in New Mexico, and wrote a biography of Pablita Velarde. Her work on New Deal programs was part of an ongoing study of Native American mural painting. Hyer was research director at the Institute of American Indian Arts' Center for Research and Cultural Exchange in Santa Fe.

LYNNE SEBASTIAN, PhD, is an archaeologist specializing in the American Southwest. Her fieldwork, carried out in New Mexico, Colorado, Utah, and Arizona, has included nearly the full range of Anasazi development from Basketmaker III through Pueblo III. In addition to excavation and survey reports, her publications include an overview of the archaeology of southeastern New Mexico, a book on archaeological uses of predictive modeling, and various articles on Chacoan archeology. Another book was published by Cambridge University Press about the political and economic structure of the Chaco system. Sebastian received her PhD from the University of New Mexico in 1988 and as of 2011 continues to work in the Albuquerque area.

LOUISE TURNER, a native New Mexican, grew up in Santa Fe. She vividly remembers herself and friends following Will Shuster around town while he sketched. She received her undergraduate degrees from the University of New Mexico and has been an educator and administrator in the

United States and abroad. She is the recipient of the Princeton Prize for Distinguished Teaching. Ms. Turner was the co-author of *Will Shuster, A Santa Fe Legend*. She has also been a feature editor and writer for such magazines as *Santa Fe Lifestyle* and *Southwest Profile*.

KATHRYN A. FLYNN, as Deputy Secretary of State, compiled and edited all the New Mexico Blue Books provided by the Office of the Secretary of State from 1991–2006. The preparation of these state reference books motivated her to search and find all New Deal public art and buildings in New Mexico. Flynn grew up in Portales but has lived in Santa Fe for over forty years working in private and government settings. Earlier she obtained her Bachelor's Degree from the University of Utah and Master's degree from Southern Illinois University. Ms. Flynn wrote a column in *The Santa Fe New Mexican* for a number of years and also was a radio talk show hostess. She was married to Jack Flynn, now deceased, who was a well known New Mexico historian particularly of politics, government and religion. Since 1998, she has been the Executive Director of the National New Deal Preservation Association and its New Mexico Chapter, both non-profit organizations determined to share about the accomplishments of Roosevelt's New Deal and to save historical items from that time period the state's history (1933–1943).

ACKNOWLEDGEMENTS AND CREDITS

The following people have participated in the creation of this book and in the earlier book, *Treasures on New Mexico Trails*, also by Flynn and it is with heartfelt gratitude that she extends her appreciation to all of them for their sincere and laborious efforts.

COMPILER:

Kathryn A. Flynn

WRITERS/RESEARCHERS:

Sue Black
Phyllis Cohen
Andrew Connors
Sandra D'Emilio
Virginia Ewing*
Kathryn A. Flynn
Pauline Giglio
Sally Hyer
Rose and George Kaplan
Judy Schmutz
Lynne Sebastian
Louise Turner

CONTRIBUTORS

Many of these individuals helped locate information about the 361 WPA schools while others contributed other information based experiences or information they had based on places they had lived or people they had known. Names with an asterisk identify people who were actual participants in the New Deal programs in New Mexico.

Sam Adelo
Manuel B. Alcon
Mary Ann Anders
Jo and Joan Arvizu
Nita Baltosser
William Baker
Susan Berry
Henrietta Christmas
Barbara Copeland
Roland Dickey*
Barbara Dimond
William Dorman
Kathy Duxbury
Octavia Fellin
Sherry Fletcher
Bernard Flynn
Lynda Grasty
Michael R. Grauer
Kittu Longstreth-Brown
Thora Hagerty

Meg Harris
Kermit Hill
Van Dorn Hooker
Jed Howard
Shirley Jacobsen
Nat Kaplan*
Kay Krehbiel
Jeanne LaMarco
Ellen Landis
Virginia Lierz
Helen Lucero, PhD
Tony Lucero
William Lumpkins*
Jan Marfyak
Johnny Martinez
Ila McAfee*
Elizabeth McGordy
Joy Y. Fincke McWilliams*
John Meigs
Sally Noe
Rod Peterson
Sarah Pirkl
Mark Pringle
Mary Helen Ratje
Lynne Robertson
Murray Ryan
Kendall Schlenker
Arlene Sisneros Sena
Myrtle Stedman*
Michael Taylor
J. Paul Taylor
Dorothy Victor
Vincent Wathen*
Alicia Weber
Marta Weigle
Mary Pollard Wheeler*
Helen Willis*
Suzi Wolfe
Vincente Ximenes*

Others who have provided support:

Numerous other interested individuals and family members of the artists from various communities were likewise most helpful in the gathering of information for the creation of this book.

The board members of the National New Deal Preservation Association and its New Mexico Chapter have been extremely helpful and supportive of the compilation of this book in order to help get their mission more widely known.

Finally, the staff of six state agencies must be thanked for their cooperation, and enthusiasm during the research for this book: the Museum of Fine Arts, the State Library-Southwest Room, State Historic Preservation Office, Center for Southwest Research, Laboratory of Anthropology and the State Records and Archives.

TECHNICAL ASSISTANCE:

William Baker
Diane H. Bryan
Robert Covelli
Robyn Covelli-Hunt

INDEX

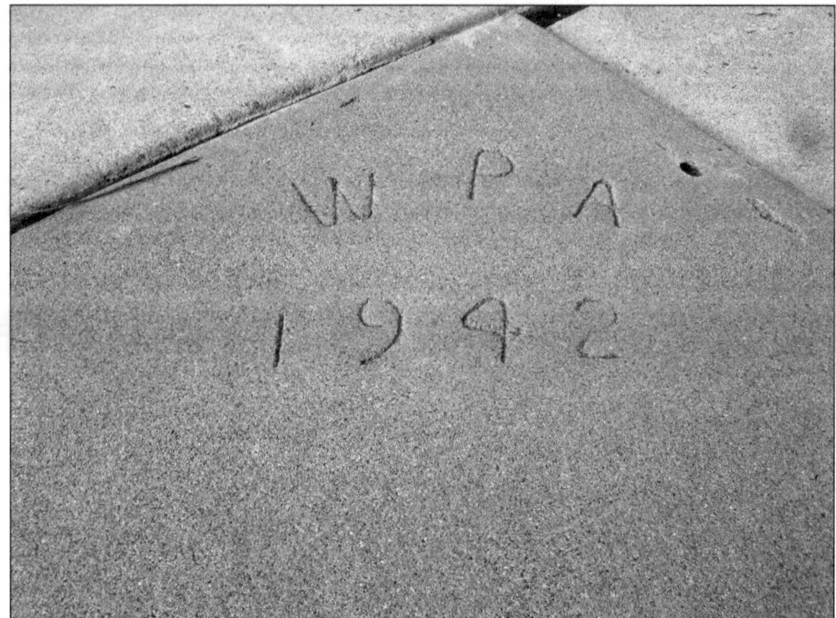

Sidewalks with "WPA" and the year were placed in towns all over this state and nation. Look for them. Use them to help you appreciate also the roads, water and sewer systems in your town and most likely also your hometown and the electricity at your family's farm or ranch. All are New Deal treasures that we are continuing to use but take for granted. Photograph by Editor.

www.ingramcontent.com/pod-product-compliance
Lightning Source LLC
LaVergne TN
LVHW081256100826
845148LV00005B/889
9780865348820